AFTER
THE MUSIC
STOPPED

ALSO BY ALAN S. BLINDER

Hard Heads, Soft Hearts
Offshoring of American Jobs
The Quiet Revolution
Downsizing in America
Asking About Prices
Central Banking in Theory and Practice
Economics: Principles and Policy

AFTER THE MUSIC STOPPED

THE FINANCIAL CRISIS,
THE RESPONSE,
AND THE WORK AHEAD

ALAN S. BLINDER

THE PENGUIN PRESS
New York
2013

THE PENGUIN PRESS
Published by the Penguin Group
Penguin Group (USA) Inc., 375 Hudson Street, New York, New York 10014, U.S.A. •
Penguin Group (Canada), 90 Eglinton Avenue East, Suite 700, Toronto, Ontario, Canada
M4P 2Y3 (a division of Pearson Penguin Canada Inc.) • Penguin Books Ltd, 80 Strand,
London WC2R 0RL, England • Penguin Ireland, 25 St. Stephen's Green, Dublin 2, Ireland
(a division of Penguin Books Ltd) • Penguin Group (Australia), 707 Collins Street, Melbourne,
Victoria 3008, Australia (a division of Pearson Australia Group Pty Ltd) • Penguin Books
India Pvt Ltd, 11 Community Centre, Panchsheel Park, New Delhi – 110 017, India •
Penguin Group (NZ), 67 Apollo Drive, Rosedale, Auckland 0632, New Zealand (a division
of Pearson New Zealand Ltd) • Penguin Books (South Africa), Rosebank Office Park,
181 Jan Smuts Avenue, Parktown North 2193, South Africa • Penguin China, B7 Jiaming
Center, 27 East Third Ring Road North, Chaoyang District, Beijing 100020, China

Penguin Books Ltd, Registered Offices:
80 Strand, London WC2R 0RL, England

First published in 2013 by The Penguin Press,
a member of Penguin Group (USA) Inc.

Diagram on page 77 from *The Deal*, issue of October 6, 2008.
By permission of The Deal LLC.

Quote from "Hey Jude" by John Lennon and Paul McCartney,
published by Sony/ATV Music Publishing. All rights reserved.

LIBRARY OF CONGRESS CATALOGING IN PUBLICATION DATA

Blinder, Alan S.
After the music stopped : the financial crisis, the response,
and the work ahead / Alan S. Blinder.
p.   cm.
Includes bibliographical references and index.
ISBN 978-1-59420-530-9
1. Global Financial Crisis, 2008–2009.   2. Financial crises—United States.
3. Finance—United States.   4. United States—Economic conditions—2009–
5. United States–Economic policy—2009–   I. Title.
HB37172008 .B55   2013
330.973—dc23   2012031025

Printed in the United States of America
3   5   7   9   10   8   6   4

DESIGNED BY AMANDA DEWEY

To Madeline

CONTENTS

|ıııııııııııııııııııııı|

PART IV. THE ROAD TO REFORM

PART V. LOOKING AHEAD

LIST OF ACRONYMS AND ABBREVIATIONS

|ıııııııııııııııııııııı|

ABCP: asset-backed commercial paper
ABS: asset-backed securities
AIG: American International Group
AIG FP: AIG Financial Products
AMLF: Asset-Backed Commercial Paper Money Market Mutual Fund
    Liquidity Facility
ANPR: Advance Notice of Proposed Rulemaking
ARM: adjustable-rate mortgage
ARRA: American Reinvestment and Recovery Act (2009)
BofA: Bank of America
CBO: Congressional Budget Office
CDO: collateralized debt obligation
CDS: credit default swaps
CEA: Council of Economic Advisers
CEO: Chief Executive Officer
CFMA: Commodity Futures Modernization Act (2000)
CFPA: Consumer Financial Protection Agency
CFPB: Consumer Financial Protection Bureau
CFTC: Commodity Futures Trading Commission
CME: Chicago Mercantile Exchange
CP: commercial paper
CPFF: Commercial Paper Funding Facility
CPI: Consumer Price Index

CPP: Capital Purchase Program

DTI: debt (service)-to-income ratio

ECB: European Central Bank

EMH: efficient markets hypothesis

ESF: Exchange Stabilization Fund

FCIC: Financial Crisis Inquiry Commission

FDIC: Federal Deposit Insurance Corporation

FHA: Federal Housing Administration

FHFA: Federal Housing Finance Agency

FICO: Fair Isaac Company

FOMC: Federal Open Market Committee

FSA: Financial Services Authority (UK)

FSLIC: Federal Savings and Loan Insurance Corporation

FSOC: Financial Stability Oversight Council

G7: Group of Seven (nations)

GAAP: generally accepted accounting principles

GAO: Government Accountability Office

GDP: gross domestic product

GLB: Gramm-Leach-Bliley Act (1999)

GSE: government-sponsored enterprise

H4H: Hope for Homeowners

HAFA: Home Affordable Foreclosure Alternatives Program

HAMP: Home Affordable Modification Program

HARP: Home Affordable Refinancing Program

HAUP: Home Affordable Unemployment Program

HHF: Hardest Hit Fund

HOLC: Home Owners' Loan Corporation

HUD: Department of Housing and Urban Development

IMF: International Monetary Fund

ISDA: International Swaps and Derivatives Association

LIBOR: London Interbank Offer Rate

LTCM: Long-Term Capital Management

LTRO: Longer-Term Refinancing Operations

LTV: loan-to-value (ratio)

MBS: mortgage-backed securities

MOM: my own money

NBER: National Bureau of Economic Research

NEC: National Economic Council

NINJA (loans): no income, no jobs, and no assets

NJTC: new jobs tax credit

OCC: Office of the Comptroller of the Currency

OFHEO: Office of Federal Housing Enterprise Oversight

OMB: Office of Management and Budget

OMT: Outright Monetary Transactions

OPM: other people's money

OTC: over the counter

OTS: Office of Thrift Supervision

PDCF: Primary Dealer Credit Facility

PIIGS: Portugal, Ireland, Italy, Greece, and Spain

QE: quantitative easing

Repo: repurchase agreement

S&L: savings and loan association

S&P: Standard and Poor's

SEC: Securities and Exchange Commission

Section 13(3): of Federal Reserve Act

SIFI: systemically important financial institution

SIV: structured investment vehicle

SPV: special purpose vehicle

TAF: Term Auction Facility

TALF: Term Asset-Backed Securities Loan Facility

TARP: Troubled Assets Relief Program

TBTF: too big to fail

TED (spread): spread between LIBOR and Treasuries

TIPS: Treasury Inflation-Protected Securities

TLGP: Temporary Liquidity Guarantee Program

TSLF: Term Securities Lending Facility

UMP: unconventional monetary policy

WaMu: Washington Mutual

PREFACE

When the music stops . . . things will be complicated.
But as long as the music is playing,
you've got to get up and dance.
We're still dancing.

Those were the immortal words on July 8, 2007, of Chuck Prince, then the CEO of Citigroup. It may be the most famous, or infamous, quotation of the entire financial crisis. Almost exactly a month later, the music stopped abruptly—and so did the dancing.

True to Prince's prophecy, things got quite complicated and very ugly—not only for Citigroup but for the entire world. The high-stakes game of musical chairs turned out to be remarkably short on seats, and large swaths of the financial industry fell rudely to the floor. The U.S. economy subsequently sank into its worst recession since the 1930s. The U.S. government, which was led at the time by a bunch of alleged free-marketeers, was called upon to ride to the rescue multiple times—not because the financial firms deserved it, but because the chaos threatened to pull all of us down into the abyss with them. They were incredible events.

ANOTHER BOOK ON THE CRISIS?

But the story of the financial crisis of 2007–2009, or at least parts of it, has been told many times, in many different ways, in a wide variety of books and articles. So why yet another work about the crisis and its aftermath?

One reason is simply that *the American people still don't quite know what hit them*, how and why it happened, or what the authorities did about it—especially why government officials took so many unusual and controversial actions. Misconceptions about the government's role are rife to this day, and they are poisoning our politics. Was government part of the problem, or part of the solution? This book attempts to answer these and related questions. The version of the story I tell focuses more on the *why* than on the *what* of the crisis and response. No one else has done that to date.

Doing so is important for several reasons. One is that *a comprehensive history of this episode has yet to be written*. A number of fine books, mostly by journalists, have examined pieces of the puzzle, sometimes in excruciating detail. The book you hold in your hands is different. It's not a work of journalism, so if you want to learn about who said what to whom when, you are best advised to look elsewhere. My purpose, instead, is to give the big picture rather than focus on just one or two pieces. One day, some ambitious historian will put everything together in a two-thousand-page tome. My version of the story is comprehensive but shorter. It is also less of a *whodunit* and more of a *why-did-they-do-it?*

An even more important reason for writing this book is that *the events recounted here are still reverberating*, both in the United States and around the world. You read about them every day, and they will pose major public policy challenges for years. The U.S. economy has not yet climbed out of the ditch into which the financial crisis and the Great Recession drove it. Unemployment remains high, the budget deficit is still huge, and the mortgage foreclosure problem festers. In Europe, the crisis is still unfolding. Some of the remedies put (or not put) into place in response to the crisis remain under vociferous, and often highly partisan, debate. That includes the Dodd-Frank financial reform act of 2010, the continuing foreclosure mess, the monstrous federal budget deficit, the Federal Reserve's ongoing efforts to boost the economy, and more. Unlike most books on the crisis, this one zeroes in more on public policy than on the mysteries of modern finance.

Finally, *this book looks to the future*. The financial crisis and ensuing recession have left us with a long agenda of unfinished business. How can and should we finish it? Furthermore, there will be financial crises in the future. Will we handle them better because of what we've learned, both economically and politically? Or will we forget quickly? Many changes—both institutional and attitudinal—were, or were not, made. What are our remaining vulnerabilities? What future problems may we have accidentally created while fighting the various fires?

WHAT'S INSIDE?

The narrative offered here is largely chronological. After all, stories are best told that way, and this is quite a story. But I deviate from chronology when doing so is important to understanding the *issues* at play. The central questions for this book are: How did we get into this mess, and how did we get out of it (to the extent we have)? Where did policy makers shine, and where did they err? What's left to be done before it's all over?

After an introductory chapter, part II describes and explains how the crisis developed and unfolded. Parts III and IV then dwell on the policy responses—first, the emergency actions that were taken to forestall catastrophe, and then the longer-term fixes that were (and were not) put into place. This section of the book ends with an important chapter that tries to unravel the essential paradox of the entire episode: that under-regulated markets ran badly off the tracks and the government rushed in to save the day, yet the government emerged as a villain. Why were the policy successes (and some failures) greeted with Bronx cheers? After the review of the past and the present, part V turns to the future. How do we get out of the remaining mess? What lies ahead? What have we learned from our bitter experience?

WITH THANKS

There is a sense in which I should be thanking everyone with whom I've ever had a conversation about finance, crises, regulation, monetary policy, politics, and the like. For my views on these and related matters have evolved over decades of watching and reading, talking and thinking, writing and teaching—and working in academia, finance, and government. But more directly pertinent to this work, I am deeply grateful to a number of public officials, financial experts, journalists, and scholars who helped me with conversations or correspondence about particular matters raised in the book, or who offered useful comments or suggestions on earlier drafts of the manuscript. Sincere thanks go to Ben Bernanke, Scott Blinder, Dan Clawson, John Duca, William Dudley, Stephen Friedman, Timothy Geithner, Erica Groschen, Robert Hoyt, Nobuhiro Kiyotaki, Edward Knight, Sebastian Mallaby, Michael Morandi, Craig Perry, Ricardo Reis, Robert Rubin, David Smith, Launny Steffens, Lawrence Summers, Phillip Swagel, and Paul Willen for taking the time to share their knowledge. Philip Freidman, in particular, must be singled out for reviewing the entire manuscript and offering numerous valuable suggestions. Importantly, none of these people should be associated with any of the conclusions I've reached. I know that several of them disagree with some important particulars. Blame everything on me.

Most of the book was written during a sabbatical year from Princeton University in 2011–2012, about half of which was spent at the Russell Sage Foundation in New York—to which I am truly indebted. From its president, Eric Wanner, on down, Russell Sage deserves high praise for providing the perfect work environment for a visiting scholar. In particular, Galo Falchettore, Claire Gabriel, and Katie Winograd provided useful assistance on the manuscript. Without the free time to ruminate and write, I would probably still have a rough draft sitting on my hard drive.

My research at Princeton has long been supported by the Griswold Center for Economic Policy Studies, whose generous support continued through the writing of this book. A big *thank-you* is due. I am also indebted to my student research assistants—Armando Asuncion-Cruz, who started it all off, and Joanne Im and Kevin Ma, who finished it up—and even more indebted to my longtime, terrific assistant, Kathleen Hurley, who manages to get everything done in less time than seems humanly possible—and always with a smile.

When the time came to turn the manuscript into an actual book, my first (and wise) stop was at the offices of John Brockman, who became my literary agent and steered me in a number of good directions. One of them was to Penguin Press, where I acquired yet more debts to a number of fine people who do their jobs exceedingly well. My editor, Scott Moyers, was at once a big booster and a smart but friendly critic whose good judgment improved the book in numerous ways. Scott's assistant, Mally Anderson, always had the right answer to every question, and delivered it with good cheer. Juliana Kiyan handled publicity deftly.

Finally, what can I say about my lifetime companion and wonderful wife, Madeline, to whom I owe so much? She fixed my prose and sharpened my arguments when they needed fixing or sharpening. She kept me from flying off on tangents and steered me away from rhetorical excesses and impenetrable jargon. She encouraged me when I needed encouragement and nudged me when I needed to be nudged. This book is dedicated, lovingly, to her. We were married in 1967 and, for us, the music has never stopped.

Alan S. Blinder
Princeton, New Jersey
November 2012

PART I

IT
HAPPENED
HERE

1

|||||||||||||||||||||||||||

WHAT'S A NICE ECONOMY LIKE YOU DOING IN A PLACE LIKE THIS?

We came very, very close to a global financial meltdown.

—Federal Reserve Chairman Ben S. Bernanke

Did anyone get the license plate of that truck?

That's how many Americans felt after our financial system spun out of control and ran over all of us—almost literally—in 2008. The U.S. economy was crawling along that summer, with employment drifting down, spending weakening, and the financial markets suffering through a gut-wrenching series of ups and downs—mostly downs. The economy was hardly in great shape but neither was it a disaster area. It wasn't even clear that we were headed for a recession, never mind the worst recession since the 1930s. Then came the failure of Lehman Brothers, the now-notorious Wall Street investment bank, on September 15, 2008, and everything fell apart. Yes, the license plate of that truck read: *L-E-H-M-A-N.*

Most Americans were innocent bystanders who didn't know where the truck came from, why it was driven so recklessly, or why the financial traf-fic cops didn't protect us better. As time went by, shell shock gave way to anger, and with good reason. A host of financial manipulations that ordi-nary people did not understand, and in which they played no part, cost millions of them their livelihoods and their homes, bankrupted many busi-nesses, destroyed trillions of dollars' of wealth, brought the once-mighty U.S. economy to its knees, and left all levels of government gasping for tax revenue. If people felt as though they were mugged, it's because they were.

The financial "accidents" that took place between the summer of 2007 and the spring of 2009 had severe consequences, which Americans experi-enced firsthand. But most citizens are baffled, and many are extremely displeased, by what their government did in response to the crisis. They question the justice of the seemingly large costs taxpayers had to bear, and they wonder why so many reckless truck drivers are still on the road, pros-pering while other Americans suffer. Perhaps most of all, they are anxious about what the future may bring. As late as the 2012 election, a strong majority of Americans were telling pollsters that the country was still "on the wrong track" or "heading in the wrong direction." No wonder we heard populist political thunder from both the Right (the Tea Party movement) and the Left (the Occupy movement).

The United States recently completed the quadrennial spectacle we call a presidential election with a plainly angry electorate. While President Obama won reelection, no one yet knows what the 2012 election will bring in its wake. But we do know that the last chapters of the story that began in 2007 are yet to be written. So let's start by looking back. What hit us—and why?

A VERY BRIEF HISTORY OF THE FINANCIAL CRISIS AND THE GREAT RECESSION

Historical perspective accrues only with the passage of time, and we are still living through the aftermath of the frightening financial crisis and the Great Recession that followed closely on its heels.* But enough time has now elapsed, and enough dust has now settled, that some preliminary judgments can be made. Consider this book a second draft of history. There will doubtless be thirds and fourths.

It is vital that we reach some preliminary verdicts relatively quickly because Americans' well-justified anger is affecting—some would say, poisoning—our political discourse. This book concentrates on the *what* and especially the *why* of the financial crisis and its aftermath. It's a long and complicated story, but some understanding is essential for the better functioning of our democracy. So before getting enmeshed in the details, here is a very brief history of the financial crisis, the Great Recession, and the U.S. government's responses to each. It will take only four paragraphs. The fourth may surprise you.

The Supershort Version

The U.S. financial system, which had grown far too complex and far too fragile for its own good—and had far too little regulation for the public good—experienced a perfect storm during the years 2007–2009. Things started unraveling when the much-chronicled housing bubble burst, but the ensuing implosion of what I call the "bond bubble" was probably larger and more devastating. The stock market also collapsed under the strain, turning many 401(k)s into—in the dark humor of the day—"201(k)s." When America's financial structure crumbled, the damage proved to be not only deep but wide. Ruin spread to every part of the bloated financial sector. Few institutions or markets were spared, and the worst-affected ones either perished (as in the case of Lehman Brothers) or went on life support (as in the case of Citigroup). We came perilously close to what Federal Reserve Chairman Ben Bernanke called "a global financial meltdown."

Some people think of the financial markets as a kind of glorified

---

*Economists date the end of a recession as when the economy stops contracting, which came in June 2009. But the public seems to consider "recession" an approximate synonym for "hard times," which are clearly still in progress.

casino with little relevance to the *real* economy—where the jobs, factories, and shops are. But that's wrong. Finance is more like the circulatory system of the economic body. And if the blood stops flowing . . . well, you don't want to think about it. All modern economies rely on a variety of credit-granting mechanisms to circulate nutrients to the rest of the system, and the U.S. economy is more credit-dependent and "financialized" than most. So when the once-copious flows of credit diminished to mere trickles, the economy nearly experienced cardiac arrest. What had been *far too much* liquidity and credit during the boom years quickly turned into *vastly too little.* The abrupt drying-up of credit, from both banks and the so-called shadow banking system, coupled with the massive destruction of wealth in the forms of houses, stocks, and securities, produced what you might expect: less credit, less buying, and a whopping recession.

The U.S. government mobilized enormous resources to alleviate the financial distress and, more important, to fight the recession. Congress expanded the social safety net and enacted large-scale fiscal stimulus programs. The Federal Reserve dropped interest rates to the floor, created incredible amounts of liquidity, and expanded its own balance sheet by making loans, purchasing assets, and issuing guarantees the likes of which it had never done before. Many of the Fed's actions were previously unimaginable. I remember coming into class one morning in September 2008, scratching my head in disbelief and saying, "Last night the Federal Reserve, which has never regulated an insurance company, nationalized one!" The company was the infamous AIG.

Now the surprise: It worked! Not perfectly, of course. But for the most part, the financial system healed faster than most observers expected. (Remember, *healing* in this context does not mean returning to the status quo ante. We don't want to do that.) And the economy's contraction, though deep and horribly costly, turned out to be both less severe and shorter than many people had feared. Only the homebuilding sector, a small share of our economy, experienced anything close to Great Depression 2.0. For the rest, unemployment never quite reached 1983 levels, never mind 1933 levels. That doesn't mean everything was hunky-dory by, say, 2012. Far from it. But the worst, most assuredly, did *not* happen.

So that's my capsule history, and it suggests a modestly happy ending—or at least a sigh of relief. That said, we are grading on a pretty lenient curve when the good news is that the United States avoided a complete meltdown of its allegedly best-in-class financial system and a second Great Depression. In truth, U.S. macroeconomic performance since the fall of 2008 doesn't merit even the proverbial gentleman's C. It has been the worst in post–World War II American history. Give it an F instead.

Congress rewrote the rulebook of finance in 2010, trying to ensure that nothing like this will ever happen again. But the financial reforms are so new—most not yet even in effect—that no one knows how the redesigned regulatory system will work in practice, especially once it comes under stress. And bank lobbyists are fighting the reforms tooth and nail. To turn Rahm Emanuel's famous principle into a question: Did we waste this crisis or use it as a catalyst for much-needed change?* Only time will tell.

Three Critical Questions

Another aspect of the crisis motivates this book: Even today, despite numerous works on the crisis—some of them excellent—most Americans remain perplexed by what hit them. They have only a limited understanding of what the U.S. government did, or failed to do, on their behalf—and, more important, *why*. They also harbor several major misconceptions. In consequence, the Tea Party movement erupted in 2009, voters "threw the rascals out" in the elections of 2010, Occupy Wall Street exploded in 2011, economic issues were central to the hotly contested election in 2012, and trust in government is still scraping all-time lows.

This, too, is understandable. As I watched the financial crisis, the recession, and the policy responses to each of them unfold in real time, one of my biggest frustrations was how little explanation the American people

---

*Emanuel, then the designated White House chief of staff, was widely quoted in November 2008 as saying, "You never want a serious crisis to go to waste."

ever heard from their leaders, whether in or out of government. Sadly, that remains true right up to the present day. We won't restore trust in government until Americans better understand what happened to them and what was done to help.

The president of the United States possesses the biggest megaphone in the world. But President George W. Bush virtually dropped out of sight during the waning months of his administration. Can you remember even a single Bush speech on the nation's developing economic crisis? President Barack Obama has been vastly more visible, activist, and eloquent than his predecessor. Yet even he has rarely taken the time to give a speech of explanation—far less time than the American people need and deserve. The two secretaries of the Treasury during the crisis period, Henry Paulson and Timothy Geithner, have between them barely given a single coherent speech explaining what happened and—perhaps more important—why they did what they did. Federal Reserve Chairman Ben Bernanke has done more explaining, and done it better. But his audience is specialized and limited, and he tries to stick to the Fed's knitting, not the administration's.

So most of the job of explaining has been outsourced by default to the private sector. Even there, however, the supply has been inadequate. For example, while our financial industry is allegedly teeming with brilliant people who understand all this stuff, hardly any industry leaders have stepped up to explain what happened, much less to apologize—probably on advice of counsel. Journalists, academics, and the like have, of course, penned hundreds of articles and op-eds on the origins of the crisis and the responses to it—including a few by yours truly. But mass media outlets require such brevity that anything remotely resembling a comprehensive explanation of something as complex as the financial crisis is out of the question. Twelve seconds of TV time constitutes a journalistic essay.

While this book tells the story in what I hope is an intelligible manner, its more important goal is to provide a conceptual framework through which both the salient facts and the litany of policy responses can be *understood*. More concretely, I want to provide answers to the following three critical questions:

How Did We Ever Get into Such a Mess?

The objective here is not to affix blame, though some of that will inevitably (and deservedly) be done, but rather to highlight and analyze the many mistakes that were made so we don't repeat them again.

What Was Done to Mitigate the Problems and Ameliorate the Damages—and Why?

Were the policy responses—some of which were hastily designed—sensible, coherent, and well justified? Again, my purpose is not so much to second-guess the decision makers and grade their performances as to learn from their experiences, so we're better prepared the next time around. My big worry is that the policy responses of 2008–2009 are now held in such ill repute that politics will stand in the way the next time a financial crisis hits.

Did We "Waste" the Financial Crisis of 2007–2009— in Emanuel's Sense—or Did We Put It to Good Use?

Specifically, were the financial reforms enacted in 2010 well or poorly designed to create a sturdier financial structure? What did they leave out? Has the financial industry cleaned up its act? Perhaps most important, what comes next?

WHAT'S A NICE ECONOMY LIKE YOU DOING IN A PLACE LIKE THIS?

A well-known series of TV commercials brags that "what happens in Vegas stays in Vegas." But the calamities that befell the financial markets in 2007–2009 did not stay there. They soon had profound ill effects on the real economy—the places where Americans live and work, where nonfinancial companies make profits or losses, and where standards of living rise or fall. Indeed, with many Americans desperate to find work or struggling to make ends meet, we are still living with many of those effects.

The links from financial ruin to recession and unemployment are not hard to fathom. As credit becomes more expensive and, in worst cases, unavailable, businesses lose the ability to finance everyday needs—like meeting payroll, buying materials, and investing in equipment. In industries whose customers rely heavily on credit—such as for buying houses or automobiles—firms also find their sales dwindling. With sales down and costs of credit up, businesses have no choice but to scale back operations. Output falls, which means more layoffs and less hiring. And that, in turn, spells less income for consumers and therefore reduced sales at other firms. The process feeds on itself, and we get a recession. All this happened with a vengeance in 2008–2009, bringing untold misery to millions.

A Portrait of Failure

The two panels of figure 1.1 offer two versions of one part of this sad story: the sharp rise in joblessness in the United States that started early in 2008. The left panel displays the behavior of the national unemployment rate since 2003. Its steep ascent from the early months of 2008 to late 2009 depicts a national tragedy. As this book went to press, the unemployment

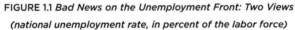

FIGURE 1.1 *Bad News on the Unemployment Front: Two Views*
(national unemployment rate, in percent of the labor force)

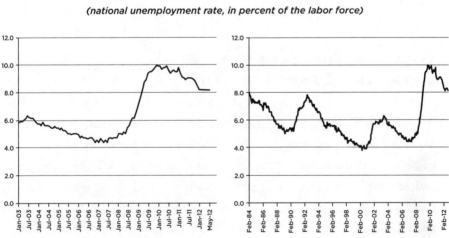

SOURCE: Bureau of Labor Statistics

rate still stood at 7.9 percent. Unemployment had been at 7.8 percent or higher for 46 consecutive months.

The right panel puts the recent stretch of miserably high unemployment into historical perspective by tracking the unemployment rate for almost thirty years. During the quarter century from February 1984 through January 2009, Americans *never* witnessed an unemployment rate as high as 8 percent *for even a single month*. An entire generation entered the labor force and worked for decades without ever experiencing an unemployment rate as high as the *lowest* rate we had from February 2009 through August 2012. The graph shows that even unemployment rates above 7 percent were rare during this twenty-five-year period. One has to go back to the spring of 1993, when today's thirty-seven-year-olds were graduating from high school, to find the previous instance. In fact, as recently as the summer of 2007, the unemployment rate was barely above 4.5 percent—a low rate we had come to think of as normal. Then came the Great Recession.

According to the U.S. Bureau of Labor Statistics, payrolls began contracting modestly in February 2008 and then with increasing ferocity after Lehman Brothers crashed and burned in September 2008. Job losses averaged a mere 46,000 per month over the first quarter of 2008, but a frightening 651,000 per month over the last quarter, and a horrific 780,000 per month over the first quarter of 2009. The labor-market pain was agonizingly deep and dismayingly long. Total employment peaked in January 2008 and then fell for a shocking twenty-five consecutive months—the longest such losing streak since the 1930s.

The total job loss was just under 8.8 million jobs, over a period during which our economy should have *added* perhaps 3.1 million jobs just to accommodate normal labor-force growth. So in that highly relevant sense, the cumulative *jobs deficit* was around 12 million by February 2010—nearly the population of Pennsylvania. Millions of families were thrown into privation and despair; many remain there. And the jobs deficit rose even higher in 2010 and 2011 as the anemic pace of job creation fell short of the roughly 125,000 jobs per month needed just to mark time with a growing population.

Figure 1.2 shows that employment crashed in 2008 and 2009, and

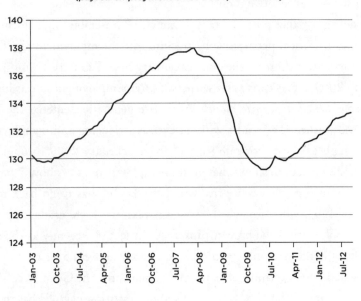

FIGURE 1.2 *A Dearth of Jobs*
(payroll employment since 2003, in millions)

SOURCE: *Bureau of Labor Statistics*

then barely crept back up in 2010 and 2011. By August 2012 total employment was back to only about May 2005 levels. That's *zero* net job growth over a period of more than seven years! The dearth of jobs is both a human and an economic tragedy that has had serious consequences already and will continue to have them for years to come.

It gets worse. Short spells of unemployment may not be terribly problematic; some are even welcome as people move or change jobs. But long spells of joblessness are devastating. Research shows that when displaced workers find new jobs, they are typically at much lower wages and that students graduating into a high-unemployment economy are burdened by a wage disadvantage that lasts for at least a decade or two.

Long-lasting unemployment is not a traditional part of the American story. In an average month during the years of 1948 to 2007, fewer than 13 percent of the unemployed were jobless for more than six months—the so-called long-term unemployed (see figure 1.3). By April 2010 this indicator of extreme labor-market stress had reached an astonishing peak above

45 percent, and it's only slightly lower today. Figure 1.3 shows that we have literally *never* seen a labor market this bad in the postwar era—not by a mile.

Jobs are something tangible. Real (that is, inflation-adjusted) gross domestic product (GDP) is, on the other hand, an abstract concept created to measure the overall size of the economy and to monitor its growth. It's our most widely used economic scoreboard. By common definition, a *recession* is a time when real GDP declines for two or more consecutive quarters.* Fortunately, that doesn't happen often. Quarterly GDP statistics date back to 1947, and during the sixty-one years from then until the start of the Great Recession, real GDP declined for two consecutive quarters only nine times. It declined for three consecutive quarters only twice, and it *never* fell for four consecutive quarters. Then came 2008–2009.

FIGURE 1.3 *Distress Signal*
(long-term unemployment as a share of total unemployment)

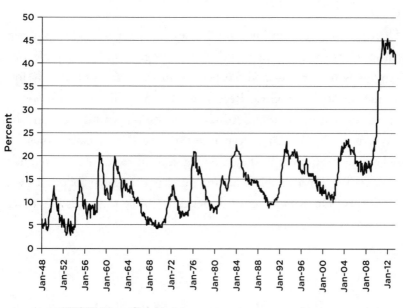

SOURCE: *Bureau of Labor Statistics*

---

*Recessions are dated officially by the National Bureau of Economic Research (NBER), a private research organization established in 1920, using a far more complicated definition. According to the NBER, the Great Recession began in 2007:4 and ended in 2009:2.

Real GDP declined in five of the six quarters that made up 2008 and the first half of 2009, including a losing streak of four straight. Whether one counts the five quarters out of six or the four in a row, that decline was the worst performance since the 1930s. The bottom literally fell out during the winter of 2008–2009, which is when the phrase "Great Depression 2.0" crept into the lexicon. All told, real GDP fell 4.7 percent. Since trend growth would have been at least 3.5 percent over that period, we probably lost over 8 percent of GDP, relative to trend. That's the equivalent of every American losing 8 percent of his or her income, or, more realistically, 10 percent of the population losing 80 percent. As Frank Sinatra might have said, it was a very bad year.

The recession of 2007–2009 is without peer in the pantheon of postwar U.S. recessions. Only the steep contractions of 1973–1975 and 1980–1982 even hold a candle, and each in its day was called "the Great Recession." All in all, it is hard to escape the conclusion that the 2008–2009 period was the worst by far in seventy years, both in terms of job loss and GDP decline.

There's more. Steep declines in GDP are normally followed by strong growth spurts as the economy makes up for lost ground. For example, our economy grew 6.2 percent and 5.6 percent in the years immediately following the previous two Great Recessions. By this additional criterion— the speed of recovery—the 2007–2009 recession stands out on the downside, too. Given such a deep recession, we should have grown by somewhere near 7 percent in the following year; instead, we managed just 2.5 percent. We got a double whammy: a sharp recession followed by a weak recovery. No wonder most Americans think the recession never ended.

The Way We Were

Things were not always so. The main story of the U.S. economy in the decades leading up to the crisis was one of growth and job creation, not of decline and job loss. Calling the years since 2008 "the new normal" represents defeatism that no one—not economists, politicians, or the public—should accept.

Look back at the first graph of this chapter, figure 1.1. The peak unemployment rate after the previous recession was only 6.3 percent, a rate we would stand up and cheer for today. And after hitting that peak in June 2003, unemployment fell steadily through late 2006, bottoming out at 4.4 percent. Net job gains during that three-plus-year period amounted to about 6 million jobs—nearly 2 million per year. So American workers benefited from a tight labor market for a protracted period. That's the sort of environment we want.*

The job market was even better during the late years of the Clinton boom. Although the U.S. economy was believed to be at full employment by 1995, it surprised us and proceeded to create about 2.8 million net new jobs in 1996, 3.4 million in 1997, another 3 million in 1998, and 3.2 million more in 1999. The unemployment rate even touched 3.9 percent for a few months in 2000. Those were the days. With jobs plentiful and employers competing actively for scarce labor resources, it was said in 1999 that if you had a pulse, you could get a job. And if you didn't, some employer would help you get one!

I recount these two happy episodes not so much to make us feel ashamed of our sorry recent performance as to make two points. The first is that it is unduly pessimistic to declare either that the American economy can't sustain job growth of 3 million a year over multiple years, or that we'll never get back to, say, 5 percent unemployment. Nonsense. Been there, done that. In fact, done both several times. So perish the thought—and I do mean *perish it*. Such job growth and unemployment targets are not the stuff of gauzy dreams. They are things we have achieved in the recent past.

Which is the second point. The years 2000 and 2007, especially

---

*The main downside of very low unemployment is concern about rising inflation. Core inflation (i.e., inflation excluding the prices of food and energy) rose a bit in 2006 but then tracked down again in 2007. This experience suggested to many economists that unemployment in the 4.5 to 5 percent range was not too low.

the latter, are not ancient history. Ask yourself what could possibly have changed so fundamentally about the U.S. labor market in six years to consign us to permanently higher unemployment? My answer is straightforward: nothing. There is not a single reason to believe that we cannot get back to within shouting distance of 5 percent unemployment again. But it will take some time; after all, we are digging out of a pretty deep hole. For reference, after the unemployment rate peaked at 10.8 percent at the end of 1982, about four years of strong growth took unemployment back down into the sixes again, and about another year brought it down into the fives. Something like that should be our target now: say, a five-year march back to 5 percent unemployment. "Five in five" makes a nice slogan. Unfortunately, we're off to a slow start.

Prelude to a Crash

Given what happened afterward, it is worth noting that, contrary to myth, the growth spurt that started petering out in 2005 was *not* powered mainly by building more houses. In fact, business investment grew at essentially the same rate as housing. In terms of share in overall GDP, homebuilding rose from 4.5 percent in 2000 to just over 6 percent in 2005. That extra 1.5 percentage points of GDP, spread out over five years, added just 0.3 percent per year to the overall GDP growth rate. Not much.

But inside the small housing sector it was a very big deal. American builders started 1.6 million new homes in 2000 but 2.1 million in 2005. That's a half million more new dwellings per year—too many, in retrospect. When homebuilding peaked in the second half of 2005, few people viewed that development with alarm. GDP was, after all, still moving up modestly: Growth averaged 2.4 percent over the second half of 2005 and the two full years of 2006 and 2007. Yes, the house-price bubble had burst and the housing sector had cratered. But maybe that was just a return to normalcy.

The economy looked to be in decent shape on the eve of the Great Recession. The unemployment rate was under 5 percent, where it had been for about two years. GDP was growing close to its assumed trend rate.

Outside of housing, the seas did not look particularly stormy. But there were hints of trouble: House prices were falling, the homebuilding industry was dying, and employment growth was meager over the last half of 2007. In addition, both American businesses and American households had saddled themselves with huge debts. If the economy tanked, these debts would be hard to repay.

Then came the slide.

As everybody knows, the collapse of homebuilding led the way. Residential construction, which is normally about 4 percent of GDP, soared to as high as 6.3 percent of GDP in 2005:4—and then started falling. According to myth, the story was simple: The house-price bubble burst and new home construction came tumbling after. But that's not actually the way it happened. In fact, spending on residential construction started to decline well *before* house prices topped out.

Sounds surprising but it's true. The data on housing show clearly that homebuilding peaked in 2005. Home prices tell a messier story, however: They peaked *either* in 2006 or in 2007, depending on what measure you use. Two major competing indexes of national average house prices are shown in figure 1.4. The upper line plots a celebrated index devised by Charles "Chip" Case of Wellesley and Robert Shiller of Yale, and now

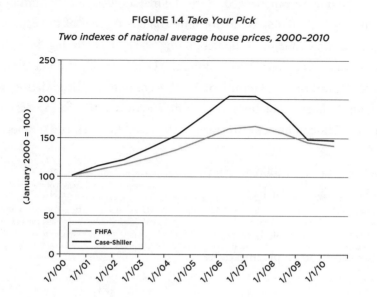

FIGURE 1.4 *Take Your Pick*

Two indexes of national average house prices, 2000–2010

maintained commercially by Standard & Poor's. The lower line plots an index maintained by the government—specifically, by the Federal Housing Finance Agency (FHFA), which is the regulator of Fannie Mae and Freddie Mac. You can see that they tell rather different stories.

According to the Case-Shiller index, home prices peaked in May 2006, but the FHFA index dates the peak a year later. That's a pretty big difference.* By either measure, however, the house-price bubble burst long *after* new home construction went into decline. So the oft-repeated story that falling prices killed homebuilding isn't right.

A simpler explanation is that homeownership simply reached an unnatural high of 69 percent of all American housing units in 2004 and 2005—up from 64 percent just a decade earlier. Just as not everyone likes vanilla ice cream, not every American wants to (or should) own a home. For some people, renting is the better option—especially when home prices soar relative to rents. But whatever the reason, the data show a remarkable decline in spending on new homes, which kept on falling for an amazing three and a half years, eventually dropping to less than half its peak value. The housing sector didn't just experience a recession; it had a depression.

But the housing collapse alone could never have caused a recession as large as the one we experienced. Both the magnitudes and the timing are off. Housing typically accounts for only about 4 percent of the economy. So the stunning collapse of homebuilding was not nearly big enough to cause a serious recession. Furthermore, the U.S. economy did not slip into a recession until the final month of 2007, according to official dating, and I will argue shortly that the recession didn't really begin in earnest until September 2008. Thus two to three *years* passed between the start of the

---

*The two indexes differ in many ways. The FHFA index is limited to mortgages that qualify for securitization by Fannie Mae and Freddie Mac. These restrictions chop off both extremes of the housing market—the *high end*, where so-called jumbo mortgages are too large for Fannie and Freddie to handle, and the *low end*, which is where most of the subprime mortgages were. Since we know from other data sources that low-end house prices inflated more than middle- and high-end prices during the bubble, the FHFA index may *understate* the boom and bust. But the Case-Shiller index puts too much weight on twenty major urban areas, on the East and West Coasts in particular, where home prices are more volatile. So it seems at least arguable that Case-Shiller *overstates* the bubble.

decline in housing and the serious decline in the overall economy. During 2006 and 2007, real GDP *rose* at about a 2.3 percent annual rate, and the unemployment rate barely budged, despite an imploding housing sector. Macroeconomists call that steady trend growth. Others call it boring. But it wasn't a recession.

Things deteriorated in the winter of 2007–2008, however. Payrolls started to decline in February 2008, beginning what would ultimately become the horrific twenty-five-month job-losing streak mentioned earlier. The unemployment rate ticked up in November 2007, beginning a long ascent that would eventually take it to a dizzying high of 10 percent in October 2009. GDP tells a different story. It decreased only slightly, on net, over the last quarter of 2007 and the first half of 2008. The U.S. economy was staggering but had not yet fallen to its knees.

Did Anyone Get the License Plate of That Truck?

When an economy is inching along, with employment drifting down, spending weakening, and its financial system reeling from a gut-wrenching year of ups and downs, that economy is in a weak position to withstand any adverse shock. And we got a whopper on September 15, 2008, when Lehman Brothers filed for bankruptcy. Immediately thereafter, the whole U.S. economy fell off the table. Look at figure 1.5. Lehman's bankruptcy came late in the third quarter of 2008. In that quarter, real GDP fell at a 3.7 percent annual rate. Then it dropped at a frightening 8.9 percent rate in the fourth quarter, and then at a rapid 5.3 percent rate in 2009:1. The graph gives the unmistakable visual impression of something sliding downhill fast—right after the truck hit us.

Job losses, which had averaged "only" 152,000 per month over the first eight months of 2008, leaped to 596,000 jobs per month over the last four, and then to 780,000 a month over the first three months of 2009. Figure 1.6, which depicts these numbers, looks downright scary—and it felt so at the time.

As jobs declined, the unemployment rate, which was just 6.2 percent

FIGURE 1.5 *Falling Off the Table I*
(real GDP growth, in percent)

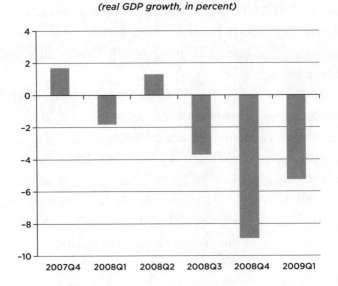

in September 2008, soared. It was a miserable time for American workers. It is only a slight exaggeration to say that everything fell apart after Lehman Day. That is why, unlike the official arbiters at the NBER, I date the start of the recession to a precise day: September 15, 2008. It was one of those

FIGURE 1.6 *Falling Off the Table II*
(change in payroll employment, in thousands)

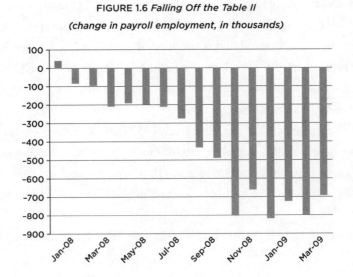

rare cases in which we know exactly what hit us: Lehman Brothers failed, kicking off a virulent financial crisis.

If you were watching data such as these in real time, the U.S. economy might have appeared to be falling into an abyss—Great Depression 2.0, if you will—from Lehman Day until sometime in February or March 2009, when the collapse hit bottom. Figures 1.7 and 1.8 extend the awful data shown in figures 1.5 and 1.6 beyond the first quarter of 2009, to see what happened next. Here you see that it was literally true—as some people were ridiculed for saying at the time—that things started getting worse at a slower rate. GDP stopped dropping and jobs were still falling, but at a slower pace. That was progress!

The visual impression left by these two figures, and many others I could show, reinforce the case that the darkest days came in February and March of 2009. (*Welcome to Washington, President Obama!*) After that the U.S. economy entered the "getting worse at a slower rate" phase, and some glimmers of light began to show. Beginning in 2009:3 for GDP but only in March 2010 for employment, the uphill climb began in earnest. Unfortunately, once an economy has fallen into such a deep hole, climbing out

FIGURE 1.7 *GDP Growth After the Fall*
(in percent)

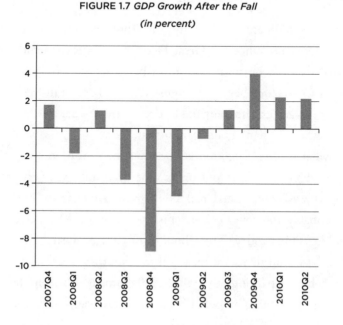

FIGURE 1.8 *Payroll Employment After the Fall*
(*monthly changes, in thousands*)

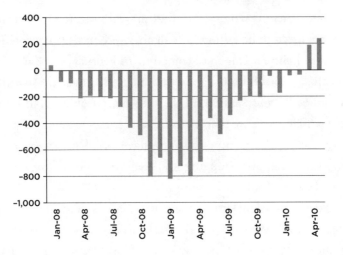

takes quite awhile. As this book went to press, we were still climbing far too slowly.

The Worst Since the Depression?

Did the years 2008 and 2009 really constitute America's worst macroeconomic performance since the Great Depression, as is frequently claimed? Well, that depends on what you mean by "since the Great Depression." The Great *Contraction* began in August 1929 and ended in March 1933. It was vastly longer and incomparably deeper than what we have suffered through recently. Thank goodness for that.

But what is often forgotten is that after the U.S. economy hit bottom in March 1933, the climb out of its superdeep hole was very rapid. Try guessing the average annual real GDP growth rate from 1933 to 1937. You're probably too low. The astonishing answer is 9.5 percent, which sounds like China today. This "boom," of course, started from a shockingly low base, and there was misery throughout.

The robust expansion of the mid-1930s came to an abrupt halt in May 1937—due to mistakes by policy makers, by the way—and "the recession within the Depression" followed. Although the 1937–1938 recession seemed like peanuts compared with the Great Contraction of 1929–1933, it was pretty violent by modern standards. So standing as America's worst recession since 1937–1938, as 2007–2009 does, is a pretty high dishonor.

What sent the U.S. economic juggernaut into a tailspin in 2008? The short answer: the financial crisis. It's now time to find out how. What made the music stop?

PART II

FINANCE
GOES MAD

2

|ıııııııııııııııııııııı|

IN THE BEGINNING ...

This financial crisis was avoidable.

—Report of the Financial Crisis Inquiry Commission

A geologist, a chemist, and an investment banker are arguing over whose profession is the oldest. The geologist points out that his science is as old as the Earth itself. The chemist scoffs at that: "Long before the Earth was formed, there were masses of swirling gasses—chemicals. Before that, there was just chaos." The investment banker smiles slyly, nursing a martini: "And who do you think created all that chaos?"

It would be emotionally satisfying to pin the blame for the crumbling of the financial system on a single culprit—such as greedy bankers, who certainly deserve their share. But it's only a share. While it is natural to crave simple explanations, complicated events are, well, complicated. It is hard to imagine how something as sweeping and multifaceted as the financial crisis could have stemmed from a single cause or had a single villain.

Which it didn't. Knowing full well that any short list will be necessarily incomplete, this chapter and the next focus on seven key weaknesses that predate the fateful summer of 2007 and that contributed mightily to the ensuing financial mess. These are the main villains of the piece. (Lesser villains will appear in later chapters.) The malevolent seven are:

1. inflated asset prices, especially of houses (the housing bubble) but also of certain securities (the bond bubble);
2. excessive leverage (heavy borrowing) throughout the financial system and the economy;
3. lax financial regulation, both in terms of what the law left unregulated and how poorly the various regulators performed their duties;
4. disgraceful banking practices in subprime and other mortgage lending;
5. the crazy-quilt of unregulated securities and derivatives that were built on these bad mortgages;
6. the abysmal performance of the statistical rating agencies, which helped the crazy-quilt get stitched together; and
7. the perverse compensation systems in many financial institutions that created powerful incentives to go for broke.

This book aims to *explain* how these factors conspired to create the financial crisis so that citizens can understand what happened to them, why their government took the actions it did, and whether those policies were wise. Toward that end, this chapter and the next take up the seven villains in turn. In each case, I illustrate how it created a vulnerability that *could* and *should* have been avoided. Yes, as the Financial Crisis Inquiry Commission (FCIC)—which Congress established to "examine the causes of the current financial and economic crisis in the United States"—concluded, this mess did not have to happen.

VILLAIN 1: DOUBLE BUBBLE, TOIL AND TROUBLE

Two bubbles blew up and burst during the last decade, combining to deliver a devastating one-two punch, first to the financial system and then to the economy. The first was the notorious house-price bubble, about which so much has been written. The second, which I'll call the bond bubble, is almost unknown by comparison. I'll begin with the more famous of the two bubbles because no one doubts that the crash of house prices after 2006 was among the major causes of the crisis and the ensuing recession. But first, let's ask a logically prior question: What is a "bubble" anyway?

What Is a Bubble?

A bubble is a *large* and *long-lasting* deviation of the price of some asset—such as a stock, a bond, or a house—from its *fundamental* value. Usually, it's an upward deviation; it is rare to hear anyone speak of a "negative bubble." Mindful of Supreme Court Justice Potter Stewart's classic definition of pornography—"I know it when I see it"—let's pause over each of the three italicized adjectives, starting with *fundamental*.

The idea here seems simple enough, though in practice it is not. In theory, the correct price of an asset depends on certain fundamentals—the things that determine an asset's inherent value to an actual or prospective owner. So, for example, we teach in financial kindergarten that the fundamental value of a share of stock is the value, *in terms of today's money*, of the dividends and capital gains that are expected to accrue to its owner *in the future*. The reason is pretty obvious. Though there may be isolated exceptions—such as buying shares in the Green Bay Packers—most people value shares in a company *only* for the money they expect those shares to bring them. Because sentimental value is nil, the fundamental determinants of stock values are dividends, their expected growth rates, and interest rates. Period.

Why interest rates? Because dividends and capital gains received in the future are worth *less* today when interest rates are higher and *more* when interest rates are lower. The reason is the time value of money: $1 received later is worth less than $1 received sooner because, if you can get your hands on money sooner, you can put it to work earning interest. When interest rates fall, this difference shrinks. The time value of money becomes less and less important. The reverse happens when interest rates rise.

A similar valuation analysis applies to houses, if we ignore emotional attachments and treat buying a house as an investment. Then the "dividends" you receive are the monthly rental fees you *save* by owning rather than renting. Since houses last for decades, most of these rental savings come far in the future. So lower interest rates imply higher fundamental values for houses, just as they do for stocks or bonds—and for basically the same reason: the time value of money.

The calculation of fundamental value for houses is not quite as straightforward as this, of course. One reason is that huge idiosyncrasies across individual houses make the precise rent that is being "saved" hard to know precisely. (*It's ten o'clock. Do you know how much your house would rent for?*) Furthermore, perhaps even more so than with shares of the Green Bay Packers, genuine nonmonetary benefits may accompany homeownership. A house is, after all, something personal—you live in it. It may be worth more to you than the rent you save each month.

The next italicized word is *large*. It has been said that the one thing we really know about speculative markets is that prices go up and down. Small asset-price movements that are part of the normal background noise certainly don't merit the label "bubble." But where does *small* end and *large* begin? Therein lies the second difficulty in recognizing and measuring a bubble in real time. Sometimes a bubble is called too soon, and sometimes a bubble is not recognized until it's too late.

Suppose some outside observer calculates that the fundamental value of a particular house is $300,000. If it then sells for $330,000, is that evidence of a housing bubble? Probably not, because a 10 percent price deviation is not large enough, relative to the inherent uncertainties in estimating a house's fundamental value, to declare it a bubbly valuation. Maybe the buyer just fell in love with it. But what about a 20 percent deviation? Or 30 percent? Where do we draw the line? Like Potter Stewart and pornography, the existence of a bubble may be in the eyes of the beholder.

Finally, consider the term *long-lasting*. Some asset prices—but not usually house prices—bounce around a lot on a daily basis. If the price of some stock soars 50 percent in a week because of an unfounded rumor, and then falls back down to earth, we would not normally call that a bubble because the event was so fleeting. "Long-lasting" means that the price stays elevated long enough that it's easily confused with a higher fundamental value.

So that's my admittedly squishy definition of a bubble: a *large* and *long-lasting* deviation of the price of an asset from its *fundamental* value. And like Mr. Justice Stewart, you are supposed to recognize one when you see one.

Inevitably, however, not everyone sees things the same way. Furthermore, bubbles don't just emerge spontaneously. More often than not, the fundamentals are becoming more favorable as the bubble inflates. For example, in the case of houses, population may be growing or interest rates may be falling. Bubbles typically arise from either exaggeration or unwarranted extrapolation of genuinely favorable trends. The upshot is that reasonable people can and do disagree over what portion of any asset-price increase constitutes a bubble and what portion reflects improved fundamentals. During a bubble, we often hear stories about how some grand new era makes previous valuation standards obsolete. Remember how the Internet was going to create a whole New Economy with different rules that made eyeballs more important than profits? It didn't.

The Housing Bubble

All that said, there can be little doubt that the United States experienced a pretty gigantic housing bubble that blew up and then burst with disastrous consequences in, roughly, the years 2000–2009. Let's look at some of the evidence, starting with the remarkable figure 2.1 on the next page, which is due to the efforts of Robert Shiller, perhaps our nation's most perspicacious chronicler of the housing bubble.

Notice two things about this graph. First, the data go all the way back to 1890—over 120 years! That should be long enough to give us historical perspective. Second, the graph plots *real* house prices—that is, house prices deflated by the Consumer Price Index (CPI). In plain English, what we see here is the history of house prices *relative to the prices of other things* that consumers buy. That is why, for example, you don't see price declines during the Great Depression. House prices did fall quite a bit then, but so did other prices. Ranges in which the graph is relatively flat—such as the half century from the late 1940s to the late 1990s—connote periods when house prices moved more or less in tandem with other prices.

FIGURE 2.1 *Real House Prices: The Long View*
(index, 1890 = 100)

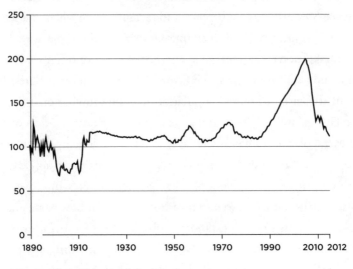

SOURCE: *Robert Shiller and author's calculations.*

Now compare the value of the index in 1890 with its value in the 1990s. The two look about the same. Specifically, the index, which is constructed to start at 100 in 1890, averages about 110 in the years 1995–1997. That historical comparison reveals a stunning—and virtually unknown—fact: On balance, the *relative* prices of houses in America barely changed over more than a century! To be precise, the average annual *relative* price increase from 1890 to 1997 was just 0.09 of 1 percent. You don't get rich on that.

Then things changed dramatically. After 2000 the graph gives the visual impression of a rocket ship taking off. According to the Case-Shiller index, real house prices soared by an astounding 85 percent between 1997 and 2006—and then came crashing down to earth from 2006 to 2012. America had never seen anything like it. Did this huge run-up and crash constitute a bubble? I think Mr. Justice Stewart would have said yes. It was certainly large, long-lasting, and a sharp deviation from fundamental value.

Such judgments are, however, all too easy to make with the incredible clarity of hindsight. The tougher and more important question is whether and when the bubble should have been recognized by the people of the day. Notice that during the hundred-plus years prior to the big housing bubble, Shiller's index rose to as high as 124 in 1894 and 128 in 1989, and fell to as low as about 66 in 1921 and 69 in 1942. So while the data exhibit no *long-run trend* for over a century, there were some very conspicuous ups and downs. For example, real house prices rose almost 60 percent from 1942 to 1947 and, more recently, jumped over 20 percent from 1984 to 1989.

Now, imagine yourself living in 2002. Real house prices are up almost 30 percent over the past five years. Are you in a house-price bubble? Maybe—but only a few contemporary observers thought so. Paul Krugman began mentioning the possibility of a housing bubble in his *New York Times* columns in 2001 and 2002. The *Economist* magazine, which seems to see bubbles everywhere, was hinting at such in 2002. The clearest early call of a housing bubble that I could find came from economist Dean Baker, who concluded in a 2002 paper that "the only plausible explanation for the sudden surge in home prices is the existence of a housing bubble." By 2003 magazines like the *Economist, Barron's,* and *Money* began carrying articles about a possible housing bubble. But not even Shiller seemed convinced at the time. By 2004 media stories about a possible bursting of the housing bubble were becoming commonplace. It was then that the now-renowned economic pessimist Nouriel Roubini began warning of serious troubles ahead.

It is not hard to understand why most of us—including me—missed the early stages of the house-price bubble. America had witnessed comparable price increases in its history. Mortgage interest rates had fallen, which should boost house prices for perfectly conventional *fundamental* reasons. Judgment was further clouded by a detail I mentioned in the last chapter: The Case-Shiller index shown in figure 2.1 is not the only measure of house prices, maybe not even the best. As we saw in the previous chapter, the government's price index rose considerably less than Case-Shiller.

Concentrating now on the shorter period from 2000 to 2010, figure 2.2 displays the two indexes again, now with both deflated by the CPI. We see once again that the price run-up from 2000 to 2006 was *much smaller* when measured by the official FHFA index than when measured by Case-Shiller. The disagreement is not minor: Case-Shiller says real prices rose about 72 percent from January 2000 to January 2006, while FHFA puts the increase at just 34 percent.

Of course, Americans were not studying either index in real time. They were, however, witnessing the actual behavior of house prices in their own neighborhoods. So what matters is which of the indexes offered the more *accurate* representation of reality during the bubble period. Unfortunately, even experts disagree about that.

One further important point is buried in figure 2.2. Even by the time real house prices started to flatten out in May 2009, they had retreated back to only about 2001 levels, not to 1997 levels. (They later fell more.) So, even with the magnificent wisdom of hindsight, it is not obvious that house prices were bubbly in 2002 or 2003. How much harder, then, must it have been to tell in real time?

As late as October 2005, as keen an observer as Ben Bernanke, who was then Chairman of President Bush's Council of Economic Advisers,

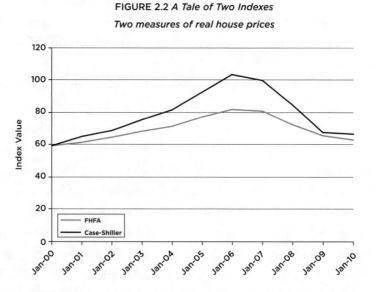

FIGURE 2.2 *A Tale of Two Indexes*
Two measures of real house prices

SOURCES: *Standard & Poor's and Federal Housing Finance Agency (deflated by the author)*

declared that while "house prices have risen by nearly 25 percent over the past two years . . . these price increases largely reflect strong economic fundamentals." While Bernanke was wrong—prices in the Capitol Hill area, where Bernanke bought a house in May 2004, were peaking just about then—he was not alone in this judgment. A skeptical *Wall Street Journal* article from July 2005 was titled, "What Housing Bubble?" And as late as 2008, two housing experts published a book titled, *Houseonomics: Why Owning a Home Is Still a Great Investment*. The book's index has no entry for "bubble."

So, yes, we experienced a house-price bubble and bust of historic proportions in the 2000s. But if you were living through it in real time, it wasn't obvious that we were in a bubble until sometime after 2003, maybe not until after 2005. That said, it was pretty clear by 2006–2007 that the house-price bubble had blown up into something large and dangerous.

Big bubbles leave their marks on economies, not just on financial markets. The nineteenth-century railroad bubble left us with plenty of unused track; the Internet bubble of the late 1990s left us with thousands of miles of unused fiber optic cable; and the house-price bubble left us with a glut of houses, many of which are now vacant, and many more of which are "underwater"—that is, worth less than their mortgages.

Figure 2.3 displays the most scrutinized measure of homebuilding activity: new housing starts. We see quite dramatically that homebuilding is a boom-and-bust industry—with a particularly large bust after 2006. Housing starts soared from a recession-induced low of around 800,000 units per year in January 1991 to a stunning peak of almost 2.3 million units per year in January 2006, and then fell off a cliff—bottoming out at under 500,000 units per year in April 2009, the lowest number in the history of a series that dates back to January 1959. It was quite a roller-coaster ride.

The data thus paint two vivid and remarkably consistent pictures—one for prices, the other for building activity—of a gigantic housing bubble that blew up gradually and then imploded ferociously. It would have been asking a lot of people to recognize the housing bubble and the dangers inherent therein by, say, 2002–2003. But by 2006–2007, the bubble should have been obvious. Apparently, it wasn't.

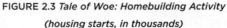

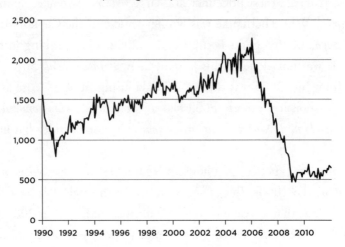

FIGURE 2.3 *Tale of Woe: Homebuilding Activity*
(housing starts, in thousands)

This quick perusal of the facts leaves us with a nagging question: *Why?* Why did it happen? What were the major causes of the housing boom and bust? Let me offer a few likely culprits.

The first, and I think the foremost, is summarized in the famous Pogo line, "We have met the enemy and he is us." We Americans, frankly, went a little crazy about housing. In this, we were not alone. There were also major housing bubbles in the United Kingdom, Ireland, Spain, Australia, and South Africa, among others. The belief that house prices inevitably rise year after year spread like an epidemic and became part of the conventional wisdom. You allegedly *couldn't lose* by investing in houses—which would rise in value by 10 percent or so a year *forever.* Never mind the history shown in figure 2.1. So too many Americans took on too much debt to buy houses they couldn't afford—and then refinanced them several times to pocket capital gains. The media fed the beast by hyping the good real estate news.

Here are two concrete examples from 2005 in California—one of the epicenters of the bubble. A survey of San Francisco homebuyers conducted by Case and Shiller found that the average price increase expected over the next *decade* was *14 percent per annum*—and about a third of the sample expected substantially more than that. The *Economist* reported a survey of Los Angeles homebuyers who expected gains of *22 percent* per annum over that same time span. Think about it: If house prices actually rose 14 percent a year for ten years, the cumulative increase would be an incredible (and I mean that literally—*not credible*) 271 percent, meaning that a $500,000 home in 2005 would be worth $1,854,000 by 2015. At 22 percent a year, the cumulative price appreciation is a jaw-dropping 630 percent, taking that same house's value up to a staggering $3,652,000. If you believed that, it made all the sense in the world to damn the torpedoes and go full speed ahead. After all, housing was a *great* investment. Where else could you earn 22 percent a year?

One fascinating question is where the belief in ever-rising house prices came from when, in fact, house prices had risen, on average, no faster than general inflation for over a century. Part of the answer was surely unwarranted extrapolation of recent trends. House prices had, after all, soared in recent years. Wouldn't they keep doing so?

Another part lies in *leverage*. A simple example will illustrate how it can distort vision. Suppose John and Jane Doe buy a $200,000 house, putting $40,000 down and taking out a $160,000 mortgage. Because they have acquired a $200,000 asset with only $40,000 in equity, we say that their real estate investment is *leveraged* 5 to 1—the asset is worth five times the equity. To keep the arithmetic simple, assume the Does have an interest-only mortgage, so that five years later they still owe the bank $160,000. And assume further—in line with historical evidence—that the house's value rises only with general inflation, which cumulates to 20 percent over the five years. At the end of five years, the Does' home will be worth 20 percent more than what they paid for it, or $240,000, and they will still owe $160,000 on their mortgage. Their *equity* in the house will therefore have risen from $40,000 to $80,000—a *doubling* of their original investment in just five years. It's unlikely they could have done that well in the stock market because they would never have used five times' leverage.

Even adjusting for inflation, something John and Jane probably would *not* do, the value of the couple's real estate investment would have risen at an annual rate of 10.8 percent in real terms. That's impressive. And remember, once adjusted for inflation, the real value of the house didn't rise at all, in this example; it all came from leverage. Many Americans who own homes have had actual experiences that mimicked the hypothetical Does' experience. Some have done it multiple times. No wonder they think homeownership is a great deal.

I find this story plausible. But was the house-price boom based *entirely* on such misconceptions? Certainly not. First of all, it wasn't all myth. As the numerical example illustrated, you really *could* earn a high real return by investing in housing, even with only historically average price increases.

Second, after the tech stock bubble burst in 2000 and the stock market crashed, many Americans were looking around for a safer, stabler place to invest their money. Houses looked like such a place.

Third, as Bernanke observed in 2005, the fundamentals for housing—such as income growth and interest rates—were strong over the years 2003 through 2006.

Fourth, banks and other lenders were practically throwing money both at prospective new homebuyers and existing homeowners who could refinance, encouraging both to lever up. (Where were the regulators, you may ask? We'll come back to that.)

Fifth, many homeowners figured out how to turn their houses into ATMs. As house prices rose they could refinance their mortgages, often to a bigger mortgage with a lower interest rate, and take out some spendable cash in the bargain.

Sixth, the Federal Reserve, trying to give the languid economy a shot in the arm, held short-term interest rates extraordinarily low in 2003 and 2004, adding fuel to the housing boom. In fact, some critics have gone so far as to lay most of the blame for the house-price bubble squarely on the central bank's doorstep. To me, that is a grotesque exaggeration; at worst, the Fed's monetary policy was a minor contributor to the boom.

But don't take my word for it. Draw your own conclusions after considering three pertinent facts: (1) The bubble started several years *before* the Fed adopted its superlow interest-rate policy in June 2003; (2) the bubble continued to inflate for at least two years *after* the Fed began *raising* interest rates in June 2004; and (3) other countries, such as the UK, experienced a house-price bubble as severe as ours or worse, even though their central banks kept interest rates much higher than the Fed throughout the 2003–2004 period. Facts like these should make you wonder how anyone can believe that loose monetary policy was the *primary* cause of the housing bubble. I wonder, too.

Anyway, one thing we *do* know about speculative bubbles—whether in houses, stocks, or anything else—is that they eventually burst. And this one did, spectacularly, starting in either 2006 or 2007, depending on which price index you use. Why then, rather than earlier or later? No one will ever know. Ask yourself why the NASDAQ bubble burst in March 2000, not sooner or later. Or why the stock market crashed in October 1987, rather than in September or November. No one will ever know those answers, either.

The metaphor I use to illustrate the bursting of bubbles is Wile E. Coyote, that hapless enemy of the Road Runner in the well-known cartoons. *(Meep, Meep!)* As you'll recall, every now and then Wile E. Coyote, in hot pursuit of the Road Runner, dashes straight off a cliff. He remains there for a while, suspended in midair, until he looks down, realizes he is supported by *nothing*, and crashes violently to the earth.

Bubble bursting is like that. At some unpredictable moment, investors start "looking down," realize that the sky-high prices they believed would never end are not supported by the fundamentals, and start selling. It is abundantly clear that the crash must come—*eventually*. Fundamentals win out in the end. But why it happens just when it does is always a mystery.

We know now that the house-price crash started in 2006–2007. Didn't anyone see it coming in, say, 2005? Yes, some people did. As noted earlier, a few Cassandras were predicting an imminent fall in house prices as early as 2002. But forecasters who are that early are like the proverbial stopped clock that shows the correct time twice a day—or, more apropos, like the pessimist who predicts that the stock market will crash every year and is eventually right.

The Wile E. Coyote of house prices did not fall from the sky without warning. By 2004–2005 a vigorous national and international debate over whether house prices were too bubbly was in train. Some said yes, others said no. Most of our policy makers turned out to be on the wrong side of this debate—the no side. But here's the rub: By the end of 2005, it was already too late for the housing bubble not to end badly. That, too, is part of the sad-but-true chronology of most bubbles: It is extremely difficult to recognize them early enough to do much good. By the time a bubble is widely recognized, it's too late. Such was the case with the housing bubble.

The Bond Bubble

However, housing was not the only bubble to inflate and blow up during the last decade, maybe not even the most damaging one. There was also a gigantic bond bubble that you may never have heard of.

Bonds and other *fixed-income securities* derive their names from the fact that the borrower is legally obliged to pay the lender a *fixed* number of dollars (or euros, or pounds, or whatever) at dates set in advance. Should the borrowing company fare exceptionally well during the decade, the lender will not share in its prosperity—it will just receive the promised interest payments. Similarly, if the business does poorly, the lender will not share in the downside—unless the borrower defaults. This fixity of the income stream contrasts starkly with common stocks, where dividends and capital gains rise and fall with the fortunes of companies and are not specified in advance.

The fundamental value of a fixed-income security is easy to compute *in the absence of default risk:* One need compute only the present values of all the future flows of interest and principal, which are *fixed* and *known*—and then add them up. Because of the time value of money, lower interest rates make those future flows worth more, implying higher bond prices.

For U.S. Treasury bonds, which carry no risk of default, the fundamentals are only the stated ("coupon") rate of interest and the current market rate of interest. When the market interest rate falls, the bond's fundamental value rises—and the bond's value falls when the market interest rate rises. That's it. But for any other type of bond there is some risk of default.

Default risk both complicates valuation and opens up the possibility of bubbles. In particular, the fundamentals for a corporate bond or a mortgage-backed security (MBS) are not only the stated coupon interest payments and the corresponding risk-free Treasury rate, but also the *perceived probability of loss from default.* Underestimating the risk of default is therefore tantamount to overestimating the value of the bond. And that's what can give rise to bubbles. The bubble in house prices had as its counterpart a bubble in MBS because investors falsely believed that the probabilities of mortgage default were tiny.

Just as the fundamentals for, say, stocks and houses are often improving as a bubble inflates, the same is true of bonds and other fixed-income securities. During prosperous times, default rates drop to very low levels. Investors then deduce that rational interest-rate spreads over Treasuries— just enough to compensate lenders for the default risks they bear—should also drop to very low levels. The trouble is, how low is low? Markets sometimes get carried away.

DEFAULT RISK AND INTEREST-RATE SPREADS

One key respect in which fixed-income securities differ is their *risk of default.* There is no such risk on U.S. government securities. Dating back to fundamental decisions made by Alexander Hamilton, the nation's first secretary of the Treasury, the U.S. government has always paid its debts in full and on time. Investors assume it always will. So Treasuries are considered *risk-free* securities.

Moving up the risk spectrum, the debts of the nation's leading corporations carry some small risk of default. In order to induce investors to buy their securities, corporations must therefore pay somewhat higher interest rates than the Treasury. The lesson generalizes: *Riskier borrowers pay higher interest rates than safer borrowers* in order to compensate lenders for the risk they bear. For example, "junk bonds"—the debts of less-than-blue-chip companies— carry higher interest rates than, say, the bonds of IBM or AT&T. And the bonds of emerging-market nations carry higher interest rates than U.S. government bonds.

The gap between the interest rate on a risky bond and the corresponding risk-free Treasury rate is called the *risk premium*, or *spread*, on that bond. For example, if a 30-year Treasury bond pays 3 percent per annum, and the 30-year bond of some corporation pays 5 percent, we say that the spread on that particular bond is 2 percentage points (or 200 basis points) over Treasuries. Notice that this spread, which is determined by supply and demand every day in the marketplace, compensates the investor for a 2 percent annual expected loss from default. The clear implication is that when defaults are perceived as more (or less) likely, risk spreads will widen (or narrow).

In the years leading up to the financial crisis, many spreads narrowed remarkably—perhaps unrealistically—suggesting that default risk was negligible. Then, as the crisis exploded and deepened, risk spreads skyrocketed. Finally, once the financial system started to return to normal after March 2009, risk spreads narrowed again.

The default experience with home mortgages during the boom is a poignant case in point, especially in view of the subsequent bust. Over the period from 1991 through 2001, banks lost only 0.15 percent (15 basis points) on home mortgages. Think about what that means: For every million dollars in outstanding mortgage balances, banks lost an average of $1,500! That's nothing. In short, home mortgages were an exceptionally safe form of lending for over a decade. Then they got even safer.

Figure 2.4 shows the behavior of bank loss rates on residential mortgages over the period 1991–2004. Notice the vertical scale used for the graph. What looks like a big spike in loss rates in the third quarter of 2001 is a paltry 0.45 percent. With a few other brief upward blips, the loss rate fell from 0.24 percent in 1992 to just 0.10 percent in 2004—and hit a

FIGURE 2.4 *Safety in Numbers*

(loss rates on home mortgages, 1991–2004, in percent)

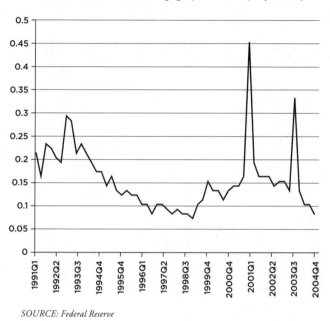

SOURCE: *Federal Reserve*

puny 0.08 percent in the fourth quarter of 2004, the lowest ever. Actual defaults in those years were, in a word, negligible.

Now, imagine yourself as a banker in 2005. House prices have been soaring for eight years or so, with nary a break in the seemingly inexorable upward trend. Mortgage delinquencies and defaults have plummeted to historic lows. From your perch, mortgage lending, which was always a safe form of lending, looks safer than ever—a veritable walk in the park. Or imagine yourself as an investor, listening to a bond salesman tout the virtues of MBS. *(Mortgages never default.)* Sounds like a very-low-risk investment that pays more than Treasuries, right? Well, it was—until it wasn't.

You know what happened next, and figure 2.5 shows you. Here I have extended *exactly* the same data series through the year 2011, adjusting the scale for the much higher loss rates. On this larger scale, the two blips that stood out in figure 2.4 are barely noticeable. You see now that the superlow delinquency rates continued for a while longer, but then reversed with a

FIGURE 2.5 *Unsafety in Numbers*
(loss rates on home mortgages, 1991–2011, in percent)

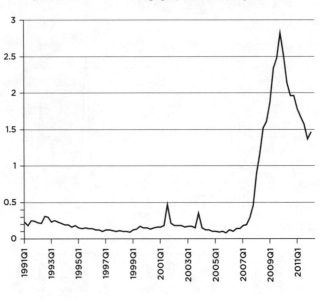

SOURCE: *Federal Reserve*

vengeance starting in 2006. By 2008 mortgage lending didn't look so safe anymore. And then things got much worse. Imagine yourself walking into a bank for a mortgage in 2009, or listening to a sales pitch for MBS. Times had indeed changed.

My point here is not to argue that bankers were foolish—especially since the bursting of the bond bubble caught so many other people by surprise, too. In fairness, no one should have been expected to foresee accurately the truly unprecedented collapse of the residential mortgage market. It was bigger than your worst nightmare.

But I *am* claiming that neither bankers nor other investors should have extrapolated the superlow default rates of 2003–2006, which in many cases were unprecedented, indefinitely into the future—especially as so many of the underlying mortgages were, to put it politely, junk. But many short-sighted investors apparently did just that. For example, many fancy mathematical models of risk were based on only three years' worth of data or less. Three years! Of course, *underestimating* the probabilities of default led to risk spreads (over Treasuries) that were far *too small*, and, therefore, to bond prices that were far *too high*. The result? A huge bond bubble.

I used residential mortgages as my example because the home mortgage collapse was at the epicenter of the financial earthquake that struck in 2007. However, the bond bubble was by no means limited to mortgages. It was ubiquitous.

During the years 2004–2006, I occasionally spoke to financial market audiences about the dangers lurking in the bond bubble. My belief, which was hardly unique to me, was that risk spreads were irrationally small and therefore had to widen. The bond market was like Wile E. Coyote suspended in midair. But, of course, I had no idea when the bust would come. Needless to say, such dour—and unspecific—warnings were widely ignored.

I remember one such speech vividly. It was to a hotel ballroom full of stockbrokers, sometime in 2005. I had read in the newspaper that morning that Colombian government bonds were paying only 100 basis points above U.S. Treasuries, which struck me as nutty. Sure, the Colombians were doing much better at managing their economy, and I claimed no special expertise about the country. But a mere 100 basis points over Treasuries, which implied a 1 percent expected loss rate per annum, seemed wildly optimistic. So when I came to the part of my speech about the bond-market bubble and put a picture of Wile E. Coyote on the screen, I had Colombian debt on my mind. When I asked who among the assembled brokers thought that 100 basis points was a reasonable spread over U.S. Treasuries, not a single hand went up. Then I broke the news: The market does, because that's what Colombian bonds sell for today.

By early 2006, I had grown tired of listening to myself speak about the bond bubble to deaf ears. So I gave up. Maybe I should have kept at it.

Where did the bond bubble come from? That story, I'm afraid, *does* start with the Federal Reserve's monetary policy. The U.S. economy limped, rather than leaped, out of the minirecession of 2001. GDP grew slowly at first, and employment continued to decline for nearly two years of so-called job-loss recovery. Inflation was low and falling. In fact, by 2003 the Fed was getting worried that the United States might actually slip into *deflation*. In an effort to stimulate the sluggish economy, it pushed its overnight interest rate (called the federal funds rate) all the way down to 1 percent—the lowest since 1954. The aggressive monetary policy worked, and the economy perked up. But it also meant that investors in safe assets like Treasuries were earning very little.

That, in turn, led investors to "reach for yield." If a Treasury bond would pay you only 4.5 percent interest, but a mortgage-backed security *with (allegedly) negligible default risk* would pay you 6 percent interest instead, why not sell the Treasury bond and buy the MBS, picking up an extra 150 basis points in the process? Seems like a no-brainer, right? And if default risk really is negligible, it is. But, of course, the risk wasn't negligible. Investors should never have extrapolated the amazingly favorable default experience of 2004–2006 into the indefinite future. But they did. It was the kind of thinking that led to the bond-market bubble.

As investors shifted out of Treasuries into riskier fixed-income securities—whether Columbian government bonds or MBS backed by subprime mortgages—those riskier securities were bid up in price, and hence down in yield. You had to pay more to buy the same stream of interest payments. So what was once, say, a 150-basis-point reward for bearing more risk became a 100-basis-point reward, or maybe just a 50-basis-point reward. Investors' response to dwindling yields on fixed-income securities was to try to magnify their yields by going for more *leverage*—which is the second item on my list of villains.

If bearing a little additional risk would bring you only, say, 50 basis points in additional return, you could magnify that reward to 500 basis points by making the investment with 10-to-1 leverage. Now you're talking real money. I'll explain how that worked shortly, but first let's pause for a moment to think about remedies—or at least palliatives.

Can we prevent asset-price bubbles in the future? Here, unfortunately, the answer is mostly no. Speculative markets have succumbed to occasional bubbles for as long as there have been speculative markets. Indeed, one of the first common stocks ever issued, in the South Sea Company in England, was hyped into the first stock-market bubble—the famed South Sea Bubble of 1720—which devastated, among others, a pretty smart fellow named Isaac Newton. And the Dutch had managed to grow a gigantic bubble in—of all things—tulip bulbs almost a century earlier.

No, while we may be lucky enough to nip a few bubbles in the bud, we will never stamp them out. The herding behavior that produces them may well be programmed into our DNA. Our best hope is to minimize the consequences when bubbles go splat—as they inevitably will. And that's worth doing.

VILLAIN 2: LEVERAGE, HANDLED WITHOUT CARE

I emphasized leverage as a way to magnify investment returns. There is nothing wrong with leverage per se. Like a little wine, a little leverage can be good for you. But just as with consumption of alcoholic beverages, excesses can lead to disaster because leverage is the proverbial double-edged sword. It does magnify returns on the upside, which is what investors want. But it also magnifies losses on the downside, which can be fatal. So a company, investor, or household operating with high leverage should be labeled FRAGILE: HANDLE WITH CARE. Its shock absorbers may not be resilient. Unfortunately, by 2007 leverage was everywhere in the U.S. economy.

Leverage at Home

Start with American homebuyers. Back in the day, people used to purchase homes with 20 percent down, as in our earlier example of 5-to-1 leverage. But during the heady days of the real estate boom, when *you couldn't lose* in real estate, that old rule of thumb came to be seen as outmoded. Mortgages with 5 percent down or less became common. Twenty-to-one leverage is dangerous enough: If the house's value declines a mere 5 percent, you're wiped out. But sometimes even the down payment was borrowed, perhaps via a second mortgage. A homeowner with no money down has, in effect, infinite leverage. Even the slightest loss will put him underwater. In fact, he's not an "owner" in any real sense as his equity in the house is zero.

LEVERAGE AND FINANCIAL RETURNS

Leverage refers to the use of borrowed funds to purchase assets. The word itself derives from Archimedes, who famously declared that he could move the Earth with a large enough lever. (One wonders where he thought he would place the fulcrum!) The important point for present purposes is that leverage magnifies both gains on the way up *and* losses on the way down. To illustrate this general principle, consider the contrasting investment styles of Jane Doe and John Dough.

Jane, who craves safety, invests $1 million in one-year corporate bonds paying 6 percent interest. At the end of the year, she gets back her $1 million in principal plus $60,000 in interest. Since what she receives is 6 percent more than what she originally paid, her rate of return is, naturally, 6 percent.

John, who takes more risk, commits $1 million of his own money to buy those same bonds. But he *leverages* his investment ten times by borrowing another $9 million from a bank at 3 percent interest—investing the entire $10 million in the bonds. At year's end, John gets back his $10 millon in principal plus $600,000 in interest, or $10,600,000 in total. He repays the bank $9 million in principal plus $270,000 in interest, or $9,270,000 in total. Hence, his net return is $10,600,000 − $9,270,000 = $1,330,000 on a $1 million investment. Thus, John's rate of return is 33 percent—five and a half times as high as Jane's.

So, is John, who uses leverage, a smarter investor than Jane, who does not? Maybe not. Suppose the bond falls 5 percent in value during the year, and Jane and John need to sell. Now Jane has only $950,000 in principal plus the $60,000 in interest, or $1,010,000 in total, for a paltry rate of return of 1 percent. John will get back $9,500,000 in principal plus $600,000 in interest, or $10,100,000 in total. But he will still have to pay the bank $9,270,000, leaving him with only $830,000 of his original $1 million investment. So John's rate of return is *minus* 17 percent. Now he doesn't look so smart.

The point is that John's munificent reward on the upside—33 percent instead of Jane's 6 percent—is not evidence of superior investment talent. It merely compensates him for the risk he takes on the downside—earning *minus* 17 percent instead of 1 percent. Investors don't reap rewards without taking risk—and that includes people who refinance their houses.

He's more of a speculator, betting on rising house prices and doomed if they fall.

The dangers of leverage notwithstanding, there was a bit of a debt explosion between 2000 and 2008. Figure 2.6 shows that total household debt (mortgage plus personal) rose from about 100 percent of GDP to about 140 percent in only eight years. The lion's share of that increase came in mortgage indebtedness. American households were levering up.

FIGURE 2.6 *Rising Debt Burdens*
(household debt as percent of GDP, 1952-2009)

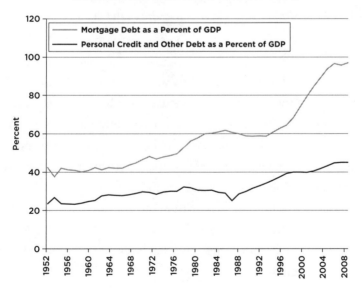

Leverage at the Bank

So were the banks. Banking has always been a leveraged business. Most people don't think of it this way, but a bank "borrows" money from its depositors and "invests" those funds in, say, loans. If a bank's capital amounts to 10 percent of its assets, the bank is leveraged 10 to 1. That's pretty normal—and also pretty safe, because loan losses rarely come close to 10 percent. But during the boom, too many of our leading banks employed legal and accounting gimmicks to push their leverage higher. One way they did so was by creating off-balance-sheet entities such as *structured investment vehicles* (SIVs)—which almost no one had ever heard of before the crisis but whose collapses made the crisis much worse.

Here's how SIVs worked—and then failed to work. Table 2.1 is the balance sheet of Big-But-Simple Bank (BBSB). This old-fashioned bank has taken $10 billion of shareholders' equity, leveraged it 10 to 1 by raising $90 billion in deposits, and made $100 billion worth of loans. As long as its loan losses don't exceed 10 percent, it's safe.

TABLE 2.1 Balance Sheet of Big-But-Simple Bank (BBSB)

Assets	Liabilities and Net Worth
Loans $100 billion	Deposits $90 billion
	Equity $10 billion

But it's also stodgy. If the managers want to grow the bank—and, not incidentally, their own salaries and bonuses—without raising more capital, the bank can sponsor a SIV and sell it, say, $50 billion of the bank's loans. Since the bank gives a tacit or explicit guarantee against most loan losses, the SIV is apparently in a safe position. Perhaps it holds just $1 billion in capital, raising the other $49 billion it needs in the commercial paper market, where top-rated companies go to raise short-term funding. That would create the balance sheet shown in table 2.2. The SIV is leveraged 50 to 1, which may seem high. But believe it or not, actual SIVs were often leveraged even more!

TABLE 2.2 Balance Sheet of BBSB's SIV

Assets	Liabilities and Net Worth	
Loans $50 billion	Commercial paper $49 billion	
	Equity	$1 billion

Meanwhile, back at the bank, BBSB has sold off $50 billion of its loans and received in return $49 billion in cash and $1 billion in stock in the SIV. But it won't just sit on the cash. When it lends out the $49 billion, its balance sheet becomes:

TABLE 2.3 New Balance Sheet of BBSB

Assets		Liabilities and Net Worth	
Loans	$99 billion	Deposits	$90 billion
Stock in SIV $1 billion		Equity	$10 billion

It still appears to be leveraged 10 to 1. But is it? If we consolidate the two balance sheets, we get this:

TABLE 2.4 Consolidated Balance Sheet of BBSB and Its SIV

Assets	Liabilities and Net Worth	
Loans $149 billion	Deposits	$90 billion
	Commercial paper $49 billion	
	Equity	$10 billion

Isn't accounting wonderful? Since the SIV is the dependent child of the parent bank, the organization's true leverage is now 14.9 to 1, as seen in table 2.4. However, it reports only 9.9 to 1 to its regulators (see table 2.3). That's what it pays its accountants and lawyers for.

All's well as long as the SIV, with its 50-to-1 leverage, stays solvent.

Unfortunately, if things turn sour, SIVs have hardly any capital to buffer them against loan losses. Once losses surpass 2 percent, this hypothetical SIV is wiped out. At that point the losses, in effect, accrue to the bank. In terms of the economics rather than the accounting, the bank's real balance was always table 2.4 (with about 15-to-1 leverage), not table 2.3 (with about 10-to-1 leverage). The SIV was a legal and accounting dodge to avoid leverage limits.

Leverage on Wall Street

Leverage numbers like the 15 to 1 in our banking example were chump change compared to what the big investment banks were doing prior to the meltdown. Venerable firms like Bear Stearns, Lehman Brothers, Merrill Lynch, Morgan Stanley, and Goldman Sachs (the old Big Five) operated with 30-to-1 or even 40-to-1 leverage. Think about what that means: With 40-to-1 leverage, a mere 2.5 percent decline in the value of your assets wipes out all shareholder value. That's a pretty risky way to run a business. What were they thinking? Where were the regulators?

The result of extreme leverage is predictable, though its timing never is. When asset values dropped after the housing and fixed-income bubbles burst, many of these highly leveraged firms were ill prepared to absorb losses. Lehman, of course, perished. Bear and Merrill were absorbed into commercial banks in shotgun marriages. Morgan Stanley and Goldman hid behind the Fed's protective skirts by becoming bank holding companies, at least de jure.

But even high leverage was apparently not enough to sate their hearty appetites for risk. If you look back at the liabilities side of BBSB's balance sheet in table 2.1, you will see that the bank funded itself exclusively by deposits and equity. That's quite unrealistic for big money-center banks, which have multiple and complex sources of funds. Nonetheless, commercial banks *do* have deposits—that's why we call them banks. Investment banks do not. They fund themselves almost entirely by borrowing.

Remember, with 40-to-1 leverage, capital constitutes a mere 2.5 percent of assets. They must borrow the other 97.5 percent. Some of this borrowing is long-term—bonds, more or less. But prior to the crisis, and still today, a great deal was and is very short-term, much of it overnight. For example, Bear Stearns' year-end 2006 balance sheet listed only 16 percent of its liabilities as long-term borrowings. Its short-term borrowings were more than eight times its equity. Its reported leverage, by the way, was 29 to 1.

Is the mix of short-term versus long-term financing a mere detail, of interest only to green eyeshades? Hardly. If Risky Investment Bank (RIB) borrows by selling a 10-year bond, that bit of funding is *guaranteed* to be there for ten years. But interest rates on bonds are far higher than interest rates on overnight, collateralized loans called repurchase agreements ("repos"). RIB may find it more attractive to borrow cheaply in the market for repos. But here's the catch: If RIB borrows overnight via repos, *it must return to the capital markets to borrow every single day.* Should the markets view RIB as creditworthy on Tuesday but risky on Wednesday, the company is in big trouble. In fact, the inability to roll over short-term borrowing is the modern version of a run on the bank. Such runs more or less killed both Bear Stearns and Lehman Brothers in 2008, and almost killed Merrill Lynch, Morgan Stanley, and Goldman Sachs. All five were playing with fire.

Synthetic Leverage

Finally, let's not forget about derivatives. Derivatives serve many purposes, some of them valuable. But one common purpose is to create lots of *synthetic leverage*, which is often embedded in the design of the contract.

The most familiar example of a derivative, a stock option, provides a clear example. At the end of February 2012, Google shares were selling for about $610. On that same day, a seven-month *call option*, giving the buyer the right but not the obligation, to buy Google at $610 per share (the "strike price") was selling for about $48 (the "option premium"). Think about what that meant: If Google shares were worth $658 in September 2012, the option-buyer would just break even: She could acquire shares of Google by paying only the $610 strike price. That, plus the $48 option premium she paid earlier, would come to exactly the market value of the shares ($658). Ignoring the time value of money, which is small over seven months, her rate of return on the option would be exactly zero.

But what if, instead, Google shares were worth $710 in September 2012? By buying the shares at the $610 strike price, and immediately selling them at the $710 market price, she would pocket a $100 profit. Since she paid $48 for the option, her net gain would be $52, which is 108 percent of her original $48 investment—even though the shares themselves rose by only 16 percent. Nice.

But now think about the other edge of the sword. What happens if Google stock is still worth only $610 a share when the option expires? While the stock price would have remained unchanged, for a rate of return of zero, the option would have lost all its value—a 100 percent loss! Welcome to the dark side of leverage.

Table 2.5 compares six investment outcomes, depending on whether the investor buys the stock or the call option and on whether Google shares wind up at $610, $658, or $710. The strong magnification of returns by the option—whether up or down—is evident. As the performance of the underlying stock ranges from no gain to a 16 percent appreciation, the rate of return on the option ranges from *minus* 100 percent to *plus* 108 percent. It behaves very much like a highly leveraged investment even though no borrowing is involved. Hence, the leverage is "synthetic."

TABLE 2.5 Embedded Leverage: An Example

Value of underlying stock	$610	$658	$710
BUY THE STOCK			
Terminal value of investment	$610	$658	$710
Rate of return	0	8%	16%
BUY THE OPTION			
Terminal value of investment	0	$48	$100
Rate of return	-100%	0	108%

There's nothing inherently wrong with this synthetic leverage, as long as it's understood and managed. But many of the newfangled derivatives that played such large roles in the crisis are vastly more complicated than this simple stock option—and some were poorly understood. They amounted to placing high-risk bets on such things as whether the losses in a mortgage pool would exceed certain thresholds or whether a company would default on its bonded debt. They all shared the common element illustrated by table 2.5, however: They created *synthetic leverage*, sometimes in stunningly large amounts. So when the bubble in MBS burst, a far bigger bubble in leveraged bets on MBS burst at the same time—making one big mess.

Letting Our Guard Down—or Worse

Leverage was *everywhere.* Indeed, often leverage was piled on top of leverage—as when companies with highly levered balance sheets bought derivatives with high synthetic leverage. The hint here for regulatory reform is too obvious to miss: *We need a financial system with much less leverage.*

A financial system that is highly leveraged and betting massively on the continuation of bubbles is a two-pronged accident waiting to happen. But that wasn't all. A nation can put safeguards in place, just in case— things like regulation and prudent lending standards. But in early twenty-first-century America, we didn't—as we will see next.

3

|||||||||||||||||||||||||||||||

THE HOUSE OF CARDS

House built on a weak foundation will not stand, oh no.

—FROM "HOSANNA," BY HARRY BELAFONTE

When foxes are left to guard chicken coops, the chickens are in mortal danger. When the foxes have legions of accomplices, the perils are commensurately greater. And when both ideology and incentives conspire to make the authorities look the other way, well, chicken dinner is served. Sadly, that was the case in America during the boom years, when regulators stopped regulating, underwriters stopped underwriting, and financial engineering ran amok.

The first two villains were bubbles and leverage. We now turn our attention to the other five members of the hall of shame, beginning with the abysmal performances of the nation's financial regulatory agencies.

VILLAIN 3: WHERE WERE THE REGULATORS?

Contrary to the complaints you often hear from the financial industry, we have regulations for good reasons. One is to prevent collapses such as the one we suffered through. Another is to limit contagion from one sick institution to another. A third is to minimize costs to the taxpayer. A fourth is to ensure square dealing. There are others. The rationale for financial regulation is often summarized under the trade jargon banner of ensuring the *safe and sound* operation of banks and other financial institutions.

Of course, saying that there are persuasive rationales for financial regulations is not to claim that all financial regulations are well designed and well executed. On the contrary, regulatory failures were legion in the years leading up to the crisis.

Bank Regulators, Reduced

The Federal Reserve is the *primus inter pares* of the four federal banking regulators. It was led for more than eighteen years by Alan Greenspan, a self-described disciple of the libertarian philosopher Ayn Rand, and proud of it.* Greenspan was, shall we say, a less-than-enthusiastic regulator. He was also, as he later confessed, unduly enamored of banks' mathematical risk models and their abilities to use them with both skill and integrity. Just like Captain Renault in *Casablanca*, he was *Shocked! Shocked!* to discover there was gambling going on.

Under the Fed's unwatchful eye, banks proliferated the SIVs we met in the previous chapter. They granted hundreds of billions of dollars' worth of embarrassingly bad subprime mortgages, many of them *designed to default* (more on this shortly). And they invested huge sums in risky assets that they portrayed as, and maybe even believed were, safe. Each of these disgraceful banking practices was, as they say, hidden in plain sight. Incurious regulators just didn't look.

Though frequently done, it is wrong to blame the regulatory breakdown entirely on the Federal Reserve. In truth, while the Fed was the most prominent of the nation's four bank regulators, it was not the biggest player. Most bankers dealt much more with regulatory personnel from the Office of the Comptroller of the Currency (OCC), the now-abolished Office of

---

*Ben Bernanke took over the chairmanship of the Federal Reserve Board in February 2006, just before the bubble started to burst. Ironically, Bernanke also characterized himself as a libertarian—before the crisis.

Thrift Supervision (OTS), and the FDIC. And each was just as asleep at the wheel as the Fed—although Sheila Bair, chairwoman of the FDIC, put the others to shame with her prompt recognition of the impending tsunami of foreclosures. One of the great tragedies of the financial crisis is that bank regulators *could have* slammed the door on some of the more outrageous underwriting practices but didn't. Each agency was headed at the time by a Bush appointee. They were a deregulation-minded bunch of regulators who probably also got swept up in the euphoria of the day.

Where did bank regulators go wrong? In many places, but I'll emphasize just one: their exceedingly permissive attitudes toward subprime lending, an attitude that grew ever more inexplicable as time passed. Subprime mortgages constituted a mere 7 percent of all mortgages granted in 2001. Okay, maybe a small problem—although the predatory lending practices in that market were already drawing attention. But by 2005, subprime lending amounted to 20 percent of all new mortgage lending, and total outstanding subprime mortgage balances had soared to around $1.25 *trillion*. Definitely *not* a small problem.

The four banking agencies are supposed to be safety-and-soundness regulators. So charging them with dereliction of duty is not hard. First, explosive growth of any particular type of lending, especially if it takes novel forms, should set off regulators' alarm bells. It's a standard red flag that bank examiners have used forever. Did the regulators really believe that subprime mortgage lending could expand that rapidly *without* deterioration of quality?

Second, regulators were receiving plenty of unsolicited warnings. Alert journalists, for example, were writing about risky lending practices in the subprime mortgage sector as early as 2004. It was an open secret. Third, inside the Fed, the late governor Edward "Ned" Gramlich was warning Alan Greenspan that things were getting out of hand as early as 2000. And Sheila Bair, who was then a Bush Treasury official, was sounding alarms there. Finally, the four agencies kept declaring that they were getting ready to crack down on disgraceful subprime underwriting practices. But they never did—at least not until it was too late.

Why not? Historians will argue about this for some time. But some of the reasons surely were that deregulation and free-market ideology were in the air, recent default experience had been quite favorable, and the regulators may have been caught up in the Panglossian bubble mentality. None of this is meant to excuse them—in my view, the regulatory failure was inexcusable—but only to explain their astonishing passivity.

Another part of the reason may have been actual or perceived political pressures. After all, well-publicized drives to increase homeownership—including by relatively low-income families—were features of both the Clinton and Bush administrations. Remember President Bush's "ownership society"? But we give our regulators a measure of independence precisely to resist such pressures. So, again, that's not an excuse.

Finally, and perhaps most important, none of the banking regulators, nor even the quartet as a whole, saw the complete sorry picture for what it was. A large and growing share of the worst subprime mortgages were not issued by banks at all, but rather by nonbank lenders who would originate dodgy mortgages, perhaps hold them for only a matter of days, and then sell them off to securitizers (whom we will meet shortly). For example, only one of the top ten subprime mortgage originators in 2005 was a regulated commercial bank (Wells Fargo). By 2007 more than half of all subprime loans were being originated by mortgage brokers rather than by banks. Indeed, Gramlich estimated that only 20 percent of subprime loans granted in 2005 came from regularly supervised banks and thrifts.

The nonbank lenders operated beyond the purview of the federal regulatory system, which often meant that they operated with no adult supervision at all. (The severity of the problem varied state by state.) That said, federal regulators should have seen more than enough shenanigans to make them sit up and take notice. But they didn't.

The Wild and Woolly Shadow Banking System

The nonbank mortgage lenders were just one piece of what we now call the *shadow banking system*—a complex latticework of financial institutions and capital markets that are heavily involved in various aspects of borrowing and lending. There is no agreed-upon definition of the shadow banking system, but the institutions involved on the eve of the crisis included non-bank loan originators; the two government-sponsored housing agencies, Fannie Mae and Freddie Mac; other so-called private-label securitizers; the giant investment banks (who were often securitizers, too); the aforementioned SIVs; a variety of finance companies (some of which specialized in housing finance); hedge funds, private equity funds, and other asset managers; and thousands of mutual, pension, and other sorts of investment funds.

The *markets* involved included those for mortgage-backed securities (MBS), other asset-backed securities (ABS), commercial paper (CP), repurchase agreements ("repos"), and a bewildering variety of derivatives, including the notorious collateralized debt obligations (CDOs) and the ill-fated credit default swaps (CDS). (Sorry about the alphabet soup—explanations to come.)

By most estimates, the shadow banking system was far larger than the conventional banking system. Imagine leaving all that financial activity almost totally unregulated—like a bunch of wild animals running around without zookeepers. Well, actually, you don't have to imagine it. We did it.

In the case of derivatives, a little history is instructive. While their ancestry dates back centuries, modern financial derivatives really came into their own in the late 1980s and early 1990s. The International Swaps and Derivatives Association (ISDA), the industry's trade association, estimates that the notional value of outstanding privately negotiated derivatives—mostly interest-rate swaps—amounted to under $1 trillion at the end of 1987. But they grew like kudzu, to $11 trillion by the end of 1992 and a staggering $69 trillion by 2001.

All this activity was visible only to specialists, however, until a series of highly publicized derivative "accidents" called attention to the still-young industry in 1994–1995. One stemmed from a deal between Merrill Lynch and Orange County, California, which left the county with such large losses that it filed the largest municipal bankruptcy in U.S. history. Another involved a sale of derivatives by Bankers Trust to Proctor & Gamble, which led to a lawsuit by the latter and to the release of some crude and

WHAT IS A DERIVATIVE?

"Derivative" is a generic term for any security or contract whose value is *derived* from that of some *underlying* natural security, such as a stock or a bond. Instead of owning the asset, and either profiting or losing as its price rises or falls, a derivative is a bet on some aspect of its behavior. One simple example is the call option, which we examined in the last chapter. Shortly, we will examine a *credit default swap* (CDS), whose value depends on whether some underlying bond goes into default. Other common types of derivatives are written on the basis of interest rates or currency values.

In addition to the nature of the underlying security, derivatives are also classified by whether they are *standardized* and *traded on organized exchanges,* much like stock options on NYSE-listed stocks, or *customized* and *traded over the counter* (OTC), as most CDS are. Experts generally consider exchange-traded derivatives to be far safer and more transparent than OTC derivatives.

They are also far less profitable to the broker-dealers. In principle, a broker is a pure middleman who matches buyers to sellers, while a dealer takes a position for himself, either as a net buyer or a net seller. The roles are typically merged, however, because broker-dealers sell derivatives to one party and then seek a buyer for the other side of the trade. The number of big derivatives dealers in the entire world is quite small—even smaller now than before the crisis. Among U.S. firms, the lion's share of the business is conducted by just five big banks: Goldman Sachs, Morgan Stanley, JP Morgan Chase, Citigroup, and Bank of America Merrill Lynch.

Derivatives can be used either to hedge away risk or to create it—which is another key distinction. For example, an airline can use derivatives to hedge away the natural business risk that arises from needing to buy jet fuel at unknown prices in the future. But the party on the other side of the trade may be acquiring risk rather than extinguishing it—making a pure bet on whether jet fuel prices will rise or fall.

The jet fuel example brings up another important point: Most derivatives are zero-sum gambles—what one party wins, the other loses, leaving investors as a whole unaffected. Lest that make derivatives sound riskless to society as a whole, note that most derivatives embed a good deal of synthetic leverage—as explained with the stock option example earlier. So the risks, though two-sided, can be high.

Data on derivative volumes often sound scarily large—vastly larger than total world wealth, for example. The reason is that the data typically report "notional values," which are based on the underlying security, not the derivative. Our earlier stock option provides an example. The call option cost the buyer $48 per share; thus, $4,800 for a 100-share lot. But the "notional" value of the underlying securities—100 shares of Google stock—is $61,000, which is almost thirteen times greater. Should this derivative become worthless, its owner would lose $4,800, not $61,000. But $61,000 is counted as the notional value.

damning audiotapes. A third was the escapades of a single rogue trader, Nick Leeson, whose wild gambles in Singapore literally broke Barings, Britain's oldest investment bank—and wound up as a movie. An inauspicious start, you might say.

But that was nothing compared with what happened in the summer and fall of 1998, when losses at the now-infamous hedge fund Long-Term Capital Management (LTCM) helped set off a worldwide financial crisis—one that seemed monumental until it was dwarfed by the stunning events of 2007–2009. An overconfident LTCM got itself on the wrong side of a huge volume and variety of derivative bets, each of which entailed substantial amounts of synthetic leverage. On top of that, LTCM's balance sheet was itself highly leveraged. The firm was on the fast track to oblivion, probably causing lots of collateral damage in its wake, when the Federal Reserve intervened by orchestrating a private-sector bailout by Wall Street firms.

You might have thought that this near-death experience would have led to some regulation of both hedge funds and the exploding markets for derivatives. But you would have been wrong. In a famous incident earlier in 1998, Brooksley Born, then head of the CFTC, was sternly rebuked when she suggested that maybe OTC derivatives should be brought under the CFTC's regulatory umbrella. Her efforts were blocked, to put it politely, by the government's financial heavyweights at the time: Fed Chairman Alan Greenspan, Treasury Secretary Robert Rubin, Deputy Secretary Lawrence Summers, and SEC Chairman Arthur Levitt. Turf was involved, to be sure: The little CFTC apparently wanted to jump into the driver's seat without taking too many other passengers along. But it was more than just turf. The quartet criticized Born publicly, warning that regulating derivatives would create legal uncertainties, stifle valuable innovations, and send derivative trading offshore—maybe even end capitalism as we know it. She also was on the receiving end of a verbal tongue-lashing from Summers.

But didn't these gentlemen change their minds after the LTCM crisis a few months later? Amazingly, the answer is no. On the contrary, their anti-regulatory position hardened. By 2000 Born was gone from the CFTC, and Rubin, who was a bit more wary about derivatives than Summers, was gone from the Treasury. As the new Treasury secretary, Summers helped push the Commodity Futures Modernization Act of 2000 through Congress. The law explicitly removed any threat of CFTC regulation of derivatives contracts among "sophisticated parties." *Sophisticated?* The very word sounds ludicrous given the foolishness that followed. Maybe the operational word was *parties*, which broke out with reckless abandon once the regulatory DO NOT ENTER sign went up. According to the ISDA, total notional volume soared from about $70 trillion in 2001 to $445 trillion by

2007. Regardless of the merits of Born's specific ideas, derivatives should have been placed under some sort of regulatory regime. Instead, "hands off" became the law of the land.

Why did so many smart people believe these laissez-fairey tales? It's a good question. Some of the blame surely goes to the excessive faith in free markets that was the elixir of the day. Some goes to economists who believed and extolled the *efficient markets hypothesis*—and taught it to their students, many of whom wound up as financial engineers on Wall Street.

Another part almost certainly came from people's collective tendency to forget the past. When times are good, asset values are rising, and loan defaults are rare, it is all too easy to forget one of the laws of financial gravity: What goes up too fast usually comes crashing down. The late Hyman Minsky, an important but neglected economist, emphasized the forgetfulness factor in his theory of recurrent financial crises. In recent years, many Wall Streeters have taken to calling the 2007–2009 crisis a "Minsky moment."* It was quite a *moment*. Too bad traders didn't remember their Minsky before the debacle. Too bad regulators didn't, either.

THE EFFICIENT MARKETS HYPOTHESIS

The adjective "efficient" in "efficient markets" refers to how investors use information. In an efficient market, every titbit of new information is processed *correctly* and *immediately* by investors. As a result, market prices react instantly and appropriately to any relevant news about the asset in question, whether it is a share of stock, a corporate bond, a derivative, or some other vehicle. As the saying goes, there are no $100 bills left on the proverbial sidewalk for latecomers to pick up, because asset prices move up or down immediately. To profit from news, you must be jackrabbit fast; otherwise, you'll be too late. This is one rationale for the oft-cited aphorism "You can't beat the market."

---

*The term was apparently coined by economist Paul McCulley.

An even stronger form of efficiency holds that market prices do not react to irrelevant news. If this were so, prices would ignore will-o'-the-wisps, unfounded rumors, the madness of crowds, and other extraneous factors—focusing at every moment on the fundamentals. In that case, prices would never deviate from fundamental values; that is, market prices would always be "right." Under that exaggerated form of market efficiency, which critics sometimes deride as "free-market fundamentalism," there would never be asset-price bubbles.

Almost no one takes the strong form of the efficient markets hypothesis (EMH) as the literal truth, just as no physicist accepts Newtonian mechanics as 100 percent accurate. But, to extend the analogy, Newtonian physics often provides excellent approximations of reality. Similarly, economists argue over how good an approximation the EMH is in particular applications. For example, the EMH fits data on widely traded stocks rather well.

But thinly traded or poorly understood securities are another matter entirely. Case in point: Theoretical valuation models based on EMH-type reasoning were used by Wall Street financial engineers to devise and price all sorts of exotic derivatives. History records that some of these calculations proved wide of the mark.

Something New Under the Sun: CDS

In the year 2000, a creative new type of derivative called a *credit default swap* (CDS) began to emerge. Its origins can be traced back a few years earlier, to a team of bright young financial engineers at JP Morgan in the 1990s. When I was vice chairman of the Federal Reserve in the mid-1990s, the Fed staff was just educating us about this unfamiliar new instrument, and we were trying to figure out what kind of beast it was. Little did we know that it was destined to play a huge role in the upcoming financial crisis.

A CDS is an insurance contract posing as a derivative. The seller insures the buyer against loss from the default of a particular bond. If the bond does default, the insurer pays off. In return, the "policyholder" makes periodic "premium" payments to the insurer—just as you do with your life and automobile insurance policies. If the bond never defaults, which is the usual case, the seller wins and the buyer loses. But in the event of default, the seller loses big time. It's classic insurance: The insurer incurs very large losses, but only rarely.

Why have derivative contracts like that in the first place? The original reason was to allow investors to hedge against the risk of nonpayment. Suppose I own a $1 million General Motors bond and become worried that GM might default. I could go to a big insurer like AIG—to pick a nonrandom example—and purchase a CDS on the bond. Under this contract, I would agree to pay AIG periodic insurance premiums. But if GM subsequently defaulted, AIG would absorb the loss. AIG would relieve me of the risk of default—for a fee, of course. That's what insurance companies do.

In short order, however, the use of CDS for *hedging* became dwarfed by their use for *gambling*—that is, for placing bets on, for example, whether GM would default—no ownership of GM bonds required! Suppose Smith believes GM will default while Jones believes it will not; neither owns the underlying GM bond. Smith can *buy* a CDS on the bond, and Jones can *sell* one. In trade parlance, deals like those are called "naked CDS" because neither party owns the bond. And look what happens. Prior to the CDS, neither Smith nor Jones had any stake in whether GM defaulted. But after the transactions, they do. If GM defaults, Smith wins and Jones loses; and the reverse occurs if GM pays on time. Risk has been *created*, not extinguished. This evolution from hedging to gambling is typical of financial innovation. New instruments that are originally—or perhaps *allegedly*—designed to hedge away risk typically become innovative ways to *create* risk where none existed before. Total risk taking in society rises.

Three other key features of CDS are worth noting because they, too, are typical of derivatives. First, the deal embeds huge synthetic leverage. If the CDS buyer makes just a few premium payments before GM defaults, she wins a huge multiple of her investment, and the CDS seller suffers a commensurate loss. So the stakes can be very high.

Second, taken together, the two deals are *zero-sum*. What Smith wins, Jones loses, and vice versa. Enthusiasts of derivatives often trumpet this fact to argue that such bets between consenting adults pose no dangers to society as a whole. That seems right until you ask what happens if the loser can't pay. Who insures the insurer? That became the nasty question of the day in 2007–2008, when perceived counterparty risk soared. In September 2008, the government concluded that AIG would not be able to pay off its vast cadre of CDS counterparties and, in essence, nationalized the company—turning its huge liabilities into taxpayer liabilities rather than let AIG collapse.

Third, *derivatives dealers make money* on both ends of the trade. Smith and Jones probably don't even know each other. To buy or sell a CDS, they go to one of the big swaps dealers, who will find someone to take the other side of the bet—charging a fee for their work. In practice, the dealer bank will probably take the other side of the trade itself and then look to sell it. In the crisis, many of them got stuck with unsold inventory.

While there are certainly exceptions, each of these features is typical of customized derivatives, so it's worth keeping them in mind. The huge synthetic leverage embedded in derivatives enabled quantum leaps in risk taking during the boom. The huge profit margins on customized derivatives drove dealer banks into feeding frenzies to expand volume. And when things started going off track, rampant fears of counterparty default played major roles in shutting down markets.

CDS were perhaps the derivatives markets' biggest boom-bust story. ISDA data on the notional value of CDS outstanding begin only at year-end 2001—at a mere $919 billion. Before that, activity was small. By the end of 2007, CDS volume topped $62 trillion, for a staggering compound growth rate of 102 percent per annum over six years. In 2008 it was estimated that about 80 percent of CDS outstanding were "naked"— that is, were pure financial bets rather than hedges. This is a major reason why such a seemingly small corner of the credit markets—subprime mortgages—caused such widespread damage. The underlying mortgage risk was greatly magnified, not reduced, by trillions of dollars of CDS sitting atop the rickety house of cards.

Thus was the stage set for 2007. We had a financial system with serious vulnerabilities. We had deregulation-minded regulators who were more enamored of innovation than safety. We had no federal mortgage regulator at all. We had a huge and almost entirely unregulated shadow banking system that was growing like mad, both in size and in scope. We had a wild and woolly world of derivatives into which regulators were not allowed to set foot. And we had lots of subprime mortgages, already going bad. A risky brew, to say the least. As it turned out, every American, unfortunately and without knowledge or consent, had a stake in the complex gamble.

The hints for future financial reform here are clear enough; they are all embedded in the last paragraph. We need better bank regulation. We need to regulate the shadow banking system and the markets for derivatives. And we need a federal agency watching out for predatory mortgage practices. This last point brings me to the next villain in this dismal story.

Villain 4: Disgraceful Practices in Subprime Mortgage Lending

It is no secret that subprime mortgages led us into the mess. Many of them were inherently crazy, and they became the basis for even greater zaniness in the wild worlds of mortgage-backed securities and derivatives. Regulators never should have allowed so many of these disgraceful mortgages to be written. So, blame the regulators. But what about the reckless banks and nonbank lenders that granted them, and the irresponsible securitizers who bought them and then peddled dodgy mortgage-backed securities to gullible or unwary investors? Blame them, too. The tragedy begins, however, with the huge volume of risky mortgages that should never have been created in the first place.

Consider the sad case of Alberto and Rosa Ramirez, a pair of Mexican

American strawberry pickers in California whose annual income was in the $12,000 to $15,000 range and whose English was marginal at best. Egged on and assisted by an unscrupulous real estate agent looking for a big commission, the Ramirezes obtained a $720,000 mortgage from the notorious (and now bankrupt) New Century Financial Corporation to buy a $720,000 house. Yes, you read that right: They didn't put a penny down, and the mortgage was forty-eight to sixty times their annual income! The real estate agent apparently recorded their income as $12,000 *per month* and their occupations as "field technicians." Slight errors. The Ramirezes moved into their McMansion with another family, and somehow, including receiving financial help from the real estate agent, managed to hang on for a few years before defaulting and losing their home to foreclosure.

Now, here's a simple test of banking IQ: Should that mortgage have been granted? You may not be an experienced banker, but your *no* answer is correct. Unfortunately, New Century got the answer wrong in 2005 when it actually made this loan and many others like it. Other banks made similarly disgraceful loans. Yes, you are asking the right question: What were these guys smoking? Apparently, the weed was called greed. Make the loan, pocket the commission, pass it downstream, and let someone else worry about the consequences.

In fairness, not every subprime mortgage was as crazy as the Ramirezes'. Indeed, the basic ideas behind subprime lending are not bad per se. Subprime borrowers are people whose credit histories do not qualify them for conventional "prime" mortgages. For the sake of concreteness, that means their FICO scores are below 620. But, of course, some borrowers just miss the cutoff; they are "almost prime" borrowers. Some of them fall into the next category, the so-called Alt-A mortgages. Others have special mitigating circumstances (e.g., no borrowing history), or are good bets for other reasons, despite their low FICO scores. It is not necessarily foolish or irresponsible to lend money to such people, especially if house prices keep on rising. And the government was not necessarily wrong-headed to help some of these people become homeowners.

But there is a difference between serving "almost qualified" borrowers who want to own homes they can probably afford and seeking out anyone who can sign his or her name on a mortgage document. You can have too much of a good thing—and we did. The volume numbers speak for themselves. Subprime mortgage originations were a mere $35 billion (under 5 percent of total originations) in 1994 but reached a stunning $625 billion (20 percent of the total) in 2005—almost an eighteen-fold increase in just eleven years. Two possible explanations for this explosive growth suggest themselves: Either a huge number of creditworthy subprime borrowers suddenly appeared out of nowhere, or underwriting standards dropped like a stone. Take your pick.

In case you need a hint, let me tell you that "low-doc" mortgages (loan files with little documentation), "no-doc" mortgages (files with no documentation at all), and even "liar loans" (you can probably figure out what that means from the Ramirez case) became prevalent in the early- to mid-2000s. It has been estimated that almost one third of all subprime mortgages were of either the low-doc or no-doc variety. My own personal favorite candidates for the hall of shame were the so-called NINJA loans—granted to people with *no income, no jobs*, and no *assets*. No one seems to know how many NINJA loans were actually granted, but Banking 101 tells us that the prudent number was zero.

Lending to high-risk borrowers is one thing, but the structures of many of these subprime mortgages made things worse. Indeed, economist Gary Gorton, a consultant to AIG, has argued that many subprime mortgages were "designed to default." The most popular such example was the "2/28 ARM." These were 30-year adjustable-rate mortgages (ARMs) with, say, a barely affordable "teaser rate" like 8 percent for the first two years that would reset to a presumably higher rate (say, LIBOR plus 6 percent) after that.*

Very few holders of such mortgages could afford to pay the higher rates they would likely face in two years. In true bubble mentality, they were essentially betting on rising house prices. If their house values rose enough,

---

*LIBOR, the subject of a huge financial scandal in 2012, is the London Interbank Offer Rate. In 2006 it averaged over 5 percent. Hardly any subprime borrowers had any idea what LIBOR was or on what factors it depended. When the crisis struck, LIBOR soared at first.

they could refinance their mortgages two years later, pay off their old ARMs (thus avoiding the higher interest rates), and even take some cash out of the deal. But if not, they'd be unable to pay. At that point, the *lender*—not the borrower—would decide whether to issue a new mortgage or to keep the collateral. People of modest means should not subject themselves to such large financial risks. If they want to, their bankers should just say no.

There were other, even more exotic forms of subprime mortgages, like "option ARMs" and "negative amortization mortgages." With an option ARM, the borrower has a choice each month: He can make the contractual payment, which includes some amortization; he can pay only the interest, leaving the mortgage balance intact; or he can even pay *less* than the interest due, adding the unpaid amount to his principal and thus sinking deeper into debt. Presenting options like those to sophisticated people of means, who may be inclined to take calculated gambles on real estate, is fine. But they never should have been offered to unsophisticated—sometimes barely literate—borrowers who could ill afford to take a loss. It was disgraceful that they were.

The lesson here for financial regulators is one they should not have needed to learn, though they apparently did. Making loans that are "designed to default" to financially unsophisticated borrowers who likely do not know what they are getting themselves into violates every principle of sound banking—not to mention of human decency. It should have been banned, period. Yet a serious look at the data shows that mortgages designed to default could *not* have been a major cause of the crisis. Mortgages that clearly were *not* designed to default failed almost as often.

Fannie Mae and Freddie Mac, the two government-sponsored enterprises (GSEs), came relatively late to the bad-mortgage party. But once they arrived, their huge size added some kick to the punch bowl.

The GSEs were given a congressional mandate to support low- and moderate-income housing in 1992, and they started gradually dipping their toes, then their feet, then their knees into these waters in the 1990s. But it was intense competition from private-sector securitizers after, say, 2003 that really drove the GSEs to lower their underwriting standards. That was about when subprime and Alt-A mortgages started exploding, and the market shares of Fannie and Freddie began to erode. There is some debate over whether Fannie and Freddie went more heavily into subprime as a deliberate business strategy, having drunk the Kool-Aid like everyone else, or were pushed into doing so by Congress and the White House. Whatever the reason, they acquired—and guaranteed—far too much junky paper.

It is nonetheless notable that the two GSEs' overall balance sheets *shrank* slightly over the 2003–2007 period—just the time when the balance sheets of private banks and investment banks were roughly doubling in size—and that their market shares in the mortgage business fell dramatically. GSE purchases of subprime MBS actually peaked in 2004, and they were concentrated in the safest tranches. Right up to the present time, GSE mortgages have far lower default rates than non-GSE mortgages. Facts like these make it hard to see how anyone can cast Fannie and Freddie in leading roles in the run-up to the crisis, and the FCIC's majority agreed with this assessment. Others do not, however.

Villain 5: Complexity Run Amok

Why were so many bad loans made in the first place? The answer is that everyone downstream thought they had something to gain. That brings us straight to the securitizers, whom we have mentioned before. Here, in vastly oversimplified form, is how securitization of mortgages worked.

Suppose Risky Bank Corporation (RBC) has made one thousand subprime mortgage loans averaging $200,000 each—all, let us say, in the Las Vegas area. RBC's highly concentrated portfolio of $200 million in mortgage loans is, to say the least, risky. Many of these loans are probably "designed to default," and the creditworthiness of many of the borrowers is somewhat dubious. Should an economic downturn or natural disaster hit the Las Vegas market, many of these homeowners would likely stop paying, perhaps taking RBC down with them. So the bank would like to find a buyer for these loans while they are still good.

Enter Friendly Investment Bank (FIB), a securitizer from Wall Street. FIB offers RBC an attractive deal: "Sell us your $200 million in subprime mortgages. We will pay you cash immediately, which you can lend out to other borrowers. We'll then combine your mortgages with others from around the country, and package them all into well-diversified mortgage-backed securities. The MBS will be less risky than the underlying mortgages because of geographical diversification. Then we will spread the risk around by selling pieces of the security to investors all over the world." FIB is not proposing an act of altruism, of course. It stands to earn handsome fees for its services.

On the surface, this little bit of financial engineering seems to make good sense. RBC is relieved of a substantial risk that could threaten its very existence. If all goes according to plan, FIB's securitization of all those mortgages really should reduce risk in the two ways claimed. While real estate prices in Las Vegas may fall, it is highly unlikely that real estate prices would drop simultaneously in Los Angeles, Chicago, Orlando, and so on. *(What happens if they do? Don't ask.)* And with the risks parceled out to hundreds of investors all over the world, no single bank is left holding the bag. Or at least that was the theory. Unfortunately, it turned out not to work so well in practice.

There is more to the story. Many mortgage-related assets were far more complex than suggested so far. The earliest MBS were simple mortgage pools, sort of like mutual funds of mortgages. If an investment bank pooled, say, two thousand mortgages with an average interest rate of 7 percent and an average principal value of $200,000, it created a security with a par value of $400 million, which paid 7 percent interest, minus whatever small losses came from defaults. If some investor bought $1 million worth of this security, she purchased an asset whose risk characteristics were inherited directly and straightforwardly from the underlying mortgages— mainly from interest-rate fluctuations, prepayments, and defaults. For example, if the loan-loss experience on the whole pool averaged 0.5 percent, she would receive not $70,000 in interest (7 percent of $1 million), but only $65,000, reflecting her pro rata share of the losses. Investing in mortgages this way is far less risky than trying to pick individual mortgages. Good idea. If only the complexity had stopped there.

It didn't. In the years leading up to the boom, Wall Street invented and marketed a dizzying array of complex securities that, in effect, offered investors complicated combinations of *pieces* of mortgage risk—sometimes with other types of loans thrown in as well. Some of these securities were so complex that few investors understood what they really owned. Let me start with one such complexity, called *tranching*.

Instead of selling straightforward shares in the mortgage pool, as mutual funds do, FIB could "tranche" the pool—that is, slice it up. The most junior tranche, which came to be called the "toxic waste," would absorb, say, the first 8 percent of losses in the pool ($32 million)—no matter which mortgages defaulted. The middle, or "mezzanine," tranche might absorb the next 2 percent ($8 million), leaving owners of the top-rated, or "senior," tranche vulnerable only to losses above 10 percent ($40 million)—an event that seemed so unlikely as to be nearly impossible. Call the resulting three-tranche bundle of securities a CDO (collateralized debt obligation). This example is unrealistically simple, by the way. Typical CDOs had seven or eight tranches; some had more.

Now, think about what happens to the various tranches of the CDO as losses on mortgages rise from negligible to monumental. As long as loan losses remain below 8 percent, only the owners of the toxic waste take any hit. Owners of the two higher tranches continue to receive full payment. That's the outcome almost everyone expected, because losses on mortgages used to be quite low. An 8 percent loss rate was literally off the charts. But if losses rise above 8 percent, the mezzanine tranche starts to absorb every *additional* dollar of loss. And since these mezzanine tranches were often quite thin, such an event would chew through them quickly. Only once losses top 10 percent of the pool do owners of the senior tranche lose even a penny—suggesting a kind of immunity from loss. As long as the good times rolled, the junior tranche would sell at a discount for expected losses while the other two tranches sold at par—much like highly rated corporate bonds. Not incidentally, the rating agencies blessed the senior tranches with coveted—and formerly rare—AAA ratings.

Now, imagine a real mortgage meltdown, and remember that the underlying pools are stuffed with crummy mortgages *designed to default*. As more and more mortgages start to become imperiled, the perceived risks in the junior tranches rise like mad, driving down their prices. As panic sets in, investors start worrying that even the mezzanine tranches may have to absorb losses, maybe large ones. So their market values drop precipitously, too. In a worst-case scenario—which, of course, is what we had—even the senior tranches lose their immunity from losses and start falling in value. Thus, the market values of *all* MBS tranches fall—never mind those lofty AAA ratings—though by very different amounts.

And this was the *easy* stuff to figure out. In the cases of the most complex and opaque securities, nobody really knew what they contained or what they were worth—which is a surefire cause for panic once doubts creep in. Let me take the example a step further.

One day, some ingenious Wall Street rocket scientist looked at all the junior tranches, with their pitiably low credit ratings, and said to himself, "Eureka! [More likely it was an expletive.] I can turn lead into gold!" To make his idea concrete, imagine that there were five CDOs just like the one in our previous example. In each case, say, the junior tranche comprised 20 percent of the total and thus had a par value of $80 million. If you packaged all five of these junior tranches into a brand-new CDO—with a face value of $400 million—you could tranche that one, too. What does that rigmarole accomplish? Get ready; here comes the alchemy.

The lowest tranche of the resulting CDO of CDOs (which Wall Street cutely dubbed a "CDO^2") would absorb, say, the first 8 percent of losses that accumulate *across all five underlying mortgage pools*. If you viewed each of the pools as posing independent risks—a huge mistake that was nevertheless made—there was not much default risk left in the other four tranches.* They were protected by the lowest-rated tranche. Voilà! Our fi-

---

*Think about flipping a fair coin three times, with tails representing default. Your probability of getting three tails is 1:8. Unlikely, but certainly possible. But the probability of getting *six* tails in a row is 1:64, and the probability of getting nine in a row is 1:512—that is, almost impossible. Because these flips are *independent*, the probability of an all-tails "coincidence" drops precipitously as the number of flips rise. But if you just double or triple your bet on the *same* three flips, the risk does not fall. The betting odds remain 1:8.

nancial engineer has managed to turn $320 million worth of toxic-waste tranches—80 percent of the new CDO—into putatively safe assets. In a rhetorical triumph of hope over reason, the top-rated tranches of such CDO^2 were even named "super senior," indicating that they were so safe you could sell them to your grandmother.

By now you may be getting dizzy, but there is one more step. So far, we have pools of complex mortgages, many of them designed to default and much too concentrated demographically and geographically. Then they are sliced and diced into complicated CDOs, mind-boggling CDO^{2}s, and other concoctions. That's bad enough. Now, let's write complex *derivatives* on these already shaky securities, as Wall Street did with reckless abandon. For example, you could buy or sell a CDS on the CDO. That security promised to pay off if the CDO failed. And if that wasn't complicated enough, Wall Street offered other ways to place bets on either the success or failure of the subprime mortgage market. It was a remarkable casino, with no agents of the state gaming commission present.

Yes, far too much risk was taken. But my main point here is somewhat different—it's about *complexity* and understanding. Each link in the daisy chain—and there are others I have not mentioned—added complexity. And that, in turn, created *opacity*—or maybe utter confusion.

The mortgage originators knew something about their local markets and the creditworthiness of their borrowers—except in such cases as liar loans. The investment banks that did the securitizing knew less, but what did they care? They were going to pool thousands of mortgages together and sell the MBS quickly. The Wall Street financial engineers who created the CDOs and CDO^{2}s were performing mathematical exercises with complex securities; they had no clue about—and little interest in—what was inside. And the ultimate investors, ranging from sophisticated portfolio managers to treasurers of small towns in Norway, were essentially clueless. About all they knew were that some illustrious Wall Street names stood behind the securities—way behind, as it turned out—and that Standard & Poor's or Moody's had blessed them with the coveted AAA rating: safe enough for Grandma. If ignorance is bliss, there was a lot of bliss going around before the crash.

In October 2008, the *Deal* magazine published the following "wiring diagram" of how the whole system of mortgage finance looked in 2006. It was not satirical, though it looks it. Don't feel bad if you can't quite figure the whole thing out. Nobody else could, either. Complexity had run amok.

You may now be asking yourself a question: Why create such a complex system? Didn't anyone remember the KISS principle? (*Keep it simple, stupid.*) The answer is, in fact, simple, and not at all stupid: Complexity and opacity are potential sources of huge profit.

The more complex and customized the security, the harder it is to comparison shop for the best price. And without comparison shopping,

FIGURE 3.1 *Modern Finance Graphic*

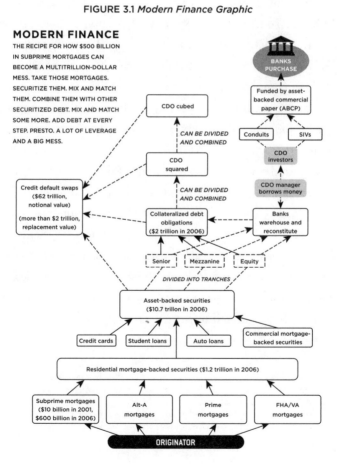

MODERN FINANCE

THE RECIPE FOR HOW $500 BILLION IN SUBPRIME MORTGAGES CAN BECOME A MULTITRILLION-DOLLAR MESS. TAKE THOSE MORTGAGES. SECURITIZE THEM. MIX AND MATCH THEM. COMBINE THEM WITH OTHER SECURITIZED DEBT. MIX AND MATCH SOME MORE. ADD DEBT AT EVERY STEP. PRESTO. A LOT OF LEVERAGE AND A BIG MESS.

BANKS PURCHASE

Funded by asset-backed commercial paper (ABCP)

CDO cubed

CAN BE DIVIDED AND COMBINED

Conduits   SIVs

CDO investors

CDO squared

CAN BE DIVIDED AND COMBINED

CDO manager borrows money

Credit default swaps ($62 trillion, notional value)

(more than $2 trillion, replacement value)

Collateralized debt obligations ($2 trillion in 2006)

Banks warehouse and reconstitute

Senior   Mezzanine   Equity

DIVIDED INTO TRANCHES

Asset-backed securities ($10.7 trillon in 2006)

Credit cards   Student loans   Auto loans   Commercial mortgage-backed securities

Residential mortgage-backed securities ($1.2 trillion in 2006)

Subprime mortgages ($10 billion in 2001, $600 billion in 2006)   Alt-A mortgages   Prime mortgages   FHA/VA mortgages

ORIGINATOR

there is little effective competition. Compare buying a customized OTC derivative on a complicated CDO^2 with buying a call option on Google stock. The broker-dealer earns a king's ransom on the former, where there is hardly any competition, and a nickel on the latter, where competition is fierce. That, of course, is why Wall Street is still fighting so hard against standardizing derivatives and trading them on organized exchanges. Standardization would spell the end of free markets, they claim. Yeah, sure, just as regulating derivatives would have done in 2000.

And opacity? That's what enables the sharpies to take advantage of the suckers. When Goldman Sachs' infamous trader, the "Fabulous" (by his own assessment) Fabrice Tourre, helped legendary hedge fund operator John Paulson bet against especially poor subprime mortgages by designing made-to-order synthetic CDO, whom do you think he envisioned as the buyers?* One of Tourre's own answers was: Belgian widows and orphans. Nice, huh? In a widely quoted e-mail, he bragged to his girlfriend that he was the "only potential survivor, the fabulous Fab . . . standing in the middle of all these complex, highly levered, exotic trades he created without necessarily understanding all the implications of those monstrosities." That's opacity for you. By the way, he added that he was "not feeling too guilty about this."

Not every trader was like Tourre, and all this might have been comical had it not ended so tragically. Here's the basic problem: Those who make and dominate the markets—"Wall Streeters," for short—love complexity and opacity as long as the party continues. It helps them make their millions—or billions. But once the music stops, their great but fair-weather friends, complexity and opacity, can become their worst enemies. As prices fall, investors start realizing that they don't really understand what they own, or what is being offered to them—not to mention "what those damn things are worth."†

---

*Goldman Sachs settled the case in July 2010, admitting to "mistakes" but not to fraud, and paying a record fine of $550 million. Tourre was put on *paid* leave from Goldman, and in August 2012 the Justice Department decided not to file criminal charges.
†This was Ben Bernanke's memorable answer when he was asked, at the Economic Club of New York in October 2007, what he would like to know that he didn't know. It was a long time before anyone knew.

The Treasury's Bob Steel, a former Goldman Sachs banker, made a colorful analogy to mad cow disease: The disease may infect only a tiny portion of the beef on the market, but the infection is so frightening that consumers shun all beef. Similarly in financial markets, Darwinian survival instincts tell traders to assume the worst, which many do. So one institution after another tries to dump its now-unwanted securities into markets where sellers are plentiful and buyers scarce. Prices naturally plummet. The panic is on, made worse by opacity.

This discussion of complexity has dropped a few hints about some of the needed financial reforms, including having simpler securities, requiring greater transparency, standardizing derivatives, trading them on organized exchanges, and requiring mortgage originators and securitizers to keep some "skin in the game" by retaining ownership of some of the mortgages rather than just passing them on like hot potatoes.

Villain 6: The Overrated Rating Agencies

One key link in the chain was the veritable flood of AAA ratings that the credit-rating agencies showered on so many senior and super senior mortgage-related securities. To put the rampant grade inflation into perspective, on the eve of the crisis only six blue-chip American corporations—names like GE, Johnson & Johnson, and Exxon Mobil—and only six of the fifty states merited the coveted Triple-A credit rating. It was the gold standard—and just as rare. So how did so much lead get labeled as gold?

The credit-rating agencies—led by Standard & Poor's, Moody's, and Fitch—were supposed to be one of the safety rails that would prevent the financial system from running off the road. Instead, they failed us, turning out to be part of the problem rather than part of the solution. Why? Sheer incompetence is one piece of the answer; the agencies simply could not *imagine* a house-price crash of the sort that occurred. But that was true of a lot of people. There were deeper problems.

One was the incentive system. Who do you think pays the rating agencies for their work? Investors? No. The government? No. Exchanges? No. It was, and still is, the *issuer* of each security. In the case of MBS, CDOs, CDO^2, and the like, that meant that the agencies' biggest customers were the Wall Street securitizers. That cozy arrangement posed several problems.

One is the natural desire of any firm to please its customers. That's not crookedness; it's good business. But in the ratings business, it means that the companies being "graded" are actually hiring and paying their own "graders." If I proposed that my students pay me for grading their work, I'd be thought crazy, corrupt, or both. Yet this remains the accepted system for paying rating agencies, even today. The Dodd-Frank Act instructs both the Securities and Exchange Commission (SEC) and the Government Accountability Office (GAO) to study other payment options. But, so far, the status quo ante still prevails.

Second, the practice of "negotiating" ratings became commonplace. Suppose our mythical investment bank, FIB, proposed a particular complicated payment structure to a rating agency, which studied it and replied that such a security would merit only a single-A rating. FIB might then respond with an obvious—and not unreasonable—question: "What would we have to do to get Triple-A?" When the rating agency answered this question, FIB could adjust the details of its proposed securitization accordingly and reapply for a rating. What else could the agency do but rate the proposed new security AAA? Again, there is nothing inherently duplicitous about this up-and-back process. That's how products get improved. But it led to an awful lot of dubiously rated AAA paper.

Third, competition among the agencies allowed—nay, invited—a pernicious form of "ratings shopping." If, say, Standard & Poor's assigned some particular security an A rating, but Moody's gave it AA, which agency do you think would get the business? Competition like that not only produces grade inflation, it also encourages (in this hypothetical example) S&P to keep pace with Moody's. That's not the sort of healthy competition Adam Smith had in mind.

Fourth, investors, regulators, and analysts alike often relied *exclusively* (or almost so) on the opinions of the rating agencies, rather than performing their own due diligence. For ordinary investors there was little choice— what else could they do, with their limited resources? But giant asset managers, regulators, and market professionals should have looked deeper. By dint of this abdication of duty, the rating agencies acquired a degree of oracular authority—a working monopoly on alleged wisdom—that they were never meant to have and certainly did not merit. Remember the old adage "Put all your eggs in one basket—then watch that basket"? Well, when it came to rating securities, the financial markets did the first but not the second.

At least three different solutions suggest themselves. One is to have some third party, such as an exchange or the SEC, hire and pay the rating agencies. Another would be to assign rating agencies randomly, as some courts do with judges. A third would be to make rating agencies more careful by giving them more legal liability. Any of these alternatives would be better than what we have now.

Villain 7: Crazy Compensation Systems

Much ink has been spilled over the truly obscene amounts of money earned by Wall Street executives, traders, and others for doing things that were not obviously in society's best interests. Anger over this obscenity is understandable. But the real problem with Wall Street pay was not its *volume*— outlandish as it was (and still is)—but rather with the way much of it was structured. Specifically, many financial companies' compensation plans created perverse incentives for key employees to take excessive risks with OPM—*other people's money*. Which is just what they did.

Consider the traders at banks, investment banks, hedge funds, and other financial companies. Darwinian selection ensures us that they are smart young people with large appetites for money and risk taking. Unfortunately, their compensation schemes exacerbate these natural tendencies by offering them the following sort of go-for-broke incentives when they place financial bets: Heads, you become richer than Croesus; tails, you get no bonus, receive instead about four times the national average salary, and may (or may not) have to look for another job. These are bright young people, not dummies, and many of them have no families to support. Faced with such skewed incentives, they place lots of big bets. If heads come up, they acquire dynastic wealth. If tails come up, OPM absorbs almost all the losses.

Whoever dreamed up this crazy compensation system? It's a good question, and the answer leads straight to the executive suite. Consider the incentives facing the CEO and other top executives of a large bank or investment bank—but, as I'll explain shortly, *not* a hedge fund. For them, it's often: Heads, you become richer than Croesus ever imagined; tails, you receive a golden parachute that still leaves you richer than Croesus. So they want to flip the big coins, too.

From the point of view of the companies' shareholders—the people who provide the OPM—this is madness. To them, the gamble looks like this: Heads, we get a share of the winnings; tails, we absorb virtually all the losses. The conclusion is clear: Traders and managers both want to flip more coins—with higher stakes—than shareholders would if they had control, which they do not. Bond holders are even more disadvantaged. They win nothing on heads. But if too many tails come up, they may lose their whole investment. The source of the problem is hardly mysterious: If you give smart people go-for-broke incentives, they will go for broke.

It was not always thus. Not so very long ago, banks shied away from big gambles on securities, and investment banks were partnerships, not corporations. In a partnership, the firm's capital belongs to the partners, so they guard it with the zeal you'd expect from people investing MOM—*my own money*. Back then, the upper echelons of Wall Street firms were not eager to let a bunch of twenty-eight-year-olds flip a lot of big coins.

Hedge funds are a kind of halfway house between the stodgy old system and the brave new system. They do use oodles of OPM. But the senior partners—the bosses—almost always have significant shares of their own personal wealth tied up in the funds. It's no accident that hedge funds operate with far less leverage than investment banks and commercial banks. Thirty-to-one leverage is simply too risky for MOM. Yet they often compensate their traders the same way. Why?

These whacky compensation schemes have puzzled me for upwards of twenty years. My worries were not assuaged when, in a 1995 conversation on this subject, a smart and famous hedge fund operator told me that the reason his firm paid its traders that way was "because everyone else does." That's always a terrible answer. When you hear it, you should grab your wallet and head for the hills. But the issue could be considered an intellectual curiosity—and apparently was—until the bottom dropped out in 2007.

Crazy compensation schemes were not limited to traders. Mortgage brokers, for example, earned their commissions by getting people to sign mortgages, even if the signatories had very poor credit standing and didn't look too likely to pay the loans back. In fact, brokers in many firms earned bigger commissions by signing up dodgier mortgages because those were the ones that paid the highest interest rates and fees. When some of these dubious mortgages subsequently defaulted, the brokers typically lost nothing. So they, too, had strong go-for-broke incentives. The push was for *quantity*, not *quality*.

As long as the costs of such foolish compensation schemes were bottled up inside firms, they were not a cause for public concern—although shareholders should have been worried about being fleeced. But that changed dramatically during the crisis, when much of the world's financial system collapsed in an orgy of irresponsible risk taking. We all went down with the ship, and dysfunctional compensation schemes were one of the reasons.

What to do? It is tempting to conclude that the government should regulate compensation practices to eliminate, or at least greatly reduce, such go-for-broke incentives. But the prospects for success in this domain are slim. I was in the Clinton administration in 1993 when we tried—

and failed miserably. The executives, lawyers, and accountants who design compensation systems are imaginative, skilled, and definitely *not* disinterested. Congress and government bureaucrats won't beat them at their own game.

Rather, fixing compensation should be the responsibility of corporate boards of directors. Those boards, I'll remind you, are supposed to represent the interests of shareholders, not managers. Quite plainly, many were asleep at the switch, with disastrous consequences. The unhappy but all-too-common combination of coziness and drowsiness in corporate boardrooms must end. Easier said than done.

A Fragile House of Cards

In summary, we Americans built a fragile house of financial cards, piece by piece, starting in the late 1990s and continuing right up until disaster struck in 2007. The intricate but precarious construction was based on asset-price bubbles, exaggerated by irresponsible leverage, encouraged by crazy compensation schemes and excessive complexity, and aided and abetted by embarrassingly bad underwriting standards, dismal performances by the statistical rating agencies, and lax financial regulation.

With a curious internal logic, each aspect of the house of cards supported the others, creating what is sometimes called a *positive feedback loop.* By bringing into the market a class of homebuyers who were formerly shut out because they weren't bankable, falling lending standards helped fuel the housing boom, especially for low-end houses. The reckless commission structure at mortgage brokers egged this process on, while ever-rising house prices kept mortgages that were "designed to default" from defaulting—as long as the music played. With default rates low, unthinking bankers could convince themselves (and others) that all this lending really was safe. And permissive regulators, instead of rapping them on the knuckles, allowed them to do so. After all, loan losses were trivial, right? Wall Street firms clamored for more and more "product" that they could turn into MBS, CDOs, CDO^2, and other sleight-of-hand—which their supercharged salesmen and traders pushed out the door like hot potatoes. The rating agencies dutifully but irresponsibly blessed these dubious constructs. If house prices kept rising, it all held together—didn't it? And, of course, leverage was present at every stage, amplifying the gains and making gamblers look like geniuses.

The house of cards not only stood, but grew. But its fragility guaranteed that it would not take much to knock it over. Here was the internal contradiction: The shell game relied on continuation of the house-price bubble, which could not go on forever. The story was bound to end badly once Wile E. Coyote succumbed to the force of gravity. And it did. Around 2006, when house prices stopped rising, the house of cards first wobbled and then collapsed.

But was the ensuing mega-mess inevitable? Absolutely not. The country would almost certainly have had a house-price bubble in any case. Take that as given. Also take it as given that Wile E. Coyote would have plummeted to earth. But . . .

- If bank regulators had cracked down on the disgraceful subprime lending practices that spread like virulent weeds between 2000 and 2006, the bubble would have been far smaller and therefore much less dangerous when it burst.
- Had Brooksley Born made more headway in her 1998 debate with Messrs. Greenspan, Rubin, Summers, and Levitt, OTC derivatives might have been subjected to some sort of regulation instead of being given a free pass in 2000. (Of course, designing such regulation was no simple task, and no one was worried about CDS then.)
- Had the leadership of America's big commercial and investment banks—not to mention households—decided to operate with less leverage and better risk-management systems, the damage would have been smaller once the bubble burst.
- Had Wall Street not concocted a system that was long on complexity and short on liquidity, the panic might have been contained.

Sadly, none of this happened. Instead, we let careless people play with dynamite, and the rest of us are still digging ourselves out of the hole. In the 1930s, Will Rogers wisecracked, "It's almost been worth this depression to find out how little our big men know." He was being facetious, of course. It wasn't worth it then and it wasn't worth it now. But we did find out how little our "big men" knew.

4

|‖‖‖‖‖‖‖‖‖‖‖‖‖‖‖‖‖|

WHEN THE
MUSIC STOPPED

*As long as the music is playing, you've got to
get up and dance. We're still dancing.*

—CHUCK PRINCE, CEO OF CITIGROUP, JULY 2007

B y 2006 the United States had built an intricate financial house of
cards—a concoction of great complexity, but also of great fragility. Like most houses of cards, this one was constructed slowly
and painstakingly. The sheer ingenuity was impressive. But when it fell, it
tumbled suddenly and chaotically. All that was necessary to trigger the collapse was the removal of one of its main supporting props. The jig was up
when house prices ended their long ascent; after that, the rest of the crumbling followed logically. Unfortunately, not many people had penetrated
the tortured logic beforehand; so few were prepared for the devastation
that ensued.

The end of the house-price bubble itself could hardly have come as a
surprise. By 2006 the "is there a bubble" debate was just about over, and
seemingly everyone was wondering how much longer the levitation act
could last. The disagreement—and it was a serious one—was over how far
house prices would fall. Optimists thought prices would just level off, end-

ing their unsustainable climb, or perhaps decline only a little. Pessimists were talking about price declines of 20 percent, 30 percent, or even more. What about the market? Futures traded on the Chicago Mercantile Exchange on September 16, 2006 indicated that investors expected a 6.4 percent decline in the Case-Shiller ten-city composite index. That proved to be way too small. In the end, the more pessimistic you were, the more prescient you were.

THE CARDS TUMBLE

The bond bubble was far less visible to most people, vastly more complicated, and appreciated by few. It also burst with devastating effect. But the bursting came in stages.

Once house prices stopped rising, subprime mortgages that had been designed to default started doing precisely that. At first, many of us wrongly believed that subprime constituted too small a corner of the financial market to do much damage to the overall economy. We soon learned better. To pick two nonrandom examples, Treasury Secretary Hank Paulson said in an April 2007 speech that the subprime mortgage problems were "largely contained." A month later, Federal Reserve Chairman Ben Bernanke told a Fed conference that "we do not expect significant spillovers from the subprime market to the rest of the economy or to the financial system."

Unfortunately, the huge amounts of leverage multiplied the damages manyfold, and the untoward degree of complexity helped spread the ruin far and wide. Financial industry executives—allegedly the smartest guys in the room—had every incentive to keep the party going for as long as they could, and they certainly tried. The regulators, still asleep at their various posts, allowed them to go on for far too long. The day of reckoning was delayed but not avoided. Why did the house of cards tumble so hard and so fast? Most of the reasons were implicit in the last two chapters.

Start by recalling our hypothetical investment bank, FIB, which convinced our hypothetical commercial bank, RBC, and probably itself as well, that mortgage-related securities reduced risk by pooling mortgages from different geographical areas and selling the resulting securities all over the globe. Unfortunately, when the house-price bubble burst, neither type of diversification worked as advertised. Why not?

First, when the *national* housing bubble burst, home prices actually did fall almost everywhere—an "impossible" event that had not occurred since the Great Depression. In fairness, few observers anticipated this virtually unprecedented collapse. (True confession: I was not one of them.) For decades, Americans had witnessed periodic housing bubbles, which blew up and popped in particular parts of the country. But when home prices fell in, say, Boston, they kept rising in, say, Los Angeles—and vice versa. The period after 2006 was different. House prices fell all over the map, undermining the trumpeted gains from geographical diversification.

That was a forgivable error. The proverbial hundred-year flood actually happened. But when the housing market began to crater, we also learned that many of the MBS were not nearly as well diversified geographically as had been claimed. In fact, it turned out that a distressingly large share of the bad mortgages came from a single state: California. Many of the rest came from Florida, Arizona, and Nevada—collectively known as the "sand states." For these and other reasons, the MBS turned out to be much riskier than advertised.

Second, the securities were not as widely distributed as had been thought. Yes, there were holders all over the world—from hamlets in Norway to Italian pension funds to billionaires in Singapore. But when the crash came, we learned that many leading financial institutions had apparently found mortgage-related assets so attractive that they still owned large concentrations of them when the bottom fell out. One reason was that there was so much profit in selling the other tranches of MBS, CDOs, and the like that investment banks were willing to hold the lowest-rated ("toxic waste") tranches themselves. The failures and near failures of such venerable firms as Bear Stearns, Lehman Brothers, Merrill Lynch, Wachovia, Citigroup, Bank of America, and others were all traceable, directly or indirectly, to excessive concentrations of mortgage-related risks.

The system began to crack in July 2007, the very month in which Chuck Prince made the now-famous statement that opened this chapter, when Bear Stearns told investors in one of its mortgage-related funds that there was "effectively no value left." The music was stopping. A variety of financial markets started twitching nervously, which should have been taken as an omen. But wishful thinking dies hard.

The real wake-up call didn't come until August 9, 2007, when BNP Paribas, a huge French bank, halted withdrawals on three of its subprime mortgage funds—citing as its reason that "the complete evaporation of liquidity in certain market segments of the US securitization market has made it impossible to value certain assets fairly." Loose translation: *Dear Customer, you can't get access to the money you thought was yours, and we have no idea how much money that is.* To people acquainted with American history, Paribas' announcement brought to mind the periodic "suspensions of specie payments" in the nineteenth century—times when some prominent bank precipitated bank runs by refusing to exchange its notes for gold or silver. The big French bank had just refused to exchange its fund shares for cash. Whether you were French or American, the signal was clear: It was time to panic. And markets dutifully did so, all over the world.

At some point, and in this case it didn't take long, the interplay of falling asset values with high leverage starts calling into question the solvency of heavily exposed financial firms like Bear and Paribas. Thus, *market-price risk*, which is already acute and getting worse, conjures up visions of *counterparty risk:* worries that firms that owe you money might not be able to pay up.

Once such seeds of doubt are sown, the scramble for liquidity begins in earnest, because, like it or not, markets are fundamentally built on trust—in particular, on trust that the other guy will pay what he owes you in full and on time. In worst cases, markets seize up. In less severe cases, enormous "flights to quality" are triggered, typically to U.S. Treasury bills. In any case, the bond bubble, which was predicated on blissfully ignoring risk, ended with a bang on August 9, 2007.

That faith in counterparties started to evaporate on that day is evidenced by the sharp rise in interbank lending rates. The key rate that everyone watches is LIBOR—the London Interbank Offer Rate—which indicates what one big bank charges another for short-term lending. This is a market restricted to the big boys: HSBC lending to Citibank, and so on. Was there actually a risk that such august financial giants might fail to repay *overnight* loans? The risk premium reflected in LIBOR said yes. After being stable for months, the LIBOR spread over Treasuries jumped by 30 basis points in just three business days. In the ultrasafe world of LIBOR, 30 basis points is a big deal. Financial lore has it that markets are alternately dominated by greed and fear. Fear was taking over.

AT THE FED'S ANNUAL WATERING HOLE

In late August of each year, most members of the Federal Open Market Committee (FOMC) doff their gray suits, don their cowboy boots (if they own any), and head off to Jackson Hole, Wyoming. There they meet with a select group of academic economists and a highly select group of bankers and Wall Streeters, for an invitation to the Jackson Hole conference is the hottest ticket in Lower Manhattan. While plenty of time is set aside for hiking and whitewater rafting, the dominant activity at Jackson Hole is shoptalk. It was in great abundance in August 2007.

The annual conclave, which is the Fed's premier event, is hosted by the Federal Reserve Bank of Kansas City, and its conference planners hit the jackpot in selecting the topic for the 2007 edition: "Housing, Housing Finance, and Monetary Policy." When the group convened on the evening of August 30, *housing* was going to the dogs, *housing finance* was cratering, and a *monetary policy* response to all this was growing increasingly urgent. Few people wanted to talk about the weather—which, as usual, was gorgeous.

Too bad the conference didn't take place four weeks earlier. At its August 7, 2007, meeting, the FOMC had concluded that "although the downside risks to growth have increased somewhat, the Committee's predominant

policy concern remains the risk that inflation will fail to moderate as expected." *How's that again?*, many of us thought when we read the statement. The predominant concern is *inflation?* Many Fed watchers blinked
in disbelief. What were those guys thinking?

Two days later in Paris, the financial world started coming apart at the
seams. The next day, the FOMC held a hurriedly arranged telephonic
meeting. This time their statement assured the financial world that the Fed
was "providing liquidity to facilitate the orderly functioning of financial
markets." (Translation: *We are pumping out cash like mad.*) But the federal
funds rate was kept right where it had been since June 2006, at 5.25 percent. Was the Fed still seeing inflation as the "predominant policy concern"? Okay, give them a break. Only three days had passed since their
August 7 meeting. The Fed would fix things soon. Right?

Wrong. The committee met telephonically again six days later, noting
correctly that "the downside risks to growth have increased." That was a
healthy step; they demoted inflation from its singular status as the predominant risk. But the FOMC still refused to cut the funds rate. (It did
reduce the less-important discount rate.) Looking back, it's hard to see how
this could have been a close call on August 16, and many Fed critics said so
at the time. But thirteen days later, as FOMC members from Washington
and around the country boarded planes to head to the beautiful Grand
Tetons, the funds rate was still stuck at 5.25 percent.

The papers economists presented at Jackson Hole that year ranged
from dour to alarmist, thereby matching the corridor conversations. Bob
Shiller warned yet again that housing would probably fall hard. He was
right. Ed Leamer of UCLA reminded everyone that housing collapses are,
historically, central ingredients in recessions. He was also right. A lunch-
time address written by the ailing Federal Reserve governor Ned Gramlich
warned that "the predictable result [in the subprime lending market] was
carnage." Right again. Even sitting Federal Reserve governor Frederic
"Rick" Mishkin, though trying to be as circumspect as he could because
the FOMC had just decided to stand pat, strongly hinted that interest rates
needed to fall. Summing up the proceedings, a pessimistic Martin Feld-

stein of Harvard observed that "if the . . . threat from the housing sector materializes with full force, the economy could suffer a very serious downturn." It did, of course.

But that was just the visible part of the conference. We learned later that Bernanke took the opportunity to cloister away several FOMC members in a small upstairs conference room to figure out what to do next—as their initial efforts were clearly inadequate. There must have been many other interesting sidebar conversations. But still, rates weren't touched until the FOMC's next regularly scheduled meeting, which was on September 18—a full forty days after Paribas Day. Yes, a lot of rain can fall in forty days and nights—and it did. The Fed cut the funds rate by 50 basis points on September 18, observing that "the tightening of credit conditions has the potential to intensify the housing correction and to restrain economic growth more generally."

That last thought was important. Before the cataclysmic failure of Lehman Brothers a year later, there were two competing views of what the crisis was all about. In the narrower, technical view, the financial world was experiencing a *liquidity crisis*—an acute one, to be sure, but still a liquidity crisis. In plain English, that meant that frightened investors and institutions wanted to get their hands on more cash than was available—partly because of the heightened counterparty risk just mentioned, partly because assets formerly deemed safe now looked risky, and partly because banks and investment funds feared that their customers might show up at the electronic door one day, seeking to make hefty withdrawals. The Paribas approach—just say no—was not an appealing way to cope with such a problem.

The dash for cash was on. The one institution in any country that can provide more cash in a hurry—in principle, in unlimited amounts—is the central bank. Both the Federal Reserve and the European Central Bank (ECB) did so massively, starting on Paribas Day, August 9, 2007. In so doing, they were performing a function that central banks have performed for centuries: serving as the "lender of last resort" in order to get their financial systems through liquidity crises. The volume of new dollars and new euros spewing forth from the world's two largest central banks was unprecedented. But the actions themselves were time-tested and routine, part of every central banker's DNA.

Back in 1873, Walter Bagehot, the sage of central banking, had instructed central banks on what to do in a liquidity crisis. His triad was *lend freely*, against *good collateral*, but at a *penalty rate*. Why? Because the acute shortage of liquidity in a panic can push even solvent institutions over the edge. Customers come in demanding their money. If the banks don't have enough cash on hand, word gets around, and bank runs start sprouting up everywhere. The disease is highly contagious.

By serving as the lender of last resort, the central bank is supposed to stop all that from happening. And every central banker in the world knew Bagehot's catechism. So that's basically what most of them did in August 2007. In fact, one can argue that the ECB stuck with the Bagehot script until late 2011. The ECB refused to cut its interest rates until October 2008 (yes, that's *2008*, not 2007), and even then it gave ground grudgingly. The 4 percent European overnight rate that prevailed in August 2007 did not fall to 3.25 percent until November 2008 and did not get as low as 2 percent until January 2009. By contrast, the Fed had virtually hit zero by December 2008.

Was this mess nothing more than a big liquidity event, as the ECB's actions suggested? Perhaps not. An alternative, and darker, view of the crisis conceptualized what was happening as a serious impairment of the economy's normal credit-granting mechanisms. On this broader view, the scarcity of liquidity was just the tip of the iceberg. The real problems lurked down the road—in gigantic losses of wealth; in massive deleveraging and possible insolvencies of major institutions; and, as just mentioned, in severe damage to the banking system, the shadow banking system, and other credit-granting mechanisms. If all that happened—and in August 2007, it hadn't happened yet—the whole economy would be in big trouble. Economies that are starved of credit fall into recessions, or worse. Businesses decline and fail. Workers lose their jobs.

THE FED SPRINGS INTO ACTION

Well, maybe not exactly "springs." Bernanke, who was a noted scholar of the Great Depression,* was slowly bringing his rather hawkish committee around to the view that this was something *big*—not just a major liquidity event, but potentially the cause for a big recession. But old habits die hard, and while the Fed was way ahead of the ECB, it was not quite there yet. At its September 18 meeting, the FOMC qualified its view that "the tightening of credit conditions has the potential to . . . restrain economic growth" by adding that "some inflation risks remain." It was a finely balanced assessment of risks—far too balanced, given the emerging realities. Just five days earlier, the Bank of England had intervened massively to save Northern Rock, a huge savings institution, from the first bank run in Britain since 1866.† Things were coming unglued in England. Our problems here were strikingly similar. Could we be far behind?

While the Fed's speed made the ECB look like the proverbial tortoise watching the hare, this particular hare wasn't actually running that fast. After its 50-basis-point rate cut on September 18, 2007, the Fed waited another six weeks—until its next regularly scheduled meeting—to move again. By that time, many mortgage-lending companies had failed, and Citigroup and others had announced major write-downs on subprime mortgages. But the Fed chipped in with only another 25 basis points on October 31—a baby step that it repeated at its next regular meeting on December 11. A number of FOMC members were less than convinced of the need for easier money.

After that, however, the Fed seemed to step it up a notch. The next day it announced two new liquidity-providing facilities. The first was a series of currency swap lines with foreign central banks, which were finding

*In one of his earliest scholarly papers, "Nonmonetary Effects of the Financial Crisis in Propagation of the Great Depression," a young Ben Bernanke wrote a long and original essay on how the breakdown of the credit markets had "helped convert the severe but not unprecedented downturn of 1929–30 into a protracted depression." The paper received a lot of attention and was published in what is probably the world's most prestigious economics journal, *American Economic Review.*
†The salvation proved temporary. Britain nationalized Northern Rock in February 2008.

themselves seriously short of dollars. In a currency swap, the Fed, say, lends dollars to the ECB in return for euros. When the dollar liquidity crisis in Europe passes, the ECB pays back the dollars and gets back the euros. The initial announcement was for just $24 billion, which was considered sizable at the time. But the swap lines eventually topped out at a whopping $583 billion in December 2008.

The second facility was the Term Auction Facility (TAF), designed to do Bagehot-type lending to banks, though for periods longer than normal—up to four weeks. The Fed's earlier attempts to lend to banks had been stymied by bankers' fears of being stigmatized by asking the central bank for a loan. Didn't that mean you were on the ropes? The TAF sought to overcome the stigma problem in two ways: It was set up as an *auction* in which any bank could show up to bid; the bank didn't need to be in bad shape. And since the bank wouldn't receive the cash for a few days, a TAF loan would not save a bank that was on the brink of disaster. TAF was important both for what it accomplished—at its peak in March 2009, it was lending $493 billion—and for its influence on subsequent policy. As we shall see, the Fed's memory of the stigma problem that led to TAF lingered on, affecting future policy decisions. TAF itself was shut down in March 2010. It was no longer needed.

But the Fed was just warming up. Over the Christmas–New Year holidays, Bernanke must have got to thinking—or to having nightmares—about the 1930s. On January 9, 2008, he convened an FOMC conference call—ostensibly to review recent developments but perhaps actually to shake the committee out of its lethargy. The minutes of that meeting noted that "the downside risks to growth had increased significantly since the time of the December FOMC meeting," but the committee was not yet ready to cut interest rates. Undaunted, Bernanke got them all on the phone again on January 21. The minutes of that call observed that "incoming information since the conference call on January 9 had reinforced the view that the outlook for economic activity was weakening." Only twelve days had elapsed between the two calls. How much could have changed?

What had changed was that the FOMC was now ready to act—

dramatically. With just one dissenter, the members agreed to announce an almost-unprecedented 75-basis-point cut in the federal funds rate early the next morning.* In the entire eighteen and a half years of the Greenspan Fed, the FOMC had moved the funds rate by 75 basis points only once—and that was an increase. Furthermore, federal funds rate announcements *always* come at *exactly* 2:15 p.m. This one came at 8:30 a.m. The Fed clearly wanted to be heard on January 22—and it was. Eight days later, at its regularly scheduled meeting, and again with one dissenter,† the FOMC dropped the funds rate another 50 basis points, down to 3 percent, leaving federal funds trading 125 basis points lower than they were only nine days previously. The Fed was on DEFCON 1.

The FOMC majority now clearly saw the task ahead of them as a two-front war, and it was gearing up for battle on both fronts. It needed to provide massive amounts of liquidity, for well-known reasons that Bagehot had articulated 135 years earlier. But it also needed to cut interest rates to fight an imminent recession, as Keynes had prescribed 72 years earlier. Chairman Bernanke did not want to preside over another episode like the 1930s. In Europe, however, overnight rates were going nowhere. The ECB was fighting the shortage of liquidity hard, maybe even harder than the Fed. But it was far from convinced that recession was in its future. At the ECB's headquarters in Frankfurt, there was lots of Bagehot but not much Keynes.

Missing Persons

Meanwhile, one might ask—as some people did—where was the United States Treasury? The approximate answer: working hard, but mostly behind the curtains. To provide some much-needed stimulus for the sluggish economy, President George W. Bush had gotten a temporary tax cut

---

*The dissenter was William Poole, president of the Federal Reserve Bank of St. Louis, who preferred to wait eight days for the next regularly scheduled meeting.
†This dissenter was Richard Fisher, president of the Federal Reserve Bank of Dallas.

through Congress in February 2008—tax cuts were his remedy for everything. After that, however, he more or less checked out, delegating management of the economy to his secretary of the Treasury, Hank Paulson.

The Bush administration looked to be a spent force by then. But Paulson seemed to be the perfect man for the job. A complex, multifaceted financial crisis, centered on Wall Street, was brewing. President Bush's two previous Treasury secretaries had been an aluminum executive and a railroad man, and the chairman of the Fed had come from the cloistered halls of academia. But Paulson had been the head of Goldman Sachs, a lion of Wall Street, a King of the Universe, a man who had spent his entire adult life in the rough-and-tumble of the financial world. (He collected birds of prey as a hobby, which, some people claimed, told you something.) Who could have been better prepared for the difficult job he now faced? Or so we thought.

Throughout this period, while the Fed was working feverishly to douse the flames that threatened to engulf Paulson's old neighborhood (and, later, even his old firm), the secretary of the Treasury was pretty quiet in public. Other than shepherding the February 2008 tax cut through Congress, the Treasury secretary seemed content to work behind the scenes, with the Fed in the visible lead chair. One major reason, of course, is that he lacked something the Fed had: money.

Fortunately, the Bernanke-led Federal Reserve had plenty of that, and it kept up the fight. On March 11, 2008, the Fed announced yet another novel way in which to serve as the lender of last resort. (There would be more to come.) The nervous markets were craving Treasury securities, especially T-bills, as a kind of security blanket. And the Fed owned lots of them. The Term Securities Lending Facility (TSLF) was designed to lend Treasury securities to the so-called primary dealers—a bunch of Wall Street firms and their foreign counterparts that helped make a market in Treasuries. As security for the loans, the Fed would take what Bagehot would have called "good collateral." Well, not all of it was supergood. Let's just say, pretty decent collateral.

The idea was straightforward. The markets were suffering from a shortage of highly liquid Treasury securities, but they had a huge surplus of other stuff. If the Fed was willing to swap T-bills for some of that other stuff, it might alleviate the liquidity squeeze. After all, T-bills can be converted into cash in seconds. And the Fed could make the swaps without expanding its balance sheet or bank reserves, the latter being the usual fodder for money-supply expansion. Hence, the TSLF was born—or, rather, announced; its first actual loan was not made until March 27. That date was exquisitely bad timing for one of the primary dealers that was fighting for its life at the time: an investment bank named Bear Stearns.

|ıııııııııııııııııııııı|

FROM BEAR TO LEHMAN: INCONSISTENCY WAS THE HOBGOBLIN

A foolish consistency is the hobgoblin of little minds.

—RALPH WALDO EMERSON

The six months between the collapse of Bear Stearns into the waiting arms of JP Morgan Chase and the collapse of Lehman Brothers into bankruptcy was interesting, in the sense of the apocryphal Chinese curse. *(May you live in interesting times.)* In March the Federal Reserve, supported by the Treasury, kicked in almost $30 billion to facilitate the shotgun marriage of Bear to JP Morgan, presumably because a disorderly failure of Bear *might have* devastated the financial system. But in September, the Federal Reserve, again with the full support of the Treasury, refused to provide any money at all to facilitate a sale of Lehman—even though Lehman's failure *did* devastate the financial system. Go figure.

These two monumental decisions were among the most eventful of the entire financial crisis. While it is hard to know which was more controversial, the decision to let Lehman fail was clearly more consequential. After all, when Lehman went under, it took the rest of us down with it.

Financial experts and historians will long debate the wisdom of saving Bear and letting Lehman go. This chapter asks why the authorities did so.

TURNING BEARISH ON BEAR

Bear Stearns was the smallest, and arguably the scrappiest, of the Big Five Wall Street investment banks. The firm had long prided itself on dancing to its own drummer. That meant, among other things, that it often pursued contrarian strategies—such as buying distressed assets, holding them until markets normalized, and then selling them for a tidy profit. So Bear's top management wasn't easily scared off when the subprime mortgage market started to falter—not even when two of its own subprime funds failed in July 2007. The firm was also very profitable, especially for its top executives. The top five took home over $1.4 billion in cash and stock sales over the years 2000–2008.

Bear was also contrarian in another sense. Ten years earlier, during the height of the 1998 financial crisis, it had earned the enmity of the other Wall Street banks when it alone refused to accept its pro rata share of the emergency buyout of what was left of the faltering hedge fund Long-Term Capital Management (LTCM). Bear's refusal left a bitter aftertaste that Wall Streeters remembered in March 2008.

One way in which Bear Stearns set its own course during the bubble was by becoming a huge player in the mortgage business, especially in the subprime mortgage business. Mortgage securitization became the largest component of Bear's fixed-income division, which was in turn the company's most profitable line of business, generating almost half the firm's revenues. For example, even though it was much smaller than its Wall Street rivals, Bear ranked in the top three in underwriting private-label mortgage-backed securities from 2000 to 2007.* In addition, a series of acquisitions and expansions had turned Bear Stearns into a full-service, vertically integrated mortgage machine. Its various divisions originated home-mortgage

---

*The term "private-label" in this context means securities *not* issued by Fannie Mae or Freddie Mac.

loans, bundled them for securitization, and sold the resulting securities—profiting at each step in the chain.

This heavy concentration in mortgage finance was one of the reasons Bear was widely considered the weakest of the so-called Bulge Bracket firms when the financial world started teetering on Paribas Day. Its image was not helped by a November 2007 front-page story in the *Wall Street Journal* describing its longtime CEO, James "Jimmy" Cayne, as a detached, marijuana-smoking executive who paid more attention to his world-class bridge game than to his company. About two months after that story appeared, Cayne was out, and Bear's president, Alan Schwartz, was elevated to the top job. Schwartz was destined to hold that job for only about two months.

Speculators in panicky markets have been aptly described as a pack of jackals looking to attack the slowest antelope in the herd. The jackals had plenty of teeth: They could pull assets out of the target firm, stop lending to it, sell the firm's stock short, or buy its CDS—thereby betting loudly on default. And did I mention, they could spread rumors that the firm was going down?

In March 2008, Bear Stearns was widely viewed as that slow antelope, with Lehman Brothers running just slightly faster. The rating agencies had called Bear's creditworthiness into question. Several notable counterparties, including Citigroup and JP Morgan Chase, had pulled away from it. Warren Spector, Bear's top expert on the firm's exotic fixed-income positions, had been purged, leaving Schwartz, an investment banker who was gamely trying to acquire bond-market expertise in a hurry, in charge. But as one of Bear's top fixed-income executives put it, his crash course "was like Bonds 101."

On Monday, March 10, 2008, rumors—vigorously denied by the company—began to circulate that Bear Stearns was experiencing liquidity problems. Other rumors held that one or more of its Wall Street rivals was spreading the rumors—it's a tough crowd. Remember that Bear, like the other Wall Street giants, financed itself to a stunning degree with cheap, very short-term credit—mainly repos. By the end of 2007, Bear was borrowing over $100 billion in the repo market; most of it overnight.

Overnight loans must, of course, be rolled over every day. Usually that's routine. But a piece of bad news, or even a *rumor* of bad news, can transform a company from a good credit risk to a bad credit risk in the eyes of the market literally overnight. One day that fateful week, a top aide informed Treasury Secretary Paulson that Bear was under severe stress and might last only another month or so. Paulson, who had been around the block a few times, replied wisely: "I don't buy that. When confidence goes, it goes." He was right. Bear Stearns didn't survive the week.

The firm opened for business Monday morning with $18 billion on hand in cash and highly liquid securities. Enough to withstand a run, right? Not even close. By the end of that day, with rumors flying, Bear's liquidity was down to $12.5 billion. It was bleeding cash. Counterparties were getting nervous about dealing with Bear, and some were refusing to do so. On Tuesday afternoon, Goldman Sachs startled Bear by declining a routine trade, and the news spread like wildfire. By Wednesday night, Bear's access to the repo market was withering away. The next morning, Alan Schwartz was on the phone with Tim Geithner, then president of the Federal Reserve Bank of New York, warning that his company was in dire straits. Dire, indeed. By Thursday night, Bear Stearns was down to $2 billion—it had run out of cash in less than a week. Bankruptcy looked imminent, even though Bear executives insisted that the company's problem was illiquidity, not insolvency.

INSOLVENCY VERSUS ILLIQUIDITY

The distinction between *insolvency* and *illiquidity* is one of those lessons that both economists and financial market participants probably learned too well. The crisis made us all rethink it.

In principle, the difference is stark. A firm is *insolvent* when the value of its liabilities exceeds the value of its assets, making its *net worth negative*. Its next stop is probably bankruptcy court. A firm is *illiquid* when it is *short on cash*, even if its balance sheet displays a healthy net worth. In such cases, the firm needs short-term credit, not euthanasia. Insolvency is a fatal disease; illiquidity is a bad cold, perhaps a *very* bad cold. It was exactly this distinction that Walter Bagehot had in mind in 1873 when he counseled central banks to lend freely (to relieve illiquidity problems) against good collateral (because only solvent institutions can post enough collateral).

But here's the problem. A company facing a severe cash squeeze—especially if its usual suppliers of funding have turned their backs on it—may be forced into fire sales of its less liquid assets. Which may mean selling them at exceptionally low prices, if, indeed, it can sell them at all. Which reduces net worth. The problem is worse if you're a financial company, for at least two reasons. One is that moving cash is your business. Your daily inflows and outflows of cash are likely to be extremely large compared with, say, a comparably sized manufacturing company. The second is that your leverage is likely to be high enough that even modest percentage declines in asset values translate into severe percentage declines in net worth. And it's *much* worse if lenders and counterparties lose confidence in you, for then the credit spigot may be turned off. That's what Paulson meant when he said, "When confidence goes, it goes."

For these reasons, a severe liquidity crunch can destroy a financial company, such as a commercial bank or an investment bank, even if its balance sheet is basically okay. Illiquidity can turn into insolvency—as happened to Bear Stearns and, later, to Lehman Brothers.

In practice, however, the distinction didn't matter much. According to rumors, a bunch of hedge funds had pulled their brokerage accounts from Bear Stearns, bought insurance on the CDS market against the bank's default, and then started shorting the stock like mad—which naturally pushed up the prices of the CDS. True or not, it looked as though a firm that had lived by the sword was about to die by the sword.

Financial firefighters from the Fed, the Treasury, the SEC, and others worked through the night that Thursday, debating the pros and cons of a "bailout" and trying to figure out how one might be done, if that was the decision from on high. The decision itself came early Friday morning before the markets opened: The Fed, using JP Morgan Chase as an intermediary, would lend Bear $13 billion to get it through to the weekend. (The number itself was not announced.) That decision was both stunning and monumental. It constituted crossing the Rubicon.

Why? Remember that Bear Stearns was not a bank. (Technically, the loan went to JP Morgan.) It had never been supervised by the Fed. Don Kohn, the Fed's vice chairman, called it "an irreversible decision that would have consequences that were very hard to say at the time." As reporter David Wessel observed, "The fact that the Fed was on the hook was such a departure from tradition that some insiders on Wall Street didn't grasp instantly what happened when Paulson and Bernanke briefed them Friday morning."

To justify its unprecedented action, the Federal Reserve invoked a little-known clause of the Federal Reserve Act, Section 13(3)—which was destined to become a very well-known clause. Section 13(3) empowered a supermajority of five of the seven governors to make emergency loans "to any individual, partnership, or corporation" under "unusual and exigent circumstances." It was an obscure power that few people knew the Fed had and which had not been used since 1936. In one of those little footnotes to history, the Federal Reserve Board had only five sitting governors at the time, and one of them (Rick Mishkin) was on a transatlantic flight. Fortunately, a post-9/11 escape hatch held that a unanimous vote would suffice if fewer than five governors were available and the need was urgent. It was urgent, so a 4–0 vote did it. That loan would prove to be the first of many uses of the now-famous Section 13(3) during the crisis. The Fed had broken the ice.

The loan to Bear Stearns, historic as it was, got the firm through only to the close of business on Friday, March 14. The Fed could still claim it was sticking with Bagehot: lending to a solvent but illiquid institution against good collateral, especially as this initial loan was paid back in full, with interest. The weekend would be devoted to another task: finding a buyer for what was left of Bear Stearns. As it turned out, there was only one feasible buyer: JP Morgan Chase. The financial giant had been serving as Bear's clearing bank in the repo market, so it knew enough about the company's assets to be able to perform the requisite due diligence rapidly. It was also interested in acquiring some of Bear's operations. Perhaps most important, JP Morgan had the "fortress balance sheet" needed to absorb Bear Stearns, with all its attendant risks.

In a remarkable swapping of roles, the Fed and the Treasury turned into a pair of investment banks, trying to broker a deal between two Wall Street firms: Bear Stearns, to which the Fed had just lent $13 billion, and JP Morgan Chase, which the Fed regulated. A sticky wicket, to be sure. And in this particular poker game, the government team didn't hold a good hand. JP Morgan's CEO, Jamie Dimon, an acclaimed deal maker, had the ace in the hole: He was the only viable bidder in what amounted to a weekend fire sale. Paulson realized that: "Because we had only one buyer and little time for due diligence, we had little negotiating leverage." So it was: Name your price, Mr. Dimon.

That weekend, a veritable army of JP Morgan bankers descended on Bear Stearns headquarters—conveniently, the two firms were almost neighbors in Midtown Manhattan—to pore over the books. They did not like some of the things they saw. In particular, Bear Stearns owned about $30 billion in dodgy mortgage-related assets that JP Morgan did not want at all. (It already had its own pile of mortgage garbage.) And that's exactly what Dimon told the Fed and the Treasury.

To Bernanke and Geithner, that $30 billion represented a major stumbling block. *Lending* to Bear Stearns via JP Morgan for a few days was one thing. While the action was highly unusual, at least Section 13(3) koshered it. But actually *buying* a portfolio of mortgage assets that JP Morgan considered too risky for its own shareholders was quite another. After all, the

Fed's effective "shareholders" were the taxpayers.* If the Fed took these questionable assets onto its own balance sheet, taxpayers would be assuming risks that Dimon didn't want his own shareholders to bear. It was not a question of legal niceties. The Fed's lawyers could easily structure the transaction as a loan, rather than as a purchase—which is what they ultimately did.† Rather, it was a substantive policy question: Was it proper for the Federal Reserve to take on that much risk? After all, the law demanded—in true Bagehot fashion—that every Federal Reserve loan be well collateralized. The Fed was not supposed to absorb losses.

The central bank, wary of stepping over the traditional Bagehot line, first tried to get the Treasury to pony up the cash. The elected government should be responsible, right? Maybe. But that would have required an act of Congress, which was plainly impossible on such short notice—and probably would not have passed in any case. Then the Fed asked the Treasury to indemnify it against losses. Treasury lawyers nixed that idea, too.

There was the Fed, stuck between the proverbial rock and a hard place. Bernanke could let Bear Stearns fail that weekend—with whatever consequences that might entail—or put his head on the chopping block by buying a $30 billion pile of dodgy mortgage-related assets of uncertain value, and putting the taxpayers at risk for any losses. He chose the latter.

That decision both sealed the deal and set the stage for much of what would come later. JP Morgan agreed to absorb the first $1 billion of losses, leaving the next $29 billion—if it came to that—for the Fed to pick up. With that guarantee in hand, JP Morgan offered to buy all of Bear Stearns' common stock for $2 a share—a price that valued the dying company at less than the market value of its Madison Avenue headquarters building! JP Morgan's board minutes later revealed that they had reduced their $4 bid to $2 "because the government would not permit a higher number . . . because of the 'moral hazard' of the federal government using taxpayer

---

*Literally, the twelve Federal Reserve Banks are private corporations whose shareholders are the member banks. But the member banks neither control the Federal Reserve Banks nor share in their profits and losses. Those go to the U.S. Treasury.

†Technically, they created a special purpose vehicle called "Maiden Lane," named for the New York Fed's address, and lent to it. Maiden Lane then bought the assets.

money to 'bail out' the investment bank's shareholders." The purchase price was later raised to $10 a share to ensure that Bear Stearns' shareholders would not vote the "merger" down. Behind the scenes, and invisible to almost everyone, the details of the shotgun marriage that had been hurriedly arranged that Sunday then took about three months for all to agree on.

THE MORAL HAZARD DEBATE

"Moral hazard" is one of those awkward phrases that is not self-descriptive. In particular, the term, which is borrowed from the insurance industry, has nothing whatsoever to do with *morality*. Rather, it's about *incentives* for risk taking, and how people may respond to them.

The central idea behind moral hazard is that people who are well insured against some risk are less likely to take pains (and incur costs) to avoid it. Here are some common nonfinancial examples: people with good insurance against flood damage may be prone to build houses in flood plains; people who are well insured against fire may not install expensive sprinkler systems; people driving cars with more safety devices may drive less carefully. Such behaviors are obviously relevant to how insurance companies price flood, fire, and automobile insurance. They must take into account that the act of insuring something may induce people to take more risk.

In financial applications, moral hazard concerns arise whenever some third party—often the government—intervenes to insure against, or lessen the consequences of, the risk of loss. For example, those who rail against the dangers of moral hazard have never been fond of deposit insurance, which eliminates the possibility that an insured depositor will suffer losses by depositing her money in an unsafe bank. They don't like government guarantees of any kind—such as the mortgage guarantees granted (for a fee) by Fannie Mae and Freddie Mac. And they certainly don't like bailouts, which, by reducing the pain of failure, make risk taking less scary—and therefore make failure more likely. Needless to say, they did not like the Bear Stearns "bailout" one little bit.

No one denies that moral hazard exists: the debate is over magnitudes and tradeoffs. Using Bear Stearns as a concrete example: Would other Wall Street firms line up for the honor of replicating Bear's experience? Many moral hazard "doves" thought this unlikely. Perhaps more important are the fates of innocent bystanders. Bernanke, Geithner, and others did not save Bear Stearns as an act of charity or forgiveness. They did it because they feared that a messy failure would do extensive damage to third parties—and to the economy itself.

That trade-off encapsulates the essence of the moral hazard debate. A bailout may mitigate serious problems today. But it may also sow the seeds of future problems by signaling to market participants that the government may bail out other firms in the future.

WHY SAVE BEAR?

The Bear Stearns "bailout," as it was immediately branded, was instantly controversial and remains so to this day. Start with the pejorative term "bailout." The Fed didn't see the operation as a bailout, and neither did Bear Stearns. After all, the stock had traded as high as $93 in February 2008. Now, in March, shareholders would get only $2 a share (which later became $10). Jimmy Cayne alone lost about a billion dollars. Furthermore, the company was not rescued; it was dead—absorbed into JP Morgan Chase. At Bear's headquarters, the feeling was more of a funeral than of a bailout. So, who actually got bailed out? Basically, it was Bear Stearns' *creditors*—mostly other financial businesses that would have lost money in a bankruptcy proceeding.

Critics immediately pounced on the Fed's decision—from all sides, including from the inside. Remember, the Treasury was still in the background—it had not put a nickel at risk. To outsiders, this looked like a Federal Reserve operation, led by Geithner with Bernanke's blessing, although Treasury Secretary Paulson was intimately involved every step of the way. Consequently, the Fed took most of the heat. But since there was enough heat to go around, Paulson took his share, too.

The moral hazard ayatollahs excoriated the "bailout" on the usual grounds. After all, anything that eased the pain of failure, according to this doctrine, would make future investors less wary of taking the kinds of imprudent risks that almost killed Bear Stearns. For example, Anna Schwartz, who had been Milton Friedman's coauthor, called it a "rogue operation." On April 3, Bernanke, Geithner, and the Treasury's Robert Steel appeared before the Senate Banking Committee to explain the Bear deal. Senator Jim Bunning (R-KY), the former Major League pitching star and perennial foe of the Fed, told them he was "very troubled" by the bailout: "That is socialism, at least that's what I was taught." He then added an ominous and prescient question: "And what's going to happen if a Merrill or a Lehman or someone like that is next?" Fortunately for Bernanke and Geithner, Bunning's question time ran out at that moment, and they did not have to provide an answer—at least not until September.

But the criticism from Fed "insiders" must have stung even more. In an April 8 statement that garnered a huge amount of attention, Paul Volcker told the Economic Club of New York that the Fed had gone to "the very edge of its lawful and implied powers, transcending certain long-embedded central banking principles and practices." That sounded like a rebuke, and given Volcker's august stature at the Fed, his words were like criticism from Mount Olympus. Breaking the Fed's usually unbreakable solidarity, Vincent Reinhart, who had been the Fed's top staffer until 2006, publicly criticized the Bear Stearns decision as "the worst policy mistake in a generation," predicting that it would set a precedent: From now on, any time a large financial institution teetered on the brink, the Fed would be expected to bring money to the table. (Could he have been thinking about Lehman?) Three months later, Richmond Federal Reserve Bank president Jeffrey Lacker, perhaps the FOMC's most conservative member, made headlines in London with a speech denouncing the Bear Stearns decision on moral hazard grounds.

As we shall see, both the moral hazard criticisms and the "bailout" charges would weigh heavily on future decisions, including the one on Lehman Brothers. But first let's ask why the Fed and the Treasury, well aware of the potential moral hazard involved, decided to bail out Bear Stearns' creditors, anyway.

The first natural thought is incorrect: that the Bear Stearns rescue was an application of the age-old *too big to fail* doctrine. The too big to fail idea is that some companies, financial or not, are simply so large that their failure, especially if abrupt, would do so much damage to other companies, to consumers, and to the overall economy that the government has to intervene in some way.* The doctrine is actually misnamed. In some cases, the preferred solution may be to lay the company to rest slowly and peacefully, with minimal disruption to other parties. So the idea should probably be called "too big to fail *messily*." But labels, once assigned, have a way of sticking. For better or for worse, this doctrine is called "too big to fail."

But didn't I just say that Bear Stearns was probably *not* too big to fail? It was, of course, a very large company, with assets of $395 billion as of November 30, 2007. But remember, it was only the *fifth-largest* Wall Street house—the others ranged in size from $691 billion (Lehman Brothers) all the way to $1.12 *trillion* (Goldman Sachs) at the time. Bear was a pup by comparison. And I haven't even mentioned the big banks or insurance companies. As of the end of 2007, there were seven bank holding companies with assets above $395 billion. The nation's largest thrift institution, Washington Mutual (WaMu), had assets of $327 billion. And four big insurance companies had assets exceeding $360 billion. These numbers

---

*The rescues of General Motors and Chrysler in 2009 were prominent nonfinancial applications of too big to fail.

were all in the public domain and were well known to financial aficionados. So, if Bear Stearns was too big to fail, then at least sixteen other financial firms were, too. If you had taken an expert opinion poll on the question
in February 2008, I believe most observers would have judged that Bear
was *below* the too big to fail threshold. I know I did.

Why, then, were the Fed and the Treasury unwilling to let Bear
Stearns go under that weekend? The primary reason was fear that Bear was
too interconnected to fail—in several respects.

First, it was closely linked to many other financial companies, especially hedge funds. One of Bear's major business lines was acting as the
prime broker for hundreds of hedge funds—executing trades, holding collateral, receiving and disbursing monies, and so forth. These funds, in
turn, accounted for a substantial share of the trading in a variety of markets. If Bear Stearns went belly-up, the authorities feared, markets all over
the world would be severely disrupted. Remember the domino theory?
That was the governing doctrine.

Second, and related, Bear Stearns was counterparty to what were probably hundreds of thousands of derivatives transactions. Nobody knew how
many. As Paulson later told the Financial Crisis Inquiry Commission
(FCIC), "If Bear had gone, there were hundreds, maybe thousands of
counterparties that all would have grabbed their collateral, would have
started trying to sell their collateral, drove down prices, create[d] even bigger losses." Notably, that was *exactly* the rationale that had been given ten
years earlier when the Fed arranged the private-sector rescue of LTCM—
an operation in which Bear, remember, refused to participate.

Third, according to Bernanke's subsequent testimony to the FCIC,
even though Bear Stearns was "not that big a firm [so it wasn't a case of too
big to fail] . . . our view was that because it was so essentially involved in
this critical repo financing market, that its failure would have brought
down that market, which would have had implications for other firms."

Fourth, Bear's risk profile was far from unique. If Bear fell, other firms
might not be far behind. As Paulson later put it, "Perhaps if Bear had been
a one-off situation, we would have let it go down. But we realized that
Bear's failure would call into question the fate of the other financial insti-

tutions that might share Bear's predicament. The market would look for the next wounded deer, then the next, and the whole system would be at serious risk." To others, of course, that argument cut exactly the opposite way: Saving Bear implied a tacit commitment to save Lehman Brothers, Merrill Lynch, Morgan Stanley, and Goldman Sachs if necessary. In fact, the government would later save three of the four.

In a nutshell, Bear Stearns was deemed to be too *interconnected* to fail. But was it true? We'll never know, although the multiple catastrophes that followed the Lehman Brothers bankruptcy six months later give the claim substantial credence. Regardless, the Federal Reserve and the Treasury *believed* it was true and acted on that belief. The Treasury, however, was still keeping its head down. And no wonder. How would you like to explain to the voting public that the government had just put $29 billion at risk to save hedge funds, derivatives traders, and the triparty repo market? *(The what?)*

The "too interconnected to fail" doctrine seemed novel and somewhat obscure at the time. And in a sense it was, although the LTCM case ten years earlier was a clear precursor. In that famous case, however, the Federal Reserve had not contributed a penny of its own money to seal the deal. Rather, it used its good offices (née arm twisting) to persuade all the major Wall Street firms except Bear to keep LTCM alive long enough that its failure would not trigger a cascade of other failures. The March 2008 Bear Stearns rescue was actually the *second* major application of the too interconnected to fail doctrine, but with an important twist: This time, the Fed put a lot of money on the line.

What were the arguments on the other side? The first has already been mentioned: The action would set a precedent, as Vince Reinhart predicted. Once the Fed got into this business, getting out would be hard.

Second, the precedent created moral hazard, not so much from top executives and shareholders of other Wall Street firms—Bear's, after all, suffered huge personal losses—but from individuals and businesses that had extended credit to a shaky Bear Stearns. They, after all, were the ones the taxpayers actually bailed out. Would they be more careful next time, or just assume that another government bailout would save their skins? If the latter, one of the checks and balances safeguarding the financial system—vigilant creditors—would be impaired.

Third, some people argued that the Bear Stearns rescue overstepped the Fed's legal authority. They were wrong: Section 13(3) clearly made the Fed's actions legal. But perhaps it was a stretch of congressional intent. Indeed, about two years later, in the Dodd-Frank Act, Congress took this power away from the Fed. As amended by Dodd-Frank, Section 13(3) no longer authorizes emergency loans to particular financial institutions—only to all "participants in [a] program or facility with broad-based eligibility."

One other important footnote to history: On Sunday, March 16, the same day that JP Morgan Chase announced its purchase of Bear Stearns and the Fed announced its approval of the deal, the Fed's Board of Governors created the Primary Dealer Credit Facility. The PDCF made it much easier to lend money to securities firms by, for example, broadening the range of eligible collateral. Bear executives maintained that they could have averted bankruptcy without requiring assistance, if they had been given access to the PDCF. Jimmy Cayne told the FCIC that the PDCF came "just about 45 minutes" too late to save his firm. No one will ever know.

FRETTING OVER FANNIE AND FREDDIE

After Bear Stearns Day, and maybe because of the Bear Stearns rescue, things went quiet for a while—sort of. Some pretense of normalcy returned to the markets, and tales of financial woe stopped dominating page 1. The S&P 500, which had dropped almost 18 percent between October 9, 2007, and March 14, 2008, gained back about half of that between March 14 and May 2. Both risk spreads and the costs of protecting against default via credit default swaps generally declined. For example, the much-watched three-month TED spread (between LIBOR and Treasuries) dropped from 204 basis points to just 77 basis points. A number of big banks and the four remaining investment banks went into the market and successfully raised capital.

Nonetheless, beneath the surface, the pot was boiling. The house-price, mortgage-finance, and foreclosure problems were getting worse, not better. No one really knew how much junk was hidden on (and off) the books of several big banks. The huge and unregulated over-the-counter (OTC) derivatives markets remained a dark and scary continent. The rapid unraveling of Bear Stearns was a warning shot that called into question the high-risk Wall Street business model of combining high leverage with precarious liquidity. Lehman Brothers replaced Bear as the slowest antelope in the herd. And then there were the two limping mortgage finance giants, Fannie Mae and Freddie Mac.

Fannie Mae (originally the Federal National Mortgage Association—FNMA) was established in 1938 as a government-sponsored enterprise to increase the flow of funds into housing and to create a liquid secondary market on which mortgage loans could be traded. It was converted into a publicly held corporation in 1968 to get it off the federal budget. Freddie Mac (originally the Federal Home Loan Mortgage Corporation—don't ask me how FHLMC became "Freddie Mac") was chartered in 1971 to compete with Fannie and, by so doing, make the secondary mortgage market more efficient. Both companies had shareholders who sought capital gains and dividends, which is what shareholders do, and executives who sought to please their shareholders, which is what corporate executives do.

All normal, except for one crucial fact: The two companies had a number of special features that left markets with the impression that they were quasi-government enterprises. Most important, the fact that Fannie and Freddie each had a line of credit from the U.S. Treasury created the presumption that if push ever came to shove, the Treasury would stand behind their debts.* There was, in fact, no explicit, *legal* guarantee of Fannie/Freddie obligations by the U.S. government. Nonetheless, there was an almost universal belief in an *implicit* guarantee: The government would never allow Fannie or Freddie to default on its debts. And, indeed, when push came to shove, it did not.

---

*In addition, Fannie and Freddie were exempt from SEC registration requirements and state and local taxes, and had several board members named by the president of the United States.

After Treasuries, Fannie's and Freddie's securities were considered the safest assets anyone could buy. Many risk-averse investors, including banks, municipalities, and foreign governments, viewed the debt obligations of Fannie and Freddie as almost as safe as Treasuries, though with higher yields—a good deal. In consequence, the mortgage twins were able to float debt at rock-bottom interest rates, below those paid by the bluest of blue-chip corporations. That advantage, in turn, gave Fannie and Freddie a heavy competitive edge in the mortgage business—which they exploited to grow into financial behemoths. The two GSEs were thus an awkward blend of public purpose and private gain that would come back to haunt taxpayers later.

Several things followed from the implicit government guarantee and the fact that Fannie and Freddie traditionally dealt only in higher-grade mortgages. As one Freddie executive said to me early in the crisis, "We own the good stuff." Relatively speaking.

First, the mortgage twins were allowed to operate with extremely high leverage and under a pretty light regulatory regime. At the end of 2007, as the housing crash was gathering steam, Fannie and Freddie were leveraged about 75 to 1. Yes, that meant that a mere 1.4 percent loss on their assets would have left both of them insolvent.

Second, by charter, Fannie and Freddie were not allowed to diversify into other asset classes. Mortgages, mortgage guarantees, and mortgage-related securities constituted roughly 100 percent of their earning assets. In some sense, these three were the same assets in different guises. Thus, in words that no one ever used, Fannie and Freddie were actually *designed to fail* if the proverbial 100-year flood ever swallowed up the housing market. When it did so after 2006, Fannie and Freddie were doomed.

Third, a change in their business strategies during the bubble left them even more vulnerable. Pressured both by affordable housing goals from the Department of Housing and Urban Development (which, in turn, came from Congress) and by competition for market share from Wall Street, and egged on by the lure of profit, Fannie and Freddie starting guaranteeing and purchasing riskier mortgages. The share of subprime MBS owned by Fannie and Freddie rose from 16 percent in 2001 to 33 percent by 2004.

No longer did the twins hold just "the good stuff." However, as Gramlich observed, "the GSEs do not play nearly as great a role in the subprime mortgage market as they do in the prime market. Many subprime mortgages do not meet the underwriting standards of Fannie Mae and Freddie Mac." Fortunately, by the time things started to fall apart in the summer of 2007, the share of the two housing GSEs in subprime MBS was back down to 17 percent. Nonetheless, that meant they were still saddled with a good share of dodgy mortgages.

A few observers have singled out losses on Fannie's and Freddie's low-income and subprime-mortgage portfolio as the *preeminent* weakness that undermined the entire financial system. For example, Peter Wallison, who was a member of the FCIC, states in his dissent that "I believe that the *sine qua non* of the financial crisis was U.S. government housing policy." Another vocal critic is *New York Times* reporter Gretchen Morgenson, who, with coauthor Joshua Rosner, claims in their book *Reckless Endangerment* that "Fannie Mae led the way in relaxing loan underwriting standards."

Most experts, however, view that characterization as a caricature. For example, the FCIC Report condemned "the business model of Fannie Mae and Freddie Mac (the GSEs), as private-sector, publicly traded, profit-making companies with implicit government backing and a public mission, [as] fundamentally flawed." Nonetheless, it concluded that "GSE mortgage securities essentially maintained their value throughout the crisis and did not contribute to the significant financial firm losses that were central to the financial crisis." Many other financial experts with whom I have discussed this matter see Fannie and Freddie as supporting actors, far from the star of the show. So do I.

However large or small their role in the crisis, no one can accuse Secretary Paulson of failing to see the troubles at Fannie Mae and Freddie Mac brewing. Yet just a few days after Bear Stearns Day, the two government-sponsored enterprises' weak regulator, the Office of Federal Housing Enterprise Oversight (OFHEO), actually *reduced* the companies' capital requirements. Yes, that's right. It allowed Fannie and Freddie to operate with *even higher leverage* than before. Why? So they could provide more support to the wilting housing market. In return, the two companies promised—vaguely, with no specific numbers—to go into the market and raise more capital.

Nonetheless, you may still be wondering: *Even higher leverage?* That sounds crazy—until you recall that the financial conflagration by then had consumed virtually all of Fannie's and Freddie's private-sector competitors. When it came to housing finance, the two GSEs were essentially the only players left standing. But regardless of whether OFHEO's action was right, the move weakened Fannie's and Freddie's already-weak defenses.

Losses in the housing market continued to mount, of course, and Fannie and Freddie absorbed their share, which shrank their capital bases further. Confidence in the two GSEs sank, and so did their share prices. The cost of insuring their debt in the CDS market soared, as did their borrowing rates. It was beginning to look like a death spiral.

In mid-July 2008, Paulson asked Congress to authorize him to inject capital into Fannie Mae and Freddie Mac, and to increase their lines of credit (thereby making the *implicit* government guarantee *explicit*), just in case the Treasury had to prop them up. President Bush reluctantly approved the action. He didn't like the GSEs, but he knew they were essential to the foundering housing finance markets: "The first order of business, he said, was 'save their ass.'" Using a slightly less colorful metaphor that would soon come back to haunt him, Paulson told a Senate committee that he needed a "bazooka." Why such heavy artillery? Because, in his words, "If you've got a squirt gun in your pocket, you may have to take it out. If you've got a bazooka, and people know you have it, you may not have to take it out."

In late July, Congress gave Paulson the bazooka he requested. It also increased the Treasury's lines of credit to Fannie and Freddie, and strengthened their regulator. OFHEO was replaced by the new Federal Housing Finance Agency (FHFA), which, among other things, was granted the power to put Fannie and Freddie into conservatorship or receivership, if necessary. Within weeks, Paulson would be firing the bazooka he said might not be used.

On September 7, the government placed both Fannie and Freddie into conservatorship. The impossible had happened again. "Conserve" was the right word. By August 2012, the government had spent about $140 billion, net, to keep Fannie and Freddie alive and functioning, but was expecting to recoup most of that—eventually. Paulson and Bernanke must have sighed in deep relief that day in September 2008. As the Treasury secretary recounted in his memoir, "The GSE crisis left me dead tired. I told [White House Chief of Staff] Josh Bolten that solving [it] was the hardest thing I had ever done." But there was barely time for Paulson and Bernanke to catch their breaths. Notice the date: September 7, 2008, a week before the titanic financial system hit the iceberg. The stage was now set for the biggest melodrama of them all: the fall of Lehman Brothers.

ARMAGEDDON ACTUALLY ARRIVES

The consequences of adverse economic events are typically exaggerated by the Armageddonists—a sensation-seeking herd of pundits, seers, and journalists who make a living by predicting the worst. Prognostications of impending doom draw lots of attention, get you on TV, and sometimes even lead to best-selling books with titles like *How to Profit from the Coming Disaster in* _____. But the Armageddonists are almost always wrong. The economy and even the more mercurial financial system are more resilient than doomsayers give them credit for. Train wrecks don't often occur. Thus, OPEC did not bring the West to its knees in the 1970s, the Great Inflation of that decade did not destroy the U.S. monetary system, higher taxes in 1993 did not end capitalism as we know it, and the stock market crash of 2000–2002 did not kill anything but the stock market itself.

The fallout from the bankruptcy of Lehman Brothers was the exception that proved the rule. Just about everything got vastly worse than almost anyone anticipated, making the gloomiest prognostications the most accurate ones. And it all happened at warp speed. September 15, 2008, will surely go down as a day of infamy in economic history—and as the turning point in the crisis. The question for the ages is Why?

Lehman Brothers, much more so than Bear Stearns, was one of the grand old names of Wall Street. The 158-year-old firm had survived the

Civil War, the Panic of 1907, the stock market crash of 1929, the Great Depression, and much else. It had also been on the jackals' list of slow antelopes for years. Every financial ruction, it seemed, led to speculation that Lehman might be on the ropes. As the greatest financial crisis of them all unfolded in 2007 and 2008, it became clear that Lehman had loaded up both on mortgage-related securities, especially commercial real estate mortgages, and even on some big-ticket real estate like office buildings and shopping centers. Maybe that wasn't such a smart move for a company whose expertise was financial. But euphoria has a way of clouding judgment, and Lehman was riding the bubble with great profit.

Its heavy exposure to *commercial* real estate is what distinguished the firm from its Wall Street brethren, including Bear Stearns. In other respects, however, Lehman Brothers looked much like the other giant investment banks. In particular, it was a prime example of the new Wall Street model of high leverage and heavy reliance on low-cost, short-term borrowing to generate huge profits. At the end of the first quarter of 2008, Lehman had nearly $200 billion worth of repos outstanding. After the demise of Bear Stearns, the fragility of this heady but combustible mix grabbed the attention of many observers—certainly including Bernanke and Paulson,* but also including many speculators and short-sellers. The new Wall Street model looked shaky, and in the market's view, Lehman was probably the next to go.

On Bear Stearns Day, Lehman's CEO Richard "Dick" Fuld knew that his company was in the crosshairs, and when the stock market opened on the next Monday, Lehman's stock was, indeed, pummeled. As he later lamented to the FCIC, "Bear went down on rumors and a liquidity crisis of confidence. Immediately thereafter, the rumors and the naked short-selling came after us." It certainly did. But Lehman managed to hold things together for another six months.

Lehman's primary regulator was the same as Bear's: the somnolent SEC. After the Bear Stearns bailout, however, and especially after the Fed began lending to broker-dealers, the central bank started watching over

---

*As Paulson wrote in his memoir, "We learned a lot doing Bear Stearns, and what we learned scared us."

Lehman Brothers and the other three Wall Street giants—with supervision, stress tests, requests for data, and the like. The central bank was worried about Lehman's safety and soundness, and, even more so, the systemic risk it might pose if it failed. Among other things, Lehman was counterparty to almost a million derivatives contracts and a huge borrower in the repo market. Ominously, several of its derivative and repo counterparties began reducing their exposure to Lehman in the days and weeks after Bear; a few canceled or limited their lines of credit. As Paulson understood, when confidence goes, it goes. After Bear, confidence in Lehman Brothers looked like it was going fast.

In the first week after the Bear Stearns bailout, Fuld and other Lehman executives began to emphasize in public statements and interviews that the firm had plenty of capital and liquidity—and (mainly sotto voce) that it could now also borrow from the Fed. *Plenty of capital and liquidity, don't worry.* Wasn't that what Bear Stearns had said?

As late as its May 31, 2008, quarterly filing with the SEC, Lehman's balance sheet showed $26 billion in stockholders' equity—which it claimed was more than adequate to support $639 billion in assets. (That's leverage of 25 to 1.) It also boasted $45 billion in ready liquidity. But that same balance sheet showed about $21 billion in real estate and about $72 billion in "mortgage and asset-backed securities." No one believed all that stuff was worth $93 billion. If it was marked down by, say, 30 percent, the equity would be gone—which made the Fed and the Treasury deeply skeptical about Lehman's solvency. Worse yet, as it later came to light, Lehman was using accounting subterfuges to conceal some of its debt, thereby making its net worth and leverage look better than they actually were.

During the fateful March-to-September period, Fuld knew that his company needed to raise more capital and improve its liquidity position. But neither was easy. Lehman did succeed in raising about $15 billion in preferred stock and longer-term debt by June, but that was not nearly enough. Lehman's pool of liquidity still relied far too heavily on posting mortgage-related assets as collateral for short-term loans—the very strategy that had sunk Bear Stearns. The markets were growing wary of this strategy. How good was the collateral? Was Lehman really solvent?

At one point in July 2008, Fuld suggested that the Fed protect Lehman by turning it into a bank holding company. But Geithner rejected the idea as "gimmicky." It was a gimmick the Fed would eagerly embrace later, when the fates of Morgan Stanley and Goldman Sachs hung in the balance. Shortly after Fuld's spurned request, the New York Fed's Bill Dudley, who later succeeded Geithner as its president, proposed a Bear Stearns–like solution for Lehman, including a $55 billion loan from the Fed. It was a casual suggestion, not thoroughly researched, and apparently not taken seriously at the time—maybe not even by Dudley. In retrospect, that casual suggestion could have been an incredible bargain.

It wasn't the only idea that didn't fly. Over the summer months, a long-running negotiation for a large equity investment by the Korean Development Bank stumbled several times before finally dying at just about the time Fannie and Freddie were taken over. A flirtation with Bank of America (BofA) dragged on for a while but ultimately went nowhere because the government was unwilling to kick in any money. At one point late in the game, BofA's CEO Ken Lewis told Paulson that he could purchase Lehman only if the government would take over most of the risk connected with a $40 billion pool of dodgy assets. In retrospect, that was chicken feed, but Paulson refused. Instead, Bank of America bought Merrill Lynch—on the very day that Lehman went bankrupt.

It was the on-again-off-again romance with Barclays Capital, the British investment giant, that almost came to fruition. It started back in April 2008, when the Treasury's Bob Steel, a former Goldman banker, called his friend Bob Diamond, then president of Barclays, in London. With a directness that stunned Diamond, Steel asked, "Is there a price at which you'd be interested in Lehman? And if so, what would you need from us?" The U.S. government was back in the investment banking business. A surprised Diamond promised to think about it—and he did. Acquiring Lehman at a bargain price would give Barclays something the British firm coveted: a big seat at the Wall Street table. But the idea went nowhere for months.

By early September things had deteriorated further for Lehman, which appeared to be on the brink. It was about then that Barclays' executives decided it was time to revive the Lehman idea, provided the New York investment bank could be purchased for a song—as looked likely. Both the Treasury and the Fed approved, to put it mildly. Apart from being British—and hence not the Treasury's problem or the Fed's—Barclays was one of the few financial giants that had weathered the storm pretty well. Just as JP Morgan Chase had the balance sheet to save Bear Stearns, Barclays had the balance sheet to save Lehman Brothers—if the price was low enough. And Steel had strongly hinted that the U.S. government would not only broker the deal, but even throw in some cash. Over the frantic weekend of September 12–14, Barclays sent a team to New York, led by Diamond, to perform whatever due diligence they could in a hurry.

But things had changed between March and September. Partly because of the adverse publicity from Bear Stearns and partly because of the huge open-ended commitments made to Fannie Mae and Freddie Mac, Paulson was now drawing the proverbial line in the sand: Any deal for Lehman would have to be done *without* public money, in sharp contrast to Steel's suggestion to Diamond in April. Indeed, Paulson would later cite fear of creating moral hazard to explain the fateful decision to let Lehman go.

On a conference call with Bernanke and Geithner, Paulson "stated unequivocally that he would not support spending taxpayers' money—the Fed's included—to save Lehman. 'I'm being called Mr. Bailout,' he said. 'I can't do it again.'" To lock in his position, I suppose, Paulson's aides leaked his no-taxpayer-money pledge to the press on Thursday, September 11. By Friday it was all over the media—a fait accompli. This infuriated Geithner at the New York Fed. According to reporting by the *Wall Street Journal*'s David Wessel, Geithner "thought that publicly drawing 'a line in the sand' during a financial crisis was lunacy." He told Paulson that "the amount of public money you're going to have to spend is going up, more than you would have otherwise! Your statement is way out of line!" Estimates of how much public money the U.S. government would have had to kick in for Barclays to make a deal range anywhere between $12 billion and $60 billion. Any such number is a pittance compared with the trillions that the Fed and the Treasury committed later.

The decision to do the deal with *only* private money made the Lehman problem much harder to solve. Nonetheless, a last-ditch weekend attempt by Geithner and Paulson to cobble together an LTCM-like deal, whereby a consortium of Wall Street firms would band together to fill the hole that Barclays needed filled, almost succeeded. But, as they say, *close* only counts in horseshoes.

In the end, the problems extended beyond Lehman's dubious balance sheet. Unbeknownst to the Americans, British law required a shareholder vote to approve the transaction, and that could take a long time—far longer than Lehman was likely to survive without assistance. In the interim, *someone* would have to guarantee Lehman's debts. That was presumably Barclays, for the Fed would not do it—and that was not to be. Britain's financial regulator, the Financial Services Authority (FSA), and the Chancellor of the Exchequer, Alistair Darling, were dealing with their own problems across the Atlantic. Darling told Paulson that the UK government didn't want to "import our cancer." When Lehman failed, the Brits did so, anyway—in a big way.

A special waiver was needed to override the shareholder-vote requirement, and the FSA was not about to give one. Nor would Darling push them to do so. So, on Sunday, September 14, the Barclays deal went the way of the Bank of America and Korean Development Bank deals—nowhere. Ironically, it was the British government that wound up killing the prospect of a "private sector solution" for Lehman. Lehman filed for bankruptcy protection that night.

WHO LOST LEHMAN—AND WHY?

You could say it was the British government. But that would ignore the fact that an awful lot of water had flowed under an awful lot of bridges before that fateful Sunday.

Paulson, who was both a Republican and a markets man who formerly ran Goldman Sachs, was perhaps overly concerned about the moral hazard issue in the aftermath of Bear Stearns. Still, he had a point. Public funds had been deployed to save Bear, Fannie, and Freddie. If they were now made available to Lehman, it would imply—once again—that the U.S. government was waiting in the wings to bail out any major financial institution. Moral hazard would have proliferated, and Mr. Paulson would, indeed, have become Mr. Bailout. But, of course, he became Mr. Bailout, anyway.

These thoughts, valid as they were, represent only one side of the moral hazard ledger, however. In simplest terms, the trade-off looked like this: On one side, saving Lehman would deepen an existing moral hazard problem. On the other side, Bear Stearns had been rescued, moral hazard notwithstanding, in order to stave off possibly serious contagion to a wide variety of innocent bystanders—perhaps as many as 310 million Americans. If that was a winning argument in March, why wasn't it a winning argument when Lehman went on the chopping block in September? That was Geithner's worry. In his view, it was worth committing some public money again—*if* they could find a buyer for Lehman, as they had for Bear.

But the moral hazard argument for letting Lehman fail was not Paulson's or Bernanke's first line of defense. They first enunciated the belief that because six months had elapsed since Bear Stearns, the *markets had ample time to prepare*—both financially and psychologically—for the possible demise of Lehman Brothers. Counterparty risks were understood and accounted for, they argued. Hedges, not to mention shorts, were in place. The markets were allegedly ready for a Lehman failure, should it come. Here is what Bernanke told the House Financial Services Committee just nine days after Lehman failed:

> . . . the troubles at Lehman had been well known for some time, and investors clearly recognized—as evidenced, for example, by the high cost of insuring Lehman's debt in the market for credit default swaps—that the failure of the firm was a significant possibility. Thus, we judged that investors and counterparties had had time to take precautionary measures.

It was a sanguine view, to be sure, but it was not Bernanke's and Paulson's alone. Several prominent market "experts," including Goldman Sachs' CEO Lloyd Blankfein, voiced the same opinion. Within hours of Lehman's demise, they were proved wrong.

A third rationale held that Lehman Brothers, despite its larger size and global reach, was actually *less interconnected* with other firms than Bear Stearns had been. It was not, for example, the prime broker for hundreds of hedge funds. On this reasoning, Bear had been rescued because it was *too interconnected to fail*, especially with the repo market, not because it was *too big to fail*. One could therefore rationalize drawing a line that saved Bear but let Lehman go.

Maybe. But that line of defense always looked dubious, and it was not emphasized by the Fed. After all, Lehman was twice Bear's size, and its zillions of derivative and repo contracts connected it to numerous counterparties all over the world. Without detailed insider information on Lehman's various businesses, the actual degree of entanglement was hard for outsiders to gauge. Indeed, one wonders how well the authorities understood it. Once Lehman fell, however, the judgment was rendered quickly: Lehman Brothers turned out to be way too interconnected to fail.

Fourth, and most important, the Treasury and the Fed adopted the position that they hold to this day: that they lacked the *legal authority* to rescue Lehman. Remember, the crucial decision days were September 12–14, which came several weeks *before* Congress appropriated $700 billion for the TARP (Troubled Assets Relief Program), an appropriation that probably never would have passed without the Lehman failure. The Treasury had no slush fund with which to prop up Lehman—or so they claimed. Once the meltdown turned truly frightening, however, the Treasury quickly discovered such a fund, as we shall see.

The Fed, of course, did not require a congressional appropriation. It was authorized by Section 13(3) to lend to *anyone*—as long as the collateral on the loan was "secured to the satisfaction" of . . . whom? Why, the Fed itself! On March 14, the Fed had judged that Bear Stearns' dodgy mortgage assets—the stuff Jamie Dimon wouldn't take—met this rather lax test. But on September 14, it judged that Lehman Brothers' even worse mortgage and real estate assets did not. Why the difference? Here is how Bernanke explained it later:

> To avoid the failure of Bear Stearns, we facilitated the purchase of Bear Stearns by JP Morgan Chase by means of a Federal Reserve loan, backed by assets of Bear Stearns and a partial guarantee from JP Morgan. In the case of AIG, we judged that emergency Federal Reserve credit would be adequately secured by AIG's assets. However, neither route proved feasible in the case of the investment bank Lehman Brothers. No buyer for the firm was forthcoming, and the available collateral fell well short of the amount needed to secure a Federal Reserve loan.

In short, a loan secured by Lehman's assets would not be "secured to the satisfaction" of the Fed because Lehman was not just illiquid; it was insolvent.

Mostly for this reason, Paulson, Bernanke, and Geithner had made a fateful decision even before the last possible private buyer (Barclays) dropped out: If no private-sector solution could be found, they would let Lehman Brothers fail and deal with the consequences, *because saving Lehman with a loan from the Fed was illegal.* This critical judgment will reverberate for years. Bernanke, Geithner, and the Fed's legal staff decided that lending to Lehman—against collateral that few could honestly characterize as "good"—would stretch the law beyond its breaking point. They believed they had no choice.

The consequences of letting Lehman go down turned out to be more severe than probably anyone imagined. The financial system literally started to fall apart. Why? We'll be in a better position to answer that question after the next chapter, which examines the cascade of failures and near failures that followed the Lehman bankruptcy. But a large part of the answer is staring us right in the face already.

Bear Stearns—and to a lesser extent Fannie and Freddie—had, indeed, established a precedent. Call it moral hazard if you wish, though not many financial companies aspired to go the way of Bear. But whatever you call it, the market had acquired the view that the government was not going to let any financial giant fail messily. Market participants are marvelously adaptable people. According to one piece of folk wisdom, they can make money playing by any set of rules—as long as they know what the rules are. The Lehman decision abruptly and surprisingly tore the perceived rulebook into pieces and tossed it out the window. Market participants were thus cut adrift, no longer knowing what game they were playing. That's a formula for panic, for the replacement of greed by fear—which is exactly what happened on Lehman Day, September 15, 2008.

THE WATERSHED

There is close to universal agreement that the demise of Lehman Brothers was the watershed event of the entire financial crisis and that the decision to allow it to fail was the watershed decision. Virtually every discussion of the financial crisis divides history into two epochs: "before Lehman" and "after Lehman." As we have noted, the whole economy seemed to fall off the table immediately after September 15. The reasons, of course, emanated from the larger financial system, as we will see next.

6

|⁙⁙⁙⁙⁙⁙⁙⁙⁙⁙⁙⁙⁙⁙⁙⁙⁙⁙⁙⁙⁙|

THE PANIC OF 2008

You are about to experience the most unbelievable
week in America ever.

—Jamie Dimon, CEO of JP Morgan Chase, to his management
team on Saturday morning, September 13, 2008

All hell broke loose after Lehman Brothers failed on September 15, 2008. In rapid-fire succession, the giant insurance company American International Group (AIG) was essentially nationalized by the Federal Reserve. Merrill Lynch, America's best-known stock broker, avoided oblivion only by selling itself hastily to Bank of America. Goldman Sachs and Morgan Stanley were saved when the Fed declared them to be bank holding companies. Shares in the world's oldest money market mutual fund fell under the sacred $1 mark, thereby precipitating both a run on money funds and a collapse of the commercial paper market. America's largest thrift institution, Washington Mutual, and the nation's fourth-largest bank, Wachovia, crashed and burned. Each was sold for a pittance by the FDIC. Treasury Secretary Paulson and Fed Chairman Bernanke marched down to Capitol Hill to inform the congressional leadership that the world might end if they didn't appropriate $700 billion fast.

And more. Nobody had ever seen anything like it. Who was it that had claimed Lehman was *not* too interconnected to fail?

This chapter homes in on the critical juncture in the crisis, the historical discontinuity that made everything so much worse, the time when the music truly stopped and the partygoers scrambled for the few remaining seats. Because these incredible events carry important implications for what followed, we need to understand some of the details. But my focus is less on the events themselves and more on the questions of *why, how,* and *what did it mean?*

The correct image for what we now call "Lehman Weekend" might be a chaotic three-ring circus at which a trio of frenetic jugglers named Bernanke, Geithner, and Paulson tried to keep multiple balls in the air at once (Lehman, AIG, Merrill Lynch, and others) while an unruly herd of elephants stomped around, shaking the ground, and a stiff wind threatened to blow down the circus tent. We know how that particular circus ended: Lehman failed, AIG was rescued, Bank of America bought Merrill Lynch, and so on. But that terse summary leaves much out, and getting there was not half the fun.

THE UNINSURED INSURER

Insurance is supposed to be a boring business. Try talking about it at a cocktail party. But it wasn't boring at AIG during the housing-and-mortgage bubble, when the company decided to perform a high-wire act without a safety net. Little did we know that we would all be forced to go up on the wire with them.

AIG was a storied company. Founded in China in 1919 by the legendary C. V. Starr, the first Westerner to sell insurance in Shanghai, the company remained headquartered there until 1949, when it fled the advance of Mao Tse-tung's army and relocated to New York. Nonetheless, AIG's Asian roots ran deep—and they weren't limited to Asia. In 2004 it was the largest insurance company in the world, by stock market value, and boasted

116,000 employees in 130 countries. At the time, the AIG logo was also emblazoned across the jerseys of Britain's most famous soccer team, Manchester United, perhaps the most-watched sports franchise in the world. Those jerseys were deeply symbolic. AIG was a global franchise itself.

Starting in the late 1990s, the company discovered that it had two big competitive advantages that it could turn into huge profits. Unfortunately, exploiting them to the nth degree almost killed the company and almost cost the taxpayers a fortune.

AIG's first big advantage was its AAA credit rating—a rarity in corporate America, then held by only six companies. Having the ultimate Good Housekeeping seal of approval enabled the insurance giant to borrow more cheaply than its rivals. More important, the treasured Triple-A made AIG a plausible seller of huge volumes of credit default swaps (CDS). Remember, when a bond or CDO goes into default, the buyer of the CDS must collect his winnings from the seller. So, if you are thinking about buying a CDS, you want assurance that the seller will be around to pay off, even in hard times. And what better assurance could anyone ask for than AIG's gold-plated balance sheet with its coveted AAA rating? Until very late in the game, AIG did not even have to post collateral to its counterparties. A Triple-A credit didn't need to do that.

Good times are good as long as they roll. But rampant abuse of AIG's exorbitant privilege wound up getting the company into enormous trouble once the bubble burst. By the time AIG stopped selling CDS early in 2006, the insurance behemouth was in the unenviable position of being the dominant seller in a market that was destined to collapse.

The company's second big competitive advantage was extremely lax regulation—especially compared with the regulation of commercial banks. AIG's Financial Products subsidiary (AIG FP), where its mammoth CDS business was housed, managed to get itself regulated by the Office of Thrift Supervision (OTS) because the corporate parent company had acquired a few small savings banks. Savings banks? Aren't those the stodgy thrift institutions on the corner that take savings deposits and grant mortgages to homeowners? Seems like a funny place to lodge one of the world's largest derivatives operations. Well, AIG FP was not actually *lodged* there, but merely *lodged there for regulatory purposes.* Call it skillful regulatory shopping.

The badly overmatched OTS had, shall we say, limited expertise in the complex world of modern derivatives. *Very* limited. To the financial wizards at AIG FP, this must have looked like playing three-card monte without a cop on the beat. And they proceeded to play for stupefyingly high stakes.

There was a second respect in which regulation was lax, or perhaps nonexistent. I mentioned earlier that CDS are not classified as insurance policies, which is what they really are, but rather as derivatives, which they are, too. The seller of a CDS collects small premium payments as long as nothing goes wrong but is liable for a huge payment if the bond or CDO defaults. That's the classic profile of an insurance product; think about fire or life insurance, for example. Yet state insurance regulators around the country did not treat CDS as insurance, which turned out to be a fateful error. Not only did AIG face light *banking* regulation on its derivatives book, it also escaped *insurance* regulation.

One consequence, which turned out to be crucial, was that the insurance regulators did not force AIG to hold any capital reserves against potential losses—as they routinely do for policies as simple as life or fire insurance. *None. Nada. Zero.* And as noted, the firm wasn't posting collateral, either. What about the derivatives regulators? Well, as you may recall, there weren't any. The terribly misguided Commodity Futures Modernization Act had explicitly banned the regulation of derivatives in 2000.

To AIG's executives, the situation presented a virtual license to print money—with nobody watching the printing presses. As Bernanke later put it, "AIG exploited a huge gap in the regulatory system. There was no oversight of the financial products division. This was a hedge fund, basically, that was attached to a large and stable insurance company, made huge numbers of irresponsible bets." He added, "If there's a single episode in this entire 18 months that has made me more angry, I can't think of one, than AIG."

Between 1998, when it wrote its first CDS, and 2007, AIG accumulated a half-trillion-dollar position in credit risk—all on one side of the bet (betting *against* defaults). Not only that, the CDS business was highly concentrated; most of AIG's deals were with just five big Wall Street banks as counterparties. And virtually none of it was hedged.

Think about that for a moment. AIG had taken on a titanic volume of risk. The risks were concentrated in a few counterparties and were probably highly correlated from one CDS to the next, because if one batch of subprime mortgages went bad, others would likely follow. The company neither hedged those risks nor set aside capital reserves against them, as a prudent insurance company would have done. Nor did it post collateral, as a derivatives counterparty would have done. This combination of high risk and low safeguards—by an *insurance* company, no less!—must have been one of the greatest, if not *the* greatest, failures of risk management, and of corporate governance more generally, in history. Where were the risk managers? Where were the auditors? Where was AIG's board of directors? And where, by the way, were the regulators? The answers to all four questions appear to be the same: nowhere to be found.

AIG had apparently drunk the Kool-Aid. Despite the huge risks to which it had exposed itself, the company, amazingly, still thought it stood in an extremely safe position—as if its CDS on subprime mortgage-backed securities were like life insurance policies written on a broad pool of healthy individuals. They were AAA tranches, weren't they? Only in 2005 did AIG start worrying about how much risk it had taken on. Only in early 2006 did it stop writing new CDS. (Unfortunately for the world, others stepped in to fill the gap left by AIG's departure.) As late as August 2007, with things already heading south, Joseph Cassano, who ran AIG FP, stated publicly, "It is hard for us, without being flippant, to even see a scenario within any kind of realm or reason that would see us losing $1 in any of those transactions." Flippant? One dollar turned out to be a rather large underestimate of AIG's losses. But Cassano's boss at the time, Martin Sullivan, concurred: "That's why I'm sleeping a bit easier at night." Sullivan must have been a sound sleeper.

The shoes started dropping in July 2007, when declines in the values of the securities AIG insured led to collateral calls from counterparties—especially from its biggest counterparty, Goldman Sachs. Things got worse after Paribas Day (August 9, 2007), when a wave of nervousness swept over markets worldwide. AIG was woefully unprepared to post more collateral against its massive volume of outstanding CDS, and it fought the collateral calls as best it could. In particular, it engaged in a running battle with Goldman Sachs over the valuations, or "marks," of the underlying mortgage securities—with Goldman arguing for lower marks, and AIG, led by Cassano, arguing for higher ones. That battle would continue right up to AIG's demise, which was precipitated by—you guessed it—more collateral calls.

Cassano was forced to resign in February 2008 but was retained as a consultant for $1 million a month. Yes, that was $1 million per *month*. You start to see why the AIG case made a lot of people angry. Still, both dissatisfaction with AIG's management and losses at AIG FP mounted. In June 2008, Sullivan was replaced as CEO by one of AIG's board members, Robert Willumstad, a distinguished veteran banker who looked as though he were sent from central casting. But, just like Alan Schwartz at Bear Stearns, he was taking the helm of a ship that was taking on water fast.

Willumstad and Geithner had earlier discussed the possibility of giving AIG access to the Federal Reserve's discount window; at one of those meetings Willumstad left Geithner documents that showed that AIG had $2.7 *trillion* in notional exposure on derivatives, including $1 trillion concentrated in just twelve major institutions. Scary stuff. But it was only on Thursday, September 11, that AIG's new chief first alerted the New York Fed president that the company was having serious trouble getting access to credit markets. Funders were not eager to lend to a company that was on the losing side of so many big bets. According to reporting by David Wessel, "Geithner was stunned. While AIG was on the worry list, it wasn't thought to be in imminent danger." The New York Fed chief also "couldn't imagine that an insurance company posed such a big risk to the financial system that the Fed should bail it out." How about a giant, casinolike hedge fund hiding inside an insurance company?

By Lehman Weekend, AIG had been forced to post about $19 billion worth of collateral to its CDS counterparties, $7.6 billion to Goldman Sachs alone, and both Moody's and S&P were warning about a potential downgrade of AIG's cherished AAA credit rating. Such a downgrade would trigger automatic calls for more collateral—collateral that AIG did not have. By then, with the OTS both asleep at the switch and way out of its depth, the Fed had taken over as AIG's tacit regulator—or was it the insurer's savior? Unfortunately, the attention of Bernanke, Geithner, and Paulson that weekend was consumed by Lehman Brothers. AIG was a much bigger company, and it was coming apart at the seams.* But it was almost an afterthought that fateful weekend. Ironically, AIG's death spiral was a kind of liquidity run, somewhat like the one killing Lehman that very weekend.

At an emergency meeting with New York Fed officials on Friday, September 12, AIG executives reported that a severe liquidity squeeze was threatening the firm's survival. Later that evening, a staffer e-mailed the New York Fed's Bill Dudley to report that there was "more panic from [hedge funds]. Now focus is on AIG. I am hearing worse than LEH [Lehman]. Every bank and dealer has exposure to them." That sure sounded like a classic case of systemic risk. The ominous words "worse than LEH" must have grabbed Dudley's attention.

Geithner, Dudley, and others at the New York Fed were quickly learning a lot they didn't know about AIG. (Remember, they had never regulated the insurer.) But the Fed was dubious about invoking Section 13(3) to lend to AIG when it had no intention of doing so for Lehman. It also believed (or was it *hoped?*) that some sort of private-sector solution—whether a buyout or an infusion of capital—would emerge. After all, AIG looked very different from Lehman, which in the Fed's eyes was an investment bank with no remaining franchise value. AIG, by contrast, had a large number of healthy insurance businesses that were not infected by the disease at AIG FP. Couldn't they be sold? Indeed, Willumstad was actively

---

*AIG had almost $1.1 trillion in assets at the time, compared with $640 billion for Lehman.

courting a number of prospective investors. Surely, *some* private deal to save AIG would be struck.

Unfortunately, it didn't happen by the time Lehman filed for bankruptcy that Sunday night. And after that, it was too late. Whatever slim hope there might have been for a private-sector solution prior to the Lehman bankruptcy vanished into the mist, as every major financial institution in the world turned inward, focusing on self-preservation. AIG first gave up trying to raise fresh capital, and then gave up trying to persuade a syndicate of banks to lend it $75 billion. The hundred-year flood was engulfing every major financial institution. It was every man for himself.

The next morning, all three major rating agencies downgraded AIG's credit ratings, triggering an additional $13 billion in collateral calls. Their actions seemed perfectly in line with the markets' jaundiced view that the agencies show up at the battlefield after the fighting is over and shoot the wounded. AIG's stock dropped about 60 percent in a single day. Having once sold for $146 a share, the stock closed under $5.

On Tuesday, September 16—which, by unhappy coincidence, was a Federal Open Market Committee meeting day—the Federal Reserve Board overcame its reluctance to invoke Section 13(3) and extended a massive $85 billion loan to AIG. The loan deviated quite a bit from Bagehot's classic principles. Among other things, the Fed was clearly worried about AIG's solvency, not just its liquidity. As collateral on the loan, the Fed took assets of the parent company, not assets of AIG FP, plus the stock of most of AIG's regulated insurance subsidiaries. Pretty good collateral. As partial payment, the Fed also took convertible preferred stock, which, if converted, would give the Fed ownership of 79.9 percent of AIG's common stock.* This last provision meant that AIG was, in effect, *nationalized* by a government agency (the Fed) that had never regulated it and that had not sought congressional approval to do so. Very strange.

---

*Why 79.9 percent? Because at 80 percent, generally accepted accounting principles (GAAP) would require that all AIG's debts be consolidated onto the federal government's balance sheet—and there is no such thing! Holding the ownership below 80 percent preserved AIG's existence as a private company with one very large shareholder.

But even $85 billion, an almost unimaginable sum at the time, quickly proved inadequate to the task. AIG told the Fed that it anticipated needing $4 billion on the day of the bailout. It actually drew $14 billion, as its normal sources of credit began to dry up and it had to post collateral. Another $23 billion flowed out over the next few days. The loan commitment was soon raised to about $135 billion using TARP money, and eventually reached $182 billion—a truly staggering sum. Amazingly, the loan to AIG now looks likely to be paid back in full, with a profit to the government on the stock. At the time, however, it looked like a huge, bad loan to a failing company.

While there is heated competition for the dubious distinction, the AIG bailout may be the most reviled of all the emergency actions taken by the Federal Reserve and the Treasury during the crisis, even though it was one of the most important. One reason was its sheer magnitude. Before the TARP bailout pool (which is discussed in the next chapter), $182 billion was an unimaginable sum. Remember, the Bear Stearns deal had been done for "just" $29 billion. Another reason was the audacity of the Fed's actions: "With AIG, the Federal Reserve and Treasury broke new ground. They put the U.S. taxpayer on the line for the full cost and full risk of rescuing a failing company." Not to mention virtually nationalizing AIG. A third reason was that a significant share of the original loan passed through directly to Goldman Sachs, making it look like a backdoor deal for Goldman, Paulson's former firm.

But the biggest reason may have been the embarrassingly large bonuses that were subsequently paid to about four hundred employees of AIG FP, including some highly paid traders and executives—seven of whom were supposed to receive more than $4 million each. Ordinary Americans have no idea what a CDS is, and they cannot really get their arms around a number like $182 billion. (Can anyone?) But they do understand the injustice of paying $165 million in bonuses to people who run a company into the ground, especially when taxpayers are left holding the bag.

The bonuses had been approved by AIG's board in March 2008, long before the company was nationalized. But they became a public relations disaster for the fledgling Obama administration a year later, when the company filed documents revealing them. The administration seemed to be clumsily of two minds (maybe more) on the issue of whether these bonuses should be paid. On March 15, 2009, National Economic Council director Larry Summers expressed outrage on the Sunday talk shows. On ABC, he opined, "There are a lot of terrible things that have happened in the last 18 months, but what's happened at AIG is the most outrageous." But on the other hand, he observed on CBS that "We're not a country where contracts just get abrogated willy-nilly." Both statements are true, but they send a rather garbled message.

The president himself declared that he wanted Secretary Tim Geithner to "use any legal means necessary to rescind the AIG bonuses." But "any legal means" proved to be a stern test. According to journalist Noam Scheiber, "After administration lawyers could find no legal reason to stop the $165 million in bonuses . . . an aide suggested that Geithner put a stop to them anyway. The secretary shot him a look befitting the teller of a racist joke: pure, affronted disbelief." In the end, Geithner and Summers concluded that a contract is a contract. The AIG bonuses were paid. In response to the public furor, however, the AIG employees returned over 25 percent of the money.

All that said, the most serious *economic* (as opposed to public relations) issue posed by the AIG bailout was probably the decision to pay off AIG's creditors one hundred cents on the dollar, rather than impose any losses on them—which is sometimes called "bailing in" or giving them "a haircut." Goldman Sachs was just the most prominent example; all of AIG's counterparties and creditors were treated the same way. As were Fannie Mae's and Freddie Mac's creditors just days earlier. As were Bear Stearns' creditors six months earlier. It is here that moral hazard rears its ugliest head.

No one would ever want to replicate the uncomfortable—and, in some cases, disastrous—fates of AIG's top executives, its shareholders, and many of its employees. That was never the moral hazard worry. But when creditors who lent to, and counterparties who dealt with, AIG without bothering to worry about its creditworthiness are bailed out 100 percent, the government is inviting creditors and counterparties of other companies to assume the same. That's where the real moral hazard issue lurks, and it has prompted many second-guessers to assert that the Fed and the Treasury should have imposed haircuts on AIG's creditors rather than let taxpayers shoulder the entire risk. Should they have?

One's sense of justice cries out: *Yes!* And the FDIC's Sheila Bair argued the point vociferously with Paulson and Bernanke at the time. Looking back years later, she concluded, "There's no reason in the world why [AIG's] counterparties couldn't have taken a 10 percent haircut." It's hard not to sympathize with Bair's point of view. One hundred cents on the dollar does seem outrageous.

But now think about the sheer legal and logistical difficulties of arranging haircuts in real time. Who would negotiate with AIG's numerous counterparties? What if some of them wouldn't accept haircuts voluntarily—as the Fed and the Treasury believed? Would we then "abrogate contracts willy-nilly," to use Summers's phrase? Even when the counterparties were not American entities? Furthermore, the threat of sending AIG into Chapter 11 just wasn't credible amid the panic that started on Lehman Day. The Fed and the Treasury needed to save the sinking ship, not sink it faster. Creditors knew that.

Remember also that Bernanke, Geithner, and Paulson were making decisions on very compressed time scales. At first they were preoccupied by Lehman Brothers and did not have the time to master the dumbfounding (and almost unbelievable) details of the AIG situation. Then, once Lehman failed, they found themselves standing in the middle of the biggest, most complex financial meltdown anyone had ever seen. Like the crew of a sinking vessel, they were rushing around trying to save as many passengers as possible. In a situation like that, loading up the lifeboats to their fullest capacity—or even beyond—without worrying whether some undeserving parties jumped in is both natural and understandable.

In a calmer, noncrisis atmosphere, haircuts might have made good sense. But the Treasury and the Fed saw confidence evaporating left and right. They did not want to add to the contagious panic that Lehman had started by imposing losses on AIG's creditors. They did not want counter-parties everywhere calling in loans, demanding cash and collateral, and refusing to deal with one another. They did not want fire sales of assets that would depress prices even further, causing yet more losses. They did not want the financial world roiled by rumors about who would be the next to go.

Making AIG's creditors whole was one way for the authorities to stanch the bleeding—or at least to try. And they took it. As Geithner later explained to Congress:

> Once a company refuses to meet its full obligations to a customer, other customers will quickly find other places to do business. If we had sought to force counterparties to accept less than they were legally entitled to, market participants would have lost confidence in AIG and the ratings agencies would have downgraded AIG again. This could have led to the company's collapse, threatened our efforts to rebuild confidence in the financial system, and meant a deeper recession, more financial turmoil, and a much higher cost for American taxpayers.

As the wise old saying goes, where you stand depends on where you sit. To many critics seated comfortably on the sidelines, paying off AIG's creditors 100 percent looked too generous and likely to invite moral hazard. But Paulson, Bernanke, and Geithner were sitting in the hot seats at the time. If the bailout was indeed an error, which is far from clear, it was a forgivable error.

That said, the decision to make AIG's creditors whole remains controversial to this day. It may be controversial forever. At a hearing the day after the AIG bailout was announced, Congressman Barney Frank (D-MA) quipped that he might introduce a resolution declaring September 15, 2008, to have been Free Market Day. "The national commitment to the free market lasted one day," he said. "It was Monday."

CONTAGION AND FINANCIAL PANICS

From childhood, we are taught not to practice guilt by association. It's wrong. Just because little Johnnie is a jerk, that doesn't mean that his brother is—not to mention all the other little Johnnies. If one used-car salesman cheats you, that doesn't mean that all of them will. Perhaps most important, if one member of a minority group behaves badly in some respect, that does not condemn the entire group. People understand this principle intellectually, though many have a hard time internalizing it viscerally.

Financial market players do neither; they don't even try. Rather, guilt by association is one of their basic operating principles—that's where the antelope metaphor comes from. If Bear Stearns looks like it may go under, firms that in some sense *look like Bear Stearns* or are *related to Bear Stearns* come under suspicion immediately—or are convicted instantly in kangaroo court. That is the essence of *financial contagion*. One "bad apple" can make the whole group guilty until proven innocent, with unsettling results on financial markets and, much more important, on economies.

Some aspects of financial contagion are *rational*. If a bank fails, that may leave its counterparties holding the (empty) bag—as happened with Lehman Brothers and was feared in the cases of Bear Stearns and AIG. If the prices of a certain asset class (e.g., houses, stocks, or subprime mortgages) plummet, the resulting capital losses may imperil a large number of institutions. Those linkages are obvious. Other bases for rational contagion are less so. For example, in 2008 a number of big Wall Street firms operated with the same business model as Bear Stearns': combining high leverage with heavy reliance on very short-term debt. When the model failed for Bear, that called into question the safety of Lehman Brothers, Merrill Lynch, Goldman Sachs, and Morgan Stanley. By contrast, AIG was the only insurance company that harbored a gigantic hedge fund in its midst. The catastrophe at AIG did not cause investors to flee insurance companies.

When a panic strikes for *rational* reasons, the remedies are somewhat obvious, if painful. Protect or guarantee the counterparties. Try to arrest falling asset prices. Shore up—with capital, liquidity, or both—the solid firms falling victim to guilt by association.

At other times, however, financial contagion is less rational, for guilt by association can go too far. When Lehman defaulted on its commercial paper, was that really a reason to suspect that General Electric might default, too? (Well, they were both issuing commercial paper, right?) Another example is the well-known Wall Street aphorism that, in a panic, "You sell what you can, not what you want." Advice like that can spread a crash from one market to another for no good reason.

In such cases, policy makers must somehow reassure and calm markets. But how, exactly? Soothing words alone rarely work. They need to be backed up by cash—typically public cash, and sometimes a lot of it.

Policy makers may find it hard to distinguish *rational* contagion from *irrational* contagion in specific cases. Typically, they confront a blend of the two. When Lehman fell, for example, was it rational for speculators to attack Merrill Lynch and Morgan Stanley? Maybe. But what about Goldman Sachs, which was less exposed, better capitalized, and had much better risk management than Bear? Maybe not. Who really knew?

THE RUN ON THE MONEY FUNDS

Apart from the general sense of panic the Lehman bankruptcy caused, that watershed event arguably had next to nothing to do with the crisis at AIG, which would have blown up in any case. But the next big episode, the one that some observers think really started the Panic of 2008 in earnest, clearly disproved the notion that Lehman Brothers was *not* too interconnected to fail. It turned out that unbeknownst to most people, Lehman was tightly linked to the world's oldest money market mutual fund, the Reserve Primary Fund. As soon as that link was exposed, the dominoes started falling.

In a successful effort to boost what had been lagging returns, the Reserve began investing heavily in commercial paper (CP) in 2006. By September 2008, it had $785 million, or 1.2 percent of the fund, invested in Lehman Brothers' CP. The Reserve's managers felt that their investment in Lehman's highly rated paper was safe. (Remember the moral hazard: The government had engineered a rescue of Bear Stearns just six months earlier, leaving all the creditors whole.) That turned out to be a fatal miscalculation.

Within just two days after Lehman declared bankruptcy, the Reserve was flooded with redemption requests amounting to about half the fund's balances. After the close of business on Tuesday, September 16, management announced that its holdings of Lehman paper were worthless and that it was therefore forced to "break the buck"; that is, to redeem shares at less than their $1 face value. After a number of investors got out at par, and after other CP prices fell in the panicky environment, the remaining shares of the Reserve Primary Fund were worth only $0.97. A 3 percent loss doesn't sound like much compared with everything else that was happening at the time. But, in fact, it was one of the signal events of the Panic of 2008. Why?

Money market mutual funds, which (ironically) had been originated by the Reserve in 1971, were a great invention. They are like checking accounts—indeed, you can write checks on your balance—but with higher yields. The share price of a money fund never varied; it was always exactly $1, which removed any risk of capital gains or losses. This neat trick was accomplished originally by investing the funds' assets in money-market instruments that hardly ever fluctuated in value, such as short-term U.S. Treasury bills.

As time went by, and no retail money fund ever suffered losses large enough to force it to "break the buck," commercial paper and other short-term instruments came to be viewed as safe enough to be included in money funds' portfolios. And since CP paid a bit more than Treasury bills, that boosted the funds' yields. Investors, for their part, came to consider money fund balances just as safe as bank accounts, even though the former carried no FDIC guarantees. The industry flourished, and by September 2008 money funds had $3.4 trillion in outstanding balances. Let me repeat that: $3.4 *trillion*, a sum roughly equal to half of all deposits held in FDIC-insured banks at the time.

It was therefore quite a shock to the investing public to learn that shares in the Reserve Primary Fund were worth only 97 cents at the close of business on September 16, 2008. (Initial rumors had pegged the value even lower than that.) It felt like losing money in your checking account. But with one big difference: There was no deposit insurance to pay off the missing three cents. *Oh my God*, investors thought, *these are not bank accounts!*

The FDIC was set up in 1933 to prevent bank runs, and it has done so exceedingly well. If the First National Bank of Nowhere goes under, its depositors know they won't lose a cent as long as their balances are below the insured maximum, which is now $250,000. They have no reason to run on the bank. And they certainly have no reason to run on the Second National Bank next door. Not so with money funds. Shareholders in the Reserve Primary Fund *did* lose money, even if only 3 percent. They, therefore, *did* have a reason to run on the Reserve. And the resulting fears of losses at other money market funds quickly led to runs elsewhere.

This was serious business. Within days, "it was overwhelmingly clear that we were staring into the abyss—that there wasn't a bottom to this—as the outflows [from money funds] picked up steam on Wednesday and Thursday." In just a week, investors withdrew about $350 billion from prime money market funds. That meant, of course, that fund managers had to liquidate an equal volume of commercial paper, T-bills, and so on in order to meet redemption calls. But after the Lehman-induced losses at the Reserve, no fund manager wanted to buy CP—and not just Lehman's CP, *anyone's.* When the supply of something skyrockets and the demand for it crumbles, the price drops like a stone. Which is exactly what happened to commercial paper in mid-September. Yields spiked and new issuance fell sharply.

That was no mere detail. Many of America's biggest companies rely on CP for short-term borrowing to bridge routine gaps between payments and receipts—such as large cash outflows on pay days. As Geithner later told the FCIC, "A broad-based run on commercial paper markets . . . [created] the prospect of some of the largest companies in the world . . . losing the capacity to fund and access those commercial paper markets." That gave rise to rumors that blue-chip companies like General Electric and IBM might be unable to meet payroll. It was the near shutdown of the CP market that led Bernanke to declare, "We came very close to a total financial meltdown." Both the Treasury and the Fed reacted quickly to this budding catastrophe—but in the former case, not very adroitly.

Ever since Bear Stearns, Secretary Paulson had insisted that he had no slush fund to tap. The Fed had to be Mr. Moneybags. Yet, where there's a will, there's a way. After what must have been some interesting internal discussions at the Treasury, Paulson decided that the Exchange Stabilization Fund (ESF) was such a fund, after all. His putative rationale? Because some of the skittish money fund investors were foreign, "a collapse of the money fund industry could easily lead to a run on the dollar." Thin. Almost any adverse event in the United States could potentially "lead to a run on the dollar." But in the Treasury's view, the governing statute set a pretty low bar for the use of the ESF. After all, there was a panic going on, wasn't there? Didn't that imperil the dollar?

In any case, Paulson's decision to use $50 billion from the ESF to back a new insurance fund for money market balances, for which he needed President Bush's approval, was momentous in at least four respects. For openers, it was sorely needed. While there was no run on the dollar, there was a big run on the money funds and, through them, on the CP market. If there was ever a time to pull out all the stops, this was it—and the Treasury did so. Give them credit.

Second, the insurance mechanism for the money funds marked the first time the United States Treasury put its own money on the line; previously, it had hidden behind the Fed's ample skirts. *About time*, thought many observers, since decisions that put taxpayer money at risk should be made in the political domain. (Of course, Paulson had previously argued that he had no money.)

Third, using the Exchange Stabilization Fund for this purpose was quite a stretch. The ESF was set up in 1934 for a specific purpose: to stabilize the international value of the dollar when necessary by either buying or selling foreign currency. Almost always, it was neither buying nor selling, so the money just sat there. But now, without even a pretext of dealing in foreign exchange, the Treasury was going to use the ESF to insure money funds. The juxtaposition of this expansive legal reading with the letter-of-the-law attitude on lending to Lehman just days earlier makes a stark contrast. It also raises a poignant question: Why was it okay to bend the law so that the Treasury could use the ESF,* but not okay to bend it to justify a Federal Reserve loan to Lehman Brothers? Indeed, why couldn't the ESF have been used for Lehman? Historians will dote on this question for years to come. But part of the answer is clear: The two decisions were made in different milieus (political versus technocratic), under different laws, *and by different lawyers.*

Fourth, in his haste, Paulson set the original terms of the money fund guarantee in a way that if maintained, which it wasn't, might have threatened the entire U.S. banking system. Specifically, for a modest fee, he proposed insuring *all* balances in money market mutual fund accounts *regardless of the amount.* Think about that for a moment, as America's bankers did the moment the plan was announced on the morning of September 19. At the time, the FDIC insured bank account balances only up to $100,000. Now Treasury was proposing to insure accounts in one of the banks' chief competitors, the money funds, in *unlimited* amounts. I

---

*Congress subsequently banned the practice of using the ESF for money market funds in the future.

remember thinking that morning that this was crazy;* it was bound to precipitate runs on banks—something the FDIC had ended in 1934. Why would anyone keep more than $100,000 in a bank deposit when they could get *full insurance* by moving the balance to a money fund? At the FDIC, Sheila Bair apparently had the same thought, as did thousands of bankers across the country. Why would the Treasury want to do a thing like that?

The answer is simple: It didn't. The folks at the Treasury, working at warp speed in those hectic post-Lehman days, just didn't think through the consequences. They leaped first and looked second. Within days, reacting to well-justified howls of protest from bankers and their lobbyists, the Treasury corrected its error by amending the plan to insure only amounts that were *already on deposit* in money funds on September 19—not any incremental funds deposited after that date. That ended the incentive to run the banks. No harm, no foul? Maybe. But the episode didn't instill confidence in the United States Treasury.

The Fed pitched in, too, by establishing the Asset-Backed Commercial Paper Money Market Mutual Fund Liquidity Facility. (AMLF, if you must know. And try saying the full title fast.) The AMLF was created to extend nonrecourse loans at low interest rates to banks willing to purchase high-quality asset-backed commercial paper from money market funds—who needed to sell it desperately because they were experiencing runs. Let's dwell on the awkward word *nonrecourse* for a moment, because it's important and this is not the last time you'll see it.

"Nonrecourse" means that if the assets in question (in this case, commercial paper) default, the lender (in this case, the Federal Reserve) can claim back only the collateral on the loans. It cannot go after any other assets owned by the borrowers—who, in the case of the AMLF, were banks. In terms of who holds the risk, nonrecourse loans are highly skewed. The borrower owns the upside risk: If the asset appreciates in value, he

---

*Full disclosure: My interest was not purely intellectual. I was thinking about this because I am part owner of a business, Promontory Interfinancial Network, whose basis is the fact that banks—and not competitors like money funds—have deposit insurance.

pockets the gains. But the lender owns the downside risk: If, instead, the asset's value falls, he may get stuck with collateral whose value has fallen—and, thus, with losses. Lending without recourse actually puts you in an *inferior* position to buying an asset outright. It's "heads, you win; tails, I lose."

In this particular case, if the commercial paper increased in value—which actually happened as the crisis abated—the banks that borrowed from the Fed to buy CP would keep the profits. But if the CP lost value, the losses would accrue to the Fed instead. A good deal! By October 8, the Fed was lending almost $150 billion to banks to purchase asset-backed commercial paper.

In case you're wondering whether the run on the money funds created a sense of urgency at the Fed, the Federal Reserve Board announced its intention to create the AMLF on September 19, just three days after the Reserve Primary Fund broke the buck, and the facility opened for business three days after that. Trust me, six days from problem to completely novel solution is *not* the stodgy Fed's usual pace of doing business. Furthermore, it was not until January 30, 2009, that the Fed got around to announcing the detailed rules governing the AMLF. Yes, it was another case of "leap before you look." But together, the Treasury's modified money market guarantee program and the Fed's AMLF successfully ended the run on the money funds. On February 1, 2010, the Fed shut the facility down, netting a small profit on the operation. The balances had long since dwindled to zero, anyway.

But the battles to save the money market funds and the commercial paper markets did not end on September 22. On October 7, with the financial panic in full swing, the Board again invoked Section 13(3) to justify creation of the Commercial Paper Funding Facility (CPFF) to, in the Fed's words, "provide a liquidity backstop to U.S. issuers of commercial paper." Let's parse those words carefully, because the CPFF proved to be a turning point:

A "liquidity backstop"? That sounds innocent enough, but it was a vital part of a much-needed safety net. The markets were shunning asset-backed commercial paper (ABCP)—the stuff used to finance car loans, student loans, and much else—as too risky. Without ABCP, these loan markets were in peril; yet the ABCP markets were shutting down. The Fed proposed to step in and buy CP on the taxpayers' behalf, using a special purpose vehicle (SPV) to effect the transactions. In the event, the Fed made a good bet; it eventually turned a profit of over $5 billion on its CP purchases. But that wasn't its objective. The central bank was, yet again, trying to stanch the bleeding and bring a dying financial market back to life.

And the "issuers of commercial paper"? Didn't that include industrial companies like General Motors, General Electric, IBM, and AT&T—not just banks, not even just financial institutions? Yes, and the list of eligible issuers also included, as the Fed noted blandly on its fact sheet, "U.S. issuers with a foreign parent company." What the Fed was doing, in effect, was lending more or less directly to both industrial companies and foreign banks.*

Amazing. But it worked. The market for commercial paper stabilized and started functioning again. Firms and investors that had been refusing to deal with even blue-chip counterparties returned to the CP market, reassured by the Fed's backstop. By February 2010, the market was off life support and breathing on its own. The loan balances in the CPFF, which had peaked at $350 billion, were below $9 billion.

Few people realized it at the time, but the successful efforts to nurse the CP market back to health marked a crucial conceptual turning point in the Federal Reserve's policy. Prior to September 19, the Fed's focus was—by necessity—on *saving specific institutions* (or not): Bear Stearns, Lehman Brothers, AIG. Each intervention was ad hoc, and the markets had a hard time discerning any pattern or principles. (*Why Bear but not Lehman?*) But after September 19, the Fed began to shift its attention toward *saving markets*. Commercial paper was the first case; mortgage-backed securities would be the next. But that innovation would have to wait awhile.

---

*The three biggest foreign borrowers turned out to be UBS (Switzerland), Dexia (Belgium), and BNP Paribas (France).

MERRILL LYNCH:
THE CRISIS GOES RETAIL

The third ball in the air during the momentous September juggling act was Merrill Lynch. While the Lehman and AIG dramas were playing out, and before the run on the money funds, the world's largest brokerage firm was engaged in a warp-speed courtship with Bank of America. Remember, up until the eleventh hour, Bernanke, Geithner, and Paulson were hoping that Bank of America might emerge as the buyer of Lehman Brothers. But John Thain, Merrill's CEO, and especially his number two, Greg Fleming, had other ideas. Since BofA was interested in the smaller, sicker Lehman Brothers, shouldn't it be even more interested in the larger, less sickly Merrill Lynch? In the end, Thain and Fleming got the "private sector solution" for Merrill Lynch that eluded both Lehman and AIG. And they did it without government help.

Merrill Lynch needs no introduction—and that's the point. Prior to the crisis, Merrill was the largest of the five "bulge bracket" Wall Street firms in terms of employment, and nearly the largest in balance sheet size. If you asked most Americans in September 2008 (or last week for that matter) to name one brokerage firm, the most common choice would surely have been Merrill Lynch—and I have no idea who would have come in second. Alone among the Wall Street giants, Merrill, with its "thundering herd" of fifteen thousand brokers, was a household name. Who in America had not seen one of their "bullish on America" TV commercials?

When Merrill started to crash, it grabbed the attention of the public in a way that comparatively unknown firms like Bear Stearns and Lehman Brothers never could. Along with the failures of Washington Mutual (WaMu) and Wachovia quickly thereafter, the troubles at Merrill marked a new and frightening stage in the financial crisis.

Before Merrill Lynch teetered on the brink, ordinary Americans had a hard time relating to CDS, CDOs, interbank lending spreads, counterparty problems at "wholesale" banks like Bear and Lehman, and the like.

Who really knew what these firms did? Who had ever seen an office of Bear Stearns or Lehman Brothers, much less stepped into one? But once Merrill Lynch, WaMu, and Wachovia were threatened with extinction, the crisis had truly gone retail. Now ordinary brokerage accounts at Merrill branches on the corner were under siege. Now plain vanilla checking and saving accounts at two of America's biggest banks were threatened. Now the conflagration had spread beyond Wall Street and was hitting Main Street with gale force. It was no longer financial esoterica. Most Americans, after all, had at one time passed by a branch office of at least one of these three retail giants. Merrill had about 700 of them; WaMu had 2,239; and Wachovia, a stunning 3,355.

How did a legendary firm like Merrill Lynch come so close to ruin? As befits its size and scope, Merrill was involved in all things financial. But during the boom, its somewhat imperious CEO, E. Stanley "Stan" O'Neal, decided that the firm had too small a footprint in the hot markets for subprime mortgages, securitizations thereof, CDOs, and the like. He set out to fix that "problem" quickly. In 2003 O'Neal hired a hotshot mortgage securitization expert away from Credit Suisse, and within just two years Merrill Lynch was bragging to the trade that it was the "#1 global underwriter of CDOs." What a distinction! But Merrill didn't stop there. Like Bear Stearns, "Merrill sought to be a full-service producer: issuing mortgages, packaging them into securities, and then slicing and dicing them to CDOs." In December 2006, it even bought one of the nation's biggest subprime lenders, First Franklin, of San Jose, California.

Merrill's timing could hardly have been worse. When the subprime and related markets started to deteriorate in 2006, the firm was badly exposed. Two mortgage originators to which Merrill had lent money failed. In order to sell the CDOs it was still manufacturing, Merrill Lynch, like other securitizers, often had to retain the "supersenior" tranches in its own inventory—which therefore swelled dangerously. By retaining the superseniors and selling the rest, the company thought it was unloading the chaff and keeping the wheat. As one of Merrill's top fixed-income executives put it, "Everyone at the firm and most people in the industry felt that supersenior was super safe." But when the subprime and CDO markets tanked, it all became chaff. O'Neal had, indeed, succeeded in making Merrill a big player, but in a losing game.

Losses mounted in late 2007 and 2008. By September 2008, it was reported that the firm had cumulatively lost some $52 billion on its holdings of mortgage-backed securities—a sum larger than Merrill's remaining net worth. By then O'Neal was long gone, having been forced into premature retirement in October 2007. Forced, yes. But Merrill's board was duly grateful for his wonderful service. As a reward for bringing the world's largest brokerage house to the brink of oblivion, it granted him a colossal golden parachute package worth over $160 million—on top of the $91 million he had received for all his fine work in 2006. Other observers held O'Neal in somewhat less esteem. CNBC, for example, includes him on their list of "Worst American CEOs of All Time."

Regardless, as Lehman Weekend approached, Merrill still held a lot of junk, and a few of the company's top executives, led by Fleming, could read the ominous writing on the wall. As the weakest antelope in the herd, Lehman was attracting most of the jackals' attention. But Merrill Lynch might be their next prey. Fleming was determined to push Thain to act before that happened, salvaging as much value for shareholders as possible. He succeeded—barely. Thain and Bank of America's CEO Ken Lewis struck a $50 billion deal just before Lehman Brothers imploded. Had this happened just *after* . . . well, who knows?

The sale of Merrill to BofA eliminated one of the two possible suitors for Lehman, even as Thain was supposedly working with other top Wall Street CEOs to save Lehman. Slightly awkward. But Paulson, Bernanke, and Geithner smiled rather than scowled. None of them relished the thought of facing a Merrill Lynch bankruptcy. Merrill's shareholders may not have been delighted, at first, at the $29 per share price they received (in BofA stock). After all, Merrill shares had sold above $47 as recently as April. But $29 a share was 70 percent above the stock's September 12 closing price and 38 percent above Merrill's book value. Most observers thought Thain and Fleming struck a good deal—and, conversely, that

BofA's Lewis struck a bad one. What happened later made Thain's deal look even better.

Merrill Lynch lives on today, including the famous name and the fifteen-thousand-strong thundering herd, as the wealth-management division of Bank of America. It is still the world's largest brokerage, managing over $2.2 trillion in customer assets. Yet Bank of America was soon suffering from buyer's remorse. In retrospect, it overpaid for a balance sheet and legal liabilities that were worse than it realized. Merrill also brought with it yet more TARP money, which made BofA uncomfortable.

Once Merrill Lynch followed Bear Stearns into the arms of a bank, and Lehman Brothers headed off to bankruptcy court, Wall Street's former Big Five investment banks were down to two: Morgan Stanley and Goldman Sachs. Both firms were in far better shape than either Lehman or Merrill. For example, Morgan Stanley's liquidity pool exceeded $130 billion. But both firms had also been enthusiastic practitioners of the new Wall Street model that combined sky-high leverage with heavy reliance on short-term borrowing. They were therefore vulnerable to runs.

Morgan Stanley's veteran CEO, John Mack, understood which firm was the slower antelope. "As soon as we come in on Monday [September 15], we're in the eye of the storm with Merrill gone and Lehman gone. Now we're next in line," Mack later told the FCIC. Indeed, the cost of using CDS to insure against a Morgan Stanley default almost doubled that day. Shortly thereafter, the company became the target of a hedge fund run. The hedge funds were out for profit, of course; but they were also worried about the safety of the assets held by their prime broker. (This should sound familiar from the Bear Stearns episode.) They felt safer with their assets stashed in FDIC-insured banks.

Morgan Stanley started to bleed cash. But unlike Bear Stearns in March, Morgan Stanley had the new PDCF (Primary Dealer Credit Facility) to lean on in September. And lean it did. The firm borrowed $13 billion from the PDCF on Tuesday, boosted that to $27 billion on Wednesday, and then to $35 billion on Friday. That's a lot of cash. But again, when confidence goes, it goes. And it was going fast. Morgan Stanley lost cash to collateral calls, to withdrawals of funds, and to cutoffs of normal credit flows. Its liquidity pool dropped from $130 billion to $55 billion in a single week.

Similar problems were plaguing Goldman Sachs—although, as befits its status as the fastest antelope, things weren't quite as bad. According to its CEO, Lloyd Blankfein, "We had tremendous liquidity through the period. But there were systemic events going on . . . it was a more nervous position than we would have wanted . . . we were going to bed every night with more risk than any responsible manager should want to have." Goldman, of course, was also borrowing from the PDCF and elsewhere. Bernanke later told the FCIC that "We thought there was a real chance they would go under."

Once again, the Fed looked for and found a creative emergency solution. On Sunday, September 21, both Morgan Stanley and Goldman Sachs applied to the Fed to become banks (technically, bank holding companies)—something that had been anathema to both of them before. After all, being regulated like a bank would crimp their styles in many ways—not to mention bringing in a lot of prying eyes. But as the Panic of 2008 gathered force, the onerous burden of Federal Reserve regulation didn't look quite so onerous anymore—especially when stacked up against the shelter from the storm that the Fed would provide. The Fed and the Justice Department approved their applications with a wink, a nod, and blazing speed, thereby pulling the two beleaguered companies inside the Fed's safety net. That stopped the runs. The idea that Geithner had derided as a "gimmick" in the case of Lehman Brothers was now an integral part of Plan B. (Or was it Plan C? Or D?) Standards were falling.

When Wall Street opened for business on Monday, September 22, just a week after the Lehman Brothers bankruptcy, there were no big, independent investment banks left. Bear Stearns and Merrill Lynch had been absorbed into actual banks. Lehman was in the early stages of bankruptcy proceedings. Morgan Stanley and Goldman Sachs had become banks in name only. Prior to the crisis, the big investment banks had been the top dogs of finance. Theirs were the gold-plated names most of the sharpest MBAs and financial engineers wanted on their business cards. They were home to the Masters of the Universe. Then they were gone.

MORE HOUSEHOLD NAMES CRUMBLE:
WaMu AND WACHOVIA

Merrill Lynch was not the only household name to fall. Washington Mutual was the nation's largest saving and loan association—and its sixth-largest bank of any kind—at the time, with well over two thousand retail branch offices spread out over fifteen states and assets in excess of $300 billion. Through a huge series of acquisitions, the bank had become the third-largest mortgage lender in America, and CEO Kerry Killinger had declared his intention to make WaMu the Walmart of banking. If there had been a concrete definition of too big to fail at the time, Washington Mutual would surely have been situated comfortably above the line. Its failure was unthinkable.

But in September 2008, WaMu was also the unhappy holder of an inordinate volume of dicey mortgages, many of them option ARMs, the products of its own lax lending standards during the bubble. On Lehman Day, its credit ratings were lowered, and a small-scale run on the bank ensued. By September 25, WaMu had lost about 9 percent of its deposits. With more depositors sure to flee, the OTS decided to close the bank. The timing was remarkable because September 25 was a *Thursday*. Failing banks are almost always seized after the close of business on *Friday*—and reopened on Monday morning. But the OTS and the FDIC decided they couldn't wait even a single day longer. The run had to stop *then*, before it spread.

Washington Mutual became the largest bank failure in U.S. history. Its banking operations were immediately sold to JP Morgan Chase (yes, the same company that had purchased Bear Stearns), which had been interested in WaMu's footprint for months, for the bargain price of $1.9 billion. The rest of the company filed for bankruptcy protection the next day.* Neither the FDIC nor the depositors lost a penny—not even the uninsured depositors who had more than $250,000 in their accounts. But in a contro-

---

*In March 2009, what was left of WaMu sued the FDIC, partly on the basis that this price was far too low. The company abandoned the suit in December 2009, leaving shareholders to fight for whatever money they could get.

versial move, FDIC Chairman Bair decided to let the unsecured creditors of the holding company (Washington Mutual, Inc., minus its thrift) get on the bankruptcy court queue. This was a first. As noted previously, the creditors of Bear Stearns, Fannie Mae, Freddie Mac, and AIG had all been protected 100 percent. WaMu's weren't.

Bair's decision was intended to teach a moral hazard lesson and, thereby, to restore some semblance of "market discipline." She had not been happy with either the rescue of Bear Stearns or the decision to make all of AIG's creditors whole. Referring to the Treasury and the Fed, she later said, "They did not want to impose losses on bondholders, and we did. We kept saying: 'There is no insurance premium on bondholders,' you know? For the little guy on Main Street who had bank deposits, we charge banks a premium for that. . . . We don't have the same thing for bondholders." When the WaMu case rolled around, Bair *did* have a say in the decision— the biggest say—because unlike Bear and AIG, it was an FDIC-insured bank.

It was probably no coincidence that giving bondholders and other un-secured creditors haircuts also enabled the FDIC to avoid losing any money on the deal. Bair was a fierce protector of her agency. Indeed, some of her critics at the Treasury, the Fed, and elsewhere claimed that all she cared about were costs to the FDIC. But regardless of her motive, the decision to impose losses on WaMu's creditors was immediately controversial—and immediately disastrous. According to the FCIC, "Losses among [WaMu's] creditors created panic among the unsecured creditors of other struggling banks, particularly Wachovia—with serious consequences."

While Bair had her supporters, the U.S. Treasury—which was, among other things, trying to find a solution for Wachovia—certainly was not among them. As the Treasury's Neel Kashkari, a top Paulson aide, later told the FCIC, "We were saying, that's great, we can all be tough, and we can be so tough that we plunge the financial system into the Great Depression."

At the New York Fed, Geithner was furious with Bair's decision. "Yes," he said, "investors needed a reminder not to expect a government bailout, but pursuing that objective at a moment of intense financial panic was somewhere between imprudent and dangerous." Geithner tried to get Bair to change her mind, but to no avail. And according to David Wessel, "The reaction to whacking the bondholders in the middle of the Great Panic instead of bailing them out was much as Geithner feared. . . . The move raised big questions that the Fed, Treasury, and FDIC didn't answer. . . . Which investors in banks are to be protected, and which are not?"

History will long debate the wisdom of Bair's decision. Was it wise (Bair's view) or foolish (Geithner's view) to strike a blow against moral hazard in the midst of a panic? Probably not wise, at least not without loud and clear prior warning. After all, after Bear, Fannie, Freddie, and AIG, investors had come to expect the opposite. But regardless, Bair's resolution of the moral hazard dilemma came home to roost quickly, just as Geithner had feared—starting in Charlotte, North Carolina.

Wachovia, the nation's fourth-largest bank and twice the size of WaMu, was on the chopping block when WaMu went down. The problem, as usual, stemmed from subprime mortgages and related assets, some of which Wachovia had acquired in its merger with Golden West Financial, the big California thrift, in 2006. Wachovia was, in fact, the creation of a long string of mergers and acquisitions, some of which, like Golden West, it had not digested well. It was not, shall we say, the best-run bank in America.

With loan losses, especially on mortgages, large and growing, a "silent run" on Wachovia had begun, and it accelerated after WaMu went under. The run was silent because the runners were mainly sophisticated financial professionals sitting at computer keyboards, not retail depositors lining up at bank branches. On one unsettling day, the market value of Wachovia's 10-year bonds dropped from 73 cents on the dollar to 29 cents. Twenty-nine cents? That meant that the market was viewing default as imminent. The bonds of America's fourth-largest bank were now junkier than junk.

The Treasury, the Fed, and the FDIC all agreed on two things: First, Wachovia needed to be sold or otherwise secured over the weekend of September 27–28; and second, the bank had to open for business as usual on Monday morning, September 29. It was another weekend emergency-rescue operation, but this time for the bank on the corner—or, rather, the bank on thousands of corners. Wachovia then had over 3,300 branches in 21 states and over 15 million customers. If you didn't bank at Wachovia, you probably knew someone who did.

Ironically, Wachovia's CEO at the time was none other than Bob Steel, the U.S. Treasury official who had tried to convince Barclays to buy Lehman Brothers. Steel had left the Treasury just two months earlier—hired by Wachovia's board either to save the bank or to sell it. He was working on both fronts. A former investment banker, Steel had been busy shopping Wachovia around: to Goldman Sachs (no thanks), to Morgan Stanley (ditto), to Wells Fargo (could be), to Spain's Banco Santander (no), and even to struggling Citigroup—which was keenly interested because it was desperately seeking a bigger deposit base. When it came down to that fateful weekend, there were two serious suitors: Wells and Citi. That's when seriousness took a backseat, and the sales process started to resemble the Keystone cops. Let the play begin.

Prologue: Steel favored Wells. In fact, he played so hard to get with Citi's new CEO, Vikram Pandit,* that the two didn't even connect by e-mail until 4:30 a.m. (yes, *a.m.*) on Friday, September 26. Geithner, skeptical about Wells' interest, wanted to see Wachovia and Citi, a bank he supervised, married. It was never obvious to me—and perhaps not to Geithner, either—how joining two sick banks together would produce one healthy bank. But, hey, the Japanese had done it a decade earlier. Bair apparently wondered about that, too. As she later told the FCIC, "Here we were selling a troubled institution . . . to another troubled institution. I think if that deal [with Citi] had gone through, Citigroup would have had to have been bailed out again."† In fact, Bair's main interest—again—seemed to be getting a deal done that imposed minimal costs, preferably zero, on the FDIC. A worthy objective, but surely not the only one. Mean-

---

*Chuck Prince, who thought Citi should dance as long as the music played, had been fired in November 2007. Pandit was later fired in 2012.

†Citi wound up being bailed out in November, anyway.

while, at the Treasury, Paulson was forced to take a backseat because his former lieutenant, Steel, was the one selling Wachovia.

Act I: On Saturday, September 27, Wells Fargo's chairman Richard "Dick" Kovacevich gave Steel and the federal regulators what must have looked like terrific news: Wells wanted to buy all of Wachovia's stock, and it wasn't going to ask for a penny of government assistance. Unfortunately, the next day he informed Steel, the Fed, and other regulators that Wells could not make a bid over the weekend without federal assistance; they needed more time for due diligence.

Act II: The Fed contemplated tiding over Wachovia for the weekend by making another "unusual and exigent" loan under the ever-pliable Section 13(3), but didn't. After all, the FDIC was supposed to resolve teetering banks. But Bair wanted to follow the WaMu precedent: take over the bank, sell off the pieces, wipe out the stockholders, *and hand losses to the bond-holders.* Geithner hated the WaMu deal; its haircuts had panicked the markets. He blew up. Wachovia had to open on Monday even if it required government assistance—and the debt holders had to be protected. "The policy of the U.S. government is that there will be no more WaMus," he insisted. In fact, by that time Bernanke and Paulson had been to Capitol Hill to broach the idea of a $700 billion rescue fund that would eventually become the TARP.

Bair relented. In her eyes, Citigroup and Wells Fargo were now on more equal footing—either deal might require FDIC assistance. It was, as in the old joke, just a matter of price. Wells was offering to cover the first $2 billion of losses from a pool of $127 billion worth of assets, plus 80 percent of the remainder—and also to cap the FDIC's losses at $20 billion. (At that point, the balance in the Deposit Insurance Fund was $34.6 billion.) Citi offered to cover the first $42 billion in losses from a much bigger asset pool ($312 billion), leaving the FDIC to pick up only losses above that amount (and receiving $12 billion in Wachovia preferred stock in return). Bair's number crunchers decided that Wells' proposal would likely cost the FDIC somewhere between $5.6 billion and $7.2 billion, while Citi's would likely cost it nothing. Unsurprisingly, she opted for Citi—but not until

4:00 a.m. Monday, just hours before Wachovia was scheduled to open. The Fed pledged liquidity aid, if needed.

Act III: The deal was announced Monday morning: Citigroup would buy Wachovia. But the deal didn't hold. Negotiations between the two big banks dragged on and on; Steel described them as "extremely complicated and difficult." Then, on Tuesday evening, Dick Kovacevich of Wells Fargo called the Fed again with "great news. I'd love to buy Wachovia . . . and without government help." Huh? Hadn't they heard this from Kovacevich on Saturday? Allegedly, the change of heart stemmed from a new IRS ruling that made acquiring Wachovia more attractive to Wells.* Fed governor Kevin Warsh, who received Kovacevich's call, walked into Bernanke's office with the news: "You're not going to believe this." After huddling quickly, the Fed's stunned leadership decided this was the FDIC's call.

The call was predictable. Bair, who must have been delighted to get the FDIC off the hook, phoned Steel on Thursday, October 2, catching him on his cell phone on an airport tarmac. Wells is prepared to offer you $7 a share, she told him. Steel must have started to grin—that was $6 above Citi's offer. A few hours later, Wachovia's board voted unanimously to leave Citi at the altar and accept Wells Fargo's offer, instead.

Act IV: The explosion at the New York Fed might have been heard all the way to Charlotte. Geithner was livid. Not only was this another body blow to Citigroup, which needed the deposits and now looked like the gang who couldn't merge straight, but the government's deal-making credibility had been thrown into question in the bargain. "You cannot run a government in a financial crisis like this," Geithner declared. At Citigroup, Vikram Pandit was both stunned and angry. The *Wall Street Journal* reported that he "launch[ed] into a profanity-laced tirade about Bair during a conference call with Citi officials." Citigroup's stock fell 18 percent on the day of the announcement and another 43 percent within a week. Within days, Citi filed suit to stop the Wells-Wachovia merger, but the suit failed.

---

*The reason for the change of heart is in dispute. Bair says Kovacevich told her that IRS Notice 2008-83, issued just two days earlier, allowed Wells to take a bigger tax write-off. But Kovacevich told the FCIC that Wells' revised bid reflected new due diligence.

Epilogue: What a chaotic way to save a bank. Wasn't the doctrine supposed to be too big to fail *messily*? In any case, the merger held, though it created some worries about the safety of Wells Fargo, which was now a banking giant.

BAILOUTS WITHOUT END?

The Wells-Wachovia deal did not end either the panic or the parade of bank bailouts and quasi-bailouts. Far from it. Congress voted down the first Troubled Assets Relief Program (TARP) bill on Monday, September 29—the same day the ill-fated Citi-Wachovia merger was announced. Markets promptly tanked. A frightened Congress then passed a heavily modified version of TARP on Friday, October 3—the same day the Wells-Wachovia merger was announced. Just eleven days later, the first TARP money was used to start quelling the chaos. In the nick of time? We'll never know.

The FDIC pitched in with a novel program to guarantee newly issued debt of major financial institutions—not *bank deposits*, but *marketable debt*. It was dubbed the Temporary Liquidity Guarantee Program (TLGP—and I hope you're not memorizing these acronyms). For a small fee of 75 basis points, certain financial companies were authorized to float debt that was 100 percent insured by the FDIC. The eligible firms were not limited to banks; rather, they were defined in the FDIC's press release as "banks, thrifts, and certain holding companies." Hmm. *Certain holding companies?* Would it surprise you to learn that the first user of the TLGP was Goldman Sachs? By then, Goldman had been a bank for less than three weeks.*

The TLGP was unprecedented in several respects. First, the FDIC had never ventured beyond banks before. Second, throughout its seventy-five-year history, the FDIC had never insured anything but deposits—and even those were covered only up to a certain limit. Now it was going to insure, in the words of the press release, "promissory notes, commercial paper,

---

*The two biggest users of TLGP turned out to be GE and Citigroup.

inter-bank funding, and any unsecured portion of secured debt." Yes, even new corporate bonds! Wall Street knows a good deal when it sees one. Issuance under the TLGP quickly ballooned to $225 billion and peaked in May 2009 at nearly $350 billion. The last guarantees under the program did not mature until December 31, 2012.

Like the Fed and the Treasury before it, the FDIC was now way out on a limb. What justified these forays of the FDIC into entirely new domains, without an act of Congress? The answer, in short, was the *systemic risk exception*. The what?

When Congress amended the Federal Deposit Insurance Act after the savings and loan debacle in 1991, it stipulated that the agency had to use *least-cost resolution*—that is, it had to clean up each bank in the way that was cheapest to taxpayers—*unless* a systemic risk emergency was declared by the secretary of the Treasury (who had to consult with the president) and the Federal Reserve Board. In that case, the law permitted the FDIC to deviate from least-cost resolution and to "take other action or provide assistance under this section as necessary to avoid or mitigate" systemic risk. While that last phrase creates a broad remit, the criteria were meant to be stern. Remember the context back in 1991: Congress had been badly burned by the S&L crisis—Keating Five and all that—and was in no mood to give the FDIC wide discretion to toss money around without a compelling reason.

Seventeen years later, Sheila Bair felt the same way. Until October 14, she had steadfastly refused to invoke the systemic risk exception—bending it only grudgingly for Wachovia. But if the gathering post-Lehman firestorm didn't present a systemic risk emergency, probably nothing ever would. Bair, urged on by Paulson and Bernanke, agreed to boldly go where no man or woman had ever gone before. There was no particular bank to resolve at the time, but they all decided that saving the entire banking system merited a systemic risk exception. It was a stunning announcement that, among other things, implicitly repudiated Bair's decision in the WaMu case. But it helped end the nosedive. Debt guaranteed by the FDIC found a ready market.

However, it only *helped*. The crisis was far from over.

Citigroup, the giant conglomerate that was the nation's largest bank at the time, continued to founder into November. It had probably gone into the crisis burdened by more SIVs (structured investment vehicles) and other harmful off-balance-sheet entities than any other financial organization. It had failed to acquire more deposits when its attempt to buy Wachovia went awry. The initial $25 billion injection of TARP money by the Treasury (described in the next chapter) proved insufficient. And private capital in search of great investment opportunities wasn't exactly knocking on Citi's door. The bank's stock price, which had once exceeded $60 a share, had shrunk to $3.77 by the stock market close on November 21. The cost of insuring against a Citigroup default by purchasing CDS soared. Might America's biggest financial conglomerate actually go under? The markets were suggesting a frightening answer: *Yes*.

But the answer from the Treasury, the Fed, and the FDIC was an emphatic *No*. On Sunday, November 23, 2008, the three agencies issued a joint press release bailing out Citi yet again. It was another systemic risk exception. Under the terms of the deal, the Treasury and the FDIC agreed to guarantee a designated pool of $306 billion in assets "consisting of loans and securities backed by residential real estate and commercial real estate, and their associated hedges." Pause to notice the huge dollar amount: $306 billion was roughly equal to WaMu's entire balance sheet! The stakes were rising.

Under the terms of the agreement, Citi would absorb the first $29 billion in losses on the pool, plus 10 percent of any remainder. The Treasury and the FDIC would absorb the next $15 billion. Were losses yet bigger, the Fed would pick up the rest by dint of a nonrecourse loan to Citi. In return for the loan guarantees, the company issued $27 billion of preferred stock to the Treasury and the FDIC, carrying an 8 percent dividend, plus warrants on which the Treasury would ultimately profit. Citigroup, like Goldman Sachs and Morgan Stanley before it, was now essentially sheltered from the storm. Its stock rose 58 percent the next day. That was the good news. The bad news was that American taxpayers now held a lot of new risk.

The Citi bailout left just three big boats navigating the still-stormy seas. One was JP Morgan Chase—the powerhouse survivor that had acquired both Bear Stearns and WaMu at bargain prices. JP Morgan looked, and proved to be, secure. It neither wanted nor needed government aid. The second was Wells Fargo, which had just transformed itself into a megabank by acquiring the much-larger Wachovia. Would the heavy new load break the stagecoach (Wells Fargo's famous logo)? Regulators watched Wells like a hawk, but it looked, and turned out to be, okay.

And then there was the teetering Bank of America, which, by virtue of adding Merrill Lynch and the giant mortgage lender Countrywide Financial to its home-grown mortgage woes, was now the slowest antelope. Countrywide, founded by CEO Angelo Mozilo and a partner in 1969, had enjoyed phenomenal growth during the boom years. But that growth was built on high quantity, not high quality. Countrywide was, in some sense, the poster child for everything that was wrong with subprime lending. That Bank of America bought Countrywide in 2008—yes, *2008!*—is a testimonial to the strength of the boom mentality and how long it lasted, and probably also to bad business judgment.

By December 2008, BofA executives had a bad case of buyer's remorse about both the Countrywide and Merrill Lynch purchases. But the Countrywide deal was history, so bank officials turned to the Merrill Lynch deal and informed the Fed and the Treasury that they were getting cold feet. It seemed that Merrill's losses were far worse than they had thought back in September. (Yes, John Thain had made a *very* good deal.) The regulators were appalled. Shouldn't Bank of America executives have known about this before they struck the deal? Paulson told BofA's Ken Lewis that backing out of the deal would demonstrate "a colossal lack of judgment by BofA" and might induce the Fed, acting as the bank's regulator, to remove the bank's management and board. It was an unveiled threat.

Was Bank of America just looking for, as the Fed's Kevin Warsh put it, more "candy"? Maybe so. But while Bernanke and Paulson were angry, they didn't want the merger to fall through, potentially leaving both Merrill (assets of $2.2 trillion) and BofA (assets of $2.3 trillion) as expensive wards of the state.* What to do? It seemed that more "candy" was indeed in order, although none of that had been announced—despite the bank's urging—when Bank of America and Merrill Lynch closed their deal on January 1, 2009. The United States of America, incidentally, had held a presidential election by then, and Geithner had been tapped to take over for Paulson.

The regulators' bailout announcement finally came on January 16, and it was similar to the November deal for Citigroup, though the amounts were, thankfully, smaller. The pool of dodgy assets was "just" $118 billion, most of which, the press release said, had come from Merrill Lynch. Bank of America would eat the first $10 billion in losses plus 10 percent of what remained. The Treasury and the FDIC would take the next $20 billion, with the Fed picking up anything left over via a nonrecourse loan. (In the event, there wasn't anything for any government agency to pick up.) As in the Citi case, the Treasury took both preferred stock and warrants—which ultimately proved to be profitable.

The deal was naturally seen as a replay of the Citigroup bailout, and, much to its chagrin, Bank of America came to be viewed as yet another supplicant. After all that fuss, BofA asked to terminate the deal a mere four months later, after seeing that its losses would be below $10 billion. The government, however, insisted on collecting a $425 million fee for the insurance it had provided. Ironically, by 2011 Merrill Lynch was BofA's most profitable unit, by far. The rest of the bank looked pretty weak.

By the time the post-Lehman panic subsided, the wreckage was everywhere. Bear Stearns, Merrill Lynch, Goldman Sachs, Morgan Stanley, Citigroup, Bank of America, Wachovia, Washington Mutual, Fannie Mae, Freddie Mac, and others had all been rescued, in one way or another, by the federal government. A government led, by the way, by a deeply conservative Republican president, a secretary of the Treasury who hailed from Goldman Sachs and characterized himself as "a firm believer in free mar-

---

*In 2009 there was a brouhaha over whether Bernanke and Paulson had *forced* BofA to go through with the merger.

kets," and a professorial Federal Reserve chairman who called himself a libertarian.

Table 6.1 offers a shorthand summary of the amazing transformation under duress of the U.S. financial system that took place in less than a year, starting with Bear Stearns in March 2008. In fact, most of it happened in the harrowing two weeks following September 15, 2008. One word comes to mind after looking over this list: *Wow!* The face of the American financial system was changed beyond recognition. The Federal Reserve, the Treasury, and the FDIC took actions that few people could have imagined before 2008. The U.S. taxpayer was potentially on the hook for unbelievable sums. But the system, massively assisted by the U.S. government, held together. That's the unsung part of the story.

TABLE 6.1 The Big Fourteen: A Financial System Transformed

	Assets		CEO		
Name	**Late 2007**	**Late 2009**	**End of 2007**	**End of 2009**	**Major Changes**
THE INVESTMENT BANKS					
Goldman Sachs	$1.12 trillion	$849 billion	Lloyd Blankfein	Lloyd Blankfein	Became a "bank"
Morgan Stanley	$1.05 trillion	$771 billion	John Mack	John Mack	Became a "bank"
Merrill Lynch	$1.02 trillion	—	Stan O'Neal	—	Merged into BofA
Lehman Brothers	$691 billion	—	Dick Fuld	—	Bankrupt
Bear Stearns	$395 billion	—	Jimmy Cayne	—	Bought by JP Morgan Chase

Name	Assets		CEO		Major Changes
	Late 2007	Late 2009	End of 2007	End of 2009	
THE BANKS					
Bank of America	$1.72 trillion	$2.22 trillion	Ken Lewis	Brian Moynihan[a]	Acquired Merrill Lynch; bailed out
Citigroup	$2.19 trillion	$1.86 trillion	Chuck Prince	Vikram Pandit	Bailed out
JP Morgan Chase	$1.56 trillion	$2.03 trillion	Jamie Dimon	Jamie Dimon	Acquired Bear Stearns and WaMu
Wachovia	$783 billion	—	Ken Thompson	—	Failed; bought by Wells Fargo
Wells Fargo	$575 billion	$1.24 trillion	Dick Kovacevich[b]	Dick Kovacevich	Bought Wachovia
THE OTHERS					
AIG	$1.06 trillion	$848 billion	Martin Sullivan	Robert Benmosche	"Nationalized" by Federal Reserve
Fannie Mae	$883 billion	$869 billion	Daniel Mudd	Michael Williams[c]	Government conservatorship
Freddie Mac	$794 billion	$842 billion	Richard Syron	Charles Haldeman[d]	Government conservatorship
Washington Mutual	$328 billion	—	Kerry Killinger	—	Failed; bought by JP Morgan Chase

[a] Lewis retired; he was not fired.

[b] Kovacevich was actually chairman, not CEO.

[c] Mudd was replaced by Herbert Allison, who then moved to the Treasury Department.

[d] Syron was replaced by David Moffett, who served only until March 2009.

WE'RE NOT IN KANSAS ANYMORE

The post-Lehman panic spread rapidly beyond U.S. borders. The United Kingdom, of course, was deeply enmeshed in the financial crisis well before Lehman failed. It had stopped the run on Northern Rock, improvised a deposit insurance system on short notice, and either rescued or nationalized most of its big banks. Banks in Ireland lent recklessly during the property boom and were carrying huge unrealized losses prior to the Lehman bankruptcy. This "open secret" was laid bare in a very rough way when Lehman collapsed. The same was true of Iceland, on an even grander scale relative to its tiny economy. Spain was also hard-hit by the real estate collapse, though its major banks survived the crisis better than might have been expected—at least at first. (They would later be central to the European debt crisis.) Australia also weathered the storm surprisingly well.

But much of continental Europe, Asia, and Latin America had avoided serious consequences until September 15, 2008. It was only after Lehman Day that the crisis truly went global. Immediately following Lehman's filing for bankruptcy protection in New York, dominoes started falling all over the world. The global investment bank was quickly involved in about eighty insolvency proceedings in eighteen foreign countries—each with its own laws and procedures. The biggest was in the UK, where Lehman had major operations—and where the bankruptcy laws did not mesh at all well with ours. For example, under U.S. bankruptcy law, Lehman was able to continue to unwind derivatives positions after filing under Chapter 11; indeed, the U.S. broker dealer didn't actually file under Chapter 11. But under UK bankruptcy law, all these positions were frozen in place, leaving many assets and counterparties in limbo.

There is an important lesson here, too: Bankruptcy procedures differ substantially around the world, even among the small group of countries that are essential to the global financial system. And the world is not likely to reach international agreement on a common bankruptcy code anytime soon, if ever. This little detail will make it excruciatingly difficult to put a failing global bank to bed peacefully for years to come. In particular, while the Dodd-Frank Act (2010), which we'll examine later, has given the United States a sensible (albeit untested) resolution regime for systemically important financial institutions, other countries have not adopted anything like it. So the next time a big global financial institution fails, watch out. Although the authorities are striving to create international coordination, every country for itself may still be the order of the day.

On September 25, rumors circulated that Fortis, a gigantic banking-insurance-investment conglomerate based in the Benelux countries, was in trouble. Its CEO resigned, and the next day Fortis' banks suffered massive runs. European governments generally have fewer compunctions about bailouts than the U.S. government does and are well accustomed to practicing "lemon socialism." As one European central banker, looking with both wonderment and disdain at the U.S. decision to let Lehman go, wryly observed, "We don't let banks fail. We don't even let dry cleaners fail."

The governments of Belgium, the Netherlands, and Luxembourg were quick to offer support to Fortis. On September 28, they announced that the banking division would be nationalized, with the three countries investing a total of €11.2 billion in return for about two-thirds ownership. A multinational free-for-all ensued. In the end, Fortis was broken into pieces and sold off to Dutch, Belgian, and French financial companies.

Just days later, Dexia, a big Belgian bank with worldwide operations, came under severe pressure as its counterparties grew jittery about losses and Moody's downgraded its long-term debt. Dexia's appeal for state aid was quickly granted. Foreshadowing what would later happen to Citigroup and Bank of America, Dexia got both a capital injection and a state guarantee of its liabilities. The bank was subsequently restructured and put back into business. Amazingly, Dexia had to be nationalized *again* in October 2011, during the European sovereign debt crisis. A two-time loser!

At roughly the same time in Germany, Hypo Real Estate Bank, whose specialty is apparent from its name, suffered a severe liquidity run. The run was stopped only by a huge (€35 billion) line of credit hurriedly arranged by the German Finance Ministry, which included the participation of a consortium of German banks. A few days later, the banks pulled out and the deal fell apart. On October 6, 2008, the Bundesbank, hardly a fan of bailouts, arranged a new line of credit, this time for €50 billion, and again involving a consortium of banks. Official support for Hypo eventually topped €100 billion—a lot of money for a bank whose precrisis assets were only about €170 billion. In October 2009, the bank was finally nationalized.

On September 29, with the panic in full swing, Ireland stunned the world by guaranteeing *all* the liabilities—including uninsured deposits and debt instruments—of its six large banks. It was a snap decision that the country would later regret, as the banks' debts became public debts and put Ireland in an untenable fiscal position. But right or wrong, Ireland's action put pressure on other countries to follow suit. Why keep money in Country X when you could move it to Ireland and have it 100 percent guaranteed? Germany, forgetting its fetish with moral hazard, quickly caved. The U.S. considered 100 percent deposit insurance, too, but rejected the idea.*

In a truly strange tale, little Iceland had transformed itself from a small fishing economy into what amounted to a huge leveraged hedge fund during the boom—partly by raising vast amounts of deposits abroad, particularly in the UK, and investing them in risky assets. When the "fund" crashed and burned right after Lehman, all three of Iceland's big banks wound up being nationalized, the Icelandic krona fell through the floor, the stock market lost 90 percent of its value, and Iceland's economy sank into a deep recession. The UK government, whose citizens had invested so much in Iceland's banks, seized Icelandic assets in Britain. What a mess.

And so it went, in country after country. Perhaps most tragically, after Lehman the financial crisis also engulfed many emerging-market nations—which to that point had been relatively unscathed by the disruption of credit flows in the rich countries. That marked a big change from past global crises, in which one or more emerging markets usually led the way. Guillermo Ortiz, then governor of the Bank of Mexico, famously

---

*Glenn Hubbard (a Republican) and I (a Democrat) published an op-ed in the *Wall Street Journal*, "Blanket Deposit Insurance Is a Bad Idea." The bipartisan coauthorship was deliberate. *More disclosure:* I appended, in the tagline to that op-ed, a disclaimer, which I repeat here: "Mr. Blinder . . . is also affiliated with Promontory Interfinancial Network, which could be affected by changes in FDIC rules."

quipped, "This time, we did not cause it." It was clearly the United States dragging the poorer countries into the muck.

MEANWHILE, BACK AT THE RANCH . . .

The Lehman Brothers failure also marked—many economists would say *caused*—a sharp deterioration in U.S. macroeconomic performance. As noted early in this book, both employment and GDP crumbled immediately after Lehman Day. Credit dried up, companies pulled in their horns or went bankrupt, and jobs disappeared. Any thoughts that the United States might skate through the financial disruptions without a serious recession were quickly dispelled. Instead, the talk turned to speculation about Great Depression 2.0.

I remember my own changing attitudes at the time. Prior to Lehman, I was relatively optimistic—relative, that is, to the prevailing gloom and doom. In particular, while the economy was clearly somewhat wounded, I was not convinced we were headed for a serious recession. After all, real GDP growth averaged 2.2 percent in 2007 and just slightly below zero in the first two quarters of 2008. But on September 15, 2008, I turned deeply pessimistic. So did lots of other people—perhaps most important, businesspeople who make hiring and firing decisions. Layoffs skyrocketed.

The two panels of figure 6.1, one for quarterly GDP growth (on the left), the other for monthly job growth (on the right), are repeated from chapter 1. They show the dramatic worsening of an already-weak economy after September 2008. Lehman's failure precipitated a near cataclysm in the financial markets and shattered confidence everywhere. It literally changed everything—for the worse.

As mentioned earlier, the Federal Open Market Committee happened to have a meeting scheduled for September 16, the day after Lehman failed and the very day AIG was bailed out. But any sense of *macroeconomic* urgency had apparently not reached the FOMC yet, as it left interest rates unchanged—noting in its statement that "the downside risks to growth

FIGURE 6.1 *The U.S. Economy Falls Off the Table*

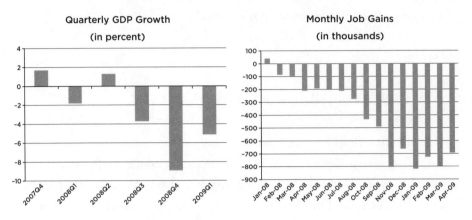

and the upside risks to inflation are both of significant concern." Really? Did that mean *equal* concern? Maybe we should cut the committee some slack, because September 16 was just one day after the implosion started. Maybe they didn't have their wits about them yet. But by the time the FOMC held an impromptu teleconference on September 29, the panic had spread far and wide, and had consumed many victims. Yet the Fed still did not touch its interest-rate weapon. The FOMC looked to be asleep at the wheel, or at least very drowsy.

But Chairman Bernanke had a trick up his sleeve. Although there was no FOMC meeting scheduled for October 8, the Fed issued a surprise 7:00 a.m. announcement that it was cutting interest rates by 50 basis points. Not only that, but the ECB, the Bank of Canada, the Bank of England, the Swedish Riksbank, and the Swiss National Bank all joined the Fed in a wave of concerted rate cutting. Coordinated interest-rate changes by multiple central banks are scarcer than hens' teeth. To a first approximation, they *never* happen because each central bank does what it thinks best for its own country, not for the world. So the coordinated rate cuts of October 8, 2008, were stunning. They symbolized, first, that the problem was global and, second, that it was no longer just financial. The health of the world economy was at stake.

One might have thought that these dramatic multicountry rate cuts would have galvanized markets around the world. My guess is that the heads of the six central banks thought so. They were surely intended to. But, in fact, the market reactions were muted, which was a testimony to how deeply depressed sentiment was at the time. The Dow Jones Industrial Average actually fell about 2 percent that day, rounding out a frightening 14.6 percent drop in six days. It was as if six central banks fired their bazookas loudly and simultaneously—and no one noticed.

While the Fed was struggling with its interest-rate policy in September, and the trio of Paulson, Bernanke, and Geithner was bailing out firms left and right, Bernanke and Paulson were also struggling with what else they could do to stem the burgeoning financial panic. They concluded it was time to visit Capitol Hill and enlist the United States Congress in the fight. Soon, a TARP was born.

PART III

PICKING UP
THE PIECES

|ıııııııııııııııııııııı|

STRETCHING OUT
THE TARP

If money isn't loosened up, this sucker could go down.

—President George W. Bush, September 24, 2008

To baseball fans, a tarp (or tarpaulin, for long) is something the grounds crew stretches across the infield to protect it from rain. The tarp is held in reserve, next to the playing field, ready to be brought out on a moment's notice if and when it is needed. Tarps are designed to save the field and, with luck, to allow the game to proceed after a brief delay. But some rain delays are long, and some games get rained out, anyway.

So it was with the much-maligned Troubled Assets Relief Program, or TARP, which Congress enacted, with extreme reluctance, in truly foul financial weather at the height of the Panic of 2008. But there is an important difference between baseball tarps and the financial TARP. Unlike the tried-and-true tarps at baseball stadiums, the TARP was not already in place, sitting at the side of the field with a practiced grounds crew ready to roll it out, when the financial storm struck. On the contrary, legislation had to be drafted and approved (after first being voted down) in a great rush, with details made up on the fly. As Treasury Secretary Paulson later put it,

"Frankly we had no choice but to fly by the seat of our pants, making it up as we went along." Nonetheless, and contrary to much political rhetoric, it worked. In fact, despite a number of missteps, it worked extraordinarily well.

The TARP may be among the most successful—but least understood—economic policy innovations in our nation's history. Even today, it has a terrible name with the body politic. For example, a Pew poll in February 2012 found that just 39 percent of Americans thought that the TARP's "major loans to banks and financial institutions to try to keep the markets secure" in 2008 were "the right thing . . . for the government to do." Fifty-two percent thought it was the wrong thing. The poll then quizzed Americans on "how much of the . . . money . . . has been paid back . . . All of the money, most of it, only some of it, or none of it?" Only 15 percent gave the correct answer at the time—either "all of it" or "most of it." By contrast, 72 percent chose either "only some of it" or "none of it." For years after the TARP's passage, and maybe still, one of the surest ways to kill a proposal in Congress was to brand it as "like the TARP" or "a permanent TARP." Why?

ORIGINS OF THE TARP

The birth of the Troubled Assets Relief Program came suddenly, like one of those deliveries in a taxicab en route to the hospital. The TARP was born in a crisis atmosphere, and even then only by scaring the dickens out of Congress. But its origins date back five or six months earlier, to a somewhat calmer period.

Immediately after the Bear Stearns rescue in March 2008, the Treasury concluded that "we had better get to work on contingency plans in case things got worse." Secretary Paulson put two bright young assistant secretaries, Phillip Swagel, an economist, and Neel Kashkari, an investment banker who came from (where else?) Goldman Sachs, in charge of drafting what became known as the "Break-the-Glass Memo." The idea was to think through some out-of-the-box plans for what the government might do if it faced a true financial meltdown. As the name suggests, a memo like that is meant to outline drastic policy options that you hope never to use.

After what Swagel described as "more than a dozen iterations" and extensive discussions both within the Treasury and with the Fed, a ten-page memo emerged on April 15, outlining four basic options:

1. buy toxic assets—which was the suggestion the Treasury heard most often from market participants, and was the one that would later give the TARP its name;
2. guarantee the assets rather than buy them—which was an option reluctantly included, under political duress, in the ultimate legislation;
3. inject capital directly into banks by buying their shares—which would become the TARP's signature program; and
4. refinance home mortgages into loans guaranteed by the government—something that was never done with TARP money to any great extent.

Based on then-current estimates of banks' losses on mortgage-related securities, Kashkari and Swagel guesstimated that a government fund of about $500 billion would do the trick. But, of course, no one at Treasury believed there was a snowball's chance in hell of getting such a fund approved in April 2008. For the moment, it was academic, and the memo was stashed away in the proverbial box labeled IN CASE OF FIRE, BREAK GLASS.

After the quasi-nationalization of AIG, which by no means stemmed the panic, Paulson decided it was time to break the glass. He feared things were spinning out of control and concluded that "we couldn't keep using duct tape and bailing wire to try to hold the system together." He was strongly supported in that judgment by Federal Reserve Chairman Bernanke, who couldn't wait for Congress to get the Fed off the hook by appropriating some money. As he told Paulson, "We can't keep doing this."

Their motives in proposing the TARP were many. First, the financial conflagration was spreading, not receding. Increasingly, this looked like "the big one" that the Break-the-Glass Memo had contemplated but hoped would never come.

Second, despite (or maybe because of) using the Exchange Stabilization Fund to stabilize the money market mutual funds, Paulson felt an acute need for a pot of money explicitly appropriated by Congress for financial firefighting. After all, who knew what might come next? The paltry $50 billion committed to the money funds wasn't nearly enough.

Third, the Fed had stuck its neck out very far to save Bear Stearns and AIG—and in other ways, too. Each option in the Break-the-Glass Memo was designed to "move the focus of financial markets policy back from the Fed to the Treasury, which would be appropriate in that the problem reflected inadequate capital rather than insufficient liquidity." In other words, public money was being committed by the nonpolitical and unelected Federal Reserve even though such decisions should be made at the political level—in Bernanke's words, "both because we at the Fed don't have the necessary resources and for reasons of democratic legitimacy."

Paulson and Bernanke were right on all three counts, although Paulson probably noticed that having the Fed as the rich uncle both put the central bank out front and enabled a Republican secretary of the Treasury to avoid begging a hostile Democratic Congress for money. Paulson viewed the measures outlined in the Break-the-Glass Memo as "an economic 9/11"—not something you look forward to.

But which of the memo's four options made the most sense? Here Bernanke and Paulson disagreed, perhaps reflecting the differing mind-sets of a nonpolitical former economics professor and a Wall Street deal maker thrust into a political world. Their disagreement turned out to be incredibly ironic.

The intellectual Federal Reserve chairman favored injecting capital directly into banks. An expert on economic history, Bernanke knew that publicly provided capital almost inevitably follows in the wake of a banking crisis. Besides, providing banks with new capital should leverage the government's money. At least in theory, each $1 of additional bank capital should support $10 or so of renewed lending. (We'll come back to that fallacious reasoning shortly.) Many financial market experts such as the famed investor George Soros and noted economists Paul Krugman and Joseph Stiglitz also urged that alternative.

But the less cerebral, more action-oriented Treasury secretary overruled Bernanke on both political and market grounds. Politically, a proposal to purchase bank shares, thus making the government a part owner of the largest banks in the country, would be decried as socialism by Republicans and vilified as gifts to fat-cat bankers by Democrats. Paulson knew it wouldn't stand a chance in Congress. Furthermore, on market grounds, even a partial nationalization of the banks would scare off private investors, to whom the Treasury and the Fed were still looking to bolster the ailing banks' capital. For these quite legitimate reasons, Paulson didn't want to talk in public about the possibility of purchasing stock in banks. In fact, he didn't even want the idea discussed *inside* the Treasury for fear that the discussions would leak. The idea was both in his head and in the Break-the-Glass Memo, however.

When it comes to political matters, and especially when dealing with Congress, the chairman of the Federal Reserve typically defers to the secretary of the Treasury, who, as the nation's chief financial officer, represents the president. Bernanke recognized this reality. When the two of them appealed to Congress for help, it was to fund Paulson's favorite idea (buying toxic assets), not Bernanke's (injecting capital), even though Bernanke had serious reservations about the former. The Fed chairman had little choice. Given the perilous crisis atmosphere, he couldn't let any daylight show between himself and the sometimes-mercurial Treasury secretary from Wall Street. But at the same time, he had to safeguard the Fed's vaunted independence. The institutional interests of the *political* Treasury and the *technocratic* Fed were not always perfectly aligned, and all TARP decisions were bound to be highly political.

An Early Halloween

The drama began in earnest at a remarkable meeting on Thursday night, September 18. The Fed chief and the Treasury secretary, having first con-

ferred with President Bush, locked arms—only figuratively, I imagine—
and marched down to Capitol Hill to meet with congressional leaders. The
senators and representatives who had been hurriedly convened in the conference room outside House Speaker Nancy Pelosi's office may not have
seen what was coming, but it turned out to be an early trick or treat.

At the time, few if any members of Congress had as dire a picture of
the financial mess as did Bernanke and Paulson. The politicians did not
yet comprehend the frightening dimensions of the unfolding disaster. They
still saw it as a Wall Street problem—it was the financial giants who were
staggering, right?—not a Main Street problem, and they were accordingly
hostile to bailouts. Importantly, they were not convinced of the need—and
certainly not of the political viability—of putting massive amounts of taxpayer money at risk to salve banks' self-inflicted wounds. Both the Bear
Stearns rescue and the AIG bailout had been extremely unpopular with
their constituents.

Using the Federal Reserve's ample balance sheet looked pretty attractive by comparison. After all, Congress didn't have to appropriate a penny;
Bernanke would take the heat if anything went wrong; and members of
Congress could berate the Fed for overstepping its authority or anything
else they didn't like, even while money flowed to banks in their districts.
The Fed's acute political exposure was, of course, exactly what Bernanke
was hoping to minimize. Where you stand depends on where you sit.

By all accounts—and members of Congress do talk!—the September 18 meeting was, shall we say, very interesting. Paulson did not antici-
pate a friendly gathering. A former Wall Street titan himself, he would be
seen by the Democrats, and soon by the whole country, as pleading to bail
out the moneyed interests. As he confided to Bernanke, "They'll kill me up
there. I'll be hung out to dry." Before Paulson left for the Hill that evening,
his chief of staff, Jim Wilkinson, warned him that "this is only going to
work if you scare the shit out of them." Crudely put, but probably sound
advice. Paulson took it.

He and Bernanke apparently did far more than merely outline their
vision of the *financial* Armageddon in store for the country if Congress

didn't act with dispatch—which would have been an easier sell because that Armageddon was already unfolding before their eyes. According to some members of Congress who were present, the two went much further and actually sketched a scenario in which civil order broke down in the United States and there was rioting on the streets. "If it doesn't pass, then heaven help us all," concluded Paulson, who is a religious man. According to eyewitnesses, there was much gulping around the big mahogany table. Paulson later wrote that Bernanke's bleak assessment of what might happen to the economy "was enough . . . to leave the members of Congress ashen-faced." Bernanke himself later said, "I kind of scared them. I kind of scared myself."

In the less polemical moments of the meeting, one presumes, Paulson outlined the TARP plan that he was planning to introduce the next morning. Under the plan he sketched, the Treasury would buy troubled assets from the banks, thereby getting them off banks' books, raising their market values, making banks healthier, and helping the economy. Hundreds of billions of dollars would be needed for this purpose (*Say that again?*), and the Treasury wanted the legislation passed within days. *(Say THAT again?)*

The congressional leadership, stunned by this apocalyptic vision, was reluctantly convinced—though they raised many questions. One prominent query would come back to haunt the Treasury again and again: What about limits on executive pay? Paulson hated the idea. But Barney Frank, who chaired the House Committee on Financial Services, insisted to him that "You aren't selling this plan to a boardroom. You are selling it to the American people." It was good advice, not taken.

As the meeting drew to a close, Harry Reid (D-NV), the Senate majority leader, expressed disbelief in the compressed timetable: "It takes me 48 hours to get Republicans to agree to flush the toilets around here." Fortunately, Mitch McConnell (R-KY), the minority leader, was frightened enough to opt for the treat rather than the trick. "I think we need to do this," he told Reid. It was a rare moment of bipartisanship, which was *not* a portent of things to come.

The mere news that this meeting had taken place ignited a strong stock market rally the next morning. But Reid, McConnell, Pelosi, and—most of all—House Minority Leader John Boehner would soon learn that their members were by no means ready to stretch a protective TARP over the financial system.

The next morning was Friday, September 19, and Paulson announced his plan at a press briefing—the same briefing at which he announced his first attempt to save the money market funds. Paulson outlined and defended the basic idea ("These illiquid assets are choking off the flow of credit that is so vitally important to our economy"), and said he was "convinced that this bold approach will cost American families far less than the alternative"—which was presumably laissez-faire. But he did not put a price tag on the TARP.

That was no accident; the Treasury had not yet decided how much to ask for. The Break-the-Glass Memo had used a pretty arbitrary $500 billion figure, which was the number Paulson had run by President Bush. But things had deteriorated since April. More money would probably be needed. That night, Paulson, Kashkari, and Kevin Fromer, the Treasury's legislative liaison, hashed over the question of how much money to ask for. Here is journalist Andrew Sorkin's account of how their conversation went:

> "What about $1 trillion?" Kashkari said.
> "We'll get killed," Paulson said grimly.
> "No way," Fromer said, incredulous at the sum. "Not going to happen. Impossible."
> "Okay," Kashkari said. "How about $700 billion?"
> . . . As he plucked numbers from thin air even Kashkari laughed at the absurdity of it all.

Five days after Paulson's press conference announcing TARP, I drove to a resort hotel near Atlantic City to give a speech to the New Jersey Bankers Association. Talk of TARP was naturally in the air, and they asked many questions about the program—most of which I couldn't answer. But one I could, with a high degree of confidence:

NJ BANKER: How did they come up with the number $700 billion?

ME: I'm pretty sure they pulled it out of thin air.

And who could blame them? No one knew how much would be enough.

THE THREE LITTLE PAGES

On Saturday, September 20, the first draft of Paulson's TARP plan emerged and was posted online. It was a stunner. Many people, including me, read it and gasped.

The request for the largest sum ever appropriated by Congress for a single program was merely three pages long. It gave the secretary of the Treasury almost complete discretion over how to use $700,000,000,000, providing only for an initial report to Congress within three months (and then semiannually after that). It described the bill's purpose as follows: "The Secretary is authorized to purchase . . . *on such terms and conditions as determined by the Secretary,* mortgage-related assets from any financial institution having its headquarters in the United States." (Emphasis added.)

That meant buying "troubled assets," right? Well, the draft defined "mortgage-related assets" as "residential and commercial mortgages and any securities, obligations, or other instruments that are based on *or related to such mortgages.*" (Emphasis again added.) *Related to?* My third cousin is related to me. The Treasury's lawyers assured Paulson that the language was broad enough to encompass even injecting capital directly into banks. It was?

And then there was the notorious Section 8, a single, audacious sentence, which I quote in its entirety because, otherwise, you might not believe me:

> Decisions by the Secretary pursuant to the authority of this Act are non-reviewable and committed to agency discretion, and may not be reviewed by any court of law or any administrative agency.

I shook my head in disbelief when I read those words—and, so, apparently, did many others. You may have just done the same. *May not be reviewed by any court of law?* Isn't this the United States of America, with its vaunted system of checks and balances? Don't we pride ourselves on the rule of law, not the rule of men? Isn't ours a legalistic system where *everything* is reviewable by the courts? Didn't Chief Justice John Marshall establish the principle of judicial review more than two hundred years ago?

The need for flexibility in using TARP resources was understandable, but the arrogance displayed in the three-pager was breathtaking. What *could* they have been thinking in the Treasury Department? I'm not given to hyperbole, and I'm certainly not a constitutional lawyer. But I told an NPR interviewer at the time that the proposal showed so little respect for—and understanding of—the U.S. Constitution that Secretary Paulson deserved to be impeached just for proposing it.

Paulson later explained that congressional leaders had advised him not to draft a complete bill, but rather to send them an outline of what he wanted and let Congress write the law. "So we prepared a short, bare-bones proposal with open-ended language, knowing that members would add provisions." Fine. But then why did those three pages go through multiple revisions by the Treasury's legislative drafters and emerge in the exact format of a draft bill? And where did the idea of banning judicial review come from? Surely not from Congress.

As Paulson later put it in a magnificent understatement, "Making no provision for judicial review came across as overreaching." But the issue was not *making no provision for judicial review.* What Paulson's notorious three-pager did was *make provision for no judicial review.* His draft would have given him authority to spend $700 billion of public money any way he wished, unchecked by any court. That was an incredible departure from the way we do business in the United States, and it didn't get in there by accident.

The document raised eyebrows everywhere, even *inside* the Treasury. No limits on discretion? No oversight? No review? And just three pages long? Sorkin relates the following conversation between two Treasury aides who had not worked on the bill:

DAN JESTER TO JEREMIAH NORTON: "So, have you seen the bill?"

NORTON: "I've seen the talking points."

JESTER: "No. That is the bill!"

The firestorm was immediate. On *Meet the Press* that Sunday morning, Tom Brokaw asked Paulson, "If you were in your old job at Goldman Sachs and you took this deal to the partners, they'd send you out of the room and say, 'Come back when you've got a lot more answers,' wouldn't they?" Monday morning's *Newsweek* had Paulson on its cover page under the title "King Henry." At a Senate hearing the next day, Senator Jim Bunning, the cantankerous ultraconservative Republican from Kentucky, blasted the TARP as "financial socialism" and "un-American." Committee chairman Chris Dodd (D-CT), who supported the basic TARP idea, snapped that "this proposal is stunning and unprecedented in its scope and lack of detail. . . . It is not just our economy at risk, but our Constitution as well." Joshua Rosner, a financial consultant, told the *New York Times* that TARP should stand for "Total Abdication of Responsibility to the Public." And so it went. Paulson later admitted that the September 20 draft "turned out to be a three-page political mistake." Swagel, his economic aide, called it "a communications mistake." It was much more than either. It was an outrage.

REDESIGNING THE TARP

Congress, which was then controlled by Democrats, discarded the three-pager immediately and began drafting its own legislation from scratch, accepting the basic idea of giving a Republican secretary of the Treasury huge discretion to buy assets but bargaining with Paulson over several matters. Paulson got precious little support from his own party. If there was to be a deal, it would have to be cut between the Republican administration and congressional Democrats. Republicans in Congress, and especially in the House, would be a hindrance, not a help.

It was notable that Fed Chairman Bernanke took a backseat at this point. This was a *fiscal* policy issue (appropriation of funds), he believed, and a highly political one at that. Bernanke was going to minimize his involvement in the to-ing and fro-ing between the administration and Congress. Though working like mad behind the scenes, he seemed to recede into the shadows, letting the political Treasury take over the job of committing taxpayer money from the nonpolitical Fed. For example, the Fed chair absented himself from the highly publicized September 25 political meeting called by then presidential candidate John McCain to address the crisis. The Fed's vice chairman, Don Kohn, a Fed careerist, applauded the lower public profile. "As the Treasury stands up, the Fed stands down," he thought.

This was important. The unwillingness or inability—due to legal limitations—of the Treasury to take the lead in public had forced the publicity-shy Federal Reserve to step up to the plate repeatedly and very visibly. A number of its actions, though clearly legal under Section 13(3) of the Federal Reserve Act, put taxpayer money at risk—which is just one step away from *spending* money, a power reserved to Congress. The Fed had been pushed by necessity into the political arena, where all sorts of perils awaited it. It was rightfully eager to step out.

One political issue was particularly contentious, as Barney Frank had prophesized: executive pay. Paulson—supported by Bernanke and the New York Fed's Tim Geithner—wanted to tread lightly on the compensation issue, if, indeed, they had to address it at all. The secretary envisioned the TARP as a facility in which banks would participate willingly, even eagerly; he knew that wouldn't happen if bank executives were forced to take pay cuts. Democrats saw things differently. If the government was doing banks such a big favor by purchasing their toxic assets, shouldn't bankers be willing to accept some restrictions in return—for example, on dividends and executive pay? And even if bankers objected to pay cuts, shouldn't the public's elected representatives demand them as a matter of elementary fairness?

Paulson pushed back hard, raising an issue on which he would fixate more than once. In his own words, "To my mind, restricting compensation meant putting a preemptive stigma on the program. And that is exactly what I didn't want to do." *Stigma*. Let's think about that word. The basic idea was that banks would not sell their toxic assets to the TARP if doing so would label them as "weak sisters." Taken in isolation, that sentence makes complete sense. Indeed, the Fed had run smack into the stigma problem in 2007, when it wanted to lend massively to banks. But the focus on avoiding stigma missed a larger point. At least where the big banks were concerned—and that's where the executive pay issue was salient—the markets already knew who was strong (e.g., JP Morgan Chase) and who was weak (e.g., Citigroup). Participation or nonparticipation in TARP would tell them next to nothing new. As the accompanying box explains, signaling and stigma arise when quality differences are *unobservable*. In this case, they were painfully observable.

SIGNALING AND STIGMA

Paulson's worries about stigma were grounded in the economic theory of market *signaling*. But he misused the theory badly. I will use the hiring of workers to illustrate the concept, but the same sort of analysis applies to credit-granting decisions, hiring contractors, and much else—including distinguishing between sick and healthy banks.

The key ingredient in the theory of signaling is *unobservable* differences across people, banks, businesses, or whatever. In the labor market, there are always better and worse workers. But their superiority or inferiority may not be easy for prospective employers to discern prior to hiring. Such ignorance gives superior workers powerful incentives to set themselves apart from the rest. If they succeed, they will be hired first and at higher wages. But how do they distinguish themselves?

One way is called *signaling*. Suppose there are some

characteristics, such as stick-to-itiveness, energy, and self-discipline, that employers want in prospective hires but that are *not observable* before hiring. Employers will then prefer applicants with some *observable* characteristics that *signal* the presence of these desirable traits. One such example might be completing a college degree. If so, employers will favor college graduates. From a worker's perspective, graduating from college is a *signal* to prospective employers that you are a superior worker. The logic cuts the other way, too. You want to avoid signals of inferiority—like a police record or a spotty work history. Such things carry *stigma*.

There's that word. Paulson's worry was that coming to the TARP would be seen as an act of desperation. If, for example, taking the TARP money required a bank's executives to accept pay restrictions, asking for the money would carry such a stigma. The point was conceptually correct. But it ignored the critical adjective mentioned earlier: For the theory to apply, the bank's weakness must be *unobservable;* and in this case, it was painfully *observable*.

Markets had numerous ways to distinguish between strong and weak banks: stock prices, credit ratings, CDS spreads, analysts' reports, market chatter, and so on. No one had to watch TARP take-up rates to judge whether JP Morgan Chase was stronger or weaker than Citigroup, or whether Goldman Sachs was stronger than Morgan Stanley. And if they needed any help, the strong banks were eager to provide it. To take just one concrete example, Goldman was not worrying about stigmatizing itself when it became the first user of the FDIC's guarantee program for corporate debt. Goldman was the fastest antelope in the herd, and everyone knew it.

However, the big political issue was not any debate over correct application of the economic theory of stigma, but rather over simple notions of fair play. Ordinary Americans, and therefore their elected representatives, saw that greedy and irresponsible behavior by bankers had created a financial calamity that put the whole country at risk. Now they, the taxpayers, were being asked to pay for the sins of the bankers, who would continue to earn staggering sums. Try playing that in Peoria—or anywhere else. One Republican congressman from North Carolina illustrated the public's attitude by reading from a letter from one of his constituents: "These bailouts should be about as welcome as malaria." To which he added, "They do not see why we have to be bailing out those people whose greed . . . got them into trouble." It was a fair question. Unsurprisingly, public opinion polls ran solidly against the bank bailout.

After much wrangling, Paulson got away with surprisingly mild restrictions on executive pay in the final TARP legislation. The law disallowed golden parachutes and capped severance payments at three times base salary. (Stan O'Neal would have been appalled!) It banned giving top executives pay incentives that encouraged "unnecessary and excessive risks," but it left that determination to corporate boards, not to the Treasury. There were also clawback provisions in cases in which bonuses were "based on statements of earnings, gains, or other criteria that are later proven to be materially inaccurate." All in all, it was hardly Draconian.

But Paulson's victory was pyrrhic. The pay issue would come back to haunt him and his successor, Tim Geithner, time and again. Ironically, the TARP's seemingly relaxed attitude toward executive compensation created a much more damaging kind of stigma. Never mind weak versus strong banks. In the eyes of the public, it helped stigmatize the entire TARP as a giveaway to greedy bankers, some of whom were Paulson's friends. Later, when Geithner took over the top job, the view persisted that he was an alumnus of Goldman Sachs! This was entirely fictitious and unfair: Geithner had never worked for a private bank a single day of his life.

Paulson later admitted, "I was wrong not to have been more sensitive to the public outrage." He sure was, and it should have been obvious at the time.

Numerous other changes were made on the bumpy road toward ultimate passage of the bill. Normal judicial review was, of course, restored. The TARP money was appropriated in tranches, not all at once, with some clearly set aside for the next administration. An option to insure (rather than purchase) troubled assets was added to appease certain House Republicans. (It was never utilized.) Language on using the TARP to mitigate foreclosure was added throughout the bill—including in the definition of "troubled assets." There could be no mistaking congressional intent: Members wanted some of the bailout money going to distressed homeowners, not just to distressed banks.

Multiple layers of oversight were added, including the Congressional Oversight Panel, which wound up being headed by Elizabeth Warren, and the Special Inspector General for the TARP, who wound up being Neil Barofsky. Both proved to be zealous guardians of the public purse and thorns in the side of Secretary Paulson and later Secretary Geithner. I remember saying at the time that the TARP law created so many layers of oversight that the next secretary of the Treasury would want to give away the extraordinary powers it gave him. That proved to be a bad prophecy. But I wonder if, in retrospect, Geithner wishes he had done so.

The bill that ultimately passed Congress, the Emergency Economic Stabilization Act of 2008, ran to 451 pages, of which 261 dealt with the TARP, making that part of the Act (Title I) 87 times Paulson's original length. But nowhere in those 261 pages is there a single word about using TARP money to inject capital into banks. Nowhere. Instead, there is a catch-all phrase under which the secretary of the Treasury was authorized, after "consultation" with the chairman of the Fed and a written explanation to Congress, to purchase "any other financial instrument that the Secretary . . . determines the purchase of which is necessary to promote financial market stability."* That language allowed pretty much anything.

The road to passage proved rocky. Although the House leadership thought they had the votes on September 29, the membership surprised them by rejecting the TARP the first time around, in a 205–228 vote. Opposition came from both the Republican Right and the Democratic Left,

---

*Notice that the law did not require the Fed chairman's *approval*, only that there be *consultation*.

though for starkly different reasons. The Right was the bigger problem; more than two thirds of House Republicans voted no. Apparently, Bernanke and Paulson hadn't quite "scared the shit out of them." But the stock market soon did. The S&P 500 fell almost 9 percent the next day—destroying about $1.25 trillion of wealth, almost twice the TARP request, in a single day. That made believers out of enough House members to pass the bill by a comfortable 263–171 margin just four days later—after adding a few sweeteners to a piece of legislation that no politician could love.

As this political drama played out in Congress, something else was brewing behind the scenes—something that would make the TARP even more reviled. Paulson came to believe that capital injections were a better route than asset purchases after all, just as Bernanke had said. Some observers say the secretary, too, had believed it all along but squelched the idea because of politics. Regardless, his timing was awful—right between the two House votes.

Why? It seemed that Treasury staff work was convincing him that designing a program to purchase toxic assets was fraught with difficulties and would take too long. It would be simpler and, more important, *faster* for the government just to buy equity stakes in the banks. Doing so might even net a profit for the taxpayers in the end—which, in fact, it did. Never mind the fact that buying toxic assets near their lows would probably have netted the Treasury even larger profits.

When Paulson informed his top press officer, Michelle Davis, of his decision, she reacted with disbelief. "We haven't even gotten the bill through Congress. How are we going to explain this? We can't say that *now*." And Paulson didn't. As a result, in early October 2008, the United States Senate and House of Representatives voted to inject capital into banks while *thinking* it was voting to purchase "troubled assets," including lots of home mortgages. As if the TARP needed even more political handicaps, it would soon look like a classic case of bait and switch.

Unfurling the TARP

Why the change of heart? As I've suggested, part of the reason was technical. Designing a workable mechanism for purchasing toxic assets during a financial panic was no easy task. Let's use the simplified bank balance sheet below to illustrate why.

TABLE 7.1 Simplified Balance Sheet of Troubled Bank

Assets	Liabilities and Net Worth
Good assets $50 billion	Deposits $90 billion
Bad assets $50 billion	Equity $10 billion

While this bank has a comfortable *accounting* net worth of $10 billion more in assets than in liabilities, it looks shaky to the market, which doesn't know what the bad assets are really worth—certainly not the $50 billion carried on the books. Suppose the bad assets—mortgages, MBS, and the like—are really worth only $35 billion, a 30 percent discount to face value, which may have been realistic at the time. Then the bank's true mark-to-market balance sheet would be:

TABLE 7.2 Mark-to-Market Balance Sheet of Troubled Bank

Assets	Liabilities and Net Worth
Good assets $50 billion	Deposits $90 billion
Bad assets $35 billion	Equity -$5 billion

The true value of its assets is $5 billion short of its deposit liabilities. The bank is insolvent.

If the government now buys the bank's troubled assets at fair market value—that is, for $35 billion—it would create table 7.3. Mission *not* accomplished. Yes, the bank has unloaded its bad assets onto the taxpayer.

But it is still insolvent. Indeed, that insolvency is now clear rather than hidden behind an accounting smokescreen.

TABLE 7.3 Balance Sheet of Troubled Bank After Purchases at Market

Assets	Liabilities and Net Worth
Good assets $50 billion	Deposits $90 billion
Cash (from TARP) $35 billion	Equity -$5 billion

If, on the other hand, the government *overpays* for the assets—say it pays the full $50 billion face value—it would create table 7.4.

TABLE 7.4 Balance Sheet of Troubled Bank After Purchases at Face Value

Assets	Liabilities and Net Worth
Good assets $50 billion	Deposits $90 billion
Cash (from TARP) $50 billion	Equity $10 billion

Now the bank *is* solvent. But it has received a $15 billion gift from the taxpayers, who have paid $50 billion for dodgy assets worth $35 billion. Maybe that's not such a good idea—and the politics of overpaying might have been deadly. Critics of asset purchases raised that possibility as a prominent objection.

In reality, of course, to paraphrase Bernanke, nobody knew what those damned things were worth. With markets for toxic assets barely functioning, and without reliable market quotes, it was hard even to guess the true market values of mortgage-related assets. When the highest price bid for an asset is $20, and the lowest asking price is $60—and gaps like that were common at the time—discerning the "true" market value becomes a question for philosophers, not for economists, and certainly not for traders. The big hazard for the original TARP idea was therefore this: If Treasury offered to buy that asset at, say, $40, would it be overpaying or underpaying? How would it even know?

BID-ASK SPREADS

You remember your first Economics 101 lesson, right? Free markets clear at the point where the demand curve and the supply curve cross. Well, that's not *exactly* right.

In any given market at any given time, there normally will be a gap, or spread, between the highest price any demander is willing to pay ("the bid") and lowest price any supplier is willing to accept ("the ask"). In thick markets that are functioning smoothly, the bid-ask spread is very tight—maybe a penny on a New York Stock Exchange-traded stock. But in thin or disrupted markets, bid-ask spreads can get quite large. Indeed, the size of the bid-ask spread is often used as a handy measure of how liquid a market is. A wide bid-ask spread indicates that there is not much liquidity in the market.

When the bid-ask spread is extraordinarily wide—as in the "bid 20, ask 60" example—it is virtually impossible for anyone to discern the "true" market price. The reason is simple: A $20-$60 bid-ask spread means that the market has essentially shut down.

To economists, there is an obvious solution: Hold an auction. Buyers would be invited to come and make offers, and the highest bids would establish the market values of each troubled asset. Treasury staffers were working hard on designing such auctions. But there was a financial panic in progress. What if they held an auction and nobody showed up? Many academics and market participants harped on the near impossibility of getting the prices right. To many critics, the TARP was a backdoor way of giving banks capital by overpaying for troubled assets. Why, they asked, don't we just give them the capital *directly* and *transparently*?

And there was another major issue: Would banks show up at the auctions to sell? If they hung on to their mortgages and other troubled assets, accounting rules allowed them to *pretend* they were still solvent, as in table 7.1. They could carry many assets at face value as long as they were not for sale. But if the banks started selling their dodgy assets at auction, they would have to mark them down to market values—which might, as in the example of table 7.3, render them insolvent. Hence, the question: What if nobody showed up?

It was a fair question, and it was given further credence when Prime Minister Gordon Brown announced a capital injection system (including nationalizations) for the UK on October 8, a mere five days after President Bush signed the TARP legislation. The British government would invest the equivalent of $87 billion—more than 3 percent of British GDP—in eight big banks, taking convertible preferred shares in return so as to give taxpayers some upside if and when things turned around. Brown's approach drew huzzahs from many experts—in my view, far more than it deserved—and was sort of endorsed by a G7 meeting a few days later.

Paulson must have felt a wave of jealousy wash over him. While his opening act had been roundly panned, Brown's opened to rave reviews. I remember feeling like a member of a tiny minority group at the time. As the intellectual tide shifted strongly toward equity injections, I quipped that I was one of four people on earth who favored asset purchases. In any case, on October 12, Paulson announced a complete turnabout: The U.S. Treasury would shelve its plans to purchase troubled assets and, instead, inject capital directly into banks. Did someone say "bait and switch"?

Why the change? Were the arguments compelling—or even valid? Two days after the switch, Paulson explained to the *Washington Post*, "The facts as I know them changed. We got a bigger impact per taxpayer dollar with the equity injection so we went that route." Let's parse those words. Did any significant facts actually *change* in those nine days? Not unless you count the difficulties the Treasury staff faced in designing workable auctions—which hardly came as a surprise. The real focus must be on the phrase *bigger impact per taxpayer dollar*. That's the argument, I believe, that tipped the decision.

One crucial argument favoring capital injections over asset purchases was the alleged power of *leverage*. According to Swagel, "Secretary Paulson switched gears and came to favor injecting capital, since he well understood that directly adding capital to the banking system provided greater leverage." Look back at table 7.1. Troubled Bank is holding $10 worth of assets (think of them as loans) for each $1 of capital—a leverage ratio of 10 to 1. Some proponents of equity injections argued that more capital would be high-powered money, that each $1 of additional capital could finance some $10 of additional lending. The government would therefore get a lot more lending "bang" for each taxpayer "buck."

That argument struck me as naïve in the extreme. Bankers are required by law to maintain a minimum ratio of capital to risk-weighted assets. (Never mind risk weighting; that's a separate complicated story. Just think of it as 10 percent in the example.) Most banks were presumably under-capitalized on a mark-to-market basis at the time, even if their balance sheets, using book values, said otherwise (compare tables 7.1 and 7.2). They needed capital desperately, and most of them could not raise it in the dire circumstances of October 2008. If the government made equity invest-ments, I thought, the bankers would breathe a sigh of relief, say "thank you very much," and stuff the new capital into their balance sheets to rebuild their dangerously depleted equity and thereby to *reduce* leverage. That is certainly what I would have done in their place.

Furthermore, the post-Lehman economy was in free fall, with talk of Great Depression 2.0 in the air, making the climate for lending look pretty uninviting. Why would a perilously capitalized bank, hunkering down for survival in the greatest storm it had ever seen, lend out $10 for each new dollar of capital? Why would it lend out even $1? In fact, history records that the banks pulled in their horns. By September 2012, total bank lend-ing had still not reattained its October 2008 level.

Furthermore, as Paulson had pointed out in arguing for buying trou-bled assets in the first place, mortgage-related assets were at the heart of the problem. With no one knowing what those shunned assets were worth, nor where and when the meltdown would end, bid-ask spreads were crazily wide (as noted above) and the few transactions that actually took place were at unbelievably low prices.* As emphasized earlier, a huge mountain of

---

*Over dinner one night, a smart Wall Street friend told me about a CDO carrying an 8 percent interest coupon that was selling for 6 cents on the dollar—even though it had not yet missed a single payment. Foolishly, I did not invest in it. He probably did. It's the story of my life.

securities and derivatives had been built on top of subprime mortgages—and that whole mountain was now suspect. The chaos in markets was, in turn, undermining faith in even the biggest financial institutions, which were therefore both unable and unwilling to lend. In addition, the disappearance of the market for MBS created an acute reluctance to grant new mortgages, which continued to weigh on the weakest sector of our economy (homebuilding) and to hurt actual and prospective homeowners.

That's where buying "troubled assets" was supposed to come in. If the government entered the markets as a buyer, prices of both mortgages and MBS would almost certainly rise, and bid-ask spreads would narrow. Thus, the government wouldn't have to overpay for troubled assets (or at least not *obviously* overpay). Instead, the "true" market prices would rise. In the bid-ask example above, the government might wind up buying the asset for $40, or something like that—surely more than $20 and less than $60.

Getting the auction prices *exactly right* was probably impossible in the chaotic markets of October 2008. But getting within 10 to 15 percent of true values shouldn't have been too hard. And that should have been good enough for government work amid one of the worst financial calamities ever. Furthermore, re-creating a market for MBS and enhancing their values would have more or less automatically raised the prices of CDOs, and so on up the daisy chain that Wall Street had created. And better valuations for MBS would have meant better valuations for mortgages. What went down could go up. And remember, the housing market was the original source of the recession.

Yet there *was* a valid argument for injecting capital into banks: More bank capital was sorely needed at the time. Fortunately, at $700 billion, the TARP was big enough to do some of each. Equity injections would improve banks' capital positions *directly*, and purchases of troubled assets would help unclog markets, which would boost banks' capital *indirectly*. But it was not to be. At least at first, the TARP was used exclusively to make capital injections. Ironically, the Fed would later step in to do what the TARP was originally designed to do, with Treasury kicking in TARP money to help out. So maybe the arguments for buying troubled assets weren't so bad, after all.

No Strings

If nothing else, Paulson was a man of action. The TARP law passed on October 3; he changed its purpose completely on October 12; and he was already force-feeding capital down the throats of the nation's biggest banks on October 13.

On Sunday, October 12, the holiday weekends of nine of America's most prominent bankers—Goldman's Lloyd Blankfein, Bank of America's Ken Lewis, Citigroup's Vikram Pandit, Morgan Stanley's John Mack, JP Morgan Chase's Jamie Dimon, and so on—were interrupted by surprise phone calls from the United States Treasury. (*Honey, Hank Paulson's on the line.*) It wasn't to wish each of them a Happy Columbus Day. Rather, Paulson was calling to *invite* them (a euphemism) to a meeting at the Treasury at 3:00 p.m. the next day. He wouldn't say why, but he did make it known that the "invitation" came from both him and the chairman of the Federal Reserve Board.

When the Treasury secretary and the Fed chairman say that they would *really* like to see you, a wise banker cancels his previous plans and shows up. All of them did. Blankfein, Lewis, Pandit, Mack, Dimon, Wells Fargo's Dick Kovacevich, Merrill Lynch's John Thain, Bank of New York Mellon's Robert Kelly, and State Street Bank's Ronald Logue were seated around the table when Paulson and Bernanke walked in, accompanied by Geithner, the FDIC's Sheila Bair, and John Dugan, the Comptroller of the Currency. I assume everyone had their game faces on. The CEOs still didn't know why they were there.

Paulson started the meeting by making it clear that they were not about to get a *take-it-or-leave-it* offer. It would be a *take-it* offer, even though the government had no legal authority to compel participation—a point that weighed heavily on the officials' minds. Paulson's approach was shock and awe: "Let me be clear: If you don't take it and you aren't able to raise the capital . . . in the market, then I'm going to give you a second helping [of capital] and you're not going to like the terms." Stony silence. After Bernanke and Bair each said something, Geithner, playing the heavy, told each

executive how much money his bank would be taking—er, *requesting*—
from the TARP. Everyone, it seems, had to participate because the government would subsequently be injecting capital into hundreds of smaller
banks and needed to avoid stigmatizing the recipients. There was that word
again: *stigma*.

The numbers were enormous: $25 billion each for Citi, JP Morgan
Chase, and Wells Fargo; $15 billion for BofA; $10 billion each for Merrill,*
Goldman, and Morgan Stanley; $3 billion for BNYM; and $2 billion for
State Street. A tidy $125 billion in all. Attitudes toward accepting this lar-
gesse varied across the nine in fairly predictable ways. Citi needed the
money badly, and Pandit accepted it with alacrity, as "cheap capital." Indeed, it *was* cheap, because of those silly stigma worries. Dimon and Blankfein didn't need or want government capital, but complied with little or no
resistance, seeing the outcome as inevitable.

But Kovacevich resisted. Wells Fargo had already announced plans to
raise $25 billion privately; he didn't need or want another $25 billion from
the government. "I'm not one of you New York guys with your fancy products. Why am I in this room, talking about bailing you out?" he asked the
others rhetorically. Geithner assured him that he really *did* need another
$25 billion. Paulson was direct: "Your regulator is sitting right here. And
you're going to get a call tomorrow telling you you're undercapitalized." Yes,
as Barney Frank had sardonically noted four weeks earlier, the national
commitment to the free market had lasted one day.

As the meeting progressed, punctuated by delays to convene impromptu telephone meetings of a bunch of surprised corporate boards, the
CEOs asked lots of questions about restrictions on dividends and on—
what else?—executive pay. But in the end, each of the nine signed on the
dotted line.

The terms of the capital infusions were hardly onerous. Paulson et al.
had designed them to be attractive in order to encourage "voluntary" participation. It all would be nonvoting preferred stock, not common; the government had no interest in managing the companies. The dividend rate was

---

*Merrill was being acquired by BofA, making $25 billion for the combined company.

a mere 5 percent, half of what Warren Buffett had just charged Goldman Sachs for preferred stock. Dividend payments to common stockholders would not be banned, though they could not be increased for three years. (Well, thanks for that!) There was no requirement to increase, or even to maintain, lending volumes. That would have been hard to do with loan demand crumbling, anyway. There was no commitment whatsoever to mitigate foreclosures. Restraints on executive compensation were minimal. (President Obama would later change that, making TARP money even less popular with bankers.)

Every one of these design features quickly elicited sharp criticisms of the "bank bailout." Why was the government getting only *half* of what Warren Buffett got? Why, with so much taxpayer money committed, were no public-purpose strings attached—such as requirements to boost lending or to minimize foreclosures? Why were banks allowed to maintain dividend payments? Since money is fungible, didn't that make it possible for TARP money to be paid out to shareholders?

The answer in each case was more or less the same. The terms were made deliberately generous in order *to avoid stigma*. As Swagel put it, the capital injections "had to be the opposite of *The Sopranos* or *The Godfather*—not an attempt to intimidate banks, but instead a deal so attractive that banks would be unwise to refuse it." The Treasury wanted broad and rapid take-up, and if Goldman and JP Morgan were already members of the club, it surely could not be a bad club to join.

Paulson and Bernanke pushed the stigma argument. But Fed governor Kevin Warsh, who had come from Wall Street via the Bush administration, rejected the argument out of hand, telling Geithner, "You aren't going to fool [the markets] into thinking that everybody is equally good, bad, or indifferent." Warsh was right. Within hours after the meeting at the Treasury, Wells Fargo, JP Morgan Chase, and Goldman Sachs had each told (or leaked to) the media that they neither needed nor wanted the government capital. Thus, in one of the minor tragedies of the TARP episode, the bank Capital Purchase Program (CPP), as it was called, was twisted into a pretzel in an ill-conceived effort to avoid stigma that already existed.

The CPP's multiple design flaws had two sets of consequences—one political, the other economic. Politically, because bankers were villains in the eyes of the public and some politicians, the program's munificence made the CPP, and therefore the TARP, extremely unpopular. It was considered a giveaway to undeserving bankers even as millions of homeowners struggled to avoid foreclosure. To this day, millions of Americans believe that the money was *given to*—not *invested in*—banks. Nor do they realize that the CPP, which eventually invested $205 billion in nearly seven hundred banks, turned a tidy profit for the government.

Economically, forcing capital on banks that didn't want or need it wasted a precious resource. The first tranche of TARP money was only $250 billion;* that was projected to be absorbed entirely by the CPP. What if more money was needed? What about other uses of TARP funds—like buying troubled assets, for example? Furthermore, as I argued above, it seemed unlikely that most of the newly injected capital would spur any lending.

Oh, and There Was an Election in November

While all this was going on, the United States of America was in the critical stages of a historic presidential election. It pitted the preternaturally calm man who would be America's first black president, Senator Barack Obama, of Illinois, against a mercurial one-time war hero who would be the oldest president ever elected for a first term if he won, Senator John McCain, of Arizona. Just before Lehman Day, McCain held a 4- to 5-point lead in the Gallup poll. Shortly after the Lehman bankruptcy, the lead flipped, with Obama surging ahead by roughly 4 points (see figure 7.1). Calm looked better than mercurial.

On September 25, while the TARP was under debate, a somewhat panicky McCain suspended his campaign and suggested calling off a presidential debate, which Obama rejected. The Republican standard-bearer

---

*The law provided that President Bush could request another $100 billon if he certified that it was needed.

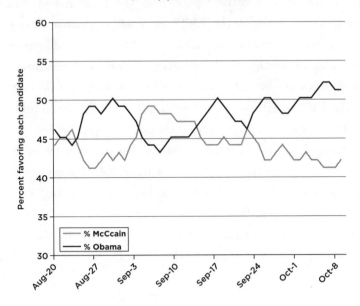

FIGURE 7.1 *Calm Beats Stormy*
(Gallup poll data, 2008)

dashed back to Washington for a crisis meeting at the White House, which he, not President Bush, called. I suppose the former war hero hoped the operation would play as "John McCain to the Rescue." But according to most participants, it turned out to be a waste of precious time.

McCain's performance played badly against his reputation for being hasty and erratic at times. Hasty, erratic, and mercurial were not what the electorate wanted during the Panic of 2008. Calm, smart, and thoughtful were more like it. Immediately after the September 25 fiasco, Obama's Gallup poll lead widened to 8 points. We didn't know it at the time, but the race was, for all intents and purposes, over. One Obama campaign aide later told journalist Noam Scheiber, "I believe we won the election in the ten days between the collapse of Lehman and the first debate. It created the sense that one guy was solid and had his feet on the ground, and the other guy was not." Obama won the popular vote on November 4 by 7.2 percentage points.

American law provides for a long transition between administrations. In this case, it was long *and agonizing*. President Bush appeared to have checked out. On any given day, many Americans didn't know whether we had one president, two presidents, or none. Secretary Paulson looked like a spent force, but he somehow had to slog through another two and a half months in office. On November 12, in one of his last official acts, Paulson made more than a few jaws drop by announcing that the TARP would not be used *at all* for its originally stated purpose: purchasing troubled assets. Not one cent! (Bait and switch squared?) He would save at least $350 billion in TARP money for his successor.

One of the jaws that dropped was my own. In a November 17 testimony to the House Financial Services Committee, I criticized the design of the CPP, the stigma argument, and the decision not to buy troubled assets. I urged Congress "to exercise its oversight authority to ensure that the Secretary of the Treasury pursues the stated goals of the legislation [which included foreclosure mitigation]. Failing that, Congress should . . . take the Secretary's checkbook away. We'll have a new Secretary of the Treasury in about two months."

A week later, that successor was named: It would be Tim Geithner, who would jump from the New York Fed's frying pan to the Treasury's fire. Geithner inherited the TARP's past decisions (in which he had been involved), an uncommitted balance of $350 billion, and all the oversight that went with TARP—a dubious inheritance, to say the least. Ironically, even before he assumed office, some bankers and financial experts were clamoring for TARP to return to its original stated purpose: buying troubled assets.

Ultimately, TARP money would be used, among other things, for more capital injections into banks, asset guarantees to save Citi and BofA, getting the Fed off the hook on AIG, foreclosure mitigation (albeit on a pitifully small scale), and the auto-industry bailout. It would never disburse more than about $430 billion of the permissible $700 billion, and never had more than about $360 billion outstanding at any one time. CBO's March 2012 estimate of the TARP's ultimate *net* cost to the taxpayers was just $32 billion, of which $22 billion will come from AIG, $19 billion will come from the auto bailout, and $16 billion will come from mortgage relief. Yes, that adds up $57 billion. Apart from these three items, the TARP turned a profit of about $25 billion. Despite many missteps, and a terrible image, it is hard not to count the TARP as a smashing success.

BETTER LATE THAN NEVER

Was that the end of the idea of having the government purchase troubled assets? Not quite. The Federal Reserve dipped its toes into those murky waters by participating in the bailouts of Citigroup in November 2008 (just days after Paulson's announcement) and Bank of America in January 2009. As described in the previous chapter, the Treasury, the Fed, and the FDIC teamed up to accept or insure mountains of dodgy assets from those two sick behemoths, with the Fed taking them as collateral for *nonrecourse loans*. That means that the Fed half-owned them—specifically, it owned only the downside. If the troubled assets rose in value, the banks owned the gains.

Right after the Citi bailout, the Fed, working closely with the Treasury, announced plans to create yet another unprecedented lending facility, the Term Asset-Backed Securities Loan Facility (TALF). The purpose of the TALF was to make nonrecourse loans to institutions willing to buy certain asset-backed securities (ABS)—the stuff no one seemed to want—up to $200 billion. You might call these "troubled assets." In fact, the Treasury backstopped the TALF with $20 billion of TARP money. Notice the risk-sharing ratio: $20 billion from the Treasury, $180 billion from the Fed.

On that same day, the Fed started buying debt obligations of Fannie Mae and Freddie Mac—marking the beginning of what would eventually be called QE1 (quantitative easing one). The central bank was clearly entering the asset-buying business on a large scale, but not with taxpayer money—or at least not directly. The Fed's gains or losses belong to taxpayers indirectly. Our central bank would eventually own a ton of this stuff.

In December 2008, the Fed published operational details on how the TALF would work. But by February 2009, it was already changing them to accept a wider set of assets as collateral—not a *better* set, but a *wider* one. This process would continue in subsequent months, making more and more assets eligible for the TALF. The Fed also said it would increase the potential loan volume under TALF to—hold on to your hats—*$1 trillion.* That was a psychological landmark: The rescue operations were adding another zero. The first TALF purchases—whoops, *loans*—started in March 2009, just as the crisis was waning. The program eventually grew to only about $70 billion, far less than the announced potential of $1 trillion.

But that wasn't all, not by a long shot. In the statement issued just after its January 28, 2009 meeting, the Federal Open Market Committee (FOMC) announced that it might add long-term Treasury securities to its QE1 asset-purchase program. Those assets were, of course, just the opposite of "troubled"; they were the safest assets money could buy. After its next meeting, on March 18, the FOMC specified that it would buy $300 billion worth of Treasuries and increase its planned purchases of GSE debt and MBS to $1.45 trillion. A cool $1.75 *trillion* in all. Breathtaking.

So, yes, the U.S. government wound up buying or half-buying—by getting only the downside risk—some $2 trillion worth of assets *eventually,* though only a small fraction of them could be called "troubled." It just didn't do it with the TARP. Yes, there were pros and cons to buying troubled assets. But maybe the original TARP idea wasn't so bad after all.

Half Full and Half Empty

Appraising the TARP is important, and historians will do so for decades to come. Among other things, the historical appraisal will influence whether we ever deploy a TARP-like rescue program again. Right now, the answer appears to be no. TARP has an undeservedly bad reputation. Why?

In my view, the program was weakened—both economically and politically—by a series of design flaws and marketing errors. These began with Paulson's ill-fated three-page bill, which was a "political mistake" and a "communications mistake," but was also much more. Indeed, it was an assault on the Constitution. The three-pager should never have seen the light of day. That it did shook public confidence in the Paulson Treasury— which was just stepping out from behind the Fed's skirts to assume the spotlight. It was a bad debut.

The errors continued with the wasteful decision to force-feed capital into banks that neither wanted nor needed it—on the foolish theory that doing so would avoid stigmatizing other TARP recipients. Pursuit of this false theory led Paulson to devise terms that were so sweet for the banks that they outraged the public. More important, the force-feeding squandered an opportunity to attach some minimum lending or foreclosure-mitigation requirements to the capital injections—which might have helped the economy recover. And by wasting TARP money on the non-needy, both Paulson and Geithner were led to husband their resources too carefully. Sorry, no money left for foreclosure mitigation or for purchasing troubled assets—which might have given TARP a better name, and also helped the recovery.

Which brings me to what I believe—though many observers do not—was the next big error: changing the central purpose of the *Troubled Assets Relief Program* from buying troubled assets to injecting capital into banks. Apart from giving the program a politically damaging bait-and-switch image, and flaunting congressional intent, this fateful decision seems to have been based on the false premise that capital injections would lead to multiple expansions of bank lending. Under crisis conditions, how could anyone have believed that?

Despite all this, the TARP worked—probably better than anyone expected. But it didn't shore up the shaky financial edifice all by itself. It had lots of help.

Many of the Fed's alphabet soup of creative lending facilities have been mentioned already. So far, I have made just passing reference to the Fed's large-scale asset purchases of both Treasury bonds and GSE debt instruments; more on them later. Then there was the FDIC's important Temporary Loan Guarantee Program, which enabled major banks and nonbanks to regain access to the credit markets. In addition, the Fed and other bank regulators collaborated on comprehensive "stress tests" of nineteen major financial institutions during the spring of 2009. As we will see later, these tests were phenomenally successful.* And there was more.

---

*The European Union tried bank stress tests later but with far less success.

To date, there have been precious few studies of the broader effects of this grab bag of financial-market policies. The only one I know of that even *attempts* to estimate the macroeconomic impacts of the entire potpourri was published in July 2010 by Mark Zandi and me. Our methodology was pretty simple—and very standard. Take a statistical model of the U.S. economy—we used the Moody's Analytics model—and simulate it both *with* and *without* the policies. The differences between the two simulations are then estimates of the effects of the policies. These estimates, of course, are only as good as the model, but ours were huge. By 2011, we estimated, real GDP was about 6 percent higher, the unemployment rate was nearly 3 percentage points lower, and 4.8 million more Americans were employed because of the financial-market policies (as compared with sticking with laissez-faire). Without these effects, and without the fiscal stimulus (the subject of the next chapter), the nightmare talk of Great Depression 2.0 might have become the frightening reality.

Oh, and did I mention that the $700 billion TARP cost the taxpayers almost nothing in the end? But hardly any Americans know that little secret.

8

|ıılıılıılıılıılıılıılıılıı|

STIMULUS, STIMULUS, WHEREFORE ART THOU, STIMULUS?

If we do not move swiftly, an economy that is already in crisis will be faced with catastrophe.

—President Barack Obama, February 5, 2009

John Maynard Keynes, the great British economist, died in 1946. But his ghost lives on. When economies around the world contracted sharply in late 2008 and early 2009, government officials started seeing visions of the 1930s and turned immediately to the teachings of Lord Keynes. For central bankers, that meant slashing interest rates to the bone and opening the monetary spigots—though the monetary systems of many countries were badly clogged by the financial mess. For presidents and prime ministers, congresses and parliaments, going Keynesian meant cutting taxes, raising public spending, or both. The idea in all cases was the same: to give total spending a badly needed boost, a *stimulus*.

But in the United States and much of Europe, the attachment to Keynesian economics was and remains skin-deep. For whatever reasons, Keynesian policies have always been controversial in the United States, and associated with the liberal side of the political spectrum—despite President Nixon's famous proclamation that "I am now a Keynesian in economics." So most Republicans opposed Keynesian stimulus from the get-go— branding fiscal stimulus as an incursion into free markets, an expansion of government, and wasteful to boot. The partisan battle over stimulus in the opening weeks of the Obama administration helped sow the seeds of the severe backlash that would come later.

KEYNESIAN ECONOMICS AND STIMULUS

Keynesian economics is based on the notion that unemployment arises when total or aggregate *demand* in an economy falls short of the economy's ability to *supply* goods and services. When products go unsold, jobs are lost.

Aggregate demand, in turn, comes from two sources: the private sector (which is the majority) and the government. At times, aggregate demand is too buoyant—goods fly off the shelves and labor is in great demand—and we get rising inflation. At other times, aggregate demand is inadequate—goods are hard to sell and jobs are hard to find. In those cases, Keynes argued in the 1930s, governments can boost employment by cutting interest rates (what we now call looser monetary policy), raising their own spending, or cutting people's taxes (what we now call looser fiscal policy). By the same logic, when there is too much demand, governments can fight actual or incipient inflation by raising interest rates (tightening monetary policy), increasing taxes, or reducing its own spending (thus tightening fiscal policy). That's part of standard Keynesian economics, too, although Keynes, writing during the Great Depression, did not emphasize it.

Setting aside the underlying theory, the central Keynesian policy idea is that the government can—and, Keynes argued, *should*—act as a kind of balance wheel, *stimulating* aggregate demand when it's too weak and restraining aggregate demand when it's too strong. For decades, American economists took for granted that most of that job should and would be done by monetary policy. Fiscal policy, they thought, was too slow, too cumbersome, and too political. And in the months after the Lehman Brothers failure, the Federal Reserve did, indeed, pull out all the stops—while fiscal policy did nothing. But what happens when, as was more or less the case by December 2008, the central bank has done almost everything it can, and yet the economy is still sinking? That's why eyes started turning toward Congress and the president—that is, toward *fiscal* stimulus—after the 2008 election.

A Terribly Timed Transition

The long transition period in 2008–2009 was terribly timed. The U.S. economy was weak and getting weaker when Senator Barack Obama was elected president on November 4, 2008. But it was in far worse shape when he was finally sworn in seventy-seven days later. According to the payroll survey, we lost 489,000 jobs in October 2008, the first full month after the Lehman bankruptcy. Then we lost another 2.3 million jobs while the president-elect waited in the wings: 803,000 in November; 661,000 in December; and 818,000 in January. The economy was sinking like a ship taking on water, and jobs were sinking with it as frightened employers pared their payrolls. No wonder the satirical newspaper the *Onion* led its November 5 edition with this tongue-in-cheek headline: "Black Man Given Nation's Worst Job."

Then another big problem got dropped into the economic hopper. Five days after the election, General Motors, once among the mightiest of America's corporations and still employing almost 100,000 people, announced that it would run out of cash around the middle of 2009 unless it received government assistance, sold assets, or was merged into another company. (GM subsequently shortened its time frame.) GM was not alone. A long streak of bad business decisions, plus effective foreign competition, plus rising oil prices, which made gas guzzlers unattractive, had brought the U.S. auto industry to its knees. Then came the severe recession, threatening to deliver the knockout blow.

On November 18, 2008, the CEOs of GM, Ford, and Chrysler all showed up at a congressional hearing trying—unsuccessfully, as it turned out—to solicit federal aid. Displaying amazingly deaf political ears, all three flew to Washington—to plead for taxpayer assistance—on their corporate jets! Appearances aside, bankruptcy for Detroit's Big Three looked like a real possibility that would have dire consequences for their dealers, suppliers, and workers. Not to mention for states like Michigan and Ohio. Not to mention for the staggering national economy.

On December 19, the ultraconservative President Bush let pragmatism trump ideology and tapped the TARP for multibillion-dollar bridge loans to both GM and Chrysler. (Ford was in better shape.) "Bridges to what?" many people asked. Well, basically, bridges to the incoming Obama administration, which was forced to add yet another big headache to its to-do list. (*The ball is in your court, Barack.*) The "auto bailout," as it would come to be called, would eventually have President Obama's name and fingerprints all over it. But in December 2008, he was not yet president.

Although Chairman Bernanke and the Fed were still working monetary policy hard, the lack of presidential leadership during those critical months hurt. Finding President Bush was a bit like playing "Where's Waldo?" You knew he was in there somewhere, but for the most part, the outgoing president was neither seen nor heard. CBS News estimated that he spent nearly a third of his time on vacation, often at his Texas ranch. It seemed like more. The president appeared to be alarmingly out of touch and had apparently delegated management of the economic crisis entirely to his secretary of the Treasury.

President-elect Obama, on the other hand, was seen *and* heard often. He was all over the media. The American public naturally turned to their new leader—who had run on a platform of "change"—with great anticipation. After all, an African American had just been elected president of the United States. Didn't that mean he could walk on water? Expectations for

Barack Obama ran so high that he could only disappoint them.* But until January 20, 2009, he didn't have the power to do anything—except to form a team and make plans.

To deal with the burgeoning economic catastrophe, President-elect Obama assembled what many at the time called a "Dream Team." For secretary of the Treasury, he tapped Tim Geithner, who was smart, deeply experienced, and battle-tested from fighting financial crises both in the Clinton Treasury and as president of the New York Fed—but who, therefore, also carried with him the political baggage from Bear Stearns, Lehman Brothers, AIG, and the rest. Geithner apparently edged out Larry Summers, who had been Bill Clinton's last secretary of the Treasury and wanted his old job back. Ironically, Geithner had followed Summers up the Treasury ladder during the Clinton administration, starting as Summers's personal assistant in 1993 and finishing as one of his undersecretaries in 2000. All the while, he had been Summers's underling—until now.

That looked like a potential problem when Obama turned around and appointed Summers to be his national economic adviser, director of the National Economic Council (NEC). Everyone knew that Summers was brilliant; if you ever forgot, he was eager to remind you. But while he was among the smartest people on earth, he was not among the best organized. He was also acerbic, domineering, and argumentative. Perhaps not the ideal character traits for the role of NEC director, who is supposed to be the "honest broker" among competing interests and personalities on the president's economic team. Pretty soon, Geithner and Summers were sparring, albeit in a generally friendly manner. According to one of their administration colleagues, "[Larry] viewed Tim as junior to him. While he respected the office, he thought of Tim at some level as a grad student who needed feedback and critiques."

For budget director, Obama nominated economist Peter Orszag. Though just forty years old, Orszag had accumulated a wealth of valuable

---

*As just one example of public opinion at the time, a mid-January *New York Times*/CBS poll found that 79 percent of Americans were optimistic about the four years under President Obama—higher than for any of the previous five new presidents—even though times were demonstrably horrible.

experience as director of the Congressional Budget Office (CBO) and was an acknowledged expert on the federal budget—and especially on health care, which would come in handy. The appointment drew nothing but applause. According to the *Washington Post*, "On Capitol Hill, the reactions to Orszag bordered on bipartisan bliss."* But it wasn't long before Orszag and Summers were practically at war.

Rounding out the quartet of top economic advisers, the president-elect nominated Christina "Christy" Romer, a University of California, Berkeley, professor who, like Bernanke, was an expert on the Great Depression, to chair his Council of Economic Advisers (CEA). Romer was virtually unknown in Washington, and she, in turn, did not know Washington. Nor did she have any preexisting relationship with Obama—unlike Austan Goolsbee, who had been the campaign's chief economic adviser and who was awkwardly placed below Romer.

The Dream Team was soon having nightmares. Orszag clashed repeatedly with Summers and was the first member of the quartet to depart (in July 2010). Romer, who showed a lot of backbone in a job with little inherent power, followed a few months later. Journalist Ron Suskind reported that she felt "increasingly isolated in her job, excluded from the broader discussion by Summers." As she left, she declared Summers to be one of her best friends, thereby ruining her reputation for honesty. Summers himself left the White House at the end of the year. Each had worked his or her fingers to the bone. Only Geithner, the *primus inter pares*, lasted two years; and he stuck it out past the 2012 election.

That settled the economic team's structure, right? Wrong. President-elect Obama then added a bunch of "czars" with special responsibilities for crucial areas of policy—and who did not report to either Geithner, Summers, or Orszag. Specifically, Nancy-Ann DeParle was named health care czar,† and Carol Browner was named energy and climate change czar. Two talented and experienced people, but aren't health care and energy/climate

---

** *Truth-in-writing notice:* Orszag was once a student of mine.
† Obama originally wanted Tom Daschle, the former Senate majority leader, to fill this role. But Daschle ran into confirmation problems.

issues of *economic* policy? How could DeParle and Browner be in charge
if there was a secretary of the Treasury and an NEC Director? A good
question—to which Summers apparently had a ready answer: They
weren't.

Finally, there was the wild card, Gene Sperling. Sperling, who had held
the top NEC post in the second Clinton administration, was given a kind of
bigshot-without-portfolio position at the Treasury—a job specifically created to give him a seat at the table. Officially, he was a counselor to the secretary. But, in fact, Sperling was granted a kind of roaming license, enabling
him to pop in on issues and meetings of his choice. Being a remarkable
bundle of energy who could outwork and outlast almost anybody, Sperling
naturally chose almost everything. When Summers departed, Sperling assumed the top NEC job.

It was a talented team, to be sure. But Summers's bull-in-a-china-shop
manner was worrisome. And with Geithner and Summers occupying the
top rungs, it all appeared—and probably was—a bit too pro–Wall Street
for the times. Besides, the players were slotted into the org chart from hell.
How would it all work? Orszag later told Suskind that it didn't: "I think
part of the problem was the lines of organization were so jumbled from the
start that no one was quite sure of their role, or what they were supposed to
be doing. What is the economic team? What is the health care team?"

There was also a further problem, which would haunt the administration time and again. In this time of trauma and deep economic anxi-
ety, with new policies flying around at warp speed, who would be the
administration's principal economic spokesman? Who would explain
things to the people? Fixing the economy was going to be a long, hard,
complicated slog. Who had the eloquence and persistence to provide a narrative to a frightened and bewildered public?

The secretary of the Treasury is the obvious choice in most administrations. But everyone soon learned that, despite his many talents, Geithner
was a terrible orator. Put him into a room to interact with a small group,
ask him to think on his feet, give him knotty problems to solve, and he
excels. I've witnessed it myself, many times. But put him in front of a mi-
crophone with a teleprompter and a large crowd watching as TV cameras

roll, and he seems to turn wooden. His clipped manner of speech and staccato delivery just don't work as oratory, and his diminutive physical stature doesn't help, either.

What about Summers, then? As a former professor, he could certainly deliver a coherent, well-organized speech, replete with alliterative adjectives, arresting adverbs, and meaningful metaphors—and he could do it all without notes. (Remember, he was brilliant.) But somehow Summers's speeches always came across as mixtures of arrogance and grouchiness. While Summers would prove to be hugely influential behind the scenes, the administration was loath to use him as its public face. Orszag may or may not have coveted the role. But he didn't get it. It fell to Romer to fill it more than anyone else on the economic team—even though the CEA chair was the lowest-ranked member of the quartet, was supposed to be the ultimate technocrat, and had no past history with Obama.

In truth, the job of principal spokesperson on *economic* policy fell to *politicos* like David Axelrod—who were not the best equipped to do it—or to President Obama himself, which meant that it mostly went begging. During the crisis and its aftermath, the eloquent young president delivered amazingly few speeches on the economy and his economic policies. No wonder the American people never really "got it," never formulated a clear mental picture of how we got into this mess, never understood how Obama's policies were supposed to get us out, and never bought the argument that things would have been much worse without the stimulus, the TARP, and all that. Instead, Obamanomics was an incoherent blur to most citizens—and not a very successful blur, at that. The president and the country would pay a steep price for his failure to communicate, to educate, and to convince.

LASER BEAM OR SCATTERSHOT?

During the transition, and intensifying after Inauguration Day 2009, the American people focused intently on their disintegrating economy. Sure, there were two wars going on and a variety of other pressing issues. But there was little doubt about what was foremost on people's minds. In James Carville's memorable words, it was the economy, stupid. A Gallup poll released right before Inauguration Day found that about 76 percent of respondents chose either the economy, unemployment, or "lack of money" as the most important problem facing the nation. The top noneconomic concern, the Iraq war, polled just 13 percent. After all, a disaster was unfolding, and Americans found themselves dragooned into being unwitting extras in a bad movie. They were looking desperately for a John Wayne character to ride to their rescue. How would the dynamic new president pull us out of the nosedive? He could pull rabbits out of hats, couldn't he?

Bill Clinton, the previous Democratic president, had famously pledged during his transition to "focus like a laser beam on the economy." It helped frame and define the Clinton presidency. Barack Obama apparently wanted no such constraining frame. He intended to do much more, including health care. So he made no such defining declaration. And it hurt him badly.

Not that focusing like a laser beam on the economy would have left Obama a lot of spare time to sharpen his golf game. The new president had to lead the economy out of the deepest recession since the 1930s— presumably with a big fiscal stimulus package. He had to make sure the economy then grew fast enough to create jobs, jobs, jobs—for nearly 3 million jobs had been lost since Lehman Day in September 2008, and another 4.3 million would disappear before payrolls finally bottomed out in February 2010.

He also had to, first, apply multiple tourniquets to the bleeding financial system, and then nurse it back to health—using whatever was left of the hated TARP, among other things. While doing so, he had to combat the coming tsunami of home mortgage foreclosures, which would otherwise throw millions of American families out of their homes. Then he almost certainly had to develop and propose sweeping reforms of the financial regulatory system, which had failed the nation badly, with horrific consequences. And he needed a plan for either bailing out the Big Three automakers or limiting the fallout from their demise. Okay, now exhale.

That was a vastly longer to-do list than Clinton had inherited. And almost every item on it would require that Obama shepherd highly controversial legislation through a contentious and highly partisan Congress. Furthermore, this list is limited to the *economic* issues that he had no choice but to deal with—the *mandatories*, you might say. But there were also the *optionals*, including big and complex issues like health care reform, which he had campaigned hard on, and energy and climate-change policies, which were also near and dear to his heart. Besides all this, there were many not-so-optional items *outside* the economic sphere, like the ongoing wars in Iraq and Afghanistan, which would just not go away. And whatever could be done about Pakistan. And ending torture and closing Guantánamo. And dealing with illegal immigration. And more.

All this would have constituted a daunting to-do list for a veteran political hand with extensive executive experience, deep Washington connections, and intimate knowledge of how to pull the levers of Congress. It was surely the toughest policy agenda to face a new president since Franklin Roosevelt in 1933. But in January 2009, it was all handed to a young, rookie president whose total national political experience consisted of two years as a U.S. senator before he went into campaign mode. Just four and a half years earlier, Barack Obama had been teaching law at the University of Chicago and serving in the Illinois State legislature.

The new president made a fateful decision early on, one that would define his presidency. He would try to be a transformational president. He would not limit himself to the must-dos; rather, he would take on other big things that needed attention. (Was this the Emanuel principle in action?: *"You never want a serious crisis to go to waste."*) Or, to put a less favorable spin on it, he would adopt a scattershot approach, trying to do everything at once, rather than "focus like a laser beam on the economy." Geithner objected, insisting to his new boss, "Your signature accomplishment is going to be preventing a Great Depression," to which Obama responded: "That's not enough for me."

It was in many ways an admirable decision. For example, Democratic presidents had been striving for universal health insurance since Truman in 1947, without success. Could this, finally, be the moment? (It was.) If so, could Obama let the moment pass? (He didn't.) But historians will long debate whether it was a wise decision. One White House aide later confessed, "No one thought we would have to take every element of the administration and dedicate it to health care both publicly and privately, which is what we ended up having to do." They should have known that.

Among its many side effects, Obama's decision to try to do everything at once meant that his personal attention, and that of his administration, would be scattered across a myriad of complex issues. It meant that the congressional circuits would be overloaded and that the new president would find his political capital spent profligately on a vast portfolio of issues. It left the public confused about what Barack Obama really stood for. What *was* this new president's agenda? "Everything" is not an answer. Most germane to the themes of this book, the lack of focus meant that the public never acquired a clear picture of President Obama's economic strategy. *(Let's see now. How does giving the uninsured health care help us out of the recession?)*

And there was one more huge problem—an insuperable barrier, actually. *Candidate* Barack Obama had declared his intention to get past the bitter partisanship that had characterized the Clinton and Bush II years. He said he wanted to be a *postpartisan* president: "If we think that we can use the same partisan playbook where we just challenge our opponent's patriotism to win an election, then the American people will lose. The times are too serious for this kind of politics." After the election, one White House aide recalled to journalist Noam Scheiber, "We all believed that the vote was so strong from the public . . . that Republicans would have to be bipartisan."

The naïveté makes me wince even today. A bipartisan tango takes two, and congressional Republicans were in no mood to dance. Rather, as Senate Minority Leader Mitch McConnell (R-KY) later admitted with startling honesty, "The single most important thing we want to achieve is for President Obama to be a one-term president." When *President* Obama met the U.S. Congress in January 2009, the Republicans were armed for bear.

Meanwhile, Back at the Fed

There were no Republican-versus-Democratic squabbles at Federal Reserve headquarters on Constitution Avenue, although the usual arguments between hawks, who always seem fixated on inflation, and doves, who agonize over unemployment, continued. By late 2008, however, the Fed's policy agenda was pretty clear. Bernanke and his colleagues were still focused on doing whatever they could to rescue the faltering financial system and to cushion the recessionary blow.

The December 16, 2008, meeting of the Federal Open Market Committee (FOMC), the last during the Bush administration, turned out to be a landmark. During the three months that had elapsed since Lehman Day, a frail U.S. economy had descended into disaster, and the Fed had taken numerous drastic actions—most of which the central bank's hawks didn't like. Prior to the December 16 meeting, market speculation was rampant about what more the Fed should, could, and would do next.

There were three main candidates: The first was more conventional open-market policy. While the federal funds rate was already down to a superlow 1 percent, the FOMC could lower it still further. The markets thought a 50-basis-point cut most likely. Second, the Committee could try to reduce longer-term interest rates by committing to holding its overnight rate low for a long time. Some called that "open-mouth policy." The idea is based on the *expectations theory of the yield curve*, which is explained in the accompanying box. Third, the Fed could keep on expanding its balance sheet, which had already soared from $924 billion the week before Lehman to $2,262 billion on December 11. Which option would the Fed choose?

It turned out to be all of the above. In the FOMC's own language, it decided to use "all available tools" to fight the recession. Of course, Bernanke was inventing tools as he went along. For openers, the federal funds rate was slashed from 1 percent to a range between 0 and 25 basis points. It was the biggest rate cut in twenty-six years and more than the markets had expected. Over the next year, the effective federal funds rate would average 16 basis points.

THE EXPECTATIONS THEORY OF THE YIELD CURVE

The idea that intermediate- and long-term interest rates depend on beliefs (or *expectations*) about what overnight interest rates (like the federal funds rate) will be in the future is called the *expectations theory of the yield curve*. It is the basis for Federal Reserve policies that make implicit or explicit commitments about future interest rates.

Here's a simple example: If one-day money costs 2 percent (annualized) today, and the market *expects* one-day money to cost 3 percent tomorrow, how much should two-day money cost today? Think about it. If you take out two consecutive one-day loans, your *expected* average cost of funds will be 2.5 percent: 2 percent for the first day and 3 percent for the next. If, instead, you borrow for two days, the appropriate interest rate should also be 2.5 percent, because two simple strategies for borrowing money for two days should cost the same.

Now let's extend the logic to a longer time frame. The one-*year* interest rate should be roughly the average of all the overnight interest rates *expected* over the next 365 days. The two-year interest rate should approximate the average *expected* overnight rate for the next 730 days, and so on. Notice the crucial role of *expectations* about the *future* in determining *current* long-term interest rates.

When the Fed declared in December 2008 that it would hold the federal funds rate near zero "for some time," it instilled the belief in market participants that the funds rate would remain near zero for . . . how long? No one knew, because the phrase "for some time" is vague. But it certainly covered *at least* three to six months. That should have driven down expected overnight rates over horizons extending out at least three to six months. Similarly, when the Fed declared in August 2011 that it would keep the funds rate near zero for almost two years,

> that should have driven down expected overnight rates covering at least two years. In that way, Fed announcements have leverage over intermediate and long rates.

Second, the Fed's postmeeting statement added words of commitment "that weak economic conditions are likely to warrant exceptionally low levels of the federal funds rate for some time." English translation: *We're going to keep the funds rate in that range for quite a while, folks.* Two meetings later, the FOMC changed the phrase "for some time" to the phrase "for an extended period," which it would use until August 2011, when it changed its verbal commitment to keep rates low to "at least through mid-2013" and later to even longer periods than that.

Third, the FOMC promised further expansions of its balance sheet—on several fronts. It would "expand its purchases of agency debt and mortgage-backed securities." It was "evaluating the potential benefits of purchasing longer-term Treasury securities." (In Fed-speak, that meant it would definitely do it.) And it would begin purchasing private assets under the TALF (Term Asset-Backed Securities Loan Facility) "early next year." (TALF purchases actually began on March 3, 2009.)

It was a trifecta, and markets stood up and cheered the Fed's aggressive response. The S&P 500 rose 5 percent that day. The Fed's hawks went along kicking and screaming (internally). The dire outlook was overwhelming their usual zeal for tighter money. The good news was that Bernanke and the FOMC doves were firmly in control. The bad news was that the Fed was nearly out of bullets. Eyes would now turn to *fiscal* policy.

PLANNING FOR FISCAL STIMULUS

The Obama transition team was busy formulating plans for a large fiscal stimulus package that would eventually become the American Reinvestment and Recovery Act of 2009 (ARRA)—the "Recovery Act" for short.

There had been a modest fiscal stimulus package under President Bush earlier in the year. The title of that bill had even used the word "stimulus," which was not then a pejorative term to Republicans. In February 2008, with the perceived risk of recession rising, Congress passed the Economic Stimulus Act of 2008, and the president eagerly signed it into law. The act adopted the standard Bush remedy for everything: No matter what the problem, cut taxes. Specifically, most American taxpayers received a one-time income tax rebate ranging from $300 to $600 for single individuals and from $600 to $1,200 for married couples. There were also several business tax breaks, aimed at spurring investment, and, as always, a few stray cats and dogs. The one-year estimated cost of the package was about $150 billion, roughly 1 percent of GDP.

During the debate over that bill, economists, led by Larry Summers, then a private (but not a quiet) citizen, developed a catchy new catechism for any effective stimulus program: Such a program should be timely, targeted, and temporary—the three *T*s. (It was the phrasing that was new, not the concepts.) The three *T*s would come back to haunt Summers and his Obama administration colleagues a year later.

Timely meant that the stimulus should be fast-acting. That dictum put a big dent into some Democrats' favorite idea: spending more money on public infrastructure. Building roads and bridges may be wonderful on the merits, many liberal economists said, but it doesn't belong in a short-term stimulus package. The spend-out rates are simply too long and shouldn't be rushed. If engineers tell us that the right amount of time to build a bridge is two years, but we rush it out in six months, would you want to cross it?

Targeted meant that the program should have a large aggregate demand "bang" for each government spending or tax cut "buck." The federal government did, after all, have a budget deficit problem on its hands. Spewing out public money on items that didn't add much to aggregate demand would widen the deficit without stimulating the economy much.

Temporary was obvious, and virtually inherent in the very idea of fiscal stimulus. Stimulus is not intended either to enlarge the public sector (as some of its critics claimed) or to shrink the revenue base (as some of those same critics desired). Rather, the basic idea behind fiscal stimulus is to boost aggregate demand in the short run *and then go away*. That way, we can stimulate the economy when necessary without damaging the long-run budget picture, which, even then, was dreadful.

While the precise amount is in dispute, there is little doubt that the 2008 tax rebates gave the U.S. economy a modest shot in the arm. But after the election, as the economy slid into what was starting to look like an abyss, that "modest" shot was clearly not enough. During the transition, Team Obama started planning for a much larger fiscal stimulus, to be introduced as one of the first acts of the incoming administration. As Goolsbee said on *Face the Nation* in November: "We're out with the dithering; we're in with a bang." *Translation: A stimulus of 1 percent of GDP was chicken feed.*

Soon Obama's stimulus plans were provoking fierce internal arguments and leaking like a sieve—or perhaps like a bunch of trial balloons. But the transition team probably had no idea what was about to hit them. To paraphrase Barney Frank again, the national commitment to bipartisanship lasted one day—not even. The era of good feeling was over even before Barack Obama was inaugurated.

According to press reports, President-elect Obama was going to ask for a stimulus package in the $700 billion to $800 billion range, roughly 5 percent of GDP. Too much, said Republicans. But liberals like Paul Krugman (publicly) and Christy Romer (privately) said it was too little. As the debate raged within the administration-in-waiting, these opposing criticisms from Left and Right may have made Obama feel that he was about in the right place.

A substantial chunk of the proposed stimulus would take the form of tax cuts, though more progressive ones than President Bush always favored. For example, the president-elect wanted (and got) a "Make Work Pay" tax credit that would be paid even to workers who earned too little to owe income taxes but who did pay payroll taxes. Republicans derided that idea as "welfare." (Wait, aren't payroll taxes *taxes*?) Another portion of the planned stimulus would go for infrastructure spending. Republicans didn't like that idea, either; it was more government spending, not tax cuts. And a third big piece would be aid to state and local governments, so they would not have to slash their payrolls and raise taxes as much. Republicans opposed that, too, claiming it would not stimulate the economy. (How come? Aren't government jobs *jobs*?)

And then there were the three *T*s. Despite some external criticisms, including some friendly fire, the administration-in-waiting argued that the need for stimulus was likely to be far less *temporary* than in past recessions—after all, this one looked like a whopper, both very long and very deep. (Good point.) That thought, in turn, made infrastructure spending a more plausible candidate for stimulus. (Also a good point.) Even if the spend-out took two years, the economy would probably still need support in 2011. Infrastructure spending would still be *timely*. Besides, Obama's team argued, they would concentrate the stimulus dollars on "shovel-ready" projects.* (Bad point. Never believe a governor or mayor who claims a project is shovel-ready.) I'll return to *targeted* shortly.

The Rocky Road to the Recovery Act

The House of Representatives eagerly went along with the new president—indeed, House members had conferred with Obama's transition team on the details. With the large Democratic majority ushered in by the 2008 election guided by the firm hand of Speaker Nancy Pelosi, the House passed the stimulus bill on January 28, 2009, by a comfortable 244–188 margin. But not a single yes vote came from a Republican—not one. Republicans decried *any* federal spending as suspect and wasteful, even in a recession, and saw saving a government job as saving something that shouldn't be saved. The Obama administration was a mere eight days old. It was a portent of things to come.

The fight was much harder in the Senate, where, as Harry Reid had explained to Hank Paulson, it take sixty votes to flush the toilets. Though in the minority, Senate Republicans used the threat of filibuster to force

---

*Obama later joked, "Shovel-ready was not as . . . uh . . . shovel-ready as we expected."

huge concessions out of Obama and the Democrats, including a variety of business tax cuts that the president didn't want and which probably wouldn't stimulate the economy much. In return, the "cooperation" they offered turned out to be exactly three votes. That isn't much, but all three votes were essential. After numerous House-Senate differences were ironed out in conference, the final Senate vote was 60–38. The price tag placed on the ARRA at the time was $787 billion, or roughly 5.5 percent of GDP, though CBO reestimates subsequently raised the cost to around $830 billion.

Several noteworthy things happened along the rocky road to passage of the Recovery Act. Two would prove to be harbingers of things to come; two would create damaging symbols; and two would severely handicap any further fiscal stimulus.

The Harbingers

The first indicator of things to come was the immediate breakdown of bipartisanship. Did I say *breakdown?* In truth, bipartisanship never got started. The first two letters of *bi*partisan connote the need for *two* parties, but President Obama never had a partner on the other side. Apparently unwilling to believe that Republicans could be that obstinate, the new president reached out to them time and time again—and got next to nothing in return.

Which was the second harbinger: Obama, new to the job and new to Washington, proved to be a terrible bargainer, giving away the store in return for a few crumbs. He aimed to please, while they aimed to destroy— which produced lopsided results at the negotiating table. Remember, the Republicans controlled neither the White House, nor the Senate, nor the House at the time. Yet they won numerous concessions. Both Obama's vain attempts at bipartisanship and his pliability at the bargaining table would become recurrent themes of his administration. Republicans reaped great political success as the "Party of No." Democrats came to see Obama as a serial capitulator.

The Symbols

One unfortunate legacy of the tarring of the Recovery Act was the tarring of the name—and even the concept—of stimulus. Never mind that Bush's 2008 tax cuts had been named the Economic *Stimulus* Act. Even before the ink was dry on the 2009 stimulus bill, Republicans were attacking it as misguided, futile, full of pork, ineffective, even a step toward socialism. Almost immediately after passage, they began a campaign to repeal it. The Republicans lacked the votes, but their campaign succeeded in giving stimulus in general, and the Recovery Act in particular, a bad name. When the economy proved to need more support in 2010, 2011, and 2012, no politician even dared utter the word "stimulus." It had become an eight-letter word—sort of like two four-letter words.

The other symbol turned out to be the number 7, or rather $700 *billion*. The Recovery Act was originally, and erroneously, priced at $787 billion. The TARP legislation, which had passed just one hundred days earlier, appropriated $700 billion (but actually spent much less). The two three-digit numbers thus both started with the numeral 7. This coincidence invited confusion, and the TARP was reviled by everyone. Pretty soon, people started thinking that the stimulus bill had given away $700 billion to bankers. For example, a 2010 CNN poll found that 54 percent of Americans believed that the stimulus helped bankers and investors rather than the middle class. In fact, the stimulus had nothing much to do with the welfare of bankers and investors per se. (The TARP, of course, did.) It was a case of guilt by mistaken association.*

I must admit that when I first heard the numerology idea set forth by an astute veteran congressman, I dismissed it as ridiculous. Was anyone confusing J. D. Drew, then the Boston Red Sox's journeyman right fielder, who wore number 7 on his back, with the New York Yankees' immortal Mickey Mantle? But as I heard the confusion idea repeated by several other

---

*Speaking of guilt by mistaken association, a Pew Center poll in July 2010 found that 47 percent of Americans thought that the TARP had been "passed and signed into law under President Obama." Only 34 percent thought it was President Bush.

politicians—all of whom are in far better touch with ordinary people than we economists are—I started to believe it. After all, Americans pay closer attention to baseball than to public policy. It would not have taken much effort to boost the size of the stimulus package to, say, $802 billion, thereby eliminating the confusion. And it was eventually scored higher than that, anyway. But who knew at the time?

The Handicaps

As mentioned earlier, one of the three *Ts* was *targeted:* A well-designed stimulus should produce a lot of bang for the buck. But when it came to targeting *jobs,* the 2009 stimulus package earned a B at best. Let me explain why.

The basic philosophy behind creating jobs through fiscal stimulus might be called "build it and they will come." Build a bigger GDP, and more jobs will come. It works because you need more labor to produce more goods and services. But it's expensive for a simple reason. The United States is a rich country, with a highly productive workforce. Specifically, in 2010 there was about $112,000 worth of GDP for each payroll job. If stimulus creates *average* jobs by raising GDP, it should therefore cost about $112,000 of GDP per job created. By no coincidence, as we'll see shortly, that number is close to the cost-per-job that the Obama administration and other macroeconomic modelers estimated for the 2009 stimulus package. Importantly, a $112,000 per job price tag doesn't mean that the stimulus package was poorly designed. That's why I gave it a B, not a D. To create jobs more cheaply, policy makers must go out of their way to *target* job creation explicitly.

How? One idea, which the incoming Obama administration considered but rejected, is called the *new jobs tax credit* (NJTC). Under such a plan, businesses would be offered, say, a $5,000 annual tax credit for each employee they *add* to their payrolls. If the average employee costs $50,000 a year, the effect is like cutting wages by 10 percent. The statistical evidence clearly shows that firms hire more workers when wages are lower, which is hardly a surprise. And estimates at the time suggested that the cost of the NJTC per job created would run in the $35,000 to $40,000 range, making it roughly three times as efficient as general fiscal stimulus.

Yet the incoming administration decided *not* to make the NJTC part of its stimulus plan—even though it is a business tax cut, which Republicans supposedly love.* Why not? There were some tricky technical issues to deal with; for example, you have to make sure businesses don't get the tax credit by firing Peter and hiring Paul. But the biggest reason appears to have been that the idea garnered so little support from the business community, which was skeptical that the NJTC would work. Many businesspeople apparently told the president-elect and his advisers that it wouldn't induce them to hire any more workers. A business tax cut without business support is dead in the political water.

But, as precious few people understand, these objections don't undercut the efficacy of the policy. Notice that the cost estimate mentioned above is, say, $40,000 for each new job actually created, even though the tax credit is only $5,000 per job. That implies that the credit is "wasted" in seven out of eight cases. Even with such a high "failure rate," the NJTC is almost three times more efficient at creating jobs than general fiscal stimulus. But the argument was too subtle by half. Try explaining it to a politician who is hearing negligible support from businesspeople in his home district, who prefer getting cash with no strings attached.

The second big handicap was a self-inflicted wound. On January 10, 2009, in response to mounting criticism, the Obama transition team released a study of the likely effects of its proposed stimulus program, coauthored by Christy Romer and Jared Bernstein, who would soon be Vice President Joe Biden's chief economic adviser. Romer and Bernstein used conventional methods, similar to those of the CBO and other Keynesian macroeconomic modelers, and came to conventional conclusions. In particular, subject to admittedly large margins of error, they estimated that the stimulus package would raise real GDP at the end of 2010 by 3.7 percent and save or create nearly 3.7 million jobs. If you did the math, that came to

---

*In 2011 the president did propose a variant as part of his American Jobs Act. Republicans rejected it.

about $118,000 per job—right in line with the economy-wide average mentioned above. In other words, theirs was a credible jobs estimate, not braggadocio. It did not imply miracles.

But here was their mistake. They translated this estimated jobs gain into achieving a 7 percent unemployment rate in 2010:4, instead of 8.8 percent without any stimulus. In fact, they said that if the stimulus program was enacted, the unemployment rate would never go above 8 percent. *Never above 8 percent?* It was already 7.8 percent in January 2009, though Romer and Bernstein didn't know it at the time, and it would rise to 8.9 percent by April 2009—well before any stimulus program could have appreciable effects. The 8 percent number was silly from day one.

What happened? Both GDP and jobs were sinking like stones during the transition, making the Romer-Bernstein baseline forecast obsolete before it was published. Their analytical estimate implied that the stimulus would reduce the unemployment rate by about 1.8 percentage points (7 percent versus 8.8 percent) in 2010:4, which was reasonable.* But the *actual* unemployment rate in 2010:4 turned out to be 9.6 percent, *even with the stimulus*. And unemployment peaked at a horrific 10 percent, not 8 percent.

These appeared to be large errors, and the administration paid a heavy price for them. In particular, Republicans used the Romer-Bernstein peak-unemployment estimate of 8 percent as "proof" that the stimulus failed. The actual peak rate was 10 percent, wasn't it? Yes, it was. But in the absence of the stimulus package, it would probably have been closer to 12 percent. But try proving that point to a skeptical public suffering from high unemployment—or to a hostile political opposition trying to embarrass you. The 8 percent peak-unemployment estimate was used over and over again to hammer the Obama administration in general and the stimulus program in particular. While wrong-headed, the criticism was effective. It was still used by Mitt Romney in the 2012 election campaign.

There is a moral here for policy makers—and for technicians who serve them. Don't *overstate* your likely achievements; when in doubt, *understate* them. Had the two economists claimed that unemployment would

---

*The estimate that Mark Zandi and I would make a year and a half later was 1.7 percentage points.

peak at 10 percent *with* the stimulus or 11.8 percent *without*—or, better yet, just stuck with the 1.8-percentage-point unemployment *decrease* and not mentioned any levels at all—there would have been less criticism of their work, and less of the stimulus itself.

This advice is based on some personal experience. As a member of President Clinton's original Council of Economic Advisers, I was in charge of the five-year forecast that we produced in a great hurry in January 1993. Being cautious about what we would claim, we made a forecast that turned out to be *terrible*. From 1993 to 1998, the U.S. economy vastly outperformed it in every respect. But I've never received a whit of criticism for the horrible forecast—and, more important, neither did Clinton. The economy did great, and nobody much cared about the errant forecast. Had the economy done *worse* than forecasted, however, there would have been hell to pay—as there was after 2009.

The American Reinvestment and Recovery Act

The American Reinvestment and Recovery Act (ARRA) passed the Congress on February 17, 2009, barely four weeks into the new Obama administration. That was fast work, though the process was painful. By the time the Recovery Act passed, whatever bipartisanship might have been latent in the Republican Party was gone. In round numbers, the bill was one-third tax cuts; one-third new spending, such as on unemployment benefits and infrastructure; and one-third aid to state and local governments, especially to help states pay their Medicaid bills.

In terms of the three *T*s, the ARRA scored pretty well. *Timely:* The Act was passed speedily, close to the worst months of the recession, and spending ramped up quickly. From a standing start of zero, stimulus spending leaped to over $100 billion (over $400 billion at an annual rate) by the second quarter of 2009. *Targeted:* As discussed earlier, the ARRA was about average on this score. *Temporary:* The spending rate under the ARRA peaked in the second and third quarters of 2009, and then started a gradual decline. It was negligible by late 2011.

Did the Recovery Act work more or less as expected? Opinions are divided on this matter to this day. The highly publicized study by Zandi and me, published in July 2010, argued that it did. We were, predictably, praised by Democrats and excoriated by Republicans for saying that. (Googling "Blinder Zandi" turns up tens of thousands of entries, not all of them favorable!) Our numerical estimates corresponded well to those from other macroeconomic modelers in the Keynesian tradition—such as the CBO, Macroeconomic Advisers, and IHS Global Insight. The mechanism is straightforward: More government spending (or lower taxes) increases total demand in the economy; as firms produce more to meet this higher demand, they hire more workers. Simple, right? Apparently not, for several economists of the Right begged to differ. Among other things, they argued, our models were estimated only on *past* data (that's true; what other data are there?) and did not take account of what *actually happened* after the ARRA passed. We just plugged the provisions of the stimulus package into a model of the past. (Also true.)

A February 2011 study by two politically independent economists, James Feyrer and Bruce Sacerdote, of Dartmouth College, addressed these criticisms. They assessed the effectiveness of the 2009 stimulus spending by comparing what *actually* happened to employment in states and counties that received differing amounts of ARRA money. Thus their methodology had nothing to do with Keynesian macroeconomic models estimated on historical data, and everything to do with what actually happened on the ground where the stimulus money was spent.

For the spending components of the ARRA (not the tax cuts), they estimated a $170,000 cost per job created, which is well above our estimate but within the range of estimation error. However, Feyrer and Sacerdote emphasized that the effectiveness of the spending depended sensitively on which parts you examined. In particular, they estimated that education grants to states created hardly any net new jobs. If you excluded them, the rest of the stimulus spending created jobs for under $100,000 each. Thus I read their estimates as saying that the macro models were not far from the mark. So do they.

Yet the fact that unemployment rose higher than 8 percent is still, *to this day*, used to "prove" that the stimulus package failed. During the vitriolic budget battles in 2011, Republicans constantly asserted that higher government spending "kills jobs." How, I've always wondered, is that supposed to happen? When the federal government buys something from a private contractor, how does that *destroy* jobs? How could any government, even if it tried, spend over $800 billion without creating lots of jobs?

But you don't get far in political discourse with counterfactual arguments that "it would have been even worse." In 2009 and 2010, the public saw both a large stimulus package and a terribly weak economy. Republicans assured them that the former caused the latter. Democrats made their case poorly, or not at all.

The Exploding Budget Deficit

There is another line of attack on the Recovery Act: that it raised the federal budget deficit. That is arithmetically true, of course. But the charge ignores the third of the three *T*s. Stimulus spending is inherently *temporary*. According to CBO estimates, the ARRA raised the federal budget deficit by $183 billion in fiscal year 2009, a whopping $405 billion in FY2010, and $145 billion in FY2011 (which ended on September 30, 2011). For fiscal year 2012, the CBO's budget-impact estimate is just $49 billion—with another $49 billion dribbling out over fiscal years 2013–2019. And these are all so-called static estimates; they do not include any feedback from stimulus to higher GDP and, therefore, to higher tax receipts. So the actual deficit impacts are smaller.

Yet the federal budget deficit ballooned from 3.2 percent of GDP in fiscal year 2008, a pretty normal number, to an astounding 10.1 percent of GDP in fiscal 2009—the largest deficit relative to GDP since World War II. Why? As table 8.1 shows, the lion's share of the increase in the deficit came from losses of revenue and increases in "income security" payments attributable to the shrinking economy and to government efforts, via the ARRA and the TARP, to revive it.

TABLE 8.1 Deficit Alarm

(CHANGES in the federal budget, 2008–2009, in billions of dollars)

Category	FY 2008 Budget	FY 2009 Budget	Change in Deficit
Overall deficit	$459	$1,413	**+$954**
Revenue, excluding ARRA	$2,524	$2,174	+$350
ARRA revenue	0	–$69	+$69
TARP	0	$152[a]	+$152
ARRA spending	0	$114	+$114
Income security[b]	$261	$350	+$89
Total			**+$774**

a TARP "spending" was not really spending, as virtually all of it was recouped. But it did raise the recorded deficit.

b Income security includes such categories as unemployment insurance compensation, SSI, nutrition programs, and the refundable portions of certain tax credits. Some of this was ARRA spending.

SOURCE: Congressional Budget Office, *The Budget and Economic Outlook: Fiscal Years 2011–2021*, January 2011

Okay, so it was explicable. But trillion-dollar deficits were still appalling to most Americans. They *felt* wrong. This isn't Greece—or Argentina. The U.S. government does not run budget deficits of 10 percent of GDP. With the budget deficit still stratospheric in 2010 and 2011, much of the often-raw politics was consumed by highly partisan debates over whom to blame for the deficit and how to reduce it quickly. In 2011 some Republicans even pushed for *immediate* budget balance, either by refusing to raise the national debt ceiling or by passing a balanced-budget amendment to the Constitution. Think about it: The fiscal year 2011 budget was in deficit to the tune of about $1.3 trillion, nearly 9 percent of GDP. A quick move to zero would almost certainly have led us straight into a deep recession. Yet this policy had many advocates.

It would be a rank understatement to say that the budget debates of
2010 and 2011 had a profoundly anti-Keynesian flavor. Had anyone roused
the great Cambridge don from his grave, he would surely have groused that
you don't raise taxes or reduce government spending when your economy is
in the doldrums. You do the opposite. Moreover, he would have been
shocked to hear that anyone in 2011 was still asking the question. The
Earth is not flat. The moon is not made of cheese. Evolution really happened. And you don't give your economy a short-run boost by cutting public spending.*

---

*The long-run is a different matter. There are powerful progrowth arguments for reducing government
budget deficits. I'll return to them later.

9

|iiiiiiiiiiiiiiiiiiiiiiiiii|

THE ATTACK ON
THE SPREADS

Credit is a system whereby a person who can't pay gets
another person who can't pay to guarantee that he can pay.

—CHARLES DICKENS

Credit is a coward. It struts around when times are good and lending risks are low, but runs and hides whenever risk rises. Since
credit is critical to any modern economy, that's a problem—and it
became an acute problem after Lehman Day. If we were to stave off Great
Depression 2.0, perceptions of risk had to be brought down to earth, and
that meant mounting an all-out attack on credit *spreads*.

On what? *Spreads* are a critical part of the cost of credit. Only the U.S.
government borrows at superlow Treasury rates. Everyone else pays more.
The interest-rate spread (over Treasuries) on a particular loan or fixed-
income security determines what it costs real people or real businesses to
borrow.

The remarkable widening of interest-rate spreads in 2008 was one of
the most stunning and worrisome features of the financial crisis. Indeed,
aficionados used spreads as a handy market measure of the severity of the

crisis. Consistent with this, the Federal Reserve's efforts to bring down spreads was one of the most critical aspects of its battle against the financial sickness. Many of the emergency actions the Fed adopted as it sought to set the financial system straight were designed, in one way or another, to reduce spreads. Indeed, while it took some time for everyone to realize it, the phrases "reduce spreads" and "fix the financial system" came pretty close to being synonymous. The sky-high spreads during the Panic of 2008 were more than just the canary in the coal mine. They were more like the methane gas; they had to be cleared out before the financial system could breathe freely again.

It's All in the Spreads

Why are interest-rate spreads so important? Any interest rate—whether it be on an auto loan, a home mortgage, or a corporate bond—can be thought of as the corresponding *riskless* rate (the rate at which the U.S. Treasury can borrow for the same period) plus a *risk premium*, or *spread*. For example, on April 26, 2011, AT&T, a truly blue-chip company, floated new 10-year bonds bearing an interest rate of 4.45 percent. Since the yield on 10-year Treasury bonds that day was 3.34 percent, the spread (over Treasuries) was 1.11 percent, or 111 basis points. Had the spread been higher, as it would have been during the crisis, AT&T would have had to pay more for ten-year money. Had I gone to the markets to borrow for ten years that same day (a fanciful thought!), I would have had to pay much more than 4.45 percent because I am not as good a credit as AT&T. (Actually, I might be, but bond buyers don't know that.) Thus, interest-rate spreads are crucial determinants of what it actually costs to borrow.

Risk spreads soared during the financial crisis, as did borrowing costs— for those able to borrow at all. Actually, the situation was a bit more complicated than that because Treasury rates actually *fell* as frightened investors sought the safe haven of U.S. Treasuries. To take one extreme example, during the post-Lehman panic in 2008, the yield on 6-month Treasury bills dropped from 1.80 percent on September 12 to as low as 0.82 percent on

October 10 as investors fled to safety. Over those same four weeks, the interest rate on 6-month financial-company commercial paper (CP) rose from 2.75 percent to 3.82 percent. The spread over Treasuries skyrocketed from 95 basis points (275 *minus* 180) to 300 basis points (382 *minus* 82)—a stunning increase of 205 basis points. However, because Treasury yields fell by 98 basis points, the CP rate itself rose only 107 basis points. That understated the degree of distress.

The standard analysis of *conventional* monetary policy—what we teach in textbooks and what central bankers are raised on—is predicated, roughly speaking, on *constant* risk spreads. When the Federal Reserve lowers *riskless* interest rates, like those on federal funds and T-bills, *riskier* interest rates, like those on corporate lending and auto loans, are supposed to follow suit.* The history on which we economists base our statistical models looks like that. Figure 9.1 shows the behavior of the interest rates on 10-year Treasuries (the lower line) and Moody's Baa corporate bonds (the upper line) over the period from January 1980 through June 2007, just before the crisis got started. The *spread* between these two rates is the vertical *distance* between the two lines, and the fact that they look roughly parallel means that the spread did not change much over those twenty-seven years.

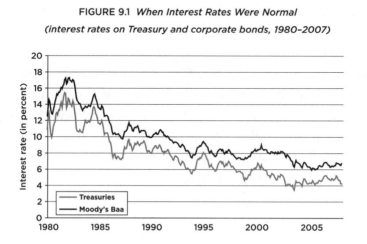

FIGURE 9.1 *When Interest Rates Were Normal*
(interest rates on Treasury and corporate bonds, 1980–2007)

*During the worst of the crisis, even federal funds were considered somewhat risky by the banks that traded them. Without any change in Fed policy, the funds rate prevailing on bank-to-bank borrowing rose from 2 percent (the Fed's target) on September 11 to 2.8 percent on September 17.

But the years 2008 and 2009 were starkly different. Risk spreads first spiked and then plummeted. Figure 9.2 displays two examples. Note that this figure, unlike the previous one, shows just the *spreads*, not the two underlying interest rates separately. (The right-hand panel of figure 9.2 corresponds to the two interest rates shown in figure 9.1.) In normal times, the lines in each panel of figure 9.2 would be roughly flat—depicting constant spreads. But no one called the years 2007–2009 normal.

FIGURE 9.2 *Spreads over Treasuries, Short-term and Long-term, 2007–2012*

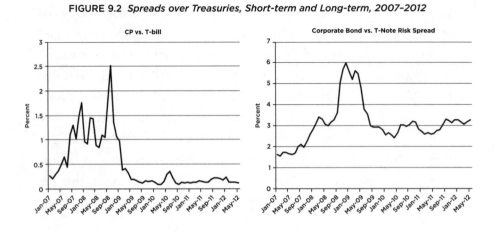

Much of *unconventional* monetary policy is designed to change risk spreads—in particular, to *reduce* spreads that have been pushed up by, for example, fear or extreme illiquidity. That's what the Federal Reserve set out to do in 2008 and 2009. And to a remarkable extent, it succeeded. Reversing the spike in spreads was tantamount to reducing the acute fears of illiquidity and insolvency that were gripping the markets at the time. To understand how the government pulled off this trick, let's start by asking where interest-rate spreads come from.

Understanding Spreads

Most borrowers pay substantially more than the U.S. Treasury to borrow money. One reason is comparative liquidity. The markets for Treasuries are the largest, broadest, and deepest in the world—the most *liquid*. If you are a hedge-fund trader, a corporate treasurer, a pension manager, or just a very rich person who may need to move large sums of money around on short notice, the Treasury markets offer you unmatchable liquidity. You can buy or sell huge amounts in minutes at known prices. So big money movers favor them, and Treasuries, therefore, trade at higher prices—thus, lower yields—than other securities.

But this is the minor reason for interest-rate spreads. The major reason is the absence of even a shred of *credit risk* when lending to the U.S. Treasury. Owning a Treasury security is like keeping money in the bank—literally, because it's the Treasury that stands behind the FDIC. No other loan is utterly riskless in dollars, not even the debts of the tiny number of corporations that still have AAA ratings.* The portion of the interest-rate spread that compensates the lender for credit risk—which is the major portion—reflects bondholders' expected losses. So, for example, if the holder of a corporate bond stands a 10 percent chance of losing 20 percent of his money each year, the *risk spread* on that bond should be about 10 percent of 20 percent, or 2 percent.

In discussing the bond bubble, I emphasized that spreads can shrink too low. That was the problem in 2005–2006. But they can also rise too high—as many people argued they did during the Panic of 2008. When spreads "blow out" (as market professionals put it), borrowing becomes prohibitively expensive, credit dries up, and economies are brought to their knees. Huge spreads often connote few transactions—markets are drying up. Most of the extraordinary financial-rescue operations can be under-

---

*Euro loans to supersafe countries like Germany and the Netherlands are probably just as safe—in euro. But to a dollar-based investor, they have currency risk.

stood as efforts to reduce excessive spreads, and thereby to mitigate the lending collapses that typically accompany them.

There are three basic ways to reduce excessive spreads, and they are by no means mutually exclusive. First, the government can take steps to reduce perceptions of risk, either risk in the overall economy or risk in holding specific securities. Improving the macroeconomic picture is a prime example of the former; it's one thing expansionary monetary and fiscal policies are supposed to do. Mitigating the foreclosure problem is a good example of the latter. Second, the government can guarantee debts, so that private investors don't bear the credit risk, or don't bear as much. Third, the government can buy some of the risky securities, thereby driving their prices *up* and their yields *down*. In the crisis, the U.S. government did all three.

One clear example of the third approach—buying assets—was the Fed's Commercial Paper Funding Facility (CPFF), discussed earlier. It was explicitly designed to bring down the extraordinary spread shown in the left-hand panel of figure 9.2—between financial companies' commercial paper (CP) and Treasury bills—by purchasing CP. As you can see, it worked splendidly. Hank Paulson's capital injections into banks were intended, in part, to ensure counterparties that it was safe to lend to banks, thereby lowering perceived risk in the interbank market. That worked, too. The FDIC's Temporary Liquidity Guarantee Program (TLGP) was put in place to enable large financial institutions to float long-term bonds at smaller spreads over Treasuries. It literally took the risk out of these assets. And so on. It was all about the spreads.

The Fed graduated from the first to the second stage of crisis fighting when it migrated from ad hoc emergency rescues of ailing financial institutions to a broader focus on attacking the spreads, beginning with the CPFF in October 2008. It was an important transition. When the central bank's rescue efforts moved away from *saving distressed institutions* (Bear Stearns, AIG, Citigroup, etc.) toward *saving distressed markets* (commercial paper, mortgage-backed securities, etc.), it was shifting its attention away from damage control and toward curing the illness. A number of the Fed's spread-shrinking initiatives fall under the general heading of *unconventional monetary policy.*

Unconventional Monetary Policy: A Quick Tour

Conventional monetary policy consists of raising or lowering the federal funds rate (a virtually riskless rate) in order to manage the state of aggregate demand. Normally, the Federal Reserve does this by selling or buying Treasury securities (which are riskless) in the open market. Anything else the central bank does, including any of a variety of quantitative easing policies, can be considered *unconventional* monetary policy. And the Federal Reserve has done plenty that's unconventional since 2008.

When would a central bank resort to unconventional monetary policy? Mainly when its scope for conventional monetary policy is (or is nearly) exhausted; that is, when the policy interest rate gets close to zero. Unconventional monetary policy can be complicated, but its goals are simple. They might be (a) stimulating aggregate demand; (b) repairing the wounded financial system, and so restoring aggregate demand; or (c) combating a financial panic, and thereby limiting the damage to aggregate demand. Do you see a pattern there?

Since *unconventional* monetary policy is anything that is *not conventional*, it comes in a virtually infinite variety of shapes and sizes. Which ones did the Fed deploy and why? And which ones has the Fed resisted?

Make a Verbal Commitment

Perhaps the simplest unconventional monetary policy is *making a verbal commitment* to keep short-term interest rates low for a protracted period of time. Other than uttering a few words, the central bank doesn't do a thing; the market does all the work for it. Remember the basic idea: By promising to hold the federal funds rate low for a long while, the Fed can push down intermediate- and longer-term interest rates because these longer rates reflect expectations of where the funds rate is headed in the future. For example, in September 2012, the Fed committed itself to maintaining a superlow federal funds rate "at least through mid-2015." Just saying that pushed down longer-term interest rates.

Here's a simple example of how such a policy works. Suppose the Fed wants to drive the *two-year* interest rate down to 1 percent. It may be able to accomplish that by pledging to hold the *overnight* interest rate (the federal funds rate) at 1 percent *for at least* two years. If the pledge is believed, an investment strategy of purchasing federal funds 730 days in a row would be expected to yield a 1 percent annualized return. That should also be the expected annualized return on a different investment strategy: buying a 2-year Treasury bond and holding it to maturity. In that way, verbal commitments by the Fed—as long as they are *believed*—can push down long- and medium-term interest rates.

The Fed employed such verbal commitments both during and after the crisis. As mentioned in the previous chapter, the FOMC promised to hold the federal funds rate in the 0-to-25-basis-points range "for some time" in December 2008, changing those words to "for an extended period" three months later. The FOMC then stuck with that phrase until August 2011, when it replaced the vague "extended period" language (how long was that?) with a more precise commitment to hold the current federal funds rate "at least through mid-2013." That decision marked a major departure from previous Fed practice because it virtually tied the FOMC's hands for nearly two years—a commitment that a number of FOMC members found objectionable.* In September 2012, it stretched its commitment into mid-2015. All these cases had the same purpose: to push intermediate-term interest rates down.

Notice that a successful verbal commitment relies on two key ingredients: First, the Fed's pledge must be believed. Second, the expectations theory of the term structure—which holds that long rates are averages of *expected* overnight rates—must be approximately true. That's where the

---

*The vote was 7 in favor, 3 opposed. Such a wide split is highly unusual on the consensus-bound FOMC.

bad news comes in: Mountains of empirical evidence show that the expectations theory, though logical, works poorly in practice. It looks like a weak reed on which to stand. That said, it seemed to work pretty well in 2009, 2011, and 2012.

Raise the Inflation Target

A very different sort of unconventional monetary policy, suggested years ago by Paul Krugman for Japan and more recently by Ken Rogoff (and Krugman again) for the United States, is to raise the central bank's target inflation rate. The idea here is that *real* interest rates, not *nominal* interest rates, matter most for spending decisions. Since the real interest rate is the nominal interest rate *minus* the expected rate of inflation, *higher* expected inflation should lead to *lower* real interest rates.

Unlike other unconventional monetary policies, posting a higher central bank inflation target is not supposed to work on *spreads* at all. Rather, it is supposed to shift the whole structure of real interest rates down. Here's a realistic example: Suppose the federal funds rate is stuck at zero and expected inflation is 2 percent, as is roughly true today. Then the *real* fed funds rate is *minus* 2 percent, and it can't be pushed any lower because the nominal fed funds rate cannot drop below zero. But if the Fed could convince market participants to expect 4 percent inflation instead, the real rate would drop to *minus* 4 percent.

This makes sense in theory. But the idea gets nothing but Bronx cheers from actual central bankers, who are allergic to declaring their affection for higher inflation, even if the love affair is only temporary. Would markets believe it was temporary? Besides, it may be difficult for a central bank to deliver higher inflation when its economy is depressed. In fact, one reaction to Krugman's suggestion for Japan back in 1998 was, How in the world can the Bank of Japan (BOJ) make a credible promise to create 4 percent inflation? In fact, it has been hard-pressed to achieve even 1 percent inflation. Neither the BOJ in 1999–2000 nor the Fed in 2011–2012 was receptive to the suggestion that it post a higher inflation target.

Reduce the Interest Rate Paid on Reserves

A third form of unconventional monetary policy is to reduce the interest rate that the Fed pays banks on their excess reserves—perhaps even to a *negative* number, which would amount to charging a fee for holding excess reserves. This option requires some explaining, starting with some vocabulary. (Sorry!)

Banks hold reserve balances—essentially, checking accounts—at the Fed. These checking accounts represent idle cash, which, these days, earn banks 25 basis points per annum. Some of this idle money sits there because the Fed *requires* banks to hold reserves equal to 10 percent of their customers' transactions deposits. So, for example, when you deposit $1,000 into your checking account, the law forces your bank to add $100 to its reserve account at the Fed. Any reserves that banks hold *above* those legal requirements are called *excess reserves*, and in normal times banks keep excess reserves close to zero. But the period since Lehman Day has been anything but normal. Banks have built up a veritable mountain of excess reserves, as is clear from figure 9.3. It shows that excess reserves were negligible prior to the Lehman bankruptcy and then exploded.

Economics 101 students learn that additional bank reserves support a multiple expansion of the money supply, which in turn supports a multiple expansion of bank lending. Had that happened after September 2008, lending would have skyrocketed. But it didn't. Instead, excess reserves just sat there rather than being put to work creating money and credit. And that's where the idea of lowering the interest rate paid on excess reserves comes in. It stands to reason that if the Fed makes holding excess reserves less attractive, banks will hold fewer of them. That, in turn, should push some idle reserves out of banks, thereby creating more money and credit. Paying a lower interest rate on excess reserves wouldn't *directly* lower spreads. But if the economy improves, spreads should fall across the board.

To date, the Federal Reserve has rejected this option. It offers two main reasons. (I can be definitive on this point because I have argued for this policy over and over with FOMC members, unsuccessfully so far.) One is

FIGURE 9.3 *A New Mountain*
(excess reserves, 2007–2012)

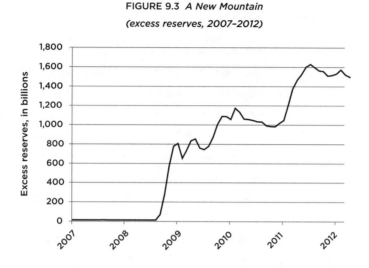

their belief that lowering the interest rate on excess reserves is a weak policy instrument. Maybe so. But that's not really an argument against it, because none of the Fed's remaining weapons pack much punch, either. Besides, several Fed spokesmen, from Chairman Bernanke on down, have repeatedly emphasized the importance of *raising* the interest rate on reserves as a tool for inducing banks to *hang on to* excess reserves. Why, then, isn't *lowering* that interest rate an effective way to induce banks to *shed* them?

The second argument is that ending interest on reserves would decimate the money market mutual fund industry. Why? Because much of the money fleeing banks' reserve accounts would be invested in the safest, most liquid assets available, such as T-bills, thereby driving their rates down to zero. Since it costs a few basis points to run a money market mutual fund, those funds and other similar arrangements might be put out of business if T-bill rates went to zero. This argument once sounded more cogent than it has since T-bill rates fell to essentially zero, anyway. Somehow, the money market funds have survived.

Peg a Longer-Term Interest Rate

Conventional monetary policy can be understood as *pegging* one particular overnight interest rate—the federal funds rate—by buying or selling reserves as necessary. By extension, the Fed could buy or sell, say, 6-month T-bills as necessary to force the 6-month Treasury rate to be, say, 15 basis points. Or it could buy or sell 2-year Treasury notes to force the 2-year rate to be, say, 1 percent. Or it could buy or sell 10-year Treasury bonds to force the 10-year rate to be 1.5 percent. And so on. The aim would be to shrink the spread between, say, the federal funds rate and some longer-term interest rate.

In principle, the Fed can peg any interest rate it wants to at whatever number it wants—*if* it is willing to buy or sell the requisite amounts of the relevant security. Indeed, during and after World War II, the Fed did peg interest rates on government bonds at extremely low levels. But doing so means that the central bank loses control over how many securities it owns and the volume of bank reserves it creates—which is just what happened during World War II. Why? Because to push a bond rate down to some target level, the central bank must stand ready to buy as many bonds as necessary to do the job—a volume of purchases it cannot know in advance. That's the main reason why central bankers shun the idea. They are taught in central banking kindergarten *never, ever* to lose control of their balance sheet because that might cost them control of bank reserves and the money supply.

That said, the Fed did lose control of its balance sheet *somewhat* when it instituted "QE3" in September 2012. This brings us to . . .

VARIETIES OF QUANTITATIVE EASING

The Fed's favorite unconventional weapon has been *quantitative easing* (QE), a term that encompasses a variety of ways to use the central bank's balance sheet to improve financial conditions. Since the Fed has deployed this weapon multiple times and in several different ways, we need to spend a little time on it.

Since quantitative easing can take many forms, table 9.1 offers a simple two-by-two taxonomy. Quantitative easing operations might alter either the *composition* of the central bank's balance sheet (the left-hand column) or the *size* (the right-hand column). The assets that the central bank purchases to do so can be either *government* securities (or *Treasuries*, the top row) or *private-sector* securities (the bottom row).* And, of course, many specific assets fall under the general term private-sector securities. That gives us the classification scheme shown in table 9.1. And as the entries in the table suggest, the Federal Reserve has tried every one of the four alternatives since the crisis began in the fall of 2008.

TABLE 9.1 Four Varieties of Quantitative Easing

	Composition	**Size**
Treasuries	Pre-QE; Operation Twist	QE2; part of QE1
Private-sector securities	QE0	Most of QE1; QE3

The first notable changes in the *composition* of the Fed's balance sheet (the upper left cell of the table) came in the weeks and months after Bear Stearns Day in March 2008. Seeing many financial institutions desperately scrambling for liquidity, the Fed sold off some of its holdings of highly liquid Treasury bills, acquiring less liquid assets—such as loans to banks—in their place. That way, banks could obtain the liquidity they wanted by holding more T-bills, while the Fed, which has much less need for liquidity, could hold less. At this early stage of the crisis, the Fed was mistakenly conceptualizing the financial ructions as mainly technical, and therefore not meriting a monetary policy response that would boost bank reserves and the money supply. It wanted to liquefy financial markets *without*

---

*In principle, the central bank could buy something other than securities—such as stocks, or even goods and services. But marketable securities are generally the only relevant choices.

QUANTITATIVE EASING

A central bank normally eases monetary policy by reducing overnight interest rates—in the United States, that's the federal funds rate. But what happens if the bank cuts its policy interest rate all the way to zero—or virtually to zero, as the Fed did in December 2008—and the economy still needs more stimulus? Does the central bank shutter its doors and take a long vacation? Or does it try something else?

Starting with the Bank of Japan in the 1990s, a number of central banks, prominently including the Fed, have resorted to some form of *quantitative easing*. The name derives from the idea that a standard easing of monetary policy works on price—on the cost of borrowing money. When that price falls, related quantities—such as the quantities of bank reserves, money supply, and bank loans—are supposed to increase. In fact, if you remember your Economics 101, they are supposed to increase by multiple amounts—maybe as much as 10 to 1. Once the *price* (that is, the interest rate) avenue is exhausted, the central bank can still boost the quantities of bank reserves, money, and credit directly—normally by buying assets. That's what quantitative easing is all about. The idea is to push more and more reserves into banks, at essentially a zero price, in the hope that the surfeit of reserves will induce banks to make use of them (e.g., to finance new lending).

Does it work? Maybe, but maybe not quite in that way. To the extent that banks just take the newly created reserves and stuff them into their accounts at the Fed, neither the money supply nor bank credit will grow. Banks will just pile up huge idle balances of *excess* reserves—as they have since September 2008. In that case, analysts need to focus on the other side of the ledger: what the Fed *buys* with the new reserves. By purchasing certain assets, the central bank can drive their prices up and their yields down.

increasing reserves—becoming, in effect, the liquidity provider of last resort. It was not yet trying to move interest rates.

No one except me has called that operation a case of quantitative easing, so I denote it as "Pre-QE" in table 9.1. But it really was an early form of QE because it altered the composition of the Fed's balance sheet quite notably. In fact, at one point, Fed officials started worrying that they might run out of T-bills to sell.

Similarly, under the so-called Operation Twist, which the FOMC launched in September 2011 and then renewed in June 2012, the Fed sold shorter-term Treasuries and bought equal amounts of longer-dated Treasuries. Thus, it, once again, changed only the *composition* of its balance sheet, not its size. The objective of "Twist" was to reduce yields on longer-term bonds relative to those on shorter-term securities, that is, to reduce term premiums.*

The QE0 in the lower left cell of table 9.1 refers to several early episodes of quantitative easing—so early, in fact, that no one called them QE at the time. Most prominently, we saw that the Fed began buying commercial paper (CP) in October 2008 in order to breathe life into the moribund CP market. QE0 was clearly aimed at spreads—specifically, at the spread of CP over T-bills. This emergency operation constituted QE because the Fed both changed its balance sheet and increased bank reserves by buying private-sector assets.

QE1, the Fed's massive purchases of Fannie Mae and Freddie Mac bonds and MBS between late November 2008 and March 2010, was a much bigger deal, quantitatively. That's when the term "quantitative easing," a Japanese coinage, started to be used in the United States. But what we now call QE1 also included purchases of $300 billion worth of Treasuries (upper right cell). Like the CP program, the large-scale MBS purchases from 2008 to 2010 had a clear purpose: in this case, to reduce the spreads of MBS over Treasuries. And it worked. QE3 in late 2012 was essentially a repeat of the MBS part of QE1.

---

*The term "Operation Twist" is an echo of the early 1960s when Chubby Checker was more popular than he is today, and when the Fed tried to "twist" the yield curve in the same way: lowering long-term rates and raising short-term rates.

QE2, which was limited to purchases of medium- to long-term Treasury securities—$600 billion worth—was announced in December 2010 and lasted until the end of June 2011. It was intended to push down longer-term Treasury rates and, with them, other interest rates as well. No private assets were involved. Yet, curiously, QE2 turned out to be the most politically controversial of all the QE programs. Shortly after it was announced, Bernanke and the Fed were attacked from directions as diverse as the political Right, including Sarah Palin, and German finance minister Wolfgang Schauble, who should have known better. It may have been what prompted Texas governor Rick Perry, while a candidate for the Republican presidential nomination, to characterize Bernanke's policies as "almost treasonous." Treasonous? As in aiding an enemy of the state?

When I defended Bernanke and the Fed in a *Wall Street Journal* column, I, too, was attacked by Palin, who argued that "it's time for us to 'refudiate' the notion that this dangerous experiment in printing $600 billion out of thin air, with nothing to back it up, will magically fix economic problems." It was as if Palin and others had just discovered that central banks create money—and decided they didn't like it.

The furor over QE2 surprised and puzzled Fed policy makers. The policy was less radical than, say, QE1; after all, central banks have been buying (and selling) government bonds forever. It was telegraphed well in advance, so markets barely moved when it was announced. Yet the political furor was loud and long; some observers even believe it made the Fed more timid in contemplating further QE for a while. This debate raises a basic question: What's wrong with the central bank blowing up the size of its balance sheet, anyway? There are several possible answers, but the main objection revolves around inflation.

It starts by remembering how *conventional* expansionary monetary policy can lead to higher inflation. Consider the highly simplified Federal Reserve balance sheet shown in table 9.2 below. When the Fed acquires either Treasury securities or private assets *and does not offset those purchases by selling other assets*, its total assets rise. That's just arithmetic. But if *total assets* rise, so must *total liabilities*—by an equal amount. That's just accounting. For the most part, higher bank reserves are the balancing item. Under normal circumstances, these additional reserves lead to more lending, a larger money supply, an expanding economy, and eventually to higher inflation. Hence, the conventional wisdom: Increases in bank reserves are inflationary—eventually. It's straight Economics 101.

TABLE 9.2 Simplified Federal Reserve Balance Sheet

Assets	Liabilities and Net Worth
Treasury securities —Bills —Bonds	Currency
Private assets	Bank reserves
Loans	Treasury deposits
	Net Worth

But what if times are not normal? What if banks just let those additional reserves accumulate as *excess* reserves, which is exactly what they've done since Lehman Day? Then none of the rest happens. The money supply doesn't rise, nor does bank lending. So the "expansionary" monetary policy doesn't expand the economy at all. And why would banks just sit on piles of excess reserves? Mainly because they are afraid to lend.

Bearing that in mind, let's look at some recent numbers. Figures 9.4 and 9.5 display the behavior of the money supply (M2 measure) and total bank lending since 2008. Figure 9.4 shows that the money supply has expanded modestly since Lehman Day—at just under a 7 percent annualized pace. But that's a tiny fraction of the increase in bank reserves, which rose thirty-four-fold! Most of the newly created bank reserves are being held idle on banks' balance sheets. Figure 9.5 shows that total bank lending sagged badly and is still below late-2008 levels. With bank lending moribund, it is hard to see how quantitative easing could be inflationary.

Critics argue that this abnormal situation will not last forever. They are right, of course. *Eventually*, banks will conclude that it's safe to step back into the water and put those excess reserves to work. Thus excess reserves, even if they're just sitting around, are regarded as fuel for *future* inflation. But how far in the future? The bloated holdings of excess reserves depicted earlier (in figure 9.3) have already lasted more than four years—and show no signs of abating. As and when the situation normalizes, and banks start

FIGURE 9.4 *Slow and Steady*
(the money supply, M2 definition, 2008–2012, in billions)

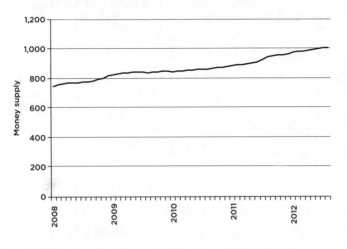

FIGURE 9.5 *Reluctant Lenders*
(total bank loans and leases, 2008–2012, in billions)

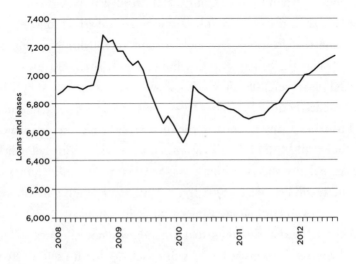

to favor lending over holding excess reserves, the Fed can start withdrawing them. Betting that large-scale asset purchases will ultimately prove inflationary is equivalent to betting on the future incompetence of the Federal Reserve.

Some of the Fed's critics take that side of the bet willingly. I do not. While the Fed is far from infallible, undoing QE purchases just isn't very hard. So it's difficult to imagine how they could muff the job that badly. (They could, I admit, muff it a little.) All the Fed has to do is *sell* what it previously *bought*. If it can't sell assets fast enough, the Fed can induce banks to hold on to their excess reserves longer by raising the interest rate it pays on them. Bernanke & Co. should be able to shrink the Fed's balance sheet without breaking a sweat.

A second risk is related to the first. If the Fed lets the U.S. money supply grow too rapidly, the value of the dollar in world markets may fall. A weaker dollar makes it easier for American businesses to sell their products to foreigners, which is nice. But it also makes it harder for foreign firms to sell their products here—which they won't think is so nice. Critics who raise this objection have a valid point, but a minor one.

First, the link between the money supply and the exchange rate is far from rock solid; indeed, it sometimes seems to work the other way around—faster money growth sometimes appreciates the dollar. Second, the argument implies that the United States is *not* entitled to pursue its own domestic monetary policy because other countries might not like it. That would come as news to the U.S. Congress, which gave the Fed no such instructions.

A third argument invoked against quantitative easing is the risk that the central bank might incur losses on its portfolio. If the central bank holds only T-bills, its portfolio is virtually immune to loss because bill prices barely move when interest rates fluctuate. But as the Fed ventures into long-term Treasuries, it runs the risk of incurring capital losses if interest rates rise. And if it owns private-sector assets, such as the Fed's huge holdings of MBS, it is exposed to possible default risk as well.

Do central bank losses matter? Probably not. Unlike a private bank, a central bank can even conduct its normal business with negative net worth.

A few have actually done so. But a central bank with no capital cushion is potentially vulnerable if, in some year, it doesn't earn enough revenue to pay its expenses. In such a case, the bank becomes beholden to its government for funds, and, if the government is hostile, central bank independence could be threatened. Needless to say, the Federal Reserve is unlikely to encounter such a problem for the foreseeable future. Its current net worth exceeds $55 billion, and its net profits (most of which it turns over to the Treasury) have lately been running around $75 billion to $80 billion *per year.** That's comparable to the combined profits of the entire oil and chemical industries. The wolf is not at the Fed's door!

Rolling the Dice: The Stress Tests

As we have seen, virtually all varieties of QE are aimed at reducing spreads—either *risk spreads* of private securities over Treasuries, or *maturity spreads* (term premiums) of longer-dated Treasury securities over shorter ones. The same was true of a variety of other financial-rescue measures taken by the Treasury, the FDIC, the Fed, and other agencies, as discussed in earlier chapters. The two graphs shown earlier (figure 9.2) suggest that it all worked. Spreads provide an objective, numerical, market-based measure of financial distress. And they started coming down rapidly in early 2009.

There were, however, some setbacks along the way. One began in the days leading up to the House of Representatives' initial negative vote on the TARP on September 29, 2008. The stock market crumbled—first on the news that TARP *might* fail and then on the fact that it actually *did* fail. The spread between three-month financial company CP and three-month T-bills rose 138 basis points between September 25 and October 6—and then remained elevated for a while after that.

A second noteworthy setback was precipitated by Treasury Secretary Geithner's unfortunate "deer in the headlights" speech on February 10,

---

*The main source of those copious profits is that the Fed earns much higher interest rates on its assets than it pays on its liabilities. The Fed's main liabilities are paper currency (Federal Reserve notes), on which it pays zero, and bank reserves, on which it pays 25 basis points.

2009—just twenty days into the Obama administration. Poor Geithner. The new president had inadvertently sandbagged him the previous day by telling a nationally televised press conference that his Treasury secretary would provide the details of the administration's banking plan the next day. But those details were not ready. When Geithner faced the press the next day, he must have felt as if he had been thrown to the lions with neither sword nor shield. Spreads rose on the day of his speech, and the stock market dropped 5 percent—not on any *bad* news, but on *not enough* news. Much worse, stock prices continued to drop for a month, falling a frightening 22 percent before they finally stopped.

In one of those ironic twists of history, President Obama called the bottom of the stock market almost to the day when he suggested at a March 3 press conference that "profit and earning ratios are starting to get to the point where buying stocks is a potentially good deal if you've got a long-term perspective." I presume it was an off-the-cuff remark, rather than a well-thought-out stock market forecast—which may be an oxymoron, in any case. But it sure sounded like the president of the United States was advising Americans to buy stock. And it turned out to be fabulous advice when the S&P 500 hit its lowest point just four trading days later. You didn't even need "a long-term perspective" to profit from Obama's sage investment advice. Over the next year, the stock market soared more than 60 percent!

The bigger, and far more important, irony about Geithner's much-decried February 10 speech is that he actually *did* announce what turned out to be the decisive step in bringing the acute phase of the financial crisis to an end. I refer to the so-called stress tests of nineteen major financial institutions,* which was a joint exercise of the four bank regulatory agencies, led by the Federal Reserve. Once the stress tests were completed and the results were announced publicly, it was mostly uphill from there, with hardly any reversals. Here is what the Secretary Geithner said in announcing the tests that day:

---

*They were not all banks. The list included GMAC, MetLife, Goldman Sachs, and Morgan Stanley. MetLife had become a bank holding company when it acquired a New Jersey bank in 2001. The other three, seeking shelter from the financial storm, had become bank holding companies hurriedly in 2008.

First, we're going to require banking institutions to go through a carefully designed comprehensive stress test, to use the medical term. We want their balance sheets cleaner, and stronger. And we are going to help this process by providing a new program of capital support for those institutions which need it.

Notice that last, very important, sentence: "we are going to help this process by providing a new program of capital support for those institutions which need it." It was a promise but also a threat: Any bank that failed its stress test, and could not raise enough fresh capital on its own, was going to get an infusion of capital from the U.S. Treasury—with plenty of strings attached. Yes, Barney Frank's "Free Market Day" was far in the past. The U.S. government now stood solidly behind these nineteen institutions, each of which was either too big or too interconnected to fail.

That reassured markets. But what about moral hazard? At this perilous point in history, hardly anyone seemed worried about that. There were far more immediate hazards to worry about—such as the potential collapse of the entire U.S. financial system, which Geithner was determined to prevent.

Here is how the stress tests were supposed to—and, in fact, did—work. Regulators would design a particularly adverse hypothetical scenario lasting for two years. After some back-and-forth with the banks, regulators would tell them what sort of loan-loss rates to assume under such stressful macroeconomic conditions. The banks would be allowed to net any projected profits over the two-year period against these projected loan losses. The net result, for each bank, would be an estimated increase or decrease in its capital over the next two years. Then regulators would judge whether the capital each bank had was enough to tide it over the adversity.

Few people imagined at the time how important the bank stress tests would prove to be. But many observers perceived the high-stakes nature of the gamble. If the estimated capital needs unearthed by the stress tests looked suspiciously low, as later happened with Europe's stress tests, markets might conclude that the government was covering up deeper problems or, worse yet, had lost its grip on reality. And therefore the markets would panic. On the other hand, if the stress tests generated capital needs that looked beyond banks' ability to raise new capital, markets might conclude that the banking system was headed for either oblivion or nationalization. And therefore panic. For the stress tests to ease market anxieties, the numbers would have to be, as in the tale of Goldilocks and the three bears, *just right*.

These risks were heavily debated inside the Obama administration, with NEC Director Summers particularly concerned and Secretary Geithner and his lieutenant Lee Sachs pushing to go ahead. As it turned out, the administration and the Fed hit the jackpot.

When the stress test results were made public on May 7, 2009, ten of the nineteen banks were ordered to raise at least some capital. In most cases, however, the capital shortfalls were small enough to fall well within the bank's capabilities. The biggest exception was GMAC, which was ordered to more than double its capital. That was no great surprise, however, since many auto loans had gone bad and GMAC had also ventured foolishly into subprime mortgages. Aggregated across all nineteen banks, the total capital shortfall was "only" about $75 billion, a number that didn't look so big when stacked up against a $180 billion bailout for AIG, a $700 billion TARP, and a $787 stimulus bill. Of the $75 billion, about $34 billion was Bank of America's share, making BofA and GMAC the only real problem children. The message from the government was clear: Large U.S. banks could now be trusted; you could deal with them with no fear.

Just as important as the bottom-line capital numbers, however, were the details that accompanied the Fed's report—details on how the tests were conducted and a surprising level of detail about the condition of each bank. Because bank supervisory data are normally guarded like nuclear secrets, this bank-by-bank detail created a whole new level of transparency. And, importantly, the numbers were judged to be credible. Yes, the regulators got it *just right*, and confidence began to come back. In fact, most bank stocks rose after the test results were announced.

The End of the Beginning

Few people realized it at the time, but the successful stress tests were a turning point. They marked the end of the acute stage of the financial crisis and the beginning of the return to normalcy—albeit just the beginning. It wouldn't be long before everyone stopped worrying about the survival of the big American banks. Not long after that, these institutions started generating profits again.

The stress tests relieved a lot of stress. But, of course, they did nothing to restructure either the financial system or the way the government regulates it. Nor were they supposed to. We turn to that story next.

PART IV

THE ROAD
TO REFORM

10

|ıııııııııııııııııııııı|

IT'S BROKE, LET'S
FIX IT: THE NEED FOR
FINANCIAL REFORM

*You've got to be very careful if you don't know where
you're going, because you might not get there.*

—YOGI BERRA

hile they were battling to end frighteningly large interest-rate
spreads, wildly high bid-ask spreads, the dramatic evaporation
of credit, and other indicators of acute financial distress, officials at the Federal Reserve, the Treasury, the FDIC, and elsewhere found
themselves running an overworked financial Emergency Medical Services team, dispatching ambulances to one roadside after another to stop
gravely wounded crash victims from bleeding to death. As they arrived on
the various crash scenes, the EMS units were generally too busy to think
about anything other than keeping the patients alive. But once the tourniquets were applied, the bleeding stopped, and some initial diagnoses were
made, the next step was to bring the patients into hospitals for the requisite
surgery.

Thus did the emergency financial rescue operations of late 2008 and early 2009 gradually morph into serious thinking about financial reform. By the spring and summer of 2009, there had been all too many crashes and casualties. A dauntingly long list of perceived ailments had accumulated, leaving plenty of work for legions of financial surgeons. For example: The financial markets seemed unduly bubble-prone. Leverage had obviously been too high and liquidity too low. Banking and other supervisors had performed badly. Glaring gaps in the regulatory apparatus had been exposed. In perhaps the most egregious case, no one seemed to have been responsible for the national mortgage market, nor to have protected gullible consumers. (Had the government been that negligent with food safety, we'd have had a lot of sick Americans.) The reasoning behind the too big to fail and too interconnected to fail doctrines was called into question as costs to taxpayers mounted. Few people could penetrate the logic behind saving Bear Stearns and letting Lehman Brothers go. And so on.

Virtually everyone seemed to agree that the status quo ante would no longer do. But what, exactly, were the financial surgeons to do once they got the patients on the operating tables? What overriding objectives and principles should guide the reconstruction of America's broken financial system in ways that ensured that "it" would not happen again? In particular, should the nation seek a wholesale redesign of the entire financial structure, analogous to what we did in the New Deal, or aim for more modest, incremental changes—fixing this, that, and the other thing?

Good questions all, and some of them had been under discussion for years. Secretary of the Treasury Paulson had put his staff to work on financial regulatory reform in 2007, leading to the *Blueprint for a Modernized Financial Regulatory Structure* in March 2008. Congressman Barney Frank (D-MA), then the newly anointed chairman of the House Financial Services Committee, gave a series of speeches on financial reform in 2007, which he followed with hearings in 2008. But apart from a few experts and an army of lobbyists, hardly anyone took notice. As is so often the case in our heavily checked and balanced system, it took a crisis to put the need for financial reform on the national agenda. And, as is its wont, America stumbled toward solutions in 2009 and 2010.

STOPPING BUBBLES? POPPING BUBBLES?

By 2009 the country had lived through notable stock market crashes in 1987 and 2000, a massive housing bubble that burst after 2006, and an absolutely frightening bond bubble that exploded in its wake. Unlike the two stock-market bubbles, the latter two spread economic ruin far beyond the financial markets. We learned that financial booms and busts could threaten the nation's economic fabric. The first order of business was to put an end to bubbles. Right?

Wrong. As noted earlier, occasional bubbles are probably an unavoidable consequence of speculative markets. They have certainly been around as long as those markets have. We humans, it appears, are prone to overconfidence, herding behavior, unwarranted extrapolation of recent trends, and contagious waves of wishful thinking—all key ingredients of bubbles. And we may be hard-wired to produce them. If so, stamping out bubbles is a loser's game. So maybe we should focus on something more achievable— such as reducing the frequency or magnitude of bubbles, or limiting the damage when they burst. Most important, and maybe most feasible, we should design a sturdier financial structure that does not crumble when big bubbles pop.

BIG THINK OR TINKERING AROUND THE EDGES?

Designing a sturdier financial structure meant different things to different people. The New Deal reforms that followed the stock market crash of 1929 and the collapse of the banking system in the early 1930s were sweeping, transformative, and in some respects radical. They created several brand-new regulatory agencies where none had existed before, such as the FDIC and the SEC. They separated banking, investment banking, and commerce, thereby changing the face of finance in America. The first-order question after the 2007–2009 financial crisis was, Should we take such a root-and-branch approach again?

Case in point: Quite a few people claimed—and still do—that repeal of the Depression-era Glass-Steagall Act was among the chief causes of the financial crisis. Glass-Steagall had separated commercial banking from investment banking in 1933, thereby pushing the high-stakes gambling on Wall Street away from the staid and stodgy banking system. Sixty-six years later, in 1999 the Gramm-Leach-Bliley Act (GLB) allowed those two businesses to get back together again, allegedly spoiling American banking and precipitating the crisis. The "obvious" solution, it was claimed, was to reconstruct Glass-Steagall barriers.

But was it true? When I hear these claims, I often ask the claimant which of the many bad things that happened before or during the crisis would have been prevented by Glass-Steagall. Their answers tend to be thin in the extreme. Indeed, they rarely extend beyond pointing to the merger that created Citigroup—as if Citi would have avoided the mess had Glass-Steagall remained in force.* The fact is that Citibank has been a central player in virtually every major banking disaster of the last several decades. Why should anyone think 2007–2009 would have been different?

Arguing that Glass-Steagall repeal was unimportant may seem surprising, even counterintuitive. But think about the travails of Bank of America, Wachovia, Washington Mutual, and even Citi that have already been discussed in this book. They did not come—or did not *mostly* come—from investment banking activities. Rather, they came from the dangerous mix of high leverage with disgraceful lending practices, precisely what has been getting banks into trouble for centuries.

Or consider the five giant investment banks prior to the crisis: Bear Stearns, Lehman Brothers, Merrill Lynch, Goldman Sachs, and Morgan Stanley. They were not creatures of Gramm-Leach-Bliley. Merrill did own a large savings bank. But Merrill Lynch Bank predated GLB by many

---

*Citibank and Travelers announced their intention to merge in April 1998. The GLB Act was signed into law by President Bill Clinton nineteen months later. Without GLB, the merger probably would not have been legal. Some observers claim that the Citi-Travelers merger was designed to force Congress's hand on Glass-Steagall.

years, was explicitly allowed under Glass-Steagall, and had virtually nothing to do with Merrill's problems. Nor would Glass-Steagall strictures have prevented any of the shenanigans at Bear Stearns, AIG, Countrywide, and the rest.

Even if I concede that repealing Glass-Steagall allowed Citi to sink deeper into the muck than it otherwise would have, which I am loath to do, the case that tearing down the Glass-Steagall walls was a *major* cause of the crisis is an urban myth. That said, myths survive—and sometimes take on lives of their own. So the idea of reinstating Glass-Steagall barriers came alive as attention turned to financial reform. So did the old idea of narrow banking, in which banks would be required to invest all their deposit monies in ultrasafe Treasury bills. There was also much talk of taking proprietary trading out of the banks, and maybe even out of too big to fail institutions entirely.

More radically, some people argued for breaking financial giants into smaller institutions, none of which would be (or could get) too big to fail. Others longed for a return to "the good old days" when investment banks were organized as partnerships, so that partners' own money was at risk. Contrast this with modern financial corporations, which mainly put OPM—other people's money—at risk. Those wistful thinkers, including some old-school investment bankers, had a point. But few experts thought the sprawling corporate genies could be stuffed back into the little old partnership bottles in the complex new world of global capital markets.

When the drive for financial reform really got going in earnest, few if any of these radical ideas were on the table. Leaders of the reform effort, both at the Treasury and in Congress, had rejected them. Instead, America would "tinker" with its financial system. However, as we shall see, some of that tinkering went far deeper than just "around the edges." The eventual reforms were substantial and thorough. Maybe we shouldn't call them tinkering at all.

Looking back at the harrowing financial collapse and many of the stunning policy responses thereto, and factoring in the public's negative reactions to both, left reformers with an extremely long and complicated to-do list. As in the Yogi Berra quotation that opens this chapter, they didn't quite know where to go or how to get there. I will not review the entire potential reform agenda here. That would occupy too many pages and bore you to tears. Besides, not all problems are created equal. Promising to be brief, I offer instead a guide to the highlights, starting with . . .

Fixing "Too Big to Fail"

Arguably, the leading item on the list was reforming, or perhaps eliminating, the too big to fail (TBTF) and too interconnected to fail doctrines, whose application during the crisis led the authorities to put hundreds of billions of public dollars on the line to save particular private companies—almost all of which had behaved badly. Needless to say, the headline-grabbing bailouts had created much public and congressional revulsion, and left legislators in a foul mood. *Never again!* But if there were to be no more bailouts, what should the authorities do instead?

One disarmingly simple approach is to adopt a policy in which every private company, no matter how large or interconnected, is allowed to fail—sort of what we did with Lehman Brothers. (*See you in bankruptcy court, folks.*) A number of moral hazard ayatollahs argue that this is exactly the right thing to do, but pretty much no one in authority does. After all, what happened after Lehman wasn't very attractive, was it?

A different approach would ensure that no company is ever allowed to grow large enough to be too big to fail. This idea has attracted some serious and high-placed advocates, including Governor Mervyn King, of the Bank of England, who declared in a June 2009 speech, "If some banks are thought to be too big to fail, then, in the words of a distinguished American economist, they are too big." A few months later, Federal Reserve Chairman Bernanke begged to differ. Asked about King's view at an October Fed conference, he expressed his preference for "a more subtle approach without losing the economic benefit of multi-function, international (financial) firms." In the ultrapolite world of central banker talk, that translated roughly to, "I think Mervyn is totally wrong."

My own view runs closer to Bernanke's than to King's. While the "keep 'em small" idea has a certain romantic allure, it encounters major problems in both the short and long runs. In the short run, history has bequeathed the United States and many other nations a number of institutions that are already TBTF—by a country mile. So it is not enough to declare that we will never allow a company to *become* TBTF. Rather, the operational issues are whether, when, and how we can and should break up *existing* TBTF institutions. In 2009, with the financial system still looking shaky, that looked awfully dangerous.

Over a longer time frame, of course, we are not slaves to history, and forcing financial giants to shrink is certainly *feasible*. The question, then, is whether it is *desirable*, given the diverse financial needs of large global corporations. Bernanke has plenty of company in thinking that it is not. Is it realistic to expect megacompanies like GE, IBM, and Apple to deal with scores of modest-sized banks? Or would they take their business to the likes of Deutsche Bank, UBS, and Banco Santander? The question answers itself. Furthermore, a country as large as the United States has gigantic firms in virtually every industry. Even a fragmented industry like retail has Walmart. Why should finance be different?

A third approach to fixing the TBTF problem is the one on which U.S. financial reform focused: devising ways to lay a giant institution to rest peacefully rather than chaotically, like Lehman Brothers. Remember, the actual doctrine is not "too big to fail," but, rather, "too big to fail *messily*." So one logical approach would be to take the messiness out.

Many ways to accomplish that objective fall under a wonkish heading called "resolution authority," because the authorities are said to "resolve" a failing institution. The FDIC has well-established and effective procedures for resolving smallish banks. But other than Wachovia and WaMu, which were sold more or less intact, the FDIC has never tried to apply those procedures to a global megabank, much less to a gigantic *nonbank* financial institution like Bear Stearns or Lehman Brothers. So, the thinking went, maybe we need a new resolution mechanism to deal with what are called *systemically important financial institutions* (SIFIs), whether or not they are banks. But what should such a mechanism look like? Answering that question turned out to occupy a lot of keen legal and financial minds for quite some time.

SYSTEMIC RISK REGULATION

Once you start thinking about resolution mechanisms, you quickly realize that the problem is broader and deeper than providing a legal alternative to bankruptcy. Do we always want to wait until a SIFI is on the verge of bankruptcy before intervening? Isn't it better to intervene sooner? Besides, systemic problems may start to arise *before* any SIFI teeters on the brink. Indeed, we witnessed exactly that in the mortgage crisis: Systemic risk in subprime mortgages was boiling up long before anyone was worried about the safety of Citigroup or Bank of America. Who would have called New Century Mortgage or even Countrywide a SIFI? When the herd moves recklessly, everyone is at risk.

This line of thinking led reformers to contemplate the need for a *systemic risk regulator,* a government agency charged with the responsibility of scouring the financial landscape for hazards that could, under adverse circumstances, become systemically important—and perhaps taking action when it finds them. Most reformers thought we needed such an agency. Here is how a systemic risk regulator might have helped us, had one existed in 2005:

The American residential mortgage market, plus the mass of securities built over it, constituted the largest financial market in the world. You might have thought a systemic risk regulator would have kept a watchful eye on it. If so, it should have seen what the banking agencies apparently missed: a lot of dodgy mortgages being granted by nonbank lenders with no federal regulation. It might then have been natural to investigate the solidity of the securities built on such mortgages. If so, the regulator *might have* noticed the questionable AAA ratings that the rating agencies were showering on these securities, but it *surely would have* uncovered the huge risk concentrations both on and off banks' balance sheets. And, unless it was totally incompetent, the systemic risk regulator would have been alarmed to learn that a single insurance company (AIG) was on the sell side of an inordinate share of all the CDS that had been issued—and that the company did not have nearly enough capital to back them. Hmm. That counterfactual really does suggest that history could have turned out much better.

While the need for a systemic risk regulator was widely acknowledged, at least three big design questions loomed: First, how do you recognize—or even define—systemic risk? (*Answer: Not easily.*) Second, should we just have a systemic risk *monitor*, responsible for raising red flags where it sees systemic risk, or a systemic risk *regulator*, which is also empowered to take action? Third, to whom should the task be assigned? The Federal Reserve? Some de novo agency? A consortium of regulators? There was no agreement on any of these questions.

HIGHER CAPITAL AND LIQUIDITY REQUIREMENTS

The crisis exposed numerous flaws in the nation's regulatory system. One painfully obvious one was that banks and other financial institutions had been allowed to operate with too much leverage; that is, with too little capital.* Capital requirements in the United States were a mixture of international (Basel) standards for large internationally active banks, and national regulations for the others. After the crisis, there was nearly universal agreement that these requirements should be higher. The only operational questions were: (1) How much higher? (2) What assets should qualify as capital for regulatory purposes? And (3) should the United States await international agreement from Basel or proceed at its own pace? These were all old and familiar issues. Not easy issues, to be sure, but familiar ones.

There was, however, at least one novel issue that had not been a major feature of financial regulation prior to the crisis: liquidity requirements. An-

---

*Remember, leverage is the ratio of assets to capital; so low capital and high leverage mean the same thing.

other painful lesson from the financial crisis was that insufficient *liquidity* can be as fatal to a financial institution as insufficient *capital*. Indeed, the line between the two is often blurry and easily breached. Think about this question: Did Bear Stearns, Lehman Brothers, and AIG founder over insolvency or illiquidity? Not easy to answer. Reformers quickly focused on new liquidity requirements as one key ingredient in regulatory reform.

Notice that, when instituted, higher liquidity and capital requirements are bound to diminish banks' profitability. A bank that earns 1 percent profit on *assets* will earn a 15 percent return on *capital*, if it is leveraged 15 to 1. But if its leverage drops to 10 to 1, that same 1 percent return on assets will translate to only a 10 percent return on capital. If a bank is forced to hold larger volumes of highly liquid assets like Treasury bills, with their low yields, its average rate of return on assets will decline. This is just arithmetic.

In 2009 traumatized banks were falling over themselves to stuff as much capital and liquid assets into their balance sheets as possible. "Market discipline"—that wonderful oxymoron—was keeping leverage down and liquidity up. But it was predictable that, as the fear factor dissipated, banks were going to dislike higher capital and liquidity requirements intensely.

PROPRIETARY TRADING AND THE VOLCKER RULE

There is a strong, though not necessarily accurate, belief that proprietary trading by commercial banks was among the root causes of the financial crisis. Was it? That's a matter of definition. If we use the conventional definition of proprietary trading—actively buying and selling assets for the banks' own accounts—there is relatively little evidence that proprietary trading got big commercial banks into the soup, and small banks never did much of it, anyway. If, on the other hand, we classify as proprietary trading the fateful decisions to retain significant volumes of their own MBS and CDOs on their balance sheets ("eating their own cooking"), there is little doubt that proprietary trading led them down the primrose path.

Critics like the estimable former Fed chairman Paul Volcker argued in 2009 and after that banks that benefit from the protective umbrella of FDIC insurance have no business using depositors' money to fund gambling operations that may foist bills onto taxpayers. Hence, *the Volcker Rule:* Commercial banks, which are insured by the FDIC, should stay out of proprietary trading. Conversely, financial institutions such as investment banks and hedge funds, which do lots of proprietary trading, should not be eligible for government bailouts. This rule would constitute a partial return to Glass-Steagall.

Volcker had a point. (Doesn't he always?) Not only is it patently unfair to ask taxpayers to cover a bank's trading losses, but it also sets up terrible "heads I win, tails you lose" incentives. Winning bets accrue to the bank's managers and shareholders; losing bets, if large enough to threaten the bank's solvency, are shared with the taxpayers. Did somebody say "moral hazard"? These are powerful arguments, coming from a man whom everyone respects.

But there are serious practical problems with the Volcker Rule. How can regulators distinguish, in concrete cases, between proprietary trading for the bank's own account and market making on behalf of a client? *(Answer: With great difficulty.)* How can they tell hedging, of which society approves, from gambling, of which it may not? *(Answer: Only by knowing the bank's entire portfolio, if even then.)** If proprietary trading is chased out of heavily supervised commercial banks, where will it go? To less-well-supervised investment banks? To totally unsupervised hedge funds? Would that make the financial system safer? *(Answer: It's not obvious.)* What if a giant *nonbank* investment house with a huge trading book was on the verge of failure? Should we follow the Lehman precedent and let it go under? *(Answer: That doesn't sound too appealing.)*

---

*In May 2012 a highly publicized case arose involving large trading losses at JP Morgan Chase. One hotly debated issue was whether the bank was taking proprietary positions or just hedging other risks.

PROPRIETARY TRADING: DO YOU KNOW IT WHEN YOU SEE IT?

One major practical problem in designing regulatory restrictions on proprietary trading is how to distinguish between trading for the bank's own account and trading for other purposes, such as market making or serving customers. Easy, you say. Just determine whose money is at risk—the bank's or the customer's. Well, that's the right starting point, but it's not quite enough.

Consider this simple example: A bank, acting as a dealer, gets a customer order on Monday to buy $10 million worth of CDS on a CDO of subprime mortgages called BS-I. But it's a thin market, so the bank doesn't have a seller at the ready. To service its customer, the bank temporarily takes the other side of the trade itself: It sells the CDS to its customer, and maybe doesn't find a real CDS seller until Thursday. Did that constitute market making for the customer? Well, I guess so. But for four days the bank held a short position in the CDS on BS-I; it was putting its own money at risk. For those four days, the trade looked and felt proprietary.

Or another example: In its role as market maker, suppose a bank has successfully matched buyers and sellers for some security. It is not directly involved on either side of the deal, and hence has no risk in the security. It's clearly not involved in proprietary trading. Now one of its customers wants to sell. If there is no immediate buyer at hand, does the bank refuse the trade? Or does it step up to the plate as a buyer for its own account, hoping to unload the position shortly? In the latter case, is it engaging in proprietary trading? What if it gets stuck holding the position?

In both these cases, and millions like them, the actual trader on the desk probably knows when he is deliberately trading for the bank's own account and when he is trying not to. But how do you devise a system of regulatory reporting that captures this knowledge? Not easily—as became clear in 2011–2012, when regulators tried to write detailed regulations promulgating the version of the Volcker Rule that became part of the Dodd-Frank Act of 2010.

Rearranging the Regulatory Deck Chairs

America had then, and has now, a befuddling array of financial regulators: two federal securities regulators (the Securities and Exchange Commission [SEC] and the Commodity Futures Trading Commission [CFTC]) that regularly did battle with each another; four federal banking regulators (the Fed, the FDIC, the Office of the Comptroller of the Currency [OCC], and the Office of Thrift Supervision [OTS]) that battled less often but still overlapped and fought over turf; fifty state banking regulators; fifty state insurance regulators; and so on. Couldn't we do the job better with fewer than 106 regulatory agencies? And despite this grotesque overpopulation, we had *no* federal insurance regulator, *no* nationwide mortgage regulator, and *no* systemic risk regulator. Whoever designed such a crazy system?

The problem went deeper than just cleaning up the messy organization chart. Because of *regulatory overlap*, many large banking organizations had to deal with the Fed, the OCC, the FDIC, the OTS, and several state banking regulators all at once. When the agencies did not agree, what was the bank to do? Because of *regulatory gaps*, no agency watched over the national mortgage market as it ran off the rails. Because of *regulatory mismatch*, the financial wizards at AIG FP were overseen by the hapless OTS, and the legions of lawyers at the SEC focused on preventing fraud rather than on safety and soundness. And so on. Everyone, it seemed, agreed that the division of regulatory labor needed changes to reduce overlaps, eliminate gaps, and assign tasks where the expertise was.

But there was no agreement on *how*. Fold the CFTC into the SEC?

The agriculture committees of the U.S. House and Senate, which had jurisdiction over the CFTC, would have none of that. Consolidate the four bank regulatory agencies into one? Well, not so fast. In the end, we reduced the four only to three (by eliminating the failed OTS). Create a national mortgage regulator and a national insurance regulator? Wouldn't that trample on states' rights? In general, rearranging the regulatory deck chairs was an area of reform into which only the brave, or politically naïve, dared tread.

Clipping the Fed's Wings?

One of the stranger aspects of the emergency-rescue phase of the financial crisis was a sharp rise in hostility toward the Federal Reserve. Through a long series of bold, creative—and, yes, often imperfect—policy actions, the Fed had been instrumental in staving off disaster. Yet in true "let no good deed go unpunished" fashion, the nation's central bank came in for withering criticism from many quarters. An amazing Gallup poll in July 2009 found that the public judged the Fed to have done the *worst* job on a list of nine federal agencies that included Homeland Security, the CIA, and even the IRS! Six months later, when President Obama nominated Ben Bernanke for a second term as the Fed's chairman, thirty senators voted against him. It was the most negative votes for a Fed chairman in history, by a wide margin.

Why the anti-Fed sentiment? In some quarters, the Fed was hated for *spending* (actually, it was *lending*) billions of taxpayer dollars to bail out undeserving bankers. Yes, they *were* undeserving, but that misses the point. If your negligent neighbor falls asleep with a lit cigarette in his mouth, setting his house on fire, he's irresponsible and guilty. But you don't want him to perish in the blaze. Nor do you want his house setting the whole neighborhood on fire. So you call in the fire department, even though it will cost taxpayers money.

Many members of Congress were appalled by the Fed's awesome display of power during the crisis. They believed either that the central bank had overstepped its legal authority, usurping powers that constitutionally belonged to Congress (by appropriating funds), or that the Federal Reserve Act granted the central bank too much unchecked and unbalanced power, which needed to be reined in. Yet regulatory-reform discussions were pointing toward giving the Fed even *more* power; for example, as the new systemic risk regulator or as the primary supervisor of all systemically important financial institutions, whether they were banks or not. Hence, the backlash against the Fed.

Proposals came from various quarters to clip the Fed's wings in many ways. Remove the Fed from its traditional role as the primary supervisor of many small- and medium-sized banks. Remove the Fed from banking supervision entirely, as several European countries had done with their central banks. Limit or end the Fed's extraordinary lending authority under Section 13(3). Make the president of the Federal Reserve Bank of New York a political appointee. Make all the Reserve Bank presidents political appointees. End private banks' right to name three members to each Reserve Bank's board of directors. Make the chairs of each of these boards political appointees. Subject the Fed's monetary policy decisions to congressional audit. And more.

It looked like perilous times ahead for the Fed. And there was another Fed power I have not yet mentioned: authority over the financial consumer protection laws.

Protecting Consumers

Duping unwary consumers has been common forever—and not just in finance. Wasn't there some business about an apple between Adam and Eve? But before the crisis, few people imagined that the failure to protect consumers from predatory lending practices could grow large enough to threaten the entire economy. We now know better.

While responsibility for enforcing the consumer protection laws was scattered across all the financial regulatory agencies, Congress had assigned most of the authority to the Federal Reserve. Why the Fed? You can interpret this assignment in one of two ways. Either Congress trusted the apolitical Fed to do the job more than it trusted the other banking agencies, or Congress believed that the banker-friendly Fed would not pursue consumer protection too vigorously. Take your pick. Maybe it was both.

But don't blame the Fed staff in either case. The people who performed these duties were competent, believed in their mission, and took their jobs seriously. Everyone knew, however, that Alan Greenspan, the Fed's chairman until 2006, was a self-proclaimed libertarian—adhering to a philosophy that believes in caveat emptor and abhors the nanny state. The problem went deeper than Greenspan's personal beliefs, however, and was more generic. Consumer affairs are destined to occupy the lowest rung on any central bank's ladder—always dwarfed in prestige and internal importance by the bank's primary missions: conducting monetary policy, regulating and supervising banks, and safeguarding the payments system. Indeed, one could argue—as many did—that it made little sense to assign primary responsibility for consumer protection to the central bank. It wasn't one of the Fed's core competencies.

In a now-celebrated 2007 article, a Harvard law professor named Elizabeth Warren proposed the creation of a new regulatory agency, which she dubbed the Financial Product Safety Commission, by clear analogy to the Consumer Product Safety Commission, to focus single-mindedly on this issue. In her words, "Financial products should be subject to the same routine safety screening that now governs the sale of every toaster, washing machine, and child's car seat sold on the American market."

The idea caught on, grabbing the attention of many Democratic legislators and candidate-then-president Barack Obama. As financial reform discussions progressed in 2009 and 2010, establishing a consumer protection bureau ranked high on the agenda. Indeed, the full name of the Dodd-Frank Act of 2010 is the Dodd-Frank Wall Street Reform *and Consumer Protection* Act (emphasis added). It is rare, indeed, that an ivory tower idea becomes the law of the land within three years. But the Consumer Financial Protection Bureau (CFPB), with its mission to protect consumers from financial legerdemain, did exactly that. For her efforts, Warren became a bête noire of the banking industry and was blocked by the Republican Party from becoming the CFPB's first director. Instead, she ran for the United States Senate from Massachusetts in 2012 and won.

WHAT ABOUT DERIVATIVES?

Let's start by recalling two starkly different views of the role of derivatives in our financial system, which I'll associate with the names of several financial luminaries.

Alan Greenspan, Bob Rubin, Larry Summers, and Arthur Levitt, you will recall, were less than enamored of the idea of letting the CFTC regulate derivatives in 1998. They successfully browbeat Brooksley Born when she broached the idea. (Levitt subsequently recanted, calling it one of the worst decisions he had ever made.) As secretary of the Treasury in 2000, Summers championed the passage of the Commodity Futures Modernization Act, an outrageous piece of legislation that actually *banned* the regulation of derivatives. The CFMA effectively decreed that this particular zoo would have no zookeepers at all. Market discipline—that old oxymoron—was supposed to take care of everything.

Looking back ruefully eleven years later, Bill Clinton wrote, "I can be fairly criticized for not making a bigger public issue out of the need to regulate financial derivatives." Of course, his Treasury Department *did* make it a big public issue. They were just on the wrong side.

Warren Buffett and Paul Volcker weren't. Buffett famously termed derivatives "financial weapons of mass destruction" in 2003. Volcker, who had been decrying financial engineering for years, once sarcastically asserted, "The most important financial innovation I've seen in the last 25 years is the automatic teller machine." In the Buffett-Volcker view, derivatives were *not* very useful but *were* very dangerous, which certainly suggests that they ought to be highly regulated.

That's quite a range of opinion, and both views contain elements of truth. But after hundreds, if not thousands, of derivatives exploded during the financial crisis—acting much like the financial WMDs Buffett had warned of—the antiregulation view was put to rout, at least temporarily. That, however, still left plenty of room between the status quo—which, with the CFMA still in effect, was zero regulation—and the Buffett-Volcker position. What to do? Before we embrace the Buffett-Volcker view too uncritically, let's remember two basic points:

The first is that derivatives can be used either to *hedge* or to *gamble*. Hedging is a way to *extinguish* risk—something we presumably don't want to impede. Gambling is a way to *create* risk—which society might (or might not) want to make more difficult. These two apparently contradictory roles of derivatives rob the notion that "derivatives are risky" of any coherent meaning. It all depends on how they are used.

To make the point concrete, consider the use of credit default swaps (CDS). If I own the bonds of BigCorp, I can reduce my risk by buying protection with a CDS. If BigCorp fails to pay up, I will lose on the bonds but collect on the CDS. So I've hedged my bet. But here's the catch: I can still buy CDS on BigCorp bonds even if I don't own any. Such so-called naked CDS amount to pure bets against the company's survival. And if Smith takes the other side of the bet by selling me the CDS, he's betting on the firm's survival. In the end, one of us will be right and the other wrong. But we have *created* risk where none existed before. For this reason, some reformers are particularly hostile to naked CDS. People are not allowed to buy fire insurance policies on their neighbors' houses, they argue. Why should they be allowed to buy default insurance on their neighbors' bonds?

The second point is that most derivative transactions are inherently zero-sum: What one party loses, the other wins. Thus it can be argued that society as a whole bears no *net* risk from derivatives. Take the previous example. When the bet settles, either Smith or I will win, and the other party will lose precisely the same amount. The country as a whole will be neither richer nor poorer because of our gamble.

True enough, but there are complications. First, the zero-sum view takes complete symmetry between winners and losers for granted. But what if, for example, the loser goes bankrupt? Then other counterparties are likely to be dragged down as well, potentially starting a chain reaction.

Second, and related, it assumes that each party posts enough collateral to cover its bets. Derivative trades typically start out worth zero to both sides, but they don't stay that way. As the odds of winning shift in favor of one party or the other, the loser is supposed to post enough collateral to the winner to insure payment. If that doesn't happen, credit risk gets piled on top of the underlying price risk.

Third, the zero-sum view ignores a critical aspect of derivatives that we discussed earlier: They often embed huge amounts of *implicit* leverage that would be hard to create explicitly. Remember, implicit leverage need not involve borrowing. Rather, it's built into the nature of the derivative contract, like a stock option that magnifies both gains and losses.

Fourth, the zero-sum view tacitly assumes that neither counterparty is a bank that is backstopped by FDIC insurance—that is, by the taxpayers. If that assumption fails, third parties can be forced to pony up.

Fifth, and finally, the zero-sum view of derivatives assumes that both parties are well informed and honest. When derivative contracts are complex, opaque, and not traded on organized exchanges, the chances of "accidents," whether from honest errors or duplicity, multiply.

That last point is critical. Think about the difference between derivatives that are *standardized* and *traded on organized exchanges* versus *over the counter* (OTC) *customized* derivatives. For exchange-traded derivatives, the price is transparent and observed continuously. OTC derivatives, in contrast, have no marketwide price data and no clearinghouse or exchange to ensure that the requisite amount of collateral is posted. Thus standardization and exchange trading breed transparency, competition, and lower trading costs, whereas customized OTC products breed higher trading costs and richer profits for the investment banks—which, of course, is why they fight so hard to keep them customized.

In any case, by 2009 the once-heated debate between Brooksley Born and "the guys" was over. Financial reform would include some regulation of derivatives. But what kind? The key issues looked likely to be, Would there would be restrictions—maybe even an outright ban—on naked CDS, and how much derivatives trading would be forced into organized exchanges? With OTC derivatives presenting a source of enormous profit to a handful of large broker-dealers, these financial behemoths had much to lose—and their army of lobbyists was girded for battle.

SHOULD HEDGE FUNDS BE REGULATED?

The financial crisis gave hedge funds a bad name, probably a worse name than they deserved. They were depicted as predators for their short selling; as excessively leveraged, and therefore a source of financial fragility; and as facilitating herding behavior, both in the bubble and in the panic after the music stopped. Maybe even as unsavory gambling dens. Nobody, it seemed, loved hedge funds—except, of course, the people who ran them, many of whom had amassed, in the apt words of a popular book on hedge funds, "more money than God." Surely anyone who had gained such an obscenely large fortune so fast must be guilty of *something*.

But the facts did not support those harsh judgments, other than the charge of obscene rewards. First, short selling probably kept the housing and bond bubbles from blowing up even bigger than they did. Why? Not because "the shorts" were socially altruistic, but because they saw it as the path to riches. Shorting is a (leveraged) way to exert selling pressure on a security, which normally pushes its price down.

Second, while there were some exceptions, hedge funds typically use leverage far less than commercial banks, and far, far less than investment banks. Why? Probably because hedge funds are partnerships, not corporations. Their managers are owners who put a great deal of their own money on the line. As such, most hedgies view 30-to-1 leverage as reckless, maybe even crazy.

Of course, some hedge funds did lose lots of money in the crash. Some went bust. But unlike the case of Long-Term Capital Management in 1998, none of them was judged to be systemically important or too big to fail in 2008–2009—which is the third reason. Losing hedge funds simply closed up shop, neither expecting taxpayer assistance nor receiving any.

Unless and until some hedge funds grow large enough to be systemically important, the case for regulating them—other than, for example, to guard against fraud—looks thin. Besides, how effectively can we regulate hedge funds, anyway, when most of them are legally domiciled in the Cayman Islands—a fact that does not enhance their reputation, by the way?

Probably the most plausible and important proposed regulation of hedge funds would be to require them to report their positions to regulators. The hedge funds hate this idea. Secrecy, after all, is often central to their business model—not to mention fleetness of foot, which means that their positions can change rapidly. Fair enough. But how can the authorities know, or even guess, whether one or several hedge funds pose a systemic risk if they don't even know what their positions are? On systemic risk grounds, then, the case for regulatory reporting appeared strong—though hedge funds had successfully resisted it in the past.

This is where the Volcker Rule's restrictions on proprietary trading by banks came in. Many observers hypothesized that if some version of the Volcker Rule were adopted, much trading activity that would have to leave the big banks would migrate to the hedge funds. These funds would therefore bulk even larger in overall trading, and therefore—at least potentially—pose more systemic risk. If that happened, it was hard to see how regulatory reporting could or should be avoided.

CAN COMPENSATION BE EFFECTIVELY REGULATED?

One of my original seven major villains is what I called "crazy compensation systems," by which I mean built-in incentives for traders to take huge risks. To oversimplify a vastly more complicated reality, too many traders earn bonuses that have a "heads I win a lot, tails I lose a little" character to them. If their bets turn out to be winners, they become fabulously wealthy.

If they lose, OPM (other people's money) absorbs almost all the losses; the traders' personal losses are minimal. Well, you know what? If you incentivize smart, risk-loving, young people to go for broke, many of them will do exactly that.

A conceptually similar problem applied to the commissions earned by mortgage brokers, which were not only keyed to loan *volume*, rather than to loan *quality*, but also often rewarded brokers for selling the riskiest mortgage products—because those were the most profitable for the company— or rather, the most profitable *unless and until they defaulted*. Rarely were commissions clawed back when mortgages became delinquent. These incentive problems were well known by 2009. What to do about them was far from obvious, however.

For openers, deciding how a firm's compensation should be structured is not something the government normally regards as part of its job, or is very good at. Employment contracts are private agreements between workers and firms. Who in America believes that the government can run businesses better than businesspeople?

Second, it is far from clear that the government can regulate pay effectively, even if it tries. Big financial companies hire fancy lawyers and accountants, not to mention clever financial engineers, who can probably devise ingenious ways to avoid the intent of pay regulations. Worse yet, some of these workarounds may have deleterious side effects. A disconcerting example of this followed the Clinton administration's ill-fated 1993 attempt to limit the tax deductibility of the pay of top executives to $1 million *unless the compensation was performance-based*. It backfired terribly. Stock options exploded, linking executive pay ever more tightly to short-run stock market performance—which encouraged an even more short-term focus. And as the stock market soared, executive pay skyrocketed.

Nonetheless, in the aftermath of the crisis, many voters were incensed about executive pay, especially CEO pay (rather than the pay of traders). Their concern was not with the *incentive structure*, which is what worried economists, but with the sheer amount of money involved. The public's ire was probably misdirected in two dimensions: It focused on CEOs rather than on traders and mortgage brokers, and it focused on the *level* of pay rather than on the *incentives* it created. But so what? The public was hopping mad, and compensation was sure to be a major political issue.

BERATING THE RATING AGENCIES

The statistical rating agencies posed a different sort of incentive problem: The agencies are hired and paid by the very firms whose securities they rate. As noted earlier, this "issuer pays" model creates a host of perverse incentives for grade inflation—such as shopping for a higher rating and the natural desire of any company to please its customers. The obvious solution to this problem—having investors, rather than issuers, pay the rating agencies—is not workable because of *free-riding*. Information just circulates too freely. If some mutual fund pays Moody's to rate a certain security, other investors will soon acquire the same information for free. So why would the original fund foot the bill in the first place?

INFORMATION AND FREE-RIDING

In the Information Age, information is one of the major factors of production, surely more important than, say, land. Many people earn their living producing, processing, and analyzing information. Yet a fundamental *free-rider* problem besets the markets for information—it's so easy to get that it's hard to own. Especially now, with electronic communications cheap and ubiquitous, it is hard—often impossible—to keep information in the corral.

Security ratings are just one example: Free-riding makes it next to impossible for asset managers to pay for ratings. Quality assessments for consumer products share the same problem: Once a Web site or a magazine rates a toaster or a telephone, almost everyone can gain access to that information for free. More generally, intellectual property is often hard, and sometimes impossible, to protect. Bits of information, after all, fly around the globe at the speed of electricity, showing no respect for borders. It's easier to steal code than to steal coal. When the producers of information and other sorts of content (e.g., rating agencies, computer programmers, musicians, etc.) can't collect fees from the *users* of that information, market function is impaired.

Different markets cope with the free-rider problem in different ways—with patents, legally protected royalty rights, encryption, and so on. But there is no foolproof solution.

This incentive problem points toward three types of fixes. One, which was championed by Senator Al Franken (D-MN), is to have the authorities assign rating agencies at random. That way, the issuer would still pay, but it would not get to choose its own grader. A second is to have some third party, such as the SEC or an exchange, hire and pay the rating agency. The third is to scare the agencies with legal liability for mistakes.*

Bringing Mortgage Finance Back to Life

And then there was the 800-pound gorilla: The entire U.S. mortgage finance system collapsed into a pile of rubble during the crisis. Fannie and Freddie were effectively nationalized. Their private-sector competitors pretty much vanished from the face of the earth. New MBS issuance, other

---

*This last approach is harder than it may seem. Ratings are opinions, which are protected by free speech.

than by Fannie and Freddie, just about disappeared. Either getting or refinancing a mortgage became very difficult unless you had the credit score of a saint and the assets of a millionaire. The entire housing finance system needed rebuilding from the ground up.

But the best way to rebuild it was by no means obvious—nor is it obvious today. In the near term, the two government-sponsored enterprises (GSEs) could continue to be run as nationalized enterprises. That was the status quo, and it could go on for a while with no problem—other than potential further taxpayer losses.* But what about the longer term? Few people in 2009 (or even now) advocated a return to the old Fannie/Freddie model, which had been exposed as an unhealthy halfway house between government and private enterprise. The GSE structure made it all too easy to privatize gains and socialize losses. No more of *that*, please.

But in which direction should we move? One path would lead toward purely private mortgage-insurance companies with no ties to the government. Another would have purely governmental institutions take over the business from Fannie and Freddie. Some of us thought that incorporating elements of both strategies might make sense: purely government insurance for special groups such as, say, low- and moderate-income borrowers or veterans, but purely private insurance for the rest of us.

More radical solutions were also broached, such as abandoning the idea that mortgages should be sold and securitized. After all, mortgage finance used to follow a simpler model wherein the banks that made the mortgages generally held them until they either matured or defaulted. As a small step in that direction, many reformers suggested "skin-in-the-game" provisions that require either the originating banks or the securitizers (or both) to hold on to some percentage of each mortgage pool—rather than selling it all off to (sometimes unsuspecting) investors.

When it came to reforming mortgage finance, there were a lot more questions than answers. Nor were there strong political or intellectual

---

*Well, not quite *no* problem. The FHFA put Fannie and Freddie into *conservatorship* in 2008. That meant that, legally, the FHFA is supposed to *conserve* value for the shareholders. The Obama administration later learned that, for example, this stipulation made it harder to refinance mortgages.

forces pushing in any particular directions—except away from the status quo ante. After the horrifying experiences of 2007–2009, hardly anyone thought the old GSE model should continue.

GETTING IT DONE

That's my selective list of the reform agenda. As I noted at the outset, it leaves out dozens, if not hundreds, of other issues. Such a long list constituted a daunting agenda for reformers in 2009–2010. And that's even before you throw in formidable barriers like the U.S. constitutional system, with its multiple checks and balances; the U.S. Congress, which was plagued by extreme partisanship; the impressive lobbying power of the financial industry, which was starting to get its mojo back; and the fact that some items on the reform agenda required international cooperation. As my grandmother would have said, *Oy vey!*

But at least we had a road map—sort of—from history. The 1933 Pecora hearings—named for the smart and feisty Ferdinand Pecora, who was chief counsel to the Senate Banking Committee—unearthed a treasure trove of damaging facts about the pre-Depression financial system. Those facts, and the political support they helped galvanize, pointed to and paved the way for fundamental financial reforms such as the Glass-Steagall separation of banking and investment banking, the creation of the FDIC and the SEC, and more. It was a virtual redo of the entire U.S. financial system.

Once the dust began to settle on the financial crisis of 2007–2009, many observers looked to the Pecora hearings as a model for what to do next: Let's have a thorough, public inquiry into what went wrong, and then use those findings to fix what was broken. It made logical sense. But things did not happen that way.

In May 2009, Congress ordered the establishment of the Financial Crisis Inquiry Commission (FCIC), with a December 2010 reporting date, to figure out what happened. Would this be Pecora 2.0? Not quite, because the U.S. Treasury could not wait for the FCIC report. Just one month after the FCIC was authorized by law, thus long before the commission could do anything substantive, the Treasury was out with its blueprint for financial reform—a document that kicked the policy debate into high gear.

The order seemed fundamentally illogical. The cure was being pre-scribed long before the diagnosis was in. But the Treasury believed it had a pretty good idea about what had caused the debacle. More important, Treasury Secretary Geithner, Federal Reserve Chairman Bernanke, and others perceived an urgent need to get at least some aspects of financial re-form in place promptly—especially new resolution authority. What would happen, they worried, if we faced another Lehman-like situation with no more legal authority than the Fed and the Treasury had in September 2008? With the scars still fresh, neither Geithner nor Bernanke wanted to find out.

The journey to the Dodd-Frank Act not only *began* (in June 2009) but actually *ended* (in July 2010), long before the FCIC report was even sub-mitted. That thirteen-month journey is the subject of the next chapter.

11

|IIIIIIIIIIIIIIIIIIIIIIIIIIIII|

WATCHING A SAUSAGE
BEING MADE

Two things you should never watch being made are laws and sausages.

—ATTRIBUTED TO OTTO VON BISMARCK

I t was going to be complicated. But complexity suits Congress just fine; members are accustomed to dealing with one-thousand-page bills. There is a downside, however. With something as mind-numbingly complex as overhauling financial regulation, public engagement was bound to be low, and public *understanding* lower yet. Even the best journalists were likely to miss much of the story. The broad public was justifiably disgusted with a system that had laid the economy low. But the changes people wanted were far from clear.

Experts, of course, were brimming with ideas. But different experts gave you different—and sometimes contradictory—solutions. Now, layer on top of all that (a) the truly titanic amounts of money at stake, (b) the proclivity of ingrained special interests to ride roughshod over the public interest, and (c) an administration heavily distracted by health reform. It looked like a field day for lobbyists.

Yet there was a potent political force to be reckoned with: the intense public anger over the financial crisis that had run the American economy into the ground. The electorate is normally a somnolent body, not easily aroused. But when it awakens in a foul mood, politicians ignore its wrath at their peril. That was the contest: America's system of government-by-lobbyist pitted against widespread public revulsion with the banking system. Might anger from both Republican and Democratic constituents be powerful enough to force bipartisan cooperation on financial reform? The answer would come soon enough: *No.*

Yet the story of financial reform had a happy ending in 2010. Somehow a pretty good bill struggled through the United States Congress. How financial reform survived is the subject of this chapter.

The Agenda

When President Obama came into office and Tim Geithner took over the reins at the Treasury, the agenda for financial reform was already long and growing longer. For convenience, table 11.1 offers a terse tabular summary of the central issues highlighted in the previous chapter. As the chapter progresses, it will serve as both a road map and a scoreboard.

Too Big to Fail

What to do about the too big to fail doctrine topped the list, both literally and figuratively. The nation and the Congress—Republicans and Democrats alike—were fed up with bailouts. A consensus, of sorts, held that the government needed new legal authority to resolve—meaning, *to euthanize*—large, complex financial institutions in an orderly manner, especially those that are not banks. (Banks fall under the FDIC's jurisdiction.) Both Geithner and Fed Chairman Bernanke were pushing hard for such authority, just as Paulson had before them. Of all the issues on the table, resolution authority looked to be the most ripe for bipartisan agreement.

Or maybe not. Some on the political Right didn't like the idea of granting such strong authority either to elected officials or to regulators. They preferred sending all such cases to the bankruptcy courts, where

TABLE 11.1 The Regulatory Reform Agenda: Major Issues

Issue/Provision	Key Aspects of the Debate
Too big to fail	• New resolution authority or use bankruptcy courts? • Break up TBTF institutions?
Systemic risk regulator	Who should do the job?
Federal Reserve reform	• Restrain Fed's Section 13(3) power? • Reduce the Fed's supervisory and regulatory powers? • More political accountability
Glass-Steagall barriers	Reinstate them?
Securitization	How to regulate the market
Capital and liquidity requirements	• How much more capital? • Dealing with off-balance-sheet entities • What measure of liquidity?
Reforming the rating agencies	• Turn agencies into public utilities? • Third-party payment?
Proprietary trading by banks	Ban or restrict it?
Regulatory agencies	• Fewer banking regulators? • Merge SEC and CFTC? • Create a national mortgage regulator?
Consumer protection	• A new, independent bureau? • Plain English documents? • Require plain vanilla and good default options?
Regulating derivatives	• Regulate OTC derivatives? • Force standardization, capital, central clearing, exchange trading? • Ban naked CDS?
Hedge funds	Should they be regulated? If so, how?
Executive compensation	How, if at all, to curb or reform it
Redesigning mortgage finance	• What comes after Fannie and Freddie? • End the originate-to-distribute model? • Better underwriting standards

judges would decide—presumably in nonpolitical ways, guided by legal precedent. Keeping politics out is desirable. So is minimizing moral hazard. But, as you may be asking yourself, didn't we try that with Lehman Brothers? I asked that question myself at the time. Nonetheless, there really were serious people arguing that Lehman was a good precedent, that bankruptcy procedures worked well! Hang on a second. Didn't it crash the entire financial system?

Both a minority on the Left and a minority on the Right favored a simpler solution to TBTF. If you don't have any systemically important financial institutions (SIFIs), you don't have to worry about resolving them, do you? So break up the financial giants. Simple, right? Actually, as we've discussed, it's not.

Systemic Risk Regulator

A second area of substantial agreement was that our financial regulatory system needed a government agency with broad responsibility for overseeing the entire financial landscape—a kind of guardian against systemic risk that would be licensed to roam across the regulatory boundaries that separate the jurisdictions of the Fed, the SEC, the FDIC, and so on. But who could do the job? And what powers should the systemic risk regulator have? As perhaps the prime candidate for the role, the Federal Reserve had both supporters (because of its broad purview, closeness to the markets, lender-of-last-resort capabilities, etc.) and detractors (because it already wielded so much power, had just failed miserably, etc.). Which brings me to . . .

Federal Reserve Reform

Some reformers wanted to give the Fed more power and responsibility. But critics of the Fed wanted to clip its wings by, for example, taking it out of bank supervision and consumer protection entirely, or imposing tighter restrictions on the central bank's ability to serve as lender of last resort under Section 13(3)—or, as they preferred to put it, to "finance bailouts." Didn't these bailouts usurp congressional authority? Weren't several key Fed officials, such as the presidents of the Reserve Banks, functioning as policy makers without having an ounce of political legitimacy? Wasn't the Fed too independent—functioning almost as a fourth branch of government? Wasn't that undemocratic?

Glass-Steagall Barriers

Reformers who assigned substantial blame for the crisis to the 1999 repeal of Glass-Steagall wanted to restore the wall between investment banking and commercial banking. Others argued that they were dead wrong.

Securitization

The Glass-Steagall issue was often confused with a different, but simpler, issue: Shouldn't the vast market for asset-based securities (ABS) come under some sort of regulation? Though details mattered, and would prove contentious, the answer was clearly yes. One oft-heard suggestion was to require originating banks, securitizers, or both to retain ownership of a percentage of what they created, thereby converting some OPM (other people's money) into MOM (my own money).

Capital and Liquidity Requirements

After the financial crisis, almost everyone believed banks should operate with thicker capital and liquidity cushions. But agreement in principle doesn't even get you to first base. The complexities of *defining* either capital or liquidity are numerous and vexing, which is why it generally takes years to negotiate international agreements at Basel. Furthermore, leverage is so closely tied to bank profitability that it touches a sensitive nerve in the industry. And an international agreement on liquidity standards would be novel. Not easy.

One related idea floating around at the time was to impose extra-high capital charges and liquidity buffers on systemically important financial institutions (SIFIs)—a kind of tax on bigness. That, of course, would require regulators to identify the SIFIs, thereby conferring official TBTF status on them. Some critics objected to naming SIFIs, both on moral hazard grounds and because acquiring such a label would give them an unfair competitive advantage: With the government standing behind them, they would be able to borrow more cheaply in capital markets. Supporters of naming countered that higher capital charges and tighter regulations would constitute major disadvantages. Being designated too big to fail would be a burden, not an honor. The market test came after Dodd-Frank was passed and regulators started compiling lists of SIFIs. It quickly became clear that companies were scrambling to stay *off* the TBTF list, if they could.

Reforming the Rating Agencies

By 2009 the credit rating agencies had virtually no defenders left; their names were mud. The agencies had performed miserably, and, at least to many observers, the incentives inherent in the issuer-pays model were perverse. But what to do about it? As I have mentioned, there were several suggestions and no consensus.

Now, take a deep breath. We are only about halfway through the table 11.1 list, but this is where we move from issues that were *moderately controversial*—leaving bipartisan agreement at least conceivable, to issues that were *supercontroversial*—making bipartisan agreement hard to imagine. Starting with:

Proprietary Trading by Banks

Risk taking had obviously been excessive in the run-up to the financial crisis. Some observers, including the formidable Paul Volcker and the prestigious Group of 30, a private group of international financial experts which he headed, claimed that proprietary trading was among the key causes of the meltdown. Others disputed this claim vehemently. As noted, much of the debate turned on how to define proprietary trading. Sadly, this case often fails the Potter Stewart test: You *don't* know it when you see it.

Rearranging the Regulatory Deck Chairs

A system that had so many different regulators and still left so much financial activity unregulated obviously needed some reorganization. For example, why have *four* federal bank regulatory agencies instead of just one? (Many reasons would soon be mustered!) And why did we need *both* an SEC *and* a CFTC—which often battled each other—to regulate the securities markets? Was the profusion of agencies grounded in some underlying legal or economic logic, or was it mainly about turf? The main answer was political: If you have multiple regulators, you need multiple congressional oversight committees, each of which is a gold mine for political contributions.

Consumer Protection

The Fed had plainly flubbed the job of consumer protection and deserved to lose control of it. It was never an essential part of running a central bank, anyway. But defenders of the status quo argued that a new independent agency with a single mission to protect consumers might be overzealous, overly harsh on banks, and therefore might undermine the safety and soundness of the banking system. Some of these critics seemed to have a soft spot for caveat emptor, anyway.

Regulating Derivatives

The formerly dominant view that derivatives are wonderful had been shattered by the crisis. No one even suggested anymore that regulating derivatives would threaten the lifeblood of capitalism. The legal ban on the regulation of derivatives was clearly headed for the dustbin of history. But the consensus ended about there. *How* to regulate *what* was entirely unclear. What *was* clear is that every detail would ignite a partisan dispute, with Democrats more regulatory and Republicans less so. This issue seemed likely to degenerate into open warfare—as it did.

Regulating Hedge Funds

Here, once again, the issue was *how* to regulate *what*. Remember, the label "hedge fund" describes a legal structure, not any particular investment activities. There are literally thousands of hedge funds, pursuing virtually every investment strategy you can think of. Furthermore, while it was clear that failure to regulate derivatives had gotten us into a lot of trouble, the same was not at all clear for hedge funds. In fact, there were defensible arguments for imposing nothing more than registration and reporting requirements. On the other hand, the public thought hedge funds were villainous, perhaps because they generated such riches for their managers.

Executive Compensation

Greedy bank executives who paid themselves outrageous bonuses were seen as even more villainous. Here the public was right to be outraged, and the AIG bonuses had made the compensation issue even more politically charged. But the practical and intellectual pitfalls to fixing the problem were enormous. Could the government design effective laws or regulations that *told* firms how to compensate their employees—or how *not* to? Not likely. The solutions might have to come from firms' boards of directors. Good luck with that.

Redesigning Mortgage Finance

And then there was what I called the 800-pound gorilla. The nation's once-vaunted mortgage finance system lay in ruin. Fannie Mae and Freddie Mac had essentially been nationalized. The rest of the MBS business had just about disappeared. Mortgages were hard to come by and residential construction had crumpled. But, of course, the housing bust would eventually end, and people would want to build and buy houses again. Since forcing everyone to pay cash was not an option, the nation would need a new system of mortgage finance—presumably one that differed from the old GSE-based system that had imploded with such devastating effect. But what would that new system look like?

THE TREASURY WEIGHS IN

Enter the United States Treasury in June 2009, with an eighty-eight-page white paper titled *Financial Regulatory Reform: A New Foundation: Rebuilding Financial Supervision and Regulation.* It covered every item on my list except the last, which was put off for later, plus a lot more. In August the Treasury backed up its white paper with a long draft bill. Unlike some of its other big policy initiatives, no one could accuse the Obama administration of following someone else's lead or taking its marching orders from Congress. The Treasury was right out front, leading the way. Its positions on the major issues are summarized in the right-hand column of table 11.2.

The Treasury proposed new legal authority for resolving SIFIs, with Treasury officials deciding when to seize a failing company but then turning the job over to the FDIC. The FDIC, in turn, could put the institution into either receivership (which would close it down in an orderly manner) or conservatorship (which might rehabilitate it). Notice that the latter approach, but not the former, could be characterized as a "bailout"—a point to which I'll return. To make this new resolution procedure more workable, SIFIs would be required to develop "living wills"—detailed plans for putting the organization's various businesses to bed peacefully—and to share them with their regulators. Yes, that's right, companies would be asked to develop plans for their own demise.

Treasury did *not* recommend more radical measures, such as breaking up large financial institutions, reintroducing Glass-Steagall barriers, or taking banks out of the proprietary trading business. Geithner and Summers thought them all bad ideas.

TABLE 11.2 The Treasury Reform Proposal

Issue/Provision	Key Aspects of the Debate	Treasury Proposal (2009)
Too big to fail	• New resolution authority or use bankruptcy courts? • Break up TBTF institutions?	• New resolution authority; FDIC as receiver *or* conservator • No • Living wills
Systemic risk regulator	Who should do the job?	Establish FSOC to advise the Fed
Federal Reserve reform	• Restrain Fed's Section 13(3) power? • Reduce the Fed's supervisory and regulatory powers? • More political accountability?	• Treasury prior approval • Increase supervisory authority; Fed to regulate and supervise SIFIs • Fed to recommend changes in "its structure and governance"
Glass-Steagall barriers	Reinstate them?	No
Securitization	How to regulate the market	5% "skin-in-the-game" for originators
Capital and liquidity requirements	• How much more capital? • Dealing with off-balance-sheet entities • What measure of liquidity?	• Higher; even higher for SIFIs • Include off-balance-sheet entities • Add a new liquidity standard; higher for SIFIs
Reforming the rating agencies	• Turn agencies into public utilities? • Third-party payment?	• Tighten SEC oversight • Reduce regulatory use of ratings
Proprietary trading by banks	Ban or restrict it?	No restrictions

Regulatory agencies	• Fewer banking regulators? • Merge SEC and CFTC? • Create a national mortgage regulator?	• Fold OTS into OCC • Keep SEC and CFTC separate • No; just an Office of National Insurance in Treasury
Consumer protection	• A new, independent bureau? • Plain-English documents? • Require plain vanilla and good default options?	• Free-standing Consumer Financial Protection Agency • Yes • Yes
Regulating derivatives	• Regulate OTC derivatives? • Force standardization, capital, central clearing, exchange trading? • Ban naked CDS?	• Regulate OTC derivatives • Capital, clearing, some standardized trading on organized venues • No
Hedge funds	Should they be regulated? If so, how?	Registration and regulatory disclosure
Executive compensation	How, if at all, to curb or reform it?	• Via regulatory guidelines • "Say on pay" • Independent comp committees
Redesigning mortgage finance	• What comes after Fannie/Freddie? • End originate-to-distribute model? • Better underwriting standards	TBD

The Treasury proposal was also extremely friendly to the Fed, which was hardly surprising since Geithner had just hopped over from the New York Fed and Summers coveted Bernanke's job—not to mention that the Fed had performed admirably. The central bank was designated as the systemic risk regulator in the Treasury plan, with a new multiagency Financial Services Oversight Council (FSOC) playing an advisory role. The Fed was also made the primary supervisor of all SIFIs, whether banks or not. Only trivial limits on the Fed's Section 13(3) emergency lending powers were recommended. And all proposals to make the Fed more politically accountable—such as turning Reserve Bank presidents into political appointees—were rejected. Instead, the Fed was asked to "propose recommendations . . . to better align its structure and governance with its authorities and responsibilities." Translation: The Fed would be asked how to reform itself.

However, the central bank would be taken out of the consumer protection business in favor of a new, independent Consumer Financial Protection Agency (CFPA) to be established along the lines suggested by Elizabeth Warren. For example, Treasury proposed that this new agency require banks to offer:

- simple, plain-English disclosures, similar to food labels, to facilitate comparison shopping by telling people "what's inside" at a glance;
- "plain vanilla" financial products (e.g., for home mortgages) that are straightforward and easy to understand; and
- good "default options" so that people who cannot make up their minds are "defaulted" into reasonable choices.

All these ideas were intended to make it easier for consumers to make intelligent choices and, failing that, to default them into such. Plainly, the banks and the Fed had not been doing that beforehand.

On the safety-and-soundness front, the Treasury proposal would saddle all banks with both higher capital requirements and a brand-new liquidity requirement—with even stiffer requirements for SIFIs. They would need to hold more capital against off-balance-sheets assets and also have to retain 5 percent of any mortgage pools they securitized. *Some* derivatives trading would be forced into central clearing mechanisms, exchanges, or both, with appropriate capital and margin requirements imposed. (Exactly *how much* turned out to be a major battleground.) But naked CDS would not be banned. Nor would executive pay be restricted by law; instead, the Treasury asked regulators to take up this matter as part of their risk-management assessments.

Two major regulatory items were conspicuously absent from the Treasury plan, though for very different reasons.

First, Treasury decided to punt on regulatory consolidation. The Office of Thrift Supervision, which, among other things, had embarrassed itself in the AIG case, was folded into the Office of the Comptroller of the Currency, but that was it. Counting the proposed new consumer protection agency, the number of bank regulators would be the same as before. Nor were the SEC and the CFTC combined. Nor was a national mortgage regulator proposed; the consumer protection agency was supposed to handle that job.

Why not a bolder approach? You could call it either cowardice or wisdom. The Obama administration recognized a legislative snake pit and avoided stepping into it. For example, the CFTC fell under the jurisdiction of the agriculture committees of the House and the Senate. You don't want to mess with those guys. Had the Treasury fought this and a series of other regulatory turf wars, they probably would have lost in Congress, wasting much political capital in the process. While academics and good-government types criticized Treasury heavily, Geithner's judgment on this matter was almost certainly sound. Tilting at windmills is not costless.

Second, the Treasury plan deliberately left the redesign of the nation's mortgage finance system in limbo. The reason was simple: They were not ready to propose a new one. The design issues for the post-Fannie/Freddie world are numerous and complex, and a comprehensive plan would take a great deal of work that Treasury (and other) staff had yet to do by June

2009.* In the meantime, Fannie and Freddie, operating virtually as government agencies, could hold down the fort. Saying that Treasury punted is not a criticism, by the way. The Geithner Treasury accomplished an astounding amount of work between Inauguration Day and June 2009. It was a wonder the folks there could still keep their eyes open.

FINANCIAL REFORM MEETS THE U.S. CONGRESS

And then it was Congress's turn. As schoolchildren, we are taught an important social studies lesson called "How a Bill Becomes a Law." You remember it. All bills originate in committees of either the House or the Senate. Once voted out of committee, they are debated and amended on the floors of the two chambers. If they pass, a conference committee irons out any differences between the Senate and House versions, and a common bill goes back to each chamber for a vote. If a majority of each house approves, it's on to the White House for the president's signature or veto.

Now forget most of that. In practice, many bills originate in the White House. House and Senate committees (and members' offices) are typically choked with lobbyists making "suggestions," cutting deals, and even drafting legislative language. At times, lobbyists act like virtual congressional staff and have near veto power that rivals the president's. The merits of the case typically take a backseat to the politics. And when huge amounts of money are at stake—and in the case of financial reform, the amounts were mind-boggling—they almost definitely do.

Furthermore, then as now, Republicans and Democrats were locked in combat. So were the House and the Senate. Without consulting the founders, the Senate uses filibuster rules to amend the Constitution to require sixty votes. Bargaining among the Senate, the House, and the White House

---

*When the Treasury finally did bite this bullet, in February 2011, it waffled by offering three options, each of which sharply reduced the government's role in providing mortgage insurance relative to the old Fannie/Freddie system.

often continues right up to the last minute, and the final vote is often taken before the final bill is drafted—not to mention read. For this and other reasons, complicated pieces of legislation are typically followed by "technical corrections" acts that fix mistakes. Sausages, indeed.

Yet financial regulatory reform succeeded in 2010 with the passage of a pretty good, albeit imperfect, 2,319-page bill that mostly tracked the original 2009 Treasury proposal. How did *that* happen? The principal credit for shepherding this ungainly and controversial piece of legislation through Congress belongs to the chairs of the two banking committees, Senator Chris Dodd (D-CT) and Congressman Barney Frank (D-MA). The law they passed bears their names: the Dodd-Frank Wall Street Reform and Consumer Protection Act.

Dodd and Frank. Two liberal Democrats from New England. Two peas in a pod, right? Wrong. The well-coiffed Dodd, who looked like a senator from central casting, and the disheveled, fast-talking Frank were a study in contrasts. Both were skilled veteran legislators and worked well together. But Dodd was smoother and more accommodating, while Frank was hard-charging, brilliant, and sometimes bombastic. Their political constraints also differed starkly.

Barney Frank represented an ultrasafe liberal district near Boston, which had voted Democratic since 1946. A favorite whipping boy of the Right wing, he was nonetheless electorally invulnerable.* The House is a fiercely partisan body where, to a first approximation, the minority might as well watch from the gallery. So Chairman Frank did not have to worry much about Republican support. And he could be pretty sure that once legislation reached the House floor, he would be backed up by Speaker Nancy Pelosi—who had the votes to pass it.

When it came to financial reform, however, Frank carried one significant piece of political baggage: He was a longtime and enthusiastic champion of Fannie Mae's and Freddie Mac's low-income housing goals. He had famously stated in 2003, for example, "I want to roll the dice a little bit

---

*Frank decided not to stand for reelection in 2012.

more in this situation towards subsidized housing." A few years later, the dice came up snake eyes.

Chris Dodd was the senior senator from a clearly blue state, though not as blue as Frank's district. (Since 1946, Connecticut had sent six Democrats and five Republicans to the U.S. Senate, though only Democrats since 1989.) Dodd had to keep his reelection prospects in mind.* Furthermore, he had been dogged since 2008 by charges that he had received special treatment on his own mortgages from Countrywide, as a "Friend of Angelo" (named for Angelo Mozilo, Countrywide's CEO).

The Senate Banking Committee had a strong bipartisan tradition, and Dodd had a good working relationship with its ranking Republican member, Senator Richard Shelby (R-AL). That was the good news. The bad news was that efforts to achieve the bipartisan consensus that Dodd wanted on his committee could delay legislation interminably. And then the bill would have to face the molasses-slow Senate floor, where the filibuster threat ruled, requiring sixty votes.

It was therefore predictable that the House would act first. A House Financial Services Committee bill that closely tracked the Treasury proposal passed the House in December 2009 on a largely party-line vote, 223–202. Among the key differences with the Treasury's White Paper were two changes that eventually found their way into Dodd-Frank. One eliminated the "conservatorship" option for resolving financial giants, leaving only receivership. That change amounted to an explicit ban on bailouts. If you fail, you fail; you just don't fail *messily.* The House also added over two hundred pages on mortgage underwriting standards—for example, requiring banks to document borrowers' ability to repay (you have to tell banks that?) and banning predatory lending.

The Senate moves at a more languid pace. The Senate Banking Committee's bill took another five months to negotiate, and even then passed the Senate on another party-line vote, 59–39. Dodd's painstaking efforts to reach bipartisan compromises bore little fruit with a Republican Party that

---

*In fact, Dodd decided not to run again in 2010.

had adopted "just say no" as its mantra. And with "only" fifty-nine votes, the bill was still vulnerable to a filibuster. The Senate version also drifted further from the Treasury's original proposal by, for example, including the Volcker Rule to ban proprietary trading by banks, some limits on the Federal Reserve, and a provision to limit debit card fees.

Ironing out the many differences between the House and Senate bills took two more difficult months before both chambers finally adopted the conference committee report in July 2010. But the 237–192 vote in the House and the 60–39 vote in the Senate each included only three "ayes" from Republicans, making it the most partisan vote on major financial-market legislation in memory. By contrast, the comprehensive Federal Deposit Insurance Corporation Improvement Act, which followed in the wake of the savings and loan debacle, cleared the House in 1991 by a whopping 344–84 margin, with overwhelming Republican support (135–29). And it passed the Senate by 68–15, with even stronger support among Republicans (32–2) than among Democrats (36–13). The starkly partisan vote on Dodd-Frank ran counter to history, which did not bode well for its future.

THE LONG AND WINDING ROAD

The rightmost column of table 11.3 summarizes the major provisions of the Dodd-Frank Act. In general, it is clear that Dodd-Frank tracks the Treasury's original proposal reasonably well. But the differences are interesting for what they tell us about the political pressures on members of Congress. Here are a few key examples:

Resolution Authority

Treasury's original idea that the FDIC could put a failing financial giant into either receivership *or* conservatorship was replaced by receivership *only*. Title II of Dodd-Frank is thus called "Orderly *Liquidation* Authority," not "Orderly *Resolution* Authority." Some banks might be too big, but they would fail anyway, for Congress was in no mood to authorize future

TABLE 11.3 The Dodd-Frank Act: Major Provisions

Issue/Provision	Key Aspects of the Debate	Treasury Proposal (2009)	Dodd-Frank Act (2010)
Too big to fail	• New resolution authority or use bankruptcy courts? • Break up TBTF institutions?	• New resolution authority; FDIC as receiver *or* conservator • No • Living wills	• New resolution authority; orderly liquidation by FDIC • No taxpayer bailouts • No • Living wills
Systemic risk regulator	Who should do the job?	FSOC to advise Fed	Fed to work for FSOC
Federal Reserve reform	• Restrain Fed's Section 13(3) power? • Reduce the Fed's supervisory and regulatory powers? • More political accountability	• Treasury prior approval • Increase supervisory authority; Fed regulates and supervises SIFIs • Fed to recommend changes in "its structure and governance"	• Limits Section 13(3) to "facilities with broad-based eligibility" • Increases supervisory authority; Fed regulates and supervises SIFIs • Audits of special credit facilities; GAO study of Fed governance
Glass-Steagall barriers	Reinstate them?	No	No
Securitization	How to regulate the market	5% "skin-in-the-game" for originators	5% "skin-in-the-game" for securitizers

Capital and liquidity requirements	• How much more capital? • Dealing with off-balance-sheet entities • What measure of liquidity?	• Higher; extra for SIFIs • Include off-balance-sheet entities • Add a new liquidity standard; higher for SIFIs	• Higher; extra for SIFIs • Include off-balance-sheet entities • Add a new liquidity standard; higher for SIFIs
Reforming the rating agencies	• Turn agencies into public utilities? • Third-party payment?	• Tighten SEC oversight • Reduce regulatory use of ratings	• Tighten SEC regulation • Reduce regulatory use of ratings • Study incentive problems
Proprietary trading by banks	Ban or restrict it?	No restrictions	Volcker Rule
Regulatory agencies	• Fewer banking regulators? • Merge SEC and CFTC? • Create a national mortgage regulator?	• Fold OTS into OCC • Keep SEC and CFTC separate • No, just Office of National Insurance in Treasury	• Fold OTS into OCC • Keep SEC and CFTC separate • No, just Office of National Insurance in Treasury
Consumer protection	• A new, independent bureau? • Plain-English documents? • Require plain vanilla and good default options?	• Free-standing Consumer Financial Protection Agency • Yes • Yes	• Consumer Financial Protection Bureau "within" but independent of the Fed • No • No

Regulating derivatives	• Regulate OTC derivatives? • Force standardization, capital, central clearing, exchange trading? • Ban naked CDS?	• Regulate OTC derivatives • Central clearing • Some standardized derivative trading in organized venues • No	• Regulate OTC derivatives • Central clearing • Some standardized derivative trading in organized venues • No
Hedge funds	Should they be regulated? If so, how?	Registration and regulatory disclosure	• Registration and regulatory disclosure • Limits on bank ownership
Executive compensation	How, if at all, to curb or reform it?	• Via regulatory guidelines • "Say on pay" • Independent comp committees	• Via regulatory guidelines • "Say on pay" • Independent comp committees
Redesigning mortgage finance	• What comes after Fannie/ Freddie? • End originate-to-distribute model? • Better underwriting standards	TBD	• TBD • Better underwriting standards

bailouts. To emphasize the point, Section 214 states clearly, "Taxpayers shall bear no losses from the exercise of any authority under this title." That's *no* losses, as in *zero*. To give this clause teeth, Congress specified that any public funds not recovered by selling the failing bank's assets "shall be the responsibility of the financial sector, through assessments." In other words, as in the old TV commercial, Uncle Sam told the financial industry: "You can pay me now or pay me later." This no-bailout language seems clear. But it hasn't stopped Republican critics of Dodd-Frank from falsely labeling the new *liquidation* authority as a vehicle for future bailouts, sometimes calling it "permanent TARP." Such talk persists to this day.

The Federal Reserve

Given that many members of Congress were hopping mad at the Fed when the reform process began, Dodd-Frank let the central bank off the hook lightly—though not quite as lightly as the Treasury had proposed. Instead of letting the Fed study its own structure and governance, that task was assigned to Congress's watchdog, the Government Accountability Office. But Congressman Ron Paul's (R-TX) call for an audit of the Fed's monetary policy was rejected, as was the proposal to make the president of the Federal Reserve Bank of New York a political appointee.

Perhaps most prominently, the Fed's authority under Section 13(3) of the Federal Reserve Act to make emergency loans to "any individual, partnership, or corporation" (the pre-Dodd-Frank wording) was restricted to lending via "facilities with broad-based eligibility" (the post-Dodd-Frank wording). The intent, once again, is to prohibit bailouts of particular companies (think Bear Stearns or AIG) while allowing the Fed to bail out whole *industries* or entire *markets* (think commercial paper or MBS). In practice, however, this policy change is less transformative than it seems. If a future Fed perceives an urgent need to save some critical financial company, it shouldn't take much effort to design a lending program "with broad-based eligibility."

Securitization

Intense lobbying by community banks got the 5 percent skin-in-the-game requirement for asset-backed securities shifted from the originating banks, where Treasury had put it, to the securitizers, namely the banking giants and Wall Street firms.

Rating Agencies

Dodd-Frank adopted Treasury's smart recommendation to excise the mandatory use of credit ratings from virtually every law and regulation. But it punted, just as Treasury had, on specifying how rating agencies should get paid. Instead, the new law asked both the GAO and the SEC to study "alternative means for compensating nationally recognized statistical rating organizations that would create incentives for accurate credit ratings." The GAO was given eighteen months to report; the SEC, three years. Go figure. In the meantime, the dubious user-pays model persists.

Volcker Rule

As mentioned earlier, a version of the Volcker Rule was embedded in Dodd-Frank, overriding objections from the Treasury and the NEC. Section 619 states that, subject to a list of exceptions, "a banking entity shall not (A) engage in proprietary trading; or (B) acquire or retain any equity, partnership, or other ownership interest in or sponsor a hedge fund or a private equity fund." That seems clear enough. But the list of exceptions runs more than seven pages, and that's not counting *de minimis* provisions.

Both Geithner and Summers initially opposed placing legal limits on banks' proprietary trading. In their view, doing so would fall somewhere between futile and damaging—and also constituted shooting at the wrong target, because proprietary trading is not what got us into trouble. But public hostility to bankers was rising, fueled among other things by those AIG bonuses. Discussions between Geithner and Volcker in the closing months of 2009 led to a version of the Volcker Rule that both of them (but not Summers) could support—and would help Dodd-Frank politically.

Then, in January 2010, Republican Scott Brown, a comparative unknown with a populist streak, stunned the political world by winning a special election to fill the Massachusetts Senate seat that had been held for thirty-seven years by Ted Kennedy—and, before that, by his revered brother. This stunning defeat in one of the bluest of blue states shocked Democrats. (It also turned out to be a portent of what was in store for them in November 2010.) To President Obama, Brown's electoral surprise suggested a few things. One was that he had to change the subject; "Stunning Republican victory" made bad headlines. Another was that the Brown election and the rising tide of public anger likely convinced the president that his stance on financial reform was being perceived as too friendly toward bankers. Perhaps he should be a bit more populist himself.

Just days later, in a memorably stage-managed White House event with (among others) Volcker, Geithner, and Summers flanking him, Obama announced his support for what he called (to Volcker's surprise) "the Volcker Rule" to take banks out of proprietary trading. You could almost see the bemused look on Volcker's face. His idea had been considered both naïve and dead for months, and the president's Damascene conversion was pretty recent. Neither Secretary Geithner nor NEC Director Summers looked particularly pleased to be there, though Geithner was resigned to the deal.

Consumer Protection

The proposed Consumer Financial Protection Agency (CFPA) ran into a buzz saw of congressional opposition from Republicans, who seemed more concerned with protecting banks than with protecting consumers—pretty amazing after the mortgage debacle. In the political wrangling, the proposed legislative requirements for plain-English forms and disclosures, plain-vanilla mortgages, and good default options all were stripped from the bill—although the CFPA might still order them. And auto financing from car dealers was exempted from the agency's authority, not on any policy grounds, I presume, but because there are so many auto dealers in every congressional district.

In a truly bizarre display of congressional creativity, a political compromise was struck between liberals, who wanted an independent proconsumer agency that would not have to go to Congress for annual appropriations, and conservatives, who wanted to keep responsibility for consumer protection within the banking agencies—which, they believed, would not bully the banks. A new Consumer Financial Protection *Bureau* (CFPB) was established "in the Federal Reserve System" (the law's words). *In?* The Fed serves as both the bureau's landlord and its source of funding, but is prohibited from interfering in the CFPB's business. Moreover, the director of the CFPB is an independent presidential appointee who reports only to Congress, not to the Federal Reserve Board or its chairman. Somewhere, Rube Goldberg is smiling.

Derivatives and the Lincoln Bill

That's not *Abe*, but *Blanche*. Blanche Lincoln was then a Democratic senator from Louisiana not known for Left-leaning views. However, she found herself in a serious primary fight with a challenger from the Left, the state's lieutenant governor, Bill Halter.* Lincoln also happened to be chair of the Senate Committee on Agriculture, which, you may recall, has jurisdiction over the CFTC and thus over derivatives trading.

As the Dodd bill meandered its way through the Senate in April 2010, waiting for the agriculture committee to drop in its derivatives piece, Lincoln pulled off a major coup by persuading the committee, on a bipartisan vote, to force banks to spin off *all* their derivatives trading, proprietary or not. The Lincoln bill not only out-Volckered Volcker on trading, it even went some way toward resuscitating the separations imposed under Glass-Steagall.

Lincoln's headline-grabbing achievement set off alarm bells at the

---

*Lincoln successfully fended off Halter's primary challenge but then lost her seat in the 2010 election.

White House, the Treasury, and the Fed—all of which swung into action to oppose the bill. Even Sheila Bair, the self-styled populist FDIC chair who often disagreed with Geithner and Summers, spoke out against the Lincoln bill—as did Volcker himself. Predictably, the banking industry declared that the bill's passage would doom American capitalism yet again. In the end, however, much of Lincoln's language survived to become Title VII of Dodd-Frank. Chris Dodd had no other choice; he needed the Republican votes in the conference committee. But banks were allowed to retain their derivatives trading in interest-rate and foreign-exchange swaps, the vast majority of the business. For bank lobbyists, it was an uncomfortably close call.

It Ain't Over 'Til It's Over

The journey to Dodd-Frank took about thirteen months and resulted in a complicated 2,319-page financial reform law. Along the arduous road to passage, reformers had to fight off hordes of bank lobbyists—sometimes successfully, sometimes not. But, despite what you learned in "How a Bill Becomes a Law," the battle was by no means over when President Obama signed Dodd-Frank into law on July 21, 2010. The lobbyists were channeling their inner Churchills: We shall fight them in the committees, we shall fight them on the floor, we shall fight them in the regulatory agencies and in the media, we shall never surrender.

The American way of regulating certainly gave the lobbyists ample opportunities. In our country, laws that involve regulations—whether they be financial, health, environmental, or anything else—must pass through many stages before they go into effect. First, of course, any proposed bill must run the gauntlet to passage by Congress in America's heavily checked and balanced system—which is what we have just discussed. Compromise and industry influence are everywhere.

But no matter how lengthy and complex the law, it is virtually never more than a skeleton. The sketchy, sometimes thematic content of each regulatory statute must be translated into concrete, detailed regulations by the agencies involved. In the case of Dodd-Frank, those agencies included the Treasury, the Federal Reserve, the OCC, the FDIC, the SEC, and the CFTC—plus the soon-to-be-established CFPB. During the process of "writing the regs," a single page of law can easily expand into dozens of pages of detailed regulations.

In principle, Congress makes all the key decisions; regulators just implement what Congress decrees. But as always, the devil is in the details. And the details matter a lot, sometimes more than the principles embodied in the law. So, in practice, regulators wind up making numerous important decisions, some of which involve piles of money. And lobbyists are always waiting in the wings with ideas they'd like written into the regs—always in the public interest, of course. When regulators are more friendly toward the industry than are legislators, the "reg writing" stage offers numerous opportunities for the affected industry to bend the law in its favor.

Typically, the first official step in the regulation-writing process is for the agency (or agencies) to issue an Advance Notice of Proposed Rulemaking (ANPR), stating their objectives, concerns, and ideas—and inviting public comment. The broad public typically has no idea what's going on, but all interested parties do. The agencies hear from them early, often, and in excruciating detail—including written public comments and numerous back-channel communications. (In fairness, the agencies typically also hear from public-interest lobbies of various sorts.)

Once the public comments have been digested, the agency or agencies proceed to write a Proposed Rule, which they publish in the *Federal Register*—inviting yet another (generally, much smaller) round of comments. If there are significant comments on the Proposed Rule, these comments, too, must be digested—possibly leading to further modifications before the Final Rule, along with full responses to the comments, is published in the *Federal Register*.

Let me use the Volcker Rule to illustrate how this process worked in one specific example.

Unlike many other cases, the controversial Volcker Rule first emerged in quite detailed form as Section 619 of Dodd-Frank, where it occupied some thirty pages. The normal ANPR stage was therefore replaced by a detailed study—conducted by the new Financial Stability Oversight Council—of how to implement the rule. In the process of conducting that study, which was completed in January 2011, the FSOC solicited public comments and got about eight thousand of them. Yes, you read that right: eight *thousand!*

These "comments," by the way, are not quick remarks like, "I like this rule except for clause 15(B)(4)(g), which should say 'often' instead of 'always.'" They often run to twenty, fifty, one hundred pages or more. Thus the agencies must have received hundreds of thousands of pages. No wonder it took them almost ten months to prepare the Proposed Rule, which finally appeared in the *Federal Register* on November 7, 2011. That rule ran to 127 pages and set a January 13, 2012, deadline for public comments. Five days after that deadline, all the key regulators were summoned to a well-publicized hearing of the House Financial Services Committee, where several Republicans urged them to scrap the entire rule. The regulators persisted, but so did their critics. Interested parties submitted more than seventeen thousand public comments on the second round. By November 2012, twenty-eight months had elapsed since the passage of Dodd-Frank, and final adoption of the Volcker Rule was nowhere in sight.

In principle, the process leading from law to Advance Notice of Proposed Rulemaking to Proposed Rule to Final Rule is admirable: It is open, democratic, and invites public input, all acting as checks on regulators. The problem is that most of the public comments—not to mention the behind-the-scenes activity—come from highly interested *private* parties and their lobbyists, not from "the public." The cumbersome rulemaking process thus gives interested parties with deep pockets, and the legislators who support them, ample opportunity to bend the intent of the law in their favor.

That's not all. Dodd-Frank required the various regulatory agencies to conduct or write more than two hundred studies and rules. It was a gargantuan task that required the agencies to hire more staff, which, of course, required bigger budgets. This gave Republicans, who wanted to repeal Dodd-Frank but couldn't, another weapon, which they eagerly embraced: Just say no again, this time to appropriation requests from the SEC and the CFTC.* Thus many deadlines for studies or rules were missed as regulators struggled under murderous workloads.

To make matters worse, Senate Republicans delayed or refused to confirm many of the top people President Obama nominated to oversee the regulatory process, including at the Treasury, the Fed, the FDIC, and especially at the new Consumer Financial Protection Bureau, where Republicans refused to confirm *anyone* as the bureau's first director unless the law was changed to their liking. This intransigence led to a constitutional confrontation in which Obama finally used his power to make recess appointments to name Richard Cordray as the CFPB's first director in January 2012—at a time when the Senate claimed it was still in session! The resulting furor delayed confirmations even further.

Amazingly, the Republicans' obstruction of financial reform has not led to any obvious political fallout, despite the fact that polling data continued to show broad popular support for the basic principles of Dodd-Frank. To cite just one example, a Lake Research poll for the AARP in July 2011 found that likely voters, once told that "there are proposals in Congress to repeal the Wall Street reform law" which has "been signed into law" but has not "fully taken effect," favored implementation over repeal by more than 3 to 1.

At some level, none of this is surprising. No one ever expected the general public to keep track of Senate confirmations or CFTC budgets. As public attention to financial reform waned, so did its influence over the political process. The White House and congressional Democrats might have drawn more attention to the cause but failed to do so. So the public fell back into its normal state of somnolence as lobbyists worked their will.

---

*The Fed and the FDIC are immune to such budgetary constraints because they fund themselves.

THE LONG WAR

The battle for financial reform still rages. Rules remain to be written, interpreted, and rewritten—not to mention implemented. For example, we won't know how the new authority for liquidating financial giants will work until we actually use it. And I have not even mentioned the difficulties of homogenizing U.S. rules with foreign rules, which are generally different and lag behind ours.

On the political front, the November 2010 midterm elections handed control of the House to a Republican Party that was and remains avowedly hostile to Dodd-Frank, with many members openly advocating repeal. Much the same was true on the Senate side of Capitol Hill, where Democrats maintained their majority in 2010 but only by a slim margin. First Senator Dodd and then Congressman Frank both left the Congress, robbing Dodd-Frank of its two most natural defenders. And President Obama was pinned down by so many other economic issues (the failure to get a budget passed, threatened defaults on the national debt, extending the payroll tax cuts . . .) that he devoted precious little attention to Dodd-Frank.

Through all of this, one group has kept its eye squarely on the ball. That's the financial industry and its legions of lobbyists, aided immensely by the U.S. Supreme Court's 2010 landmark *Citizens United* decision, which, in effect, allows corporations to make unlimited political contributions. Willie Sutton knew where the money was (in the banks), and it's still there. According to the Center for Responsive Politics, the financial industry ranked behind only the healthcare industry in lobbying expenditures over the years 2009–2012, and they were tops in political contributions in 2012. According to the center's classification, the vast majority of this cash went to conservatives rather than to liberals. Leading U.S. bankers rarely miss an opportunity to excoriate Dodd-Frank, blaming it for everything from tight credit to the scarcity of jobs to aiding foreign competitors.

Will the Dodd-Frank Act make financial crises a thing of the past? Certainly not. Will it make them rarer? Maybe; time will tell. But there are good reasons to believe it will reduce the severity and costs of future financial excesses. To paraphrase Benjamin Franklin, Dodd-Frank gives America a comprehensively, if imperfectly, reformed financial system *if we can keep it*. As of this writing, keeping it is by no means certain.

However, Dodd-Frank made no attempt to fix the nation's broken mortgage finance system. Nor did it seek a way out of the foreclosure mess, which continues to plague the U.S. financial system and acts like an albatross around the neck of the economic recovery. It is to that tragically persistent problem that we turn next.

12

|ıııııııııııııııııııı|

THE GREAT
FORECLOSURE
TRAIN WRECK

If at first you don't succeed, try, try again.

—AMERICAN FOLK SAYING

The frontal attack on interest-rate spreads waged by the Federal Reserve, the FDIC, and the Treasury in 2008–2009 was a smashing success. Give it an A. The efforts to reform financial regulation in 2009–2010 were reasonably successful, too. At least a B. But the half-hearted attack on the home mortgage foreclosure problem, engineered principally by the Bush and Obama Treasury Departments, was not successful at all. Maybe a C- or a D. And remember, the whole financial mess started with bad mortgages.

The sternest critics label the effort to stem foreclosures a total failure. That's a bit harsh. But even the most sympathetic appraisals hardly overflow with praise, and no one characterizes the effort as a success. How could they when some experts in 2012 were predicting that 10 million homes or more would enter foreclosure proceedings before it's all over? Sadly, the foreclosure problem was not only entirely *predictable*, but actually *predicted* well before the fact. Yet foreclosures more than tripled between 2006 and 2009, and the problem festers to this day. Millions of families who lost their homes have already paid a steep price; millions more will.

The cost of letting the foreclosure problem drag on has been high. Estimates suggest that a typical home loses something like half its value when it goes into foreclosure—say, $100,000. Put differently, a $100,000 loss can be avoided if the average homeowner and the average bank can find a way to avoid the average foreclosure. And that's just the money cost. In addition, foreclosures disrupt lives, create neglected properties, and leave whole neighborhoods suffering.

Watching wave after wave of foreclosures sweep across the American landscape was like watching a slow-motion train wreck take a high human toll. But unlike most train wrecks, the government was not a helpless bystander watching an inevitable disaster unfold. It had the power to do something about it—it just didn't. Dispossessed families bore the brunt, but all of us are still suffering in some measure because the foreclosure epidemic suppressed the housing market, which in turn acted like a lead weight on the struggling economy.

BARRIERS TO A SOLUTION: THE UNHOLY TRINITY

Why did we let this happen? A first, but fleeting, reason was misdiagnosis of the problem. Initially, lots of people thought the main source of the coming wave of foreclosures would be the millions of newfangled adjustable-rate mortgages (ARMs) characterized earlier as "designed to default." The belief was that many holders of subprime ARMs would find themselves unable to meet their monthly payments once mortgage rates reset after the low teaser-rate period. With house prices falling, refinancing would be next to impossible. Escalating monthly mortgage payments would lead to millions of defaults.

That happened to some extent, especially in the early days of the crisis, when interest rates surged. But it didn't last long. Soon the onset of the

Great Recession, and especially the Fed's strenuous efforts to fight it, sent interest rates tumbling. One felicitous side effect of lower rates was that many of the dreaded mortgage rate resets either never happened or turned out to push interest rates *down*. Instead of entering a brave new world of exploding ARMs, we wound up experiencing a surge of defaults for old-fashioned reasons: People who lost their jobs and faced other economic setbacks often could not keep up with their mortgage payments. It was a familiar story, just repeated on a massive scale.

Why, then, was the foreclosure problem never "solved"? There seem to have been three main barriers, all interrelated, and they exist to this day. Here is the unholy trinity that will occupy our attention in this chapter:

The Huge Expense

With millions of mortgages imperiled, the amount of money required to fix the foreclosure problem looked scarily large. Back-of-the-envelope calculations ranged from $200 billion (that's a million houses at an average of $200,000 each) *upwards*—a sum to which political leaders were unwilling to commit. Politics aside, the question was always, Is it worth it? That's a reasonable question, especially when deficits were already large and there were many other claims on public funds. The Paulson and Geithner Treasuries judged that it was not worth it. I always disagreed with that judgment, but I didn't have $200 billion to lend. Notice the verb here—it's critical. The issue was always about *lending*, not *spending*. As we'll see shortly, the net cost of avoiding millions of foreclosures might have been zero—or less.

Tampering with Property Rights

A second barrier to modifying huge numbers of mortgages is a set of knotty legal issues that no one seemed willing to tackle. Unfortunately, most and maybe all effective solutions to the foreclosure problem require some rearrangements of property rights. Some parties must be told that their legal rights are not what they thought, or that they are not going to collect what their contracts seem to entitle them to. There was, and still is, an understandable reluctance to tamper with anyone's property rights.

Here's one clear example; we'll meet others later: Many homes with subprime mortgages have second mortgages on the property. When a first mortgage goes bad, the corresponding second mortgage becomes virtually worthless, since it is junior to the first. Nonetheless, owners of these worthless seconds retain legal rights that may enable them to block refinancings of the first mortgages—unless they are paid off. *Or* unless changes in the law modify their property rights.

Objecting to tampering with property rights is entirely understandable. There are undoubtedly costs to doing so, and these costs must be weighed against the benefits of fewer foreclosures. Here again, both the Paulson and Geithner Treasuries judged those costs to be too high.

Was It Bad Politics?

American politicians came to believe that voters were dead set against bailing out borrowers whose irresponsible behavior had saddled them with unpayable mortgages. Wasn't that unfair? Wouldn't it create moral hazard? (Never mind that some borrowers were duped into killer mortgages.) Whether true or not, that belief placed a big political Do Not Enter sign in front of any pathway to mortgage modifications that involved taxpayer money—a sign that, sadly, did not come down even when the recession dragged many *responsible* homeowners into foreclosure.

As we shall see, these three problems—plus a myriad of details—made mortgage modifications look economically difficult, legally problematic, and politically toxic.

Haven't We Seen This Movie Before?

Once before in history, America experienced the frightening double whammy of a megarecession coupled with sharp declines in home prices. That was during the Great Depression. Back then, President Franklin Roosevelt and Congress reacted to the housing crisis with a burst of policy activism that put the governments of 2007–2010 to shame. The New Deal housing programs included establishing the FHA to insure home mortgages, Fannie Mae (then the FNMA, a government agency) to create a secondary market in mortgages, the Federal Home Loan Banks to provide funds to mortgage lenders, and the Federal Savings and Loan Insurance Corporation to insure deposits at thrift institutions. These innovations survive to the present day, more or less.

But I want to focus on the all-but-forgotten Depression-era housing agency, the one that was actually most instrumental in reducing the number of foreclosures in the 1930s and the only one that closed its doors after its job was done: the Home Owners' Loan Corporation (HOLC). Yes, the 2000s were different from the 1930s, but we could have created an up-to-date version of the HOLC in 2008 or 2009. Had we done that, the foreclosure problem would probably be over by now.

The HOLC was established in June 1933 as a public corporation with a single mission: to help distressed families avert foreclosures by replacing mortgages that were in or near default with new ones they could actually afford. It did so by buying up old mortgages from banks, most of which were delighted to trade dubious mortgages for government bonds that would actually be paid back, and then issuing new loans to homeowners.

The HOLC was financed by borrowing both on the capital markets and from the Treasury, and it operated on a massive scale. Within three years, it granted just over a million new mortgages, most of which were of the 15-year, fixed-rate, fully amortizing variety—a new instrument that the HOLC apparently invented. Nearly one out of every ten nonfarm homes in America became mortgaged to the federal government, which would translate to over 7.5 million today. Total lending over the HOLC's lifetime amounted to $3.5 billion—a colossal sum at the time, equal to about 5 percent of a year's GDP. The corresponding figure today would be about $800 billion.

As a public corporation focused on social goals rather than profits, the HOLC was a pliable buyer and a lenient lender. It offered banks pretty generous terms, and it tried to keep delinquent borrowers on track through debt counseling and help with budgeting. Of course, times were tough in the 1930s, and nearly 20 percent of HOLC's borrowers defaulted, anyway. So you might think it cost the taxpayers of the day a bundle. Not so. In fact, by the time the HOLC closed its books, it had netted a small profit. It was a heavy lift, but the incredible HOLC lifted it.

Relative to the size of either the economy or the federal government, the lift in 2008 or 2009 probably would have been lighter. But the governments we had then were far more timid and divided than FDR's was. Instead, as we will see, both the Bush and Obama administrations tried to do the job on the cheap. Whereas the HOLC lent out the equivalent of 5 percent of GDP, the Obama administration's foreclosure-mitigation program amounted to a tiny fraction of that—and the Bush administration spent nothing.

The HOLC precedent meant that policy makers didn't have to reinvent the wheel. Granted, contemporary mortgage finance is more complex than it was in the 1930s, when banks knew their customers and mortgagees knew their banks. A 2008 version of the HOLC would have had to deal with mortgages that were securitized and sold to buyers all over the world, and with mortgage pools that were sliced, diced, and tranched into complex derivative instruments that no one really understood. The new HOLC could not have been an exact replica of the old HOLC. But they'd have been close relatives.

All this complexity, however, bolsters rather than undermines the case for government intervention. A mortgage workout presents one set of problems when the borrower and lender can sit down together to renegotiate terms, knowing that success will make both better off. But how do you conduct a negotiation when the borrower and lender don't even know each other's names? This is one reason why so few delinquent mortgage loans have been renegotiated, even to this day. It is also one reason why strong government intervention was essential.

In a February 2008 op-ed piece in the *New York Times*, I argued for the creation of a new HOLC that would borrow and lend between $200 billion and $400 billion to refinance between 1 million and 2 million homes. And I sketched a back-of-the-envelope calculation suggesting that the new HOLC, like the original, could turn a modest profit in the end. I was not alone in doing so. Economists Paul Davidson and Alex Pollock had the idea of reviving the HOLC before I did, and Senator Chuck Schumer (D-NY) advocated something similar.

By coincidence, a few days later I attended a meeting of House Democratic leaders where the then-budding housing crisis was on the agenda. My HOLC idea came up in passing—but, believe me, only in passing. It was rejected instantly as being wildly too expensive. At that stage, the TARP was still eight months away, and neither politicians nor their constituents were thinking about committing hundreds of billions of dollars of public money. I often muse about how much better things might have been had Congress revived the HOLC idea back in 2008, when the foreclosure problem was much smaller than it subsequently, and predictably, became.

Reviving the HOLC was not the only foreclosure mitigation idea to emerge from the academy in 2008, and they didn't all come from spend-thrifty (actually *borrow*-thrifty) Democrats like me. Two weeks after my HOLC piece appeared, the *Wall Street Journal*—a newspaper not known then or now for its Left-leaning views*—published an op-ed by Martin Feldstein of Harvard, who had once chaired Ronald Reagan's Council of Economic Advisers (CEA). Feldstein offered a plan to replace 20 percent of each homeowner's mortgage with a low-interest loan from the government. The new loans would be made *with recourse*, however, so the government could go after other assets of any defaulting borrower.

In October 2008, Columbia's Glenn Hubbard, who had been George W. Bush's first CEA chairman, writing with his colleague Chris Mayer, a noted housing expert, suggested using Fannie Mae and Freddie Mac (which were by then under government control) to refinance *all* mortgages on primary residences into 30-year fixed-rate mortgages at 5.25 percent. The prevailing mortgage rate at the time was around 6.25 percent, but many older mortgages bore higher rates. As part of their plan, a new HOLC would be created to hold the underwater mortgages. Feldstein and Hubbard were

---

Full disclosure: I now write a regular op-ed column for the *Wall Street Journal*. The statement stands nonetheless.

two pillars of the Republican economics establishment. I was a labeled Democrat. The desire to get the country out of the foreclosure muck was not partisan—and the need was apparent.

Whatever the merits of these or other ideas, they were "academic" in the following sense: None of them made even a ripple on the political pond. They were all nonstarters, and mostly for the same reason: The huge amount of money the government would have to put up—not *spend*, but *borrow* and relend. The instant rejection of these and related ideas illustrates the first of our unholy trinity of barriers to solving the foreclosure problem: the unwillingness to put enough public money on the line. Amazingly, this resistance persisted even after Lehman Brothers failed and the TARP was hurriedly established.

You Gotta Have Hope

It's not as if nobody noticed the foreclosure problem. As early as August 2007, the federal government initiated the first of many attempts to mitigate it—and its first failure. Called *FHA Secure*, the new program was predicated on the prevailing belief at the time that the main problem headed our way was a wave of resets of subprime ARMs carrying low teaser rates. That view of the future seemed right in August 2007, but it proved to be wrong—as is often the case with crystal balls. In any case, FHA Secure offered holders of subprime ARMs the opportunity to refinance into FHA-guaranteed fixed-rate mortgages—*if* they were up-to-date on their mortgage payments (or had been, prior to the reset).

The program turned out to be overly complicated and never really went anywhere. When it was allowed to expire in December 2008, FHA Secure had refinanced fewer than five thousand mortgages. The program's failure contained two important design hints that, sad to say, were *not* carried over into subsequent efforts. If you want to reach large numbers of people, many of whom are barely financially literate, you must (a) market the program aggressively and (b) adhere scrupulously to the KISS principle: *Keep It Simple, Stupid.* FHA Secure was neither simple nor marketed aggressively. Unfortunately, neither were the mortgage-modification programs that followed it. That's one reason they largely failed.

Next came the *Hope Now Alliance*, which was announced with great fanfare in October 2007 and still exists today. Although nurtured and encouraged by the federal government via the Treasury and the Department of Housing and Urban Development (HUD), Hope Now is an entirely *voluntary, private* effort by a consortium of mortgage lenders, servicers, and counselors—including Fannie Mae and Freddie Mac, which were then still private companies—and a number of large banks such as Citi and JP Morgan Chase.

Hope Now focused on outreach, counseling, and encouraging delinquent borrowers to talk to their mortgage servicers about ways to become current again. It was more about minimizing lenders' prospective losses than about reducing homeowners' financial burdens.

Such a tilt is hardly surprising in a voluntary, *industry-led* effort. After all, any mortgage modification that reduces homeowners' payments must, by the inexorable laws of double-entry bookkeeping, also reduce lenders' receipts. For that simple reason, as Paulson's aide Phill Swagel put it, "avoiding more foreclosures required someone—either the government or lenders—to write a check." No one should expect lenders to volunteer for that honor with enthusiasm. Nonetheless, by now many of the mortgages modified voluntarily have reduced principal, interest payments, or both—and the program continues. According to Hope Now, by March 2012 about 4.4 million mortgages had been modified *without* government assistance.

But the most obvious lesson gleaned from Hope Now is one we knew beforehand: Voluntarism goes only so far, and often not very far when someone is being asked to act against his own self-interest. The Paulson Treasury surely understood this in 2008. While it pushed to get more mortgages modified privately, it was unwilling either to commit government funds, which it really didn't have until TARP passed, or to interfere much in private contracting. The latter brings us to the second part of the unholy trinity: property rights.

I have mentioned that it is quite difficult—maybe impossible—to solve the foreclosure problem without rearranging at least some property rights. I offered second mortgages as an example. Other examples come from the securitization process. Remember, most subprime mortgages were packaged and securitized. These securitizations created legal structures that made it difficult to break out individual mortgages for modification—especially when several legal entities stood between the original borrower (say, John Doe in Phoenix) and the ultimate lender (say, an Italian pension fund).

Cutting through such a legal morass might well entail trampling on someone's property rights. For example, economist (and hedge fund partner) John Geanakoplos and lawyer Susan Koniak proposed in 2008 that Congress pass a law overriding existing securitization contracts by giving government-appointed trustees the authority to modify mortgages. I found their idea attractive. The Bush and Obama administrations did not.

Why not? In a capitalist society, rearranging property rights outside of well-established legal channels, such as bankruptcy courts and foreclosure proceedings, is a nasty business—something to be avoided except under extreme circumstances. Some would say it's something to be avoided at all costs, period. In any case, neither Hank Paulson in the Bush administration nor Tim Geithner and Larry Summers in the Obama administration were willing to go there—and not without reason. Again, it depended on how deep you thought the problem was, relative to the sanctity of contracts.

The "hope" approach did not end with Hope Now. In July 2008, President Bush signed into law Hope for Homeowners (you can call it H4H), a program largely designed by Democratic congressional staff. This new government effort, which went into effect that October, was designed to help up to 400,000 delinquent borrowers refinance their mortgages into new FHA-guaranteed loans—*if* the original lender would forgive part of the principal on the original mortgage. That proved to be a big *if.* In practice, hardly any lenders were willing to accept write-downs of principal—which meant recognizing losses on their books. Remember, H4H was voluntary. The government would not force and did not cajole banks into taking write-downs.

For this reason, and because Hope for Homeowners was complicated, CNN reported that by March 2009 it had helped exactly *one* homeowner avoid foreclosure. One! (CNN did not report his or her name.) In what may have been the understatement of the year, an FHA official admitted that "the program isn't working terribly well." Well, I guess not—just 399,999 loan modifications short. H4H expired at the end of September 2011, having insured only 762 houses. Calling it a drop in the bucket would exaggerate its importance.

There was a fascinating subtext to all this: a running battle between Secretary of the Treasury Paulson and the FDIC's Sheila Bair. The details of their disputes over mortgages were mind-numbingly complex. (Don't worry, I won't recount them.) But the essence was that Bair wanted to take a more aggressive approach toward mortgage modifications than did Paulson, a son of Wall Street who was more worried about moral hazard and far from convinced that Bair had a workable plan. In July 2008, when the FDIC was unable to find a buyer for the failed California savings and loan association, IndyMac Bank, Bair got her chance.

IndyMac was a symbol of what had gone wrong. Originally started by Countrywide, an even more notorious mortgage lender, IndyMac was spun off as a separate entity in 1997.* Under aggressive leadership, it grew into one of the country's largest—and worst—mortgage lenders, specializing in lending to less-than-stellar credits. When the $32 billion bank went bust, the FDIC couldn't find anyone to take it off their hands at reasonable cost. Taxpayers were left holding the bag—a bag that featured a huge portfolio of dodgy mortgages in an entity that became IndyMac *Federal* Bank, with Sheila Bair as its de facto CEO.

Taking over management of the remnants of IndyMac gave Bair the opportunity to try to turn lemons into lemonade. As she stated in a press release announcing the FDIC's loan-modification program for IndyMac, "I have long supported a systematic and streamlined approach to loan modifications to put borrowers into long-term, sustainable mortgages— achieving an improved return for bankers and investors compared to foreclosure." The FDIC program tried to stave off foreclosure through

---

*IndyMac was a nickname for *I*ndependent *N*ational *M*ortgage *C*orporation. Do you think they named it to sound like Fannie Mae and Freddie Mac?

interest-rate reductions, extensions of the maturities of loans, and even principal forgiveness to reduce the so-called debt-to-income (DTI) ratio to 38 percent, which the FDIC deemed affordable.* For people seeking solutions to the foreclosure problem—and who wasn't?—the IndyMac program quickly became the one to watch.

But it was far from obvious that the IndyMac model was successful. Critics pointed to high redefault rates on modified mortgages at IndyMac—partly because the 38 percent DTI standard was too high. The Paulson Treasury worried about both adverse selection (lenders offering up their worst mortgages) and moral hazard (creating incentives that encouraged default). And then there was the "little" matter that the Bair plan would have bailed bad lenders and hedge funds out of losing positions.

Undeterred, Bair sought to take the IndyMac model nationwide. On November 14, 2008, just ten days after George W. Bush and Hank Paulson became lame ducks, and just two days after Paulson's announcement that he would not use TARP to buy any troubled assets, the FDIC chief went public with a sweeping antiforeclosure plan similar to IndyMac's. DTIs would be reduced to 31 percent (not 38 percent), interest rates could fall as low as 3 percent for five years, new loans could be extended for as long as forty years, and the government would share as much as 50 percent of the losses on refinanced mortgages that defaulted again. Bair estimated that her plan could refinance 2.2 million mortgages at a net cost to the government (after redefaults) of just $24.4 billion, which was cheap— about $11,000 per loan. She proposed to get the money from the TARP.

Consumer advocates loved the Bair plan. They loved even more her incessant questioning of why the government was so willing to bail out banks but so unwilling to bail out distressed homeowners. It was a good question that never got a satisfactory answer. Bair's slightly populist stance burnished her image as a rare and lonely hero in a sea of financial scoundrels—and, by the way, ensured her retention by the president-elect even

---

*DTI is a common measure of affordability. But it's a bad acronym. DTI is *not* the ratio of *debt* to income, but rather the ratio of what is (close to) *debt service* to income—specifically, the sum of principal and interest payments, property taxes, and insurance to household income. Only the first two of these constitute debt service.

though she was practically at war with Geithner from his days as president of the Federal Reserve Bank of New York.*

But Paulson, who held the TARP purse strings, would have none of it. If the war between Paulson and Bair had been kept under wraps until then (which it wasn't), it was now out in the open. Nor did Treasury-FDIC relations improve when Geithner replaced Paulson.

WHAT ABOUT THE TARP MONEY?

When Congress passed the TARP legislation in October 2008, there could be no doubt that foreclosure mitigation was among its chief concerns. Scanning the legislation turns up seven mentions of the word "foreclosure," mostly concentrated in two sections whose titles have unmistakable meanings: "Foreclosure mitigation efforts" (Section 109), and "Assistance to homeowners" (Section 110). For example, Section 109 instructs the secretary of the Treasury to coordinate with other federal agencies to "identify opportunities for the acquisition of troubled assets that will improve the ability of the Secretary to improve the loan modification and restructuring process." What's a "troubled asset"? The first item listed in the legal definition is "residential or commercial mortgages." *Congress to Treasury:* Look for opportunities to acquire mortgages and modify them.

Thus no sentient human being could have missed the fact that Congress wanted some of the TARP money—it didn't say how much—used to reduce the foreclosure problem. Paulson was a sentient human being, yet he did not allocate a single dollar to this purpose—presumably because he was fixated on recapitalizing the banks and planned to preserve substantial TARP money for his successor.

During the transition, the incoming Obama administration agreed with congressional Democrats to allocate $50 billion in TARP money to foreclosure mitigation, and Geithner quickly did that on becoming secre-

---

*Legally, Bair's term as FDIC chair ran well into 2010, so President Obama could not have removed her. But agency heads often depart voluntarily if they are no longer wanted.

tary of the Treasury. But comparing that with the hundreds of billions of dollars called for in the Blinder, Feldstein, Hubbard-Mayer, and other foreclosure-mitigation plans makes it clear that Geithner was trying to get the job done on the cheap. Maybe the incoming Obama administration had better ideas than these (and other) academics. But it just wasn't plausible that $50 billion, no matter how cleverly deployed, would be adequate.* If not, the Obama foreclosure initiatives were never going to be enough to solve the problem.

Why, then, did Geithner allocate so little TARP money to preventing foreclosures? The main reason was that he, Summers, and others in the administration were not convinced that there was a foreclosure-mitigation plan that could work on a large scale, was legal, and would have a large economic impact at reasonable cost. They thought there were other, more cost-effective uses of TARP money. Geithner may also have been worried that the TARP well would run dry. Paulson had left him more than half of the TARP's $700 billion. But he knew there were more banks to recapitalize, lots of "troubled assets" to buy, more potential claims on TARP such as the auto bailout—plus what Donald Rumsfeld once memorably called "unknown unknowns." Any concern about running out of TARP money proved unfounded; the Treasury never came close to using the full $700 billion. But no one knew that in January 2009.

Trying and Trying Again

As noted at the outset, the multifaceted Obama antiforeclosure efforts failed to stop the tsunami. But not for lack of trying. At the time of this writing, the administration's programs include HAMP, HARP, HAFA, HAUP, and HHF—plus a few more. (Definitions presently.) Yet new waves of foreclosures, plus a large unsold inventory of foreclosed homes, continue to depress house prices, which continue to depress new homebuilding,

---

*Actually, $75 billion was allocated, since another $25 billion was kicked in from Fannie Mae and Freddie Mac, which were by then really government agencies. In March 2012, CBO estimated that only $16 billion of the $50 billion from TARP would ever be utilized.

which continues to depress the overall economy. A highly publicized settlement with major banks over irregularities in the foreclosure process in February 2012 ironically *increased* the number of foreclosures, at least for a while, by breaking the legal logjam.

The banking plan that Treasury Secretary Geithner sketched in his first major speech on February 10, 2009, had four main components. One of them was the bank stress tests. Two others were new programs meant to accomplish the original stated purposes of the TARP: buying troubled assets. The fourth was, in Geithner's words, "a comprehensive plan to address the housing crisis." Unfortunately, he also added, "We will announce the details of this plan in the next few weeks," which led all hell to break loose in the jittery financial markets. After all, the new administration had been in office for three weeks already, and their plan was not complete!

It took Geithner only eight more days to finish the job. The housing plan, ungrammatically named *Making Home Affordable*, was announced by the president in a February 18 speech. It was supposed to help 7 million to 9 million homeowners modify or refinance their mortgages.

Its two main components were HARP and HAMP. The Home Affordable Refinancing Program (HARP) was aimed at the bigger—and presumably easier—target: refinancing the mortgages of homeowners who had managed to keep up on their payments but who were unable to refinance to a lower rate because their home values had dropped. The Home Affordable Modification Program (HAMP) was aimed at the harder cases: helping homeowners who might otherwise default by getting them mortgage modifications that enabled them to stay in their homes. How did these two programs fare?

The Home Affordable Refinancing Program

HARP's announced goal was 4 million to 5 million refinancings, all from mortgages owned or guaranteed by Fannie Mae or Freddie Mac. But HARP proved to be a tough slog, more like hand-to-hand combat than decisive air strikes. Along the way, the Treasury discovered that there were fewer eligible homeowners than they thought. By the end of July 2009, a mere 60,000 mortgages had been refinanced. By August 2011, refinancings under HARP were up to 810,000—a serious number but still way short of the administration's goal. By May 2012, the count was up to 1.3 million.

One of the difficulties the Treasury encountered was mentioned earlier: Holders of second mortgages could, and often did, block refinancing of existing first mortgages. Another problem arose when Fannie's and Freddie's regulator refused to let the companies relinquish certain property rights that made banks wary of refinancing. For example, when a bank proposes to refinance a mortgage owned by Fannie or Freddie, the GSE has the legal right to "put" the original mortgage back to the originating bank if there is even the slightest irregularity in the original documents. Bankers didn't want these loans back! The administration started to address this problem only in October 2011—a long wait.

The Home Affordable Modification Program

HAMP was, in some respects, patterned on Sheila Bair's IndyMac protocol, though Bair and Geithner continued to spar. It included a target DTI of 31 percent for the modified mortgage, lower interest rates, and incentives for mortgage servicers to engage in modifications ("mods" to the cognoscenti). The program's stated goal was to keep 3 million to 4 million imperiled homeowners in their homes by getting their mortgages modified, but the Treasury later concluded that only 2.5 million delinquent loans were actually eligible.

Just like HARP, HAMP proved to be hand-to-hand combat, one mortgage at a time. It took a long while, but by June 2012 it had successfully modified just over a million loans—out of nearly 1.9 million trial modifications started. The median savings among these successful "mods" was about $6,400 a year, which ain't hay.

In October 2010, the Treasury began implementing a modification of its modification program. Under the HAMP Principal Reduction Alternative, the government started encouraging lenders to reduce principal. Not requiring, mind you, nor even pushing very hard, just encouraging. But even encouraging principal reductions was a step forward, one the administration had mostly resisted until then. Yet by June 2012, a mere 67,000 mortgages had been modified under this program.

The Others

Bored yet? I'll be quicker on the other Obama programs, which were implemented as old problems became better understood, as new problems arose, and as results from HAMP and HARP disappointed.

The Home Affordable Foreclosure Alternatives Program

HAFA (yes, missing the *P*) was created in October 2009 to facilitate *short sales*. In a short sale, the bank agrees to accept the house in lieu of the unpaid mortgage balance. This option, of course, is attractive only to homeowners who are underwater—owing the bank more than their houses are worth. But there were many such people at the time, and there still are today. Contemporary estimates suggested that approximately one mortgage in four was underwater; so there was no shortage of potential HAFA clients. Nonetheless, by June 2012, under 57,000 short sales had been arranged. HAFA is far from a success story.

The Hardest Hit Funds

Yes, HHF, a set of state-by-state programs, was added to the government's repertoire in February 2010 in recognition of the fact that some states were hit particularly hard by the recession and the housing market collapse. HHF programs include such things as mortgage-payment assistance for unemployed homeowners, principal reductions, and funding to eliminate second mortgages. As of April 2012, $7.6 billion had been *allocated* to Hardest Hit Funds in eighteen states and the District of Columbia, but under $1 billion had been *spent*. Another slow starter.

The Home Affordable Unemployment Program

As the national unemployment problem lengthened and deepened, HAUP was added to the repertoire in July 2010. Its intent is to provide temporary reductions or suspensions of mortgage payments when homeowners lose their jobs. HAUP is a good example of adapting to the changing face of a problem. As noted earlier, the big foreclosure issue had become delinquency due to job loss, not due to interest-rate resets. HAUP sounded like a good idea. But by the end of April 2012, it had helped a mere 24,000 households.

Had enough? There are a few more programs, which I won't mention here. The purpose of this little—well, maybe not so little—*tour du programme* is to illustrate, first, that the Obama administration did not exactly ignore the foreclosure problem, and second, that progress has been slow nonetheless. The problem festers, with millions of homes in foreclosure proceedings as this is written. That means millions of miserable families and millions more worried that they might be next.

Why such slow progress? The details vary by program, of course, but a few factors are common. The first was failure to respect the KISS principle. The various programs are complex, and the details may have been poorly understood, especially by unsophisticated homeowners. Second, and related, prospective beneficiaries of these programs were made to jump through many hoops—often to make it hard for undeserving homeowners to qualify. Also, as mentioned earlier, getting second-mortgage holders to agree proved to be a vexing problem. Third, neither the GSEs nor the banks were exactly falling over one another to participate in refinancings and modifications; they needed stronger incentives—and maybe a bit more prodding, which the government did not provide. Fourth, the government did insufficient outreach. It needed to seek out eligible people and help them through the process, but it didn't. All that said, the Treasury Department seemed to get better at the job as time went on. Better, but not good.

Throughout the debate over foreclosure mitigation, a running argument raged over whether the programs should allow for, encourage, or even *require* principal reductions—which, in less-polite English, might be called partial defaults. Consumer advocates clamored for principal write-downs. Many economists insisted—and still do—that the mortgage overhang would never be solved without them. But bankers hated the idea, partly because they didn't want to give up hope of collecting the full balance on each loan, but probably more because they didn't want to recognize losses on their books. The Geithner Treasury was a bit like *Hamlet* on the issue: *To reduce principal or not to reduce principal? That was the question.* Somehow, Geithner never gave the impression that he was eager to encourage write-downs.

Notice a few things about the debate over principal reductions: First, write-downs are *expensive.* When a $250,000 mortgage balance is reduced to $200,000, either the bank or the government has to swallow $50,000—depending on who gets the bill. Perhaps more germane in practice, the new mortgage requires $200,000 in fresh financing *from someone.* In a worst case, the government might have to borrow the $200,000.

Second, principal reductions create moral hazard. If my neighbor gets his mortgage balance reduced, say, via a government-subsidized program, I may line up for a reduction, too. As usual, the moral hazard issue has validity; the government does not want to be in the business of bailing out debtors routinely. But just as in the case of the bank bailouts, moral hazard was not a show-stopper. We had an emergency on our hands.

Third, unless they are strictly voluntary, write-downs of principal amount to *rearrangements of property rights* outside of bankruptcy proceedings. In the example above, the owner of the mortgage has a legal claim to collect $250,000 from the borrower. If, say, the state comes along and "persuades" the mortgage owner to reduce this to $200,000, it is taking away some of his property rights. Tampering with property rights is not something to be taken lightly.

Notice that two of these points reprise two of the three main barriers to solving the mortgage problem highlighted at the beginning of the chapter: the need for money and the perils of altering property rights. The third was crystallized by Rick Santelli.

THE RICK SANTELLI RANT

Who? Rick Santelli is a reporter and commentator for CNBC. He's also a bit high-strung, as anyone who has watched his reports from the floors of the Chicago Board of Trade and the Chicago Mercantile Exchange (CME) can attest. And he leans Right, politically.

The day after President Obama unveiled his Making Home Affordable plan in February 2009, Santelli was on the air reporting from the CME floor, where he and the local commodity traders expressed displeasure with the plan. What happened that day made history. Here's an excerpt of what quickly became known as "the Rick Santelli rant." In his words:

> You know, the government is promoting bad behavior! . . .
>
> Why don't you put up a Web site to have people vote on the Internet as a referendum to see if we really want to subsidize the losers' mortgages? Or would we like to, at least, buy cars and buy houses in foreclosure? Give 'em to people that might have a chance to actually prosper down the road, and reward people that could carry the water instead of drink the water.
>
> [*cheers from traders*]
>
> This is America! How many of you people want to pay for your neighbor's mortgage that has an extra bathroom and can't pay their bills? Raise their hand!
>
> [*boos from the traders*]
>
> President Obama, are you listening?
>
> [*a trader in the background:* "How about we all stop paying our mortgage? It's a moral hazard."]
>
> . . .
>
> We're thinking of having a Chicago Tea Party in July. All you capitalists that want to show up to Lake Michigan, I'm going to start organizing.
>
> [*cheers*]

While most Tea Partiers probably have never heard of Rick Santelli, several of their leaders have acknowledged that those words were the origin of the Tea Party, a political movement that has channeled Right-wing discontent effectively and, in a real sense, transformed American politics.

Commodity traders are hardly representative of American society as a whole. Many of them are "go for broke" kinds of guys—yes, they are almost all guys—who take large risks every day and live with the consequences. But they also have much higher incomes than average Americans, much larger wealth cushions to fall back on when adversity strikes, and, I venture to guess, much less chance of losing their homes. Rick Santelli and his band of merry men were *not* America speaking on that day in February 2009. In fact, a Gallup poll just a few days later found that Americans *favored* "giving [federal] aid to homeowners who are in danger of losing their homes to foreclosures" by a whopping 64 percent to 33 percent margin.

Nonetheless, the Rick Santelli rant went viral, and the hostility expressed on the trading floor toward bailing out "losers" who had "an extra bathroom and can't pay their bills" struck a chord. The belief set in that Americans were not much happier about bailing out distressed homeowners than they were about bailing out distressed Wall Streeters—or commodity traders, for that matter. That, too, was blatantly false. The same Gallup poll found 59 percent to 39 percent *opposition* to giving federal aid to "U.S. banks and financial companies in danger of failing." Sheila Bair had a truer finger on the public pulse than did Rick Santelli—and was more correct on the pros and cons. But Santelli had a loud megaphone and shouted what many conservatives wanted to hear: that homeowners facing foreclosure had been irresponsible and did not deserve help.

Politicians are quick learners—even if what they learn isn't true. The Santelli rant, and others like it, made government-financed foreclosure-mitigation efforts an uphill fight. Uphill fights require strong leadership, prodigious amounts of energy and determination, and maybe huge expenditures as well. This one certainly would have. Such fights are more often lost than won. Whatever Darwinian principles select successful politicians, a desire to fall on their sword is not among of them. So few politicians were eager to sign up for "a referendum to see if we really want to subsidize the losers' mortgages." They feared, probably wrongly, that they knew how it would turn out.

THE MORE THINGS CHANGE,
THE MORE THEY STAY THE SAME

A successful effort to halt the wave of foreclosures would have had to overcome numerous complexities and legal inhibitions. It would have required the government to put hundreds of billions of taxpayer dollars at risk—though, as in the 1930s, actual losses might have been minimal. And perhaps most significantly, politicians feared it would hang albatrosses around their necks.

No wonder it didn't happen. No wonder foreclosure-mitigation efforts never got top priority. No wonder we never broke the vicious cycle that started with falling house prices, went on to collapsing financial markets, which in turn led us into recession and high unemployment, and then to massive foreclosures, and finally right back to falling house prices.

This tragedy didn't take us by surprise. The foreclosure train wreck was, as I've emphasized, not just *foreseeable* but actually *foreseen*. But we let it happen anyway, accepting the bitter fruits as if we were one of Santelli's ranters. It was, after all, the properly Social Darwinist thing to do. But here's the ultimate irony: By now, the overhang of excess houses should be a thing of the past. House prices should be recovering, and new homebuilding should be one of the sectors leading the economy out of the doldrums. How do I know? It's simple arithmetic.

We had an unsustainable housing boom from 2002 through 2006. Comparing those five halcyon years with the preceding eight, we probably overbuilt by about 1.75 million too many houses. That's what happens when you have a speculative bubble. Past bubbles have left us, for example, with too many railroads, too much fiber optic cable, and so on. This one left us with too many houses.

But think about the numbers. An extra 1.75 million houses is not much more than a year's normal production. Based on preboom norms, we have now *failed to build* about 3.5 million houses during the five bust years since 2008—a total that keeps climbing. In other words, the homebuilding *shortfall* since 2008 has been twice as large as the foolish *overbuilding* during the boom. On balance, the United States should now be experiencing a *shortage* of housing, *rising* house prices, and a homebuilding *boom*—which would be helping the economy recover.

Yet none of this has happened. Instead, the moribund housing sector has been one of the main factors keeping us in the soup for so long. Even today, with the housing sector recovering, homebuilding is a fraction of what it was, the inventory of foreclosed homes is barely below its 2011 peak, and something like 25 percent of all home sales come from foreclosures. Failure to solve the foreclosure problem is one of the reasons we have had such a weak housing sector and weak recovery for so long—and it didn't have to be that way. It is hard to resist the conclusion that we just didn't try hard enough.

13

|||||||||||||||||||||||||||

THE BACKLASH

We saved the economy, but we kind of lost the public doing it.

— TREASURY SECRETARY TIM GEITHNER, MARCH 2010

The previous chapter emphasized the gross inadequacy of our nation's policy responses to the foreclosure problem. But that was the exception that proved the rule. On balance, the years 2008–2010 were marked by extraordinary policy activism, not passivity, by the Federal Reserve and two presidential administrations. The scope and volume of these policies were enough to keep heads spinning and policy makers exhausted. And, as I mentioned at the outset, perhaps the biggest surprise of the entire episode is that they succeeded as well as they did.

But as they say in physics, every action prompts an equal and opposite reaction. Barack Obama, Ben Bernanke, Tim Geithner, and Hank Paulson were not exactly lionized for their efforts. Instead, the grab bag of largely successful policy activism in 2008–2009 produced a severe antigovernment backlash in 2009–2012, one that had huge electoral consequences in 2010 and was an albatross around Obama's neck in 2012.

Asking *why* is the central purpose of this chapter. The answer is not only relevant to our past but also to our future, because the severity of the backlash has left many observers wondering whether the U.S. government would be able to mount such an extensive and complex rescue should the music stop again.

The Policy Paradox

As the financial system and the economy slipped toward the abyss after the Lehman failure, virtually everyone in America turned toward the federal government. Banks and Wall Street sought shelter from the storm. Businesses sought the restoration of normal financing. Households sought jobs, a safety net, mortgage relief, and an end to falling home prices. State and local governments sought money to replace plummeting tax revenues.

In a humorous sign of the times, a *New Yorker* cartoon appeared in March 2009, just as the financial crisis was hitting bottom. It depicted a medieval courtyard, where an executioner was about to separate the king from his head. But a messenger rushes in shouting, "Stop! Wait! Government's no longer the problem—it's the solution." Forget the old Reaganite attitude, the cartoonist was suggesting, the federal government was saving the day.

But the notion of government-as-solution didn't last long. As soon as the financial industry was back on its feet, tycoons started bridling against excessive regulation and complaining about being treated as scapegoats. Scapegoats? How about perpetrators? President Obama was labeled a socialist and worse by arch-conservatives, who railed against "big government." By the time of the November 2010 elections, Tea Party Republicans were running—and often winning—on virulently antigovernment platforms that placed them far to the right of Ronald Reagan, whom they professed to idolize.

Think about it: The crisis was the result of a series of grievous errors, misjudgments, and even frauds by *private* companies and individuals, aided and abetted by a hands-off policy from a government unduly enamored of laissez-faire. America was plainly a victim of *too little* regulation, not *too much.* Only after the blowup in September 2008 did the formerly passive government turn interventionist—in desperation. As Paulson noted in his memoir, "I am a firm believer in free markets, and I certainly hadn't come to Washington planning to do anything to inject the government into the private sector." But he did, as did Bernanke and Geithner—neither of whom is exactly a closet socialist.

And it worked. The worst was avoided. Financial markets returned to something approximating normalcy much faster than seemed likely. There was no Great Depression 2.0. According to the estimates by Mark Zandi and me mentioned earlier, real GDP in 2011 was $1.8 *trillion* higher than it would have been without all the rescue operations. With that much more output, there were 9.8 million more jobs, and the unemployment rate was 6.5 percentage points lower. These are huge effects that transformed what might have been an utter catastrophe into something that was merely awful.

You might have thought that such a bravura performance would restore faith in government and put the advocates of laissez-faire to rout. But no. In a cruel twist on the Emanuel Principle, the coincidence in time of the horrible recession with multiple policy interventions gave the antigovernment crowd an opening to vilify the government. Which they took, with devastating effect.

Perhaps the counterfactual notion that things *would have been much worse* but for the extensive policy responses interventions is too subtle for politics. In any case, it never caught on with the public. Instead, there was a backlash against the Federal Reserve; against the Obama administration, Congress, and especially Democrats; against Keynesian economics itself, and even against economists; and most certainly against policy activism. After all, policy levers were pulled all over Washington, and the economy tanked, anyway. Right? By the same reasoning, firefighters cause fires and people age faster in Florida. But the argument caught on. Why?

Americans have long been pragmatically liberal but ideologically conservative. At the level of lip service, most of us have an inner Thomas Jefferson who makes us wary of big government. We don't trust either politicians or concentrated power—which are good ideas. We prize both free enterprise and rugged individualism—more good ideas. We tend to resent government intrusions into our lives, and we don't much like paying taxes. All of these attitudes are quintessentially American.

But when push comes to shove, Americans often turn to government to solve their problems—whether it be settling the West, building canals and later highways, ending the Great Depression, providing New Deal and Great Society safety nets, and so on. We idolize Jefferson, but we follow Hamilton. This disjuncture between talk and action was captured perfectly during the heated summer debate over health care reform in 2009 when a South Carolinian warned his congressman to "keep your government hands off my Medicare."

Therein lies the essential paradox of the great backlash. Government actions successfully mitigated some of the damage caused by letting free markets run amok. Yet, in a strange sort of guilt by association, policy activism shouldered part of the blame for the horrors that followed. And the public turned its ire against "big government," starting with the new president.

The Backlash Against the President and Congress

Figure 13.1 is a graph we have seen before; it shows monthly job losses from January 2008 through December 2010. But I now call attention to four important dates: the fall of Lehman Brothers in September 2008, the election of Barack Obama in November 2008 and his inauguration in January 2009, and the passage of the big fiscal stimulus bill in February 2009. The big picture looks pretty straightforward: The U.S. economy was in free fall from the time of the Lehman collapse through the first quarter of 2009, with terrifying rates of job loss. Then a big fiscal stimulus was passed in February, and job losses started to abate immediately and dramatically—falling from about 780,000 a month in January–March 2009 to under 40,000 a month in January–February 2010. The graph virtually conjures up an image of Barack Obama riding in on horseback to save the day.

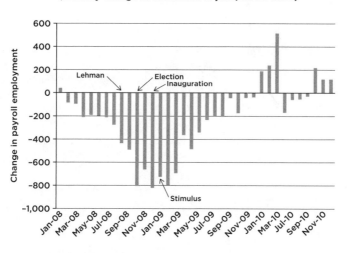

FIGURE 13.1 *Down and Up*
(monthly change in thousands of jobs, 2008–2010)

But the public didn't see it that way. What Americans saw instead was a new president elected in November 2008 on a platform that promised change. Yet the unemployment rate kept rising until October 2010. The recession, though officially declared over by the National Bureau of Economic Research in June 2009, seemed to last forever, with the economy showing precious few signs of life. Times were tough, wages and incomes stagnated, and jobs were excruciatingly hard to get. That was *change*?

Figure 13.2 shows the devastating effect on President Obama's approval rating, which began to plunge almost immediately after he took office and continued to drop into 2010. Of course, he was not up for reelection in 2010. But the entire House of Representatives was, as were thirty-seven senators—with disastrous results for the Democrats.

The angry American electorate, which had swept Democrats into power in November 2008, turned on them viciously in November 2010. Going into the election, there were 256 Democrats in the House. Coming out, there were just 193. It was the biggest seat swing by any party since 1938, and it left the House with the most Republican members since 1946. Changes in the Senate were less dramatic, but Republicans picked up 6 seats. Governorships and state legislatures also swung Republican. It was an electoral rout for the Democrats.

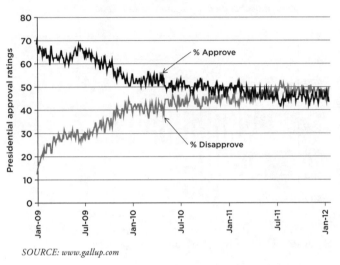

FIGURE 13.2 *To Approve or Not to Approve*

SOURCE: *www.gallup.com*

For their prodigious and largely successful economy-saving efforts, Obama and his party got a big Bronx cheer from the voters. Former president Clinton, as astute a political observer as we have, wrote, "One of the most interesting things to me [about the 2010 elections] is how easy it was to persuade so many Americans . . . to join in the government-bashing." And the government-bashing continued right through the 2012 campaign, even though President Obama won.

The Backlash Against the Fed

In the American system of government, the president and the Congress are about as visible as you can get. They are normally on the receiving end when vitriol spews from the public. The Federal Reserve was *vastly* less visible prior to the financial crisis. It did not have a high public profile at all; indeed, few Americans knew what it did. During the AIG episode in September 2008, even Barney Frank, as smart and knowledgeable a member of Congress as there was, expressed surprise to learn that the Fed has an essentially unlimited pocketbook.

Some members of Congress, mainly Republicans but also some Democrats, resented the Fed's power, even questioning its constitutionality. Anti-Fed sentiment arose from other quarters as well. Congressman Ron Paul's (R-TX) 2009 book, *End the Fed*, became a best-seller. Perhaps because of Paul's influence, but certainly because of the Fed's impressive exercise of power, America's once-invisible central bank became one of the bêtes noires of the burgeoning Tea Party movement.

But not every objection to the Fed's policies and power came from the political world. Renowned conservative economists such as John Cochrane of the University of Chicago, Allan Meltzer of Carnegie Mellon, and John Taylor of Stanford—who had been a high-ranking official in George W. Bush's Treasury—all joined the chorus of criticism. *Joined?* Maybe I should say *led*. Cochrane excoriated the bailouts. Meltzer accused Bernanke of sacrificing the Fed's hard-earned independence by working too closely with the Treasury and Congress—and also excoriated the bailouts. Taylor argued that the Fed's unprecedented policy responses were wrong-headed and had worsened, rather than mitigated, the financial crisis—and also excoriated the bailouts. The Fed was accused of fostering inflation even though the core inflation rate was drifting down. Bernanke, a Republican himself, must have been shaking his head in wonderment—and also in worry. His own party, and some of his former intellectual compatriots, were turning against him. It hurt.

When the U.S. Congress set out to reform financial regulation in 2009–2010, the Fed's head was on the chopping block. But as we have seen, the Federal Reserve, championed by its deft chairman and protected by a friendly Treasury and House Financial Services Committee, dodged virtually every bullet. On balance, the Dodd-Frank Act left the Fed more powerful than ever.

The Fed's legislative victories did not rehabilitate the central bank in its critics' eyes, however. For example, when Ron Paul sought the 2012 Republican presidential nomination, abolishing the Federal Reserve was a major plank in his platform. Some perennials are hardy.

The Backlash Against Keynesian Economics

One factor underlying the fury against the Fed was the thoroughly Keynesian behavior of Ben Bernanke and his colleagues (which, by the way, still is Keynesian). *Loose money men,* the critics screamed, *sure to cause inflation.*

Keynesian policy is often identified with the idea that governments can and should spend their way out of recessions—hence, the common association with "big government." But that is an overly narrow interpretation of Keynesianism. For one thing, governments can fight recessions by cutting taxes rather than by raising spending, which is just what Ronald Reagan and George W. Bush did—two Keynesians in deed though not in word.

More germane to the present discussion, most American Keynesians (including Bernanke) have long believed that expansionary *monetary policy* is a better way to fight recessions than expansionary *fiscal policy.* Using monetary policy to expand the economy means, principally, cutting interest rates. And, of course, the Fed cut interest rates to the bone in 2008.

One difference between fighting recessions with monetary policy rather than with fiscal policy is that the former does not increase the government budget deficit. In fact, it *reduces* the government budget deficit in at least three ways: Lower interest rates decrease the government's cost of debt service, and an expanding economy both cuts spending—for example, on unemployment benefits—and brings in more tax revenue. But relying on antirecessionary fiscal policy—cutting taxes or spending more—boosts the deficit. And that's where much of the backlash against Keynesian economics in 2009 and thereafter had its roots.

The large fiscal stimulus that Congress passed in February 2009 (the Recovery Act) *plus* the extraordinary outlays from TARP and other measures to combat the financial crisis *plus* the normal losses of tax revenue in a recession combined to raise the federal budget deficit to extraordinary heights—from a mere 1.2 percent of GDP in 2007 to a mind-boggling 10 percent of GDP in 2009. *Ten percent of GDP?* The number itself—over

$1.4 trillion in actual dollars—was a shocker. The U.S. government hadn't run budget deficits that large since World War II. In fact, the previous postwar high was Ronald Reagan's 6 percent of GDP in 1983. Even some deficit doves started raising eyebrows.

Republicans naturally piled on. Some of the same congressmen and senators who had blithely ignored deficits while George W. Bush was president* suddenly found religion and decided that "Obama's deficits" posed a clear and present danger to American prosperity—if not to its morality. Republicans opposed the February 2009 stimulus bill, almost to the man and woman. After the Recovery Act passed, they immediately began clamoring for its repeal, declaring the stimulus to have failed long before it could possibly have worked. The phrase "job-killing government spending" became John Boehner's mantra. Never mind that it made no sense.

The notion that fiscal stimulus shrinks the economy is profoundly anti-Keynesian. Keynes said exactly the opposite. Because Republicans who supported President Bush's fiscal stimulus in 2008 turned sharply against President Obama's fiscal stimulus in 2009, I guess they had to turn sharply against Keynesian economics, too. Which they did. According to the *Economist* in 2011, "If there is one ideology that unites today's Republicans, it is Keynesianism, whose nefarious influence they are determined to stamp out." Indeed, even before the new administration took office, conservatives were arguing that the best way to grow the economy is to *reduce* federal spending, not to increase it. To Keynesians, this sounded Big Brotherish in the extreme: Right is wrong. War is peace. Up is down.

Once again, the political hysteria was partially echoed and justified by voices from the academy. Stanford's Taylor and coauthors, for example, argued in a series of papers that the stimulus program had essentially no effect on aggregate demand despite costing over $800 billion. According to Taylor, the Recovery Act "did not have a significant impact in stimulating the economy." And, he added, "I do not think this finding should come as

---

*Vice President Dick Cheney famously told then Treasury secretary Paul O'Neill in 2002 that "Reagan proved that deficits don't matter."

a surprise." Not a surprise? Really? Lord Keynes would have been shocked, as was I and other modern Keynesians. How in the world can you spend that much money, even if wastefully, without creating lots of new jobs?

THE BACKLASH AGAINST
ACTIVIST POLICY

The backlashes against the Fed and against Keynesian economics each had specific, focused targets. But a broader, more encompassing charge also came thundering from the Right: just as Ronald Reagan said, government is part of the problem, not part of the solution. I mentioned earlier the attempts by some arch-conservatives to lay the blame for the financial crisis at the doorsteps of Fannie Mae and Freddie Mac. Though a thin case, it was made often. That argument was followed in short order by a concerted effort to blame the inadequate recovery on the very government policies that were speeding it along—a chant later taken up by candidate Mitt Romney in the 2012 campaign. Policy activism backfired, the critics claimed.

Taylor argued that the Fed's "unprecedented policy regime" was doing more harm than good, so "the Fed should exit from it and return to traditional monetary policy," by which he meant adherence to "the Taylor rule"—a formulaic rule for interest-rate setting. (I will examine the Fed's exit strategies in the next chapter.) But if you did the math, most versions of the Taylor rule were calling for sharply *negative* federal funds rates at the time. In fact, once Bernanke & Co. had slashed the federal funds rate to virtually zero in December 2008, the Fed looked to quantitative easing as a substitute for doing the impossible: pushing the funds rate into negative territory. Nonetheless, Taylor opposed the Fed's unconventional monetary policies, claiming that "the financial crisis was caused, prolonged, and worsened by the Fed's departure from traditional monetary policy." What he meant by "traditional monetary policy" under the extreme circumstances of 2009 was never clear—except that he favored tighter money.

Alan Greenspan, apparently unrepentant, subsequently broadened the charge. According to him, the entire panoply of activist policy responses to the financial crisis and the Great Recession undermined the economy's normal recuperative powers. While recognizing that markets can be imperfect at times, Greenspan argued that the "presumption that intervention can substitute for market flaws . . . is itself doubtful. Much intervention turns out to hobble markets rather than enhancing them. . . . I conclude that the current government activism is hampering what should be a broad-based robust economic recovery."

The notions that the Fed should close up shop and go home once the funds rate hits zero, that fiscal stimulus is either inadvisable or harmful, and that policy activism in general does more harm than good add up to a case for giving up on recession fighting and hoping for the best. Faith-based economic policy, you might call it. The arguments of Greenspan, Taylor, and others bring to mind the notorious advice that Secretary of the Treasury Andrew Mellon gave President Herbert Hoover to let the chips fall where they may: "Liquidate labor, liquidate stocks, liquidate the farmers, liquidate real estate. It will purge the rottenness out of the system. People will work harder, live a more moral life." Interestingly, Mellon went on to tell Hoover that once the Great Depression had run its natural course, "enterprising people will pick up the pieces from less competent people." Apparently, Mellon's beliefs in laissez-faire and Social Darwinism live on. But such policies will neither mitigate recessions nor shield the people from the consequences.

LEGITIMATE GRIEVANCES

Intellectuals of the Right were agitated about allegedly inflationary monetary policy, allegedly irresponsible fiscal policy, and other allegedly misguided government interventions. But intellectual opinion doesn't rule the political roost. Ordinary Americans had other things on their minds— things that were making them angry. And their anger was well justified. Here are some of the reasons why:

The Long Slump

Most important, the U.S. economy fell into a deep hole between September 2008 and June 2009, and then climbed out of it at an *agonizingly* slow pace. By the end of 2010, the unemployment rate was "down" to 9.4 percent; by October 2012, it was still 7.9 percent. Pretty bad. Supporters of activist policies argued that the economy would have been in far worse shape without the panoply of antirecessionary policies. But people see what *is*, not what *might have been*. "It could have been worse" makes a terrible platform for incumbent politicians to run on.

To make a counterfactual case stick, you have to be extremely persuasive, persistent, and convincing. Probably lucky as well. Sadly, President Obama, Secretary of the Treasury Geithner, and others were neither persuasive, persistent, convincing, nor lucky.

Innocent Victims

The shenanigans that led up to the financial crisis claimed many victims. Some probably deserved their fate. He who speculates and loses, should lose. But an unseemly amount of fraud (a legal term) and near fraud (a moral term) in the mortgage business also claimed many innocent victims. And precious little was done to help these folks straighten out their mortgages or their lives.

Nor was the damage limited to holders of subprime mortgagees. When the markets crashed, the loss of wealth was enormous. It didn't matter whether you had a mortgage—if you owned a house, its value probably tumbled. Nor did being a renter rather than a homeowner shelter you from the storm. The values of your stocks, bonds, mutual funds, and other investments probably crumbled. In total, the wealth of U.S. households fell by something on the order of $18 *trillion*. That's more than a year's GDP.

All this wealth destruction helped bring on both the terrible recession and the sluggish recovery that followed. As Americans tried to rebuild their depleted wealth, they naturally saved more. The personal saving rate (savings as a share of disposable income) rose from about 2.5 percent in 2006–

2007 to about 5.25 percent in 2008–2010. What is saved, of course, is not spent. Until 2011, battered consumers held back the recovery.

As we have noted several times, the recession took a terrible toll on jobs. Payroll employment did not bottom out until February 2010. When it did, America had 8.8 million fewer jobs than at the January 2008 peak—even though the working-age population had grown in the interim. These massive job losses shattered millions of families' incomes, not to mention their lives. And on top of this, American taxpayers were asked to bear the costs of bailing out the very financial system that had gotten them into this mess. It didn't seem fair. It wasn't.

The Punishment Didn't Fit the Crime

While many of the victims were innocent, the perpetrators of the numerous frauds and near frauds were not. Yet who was punished for their crimes? The answer seems to be: Lee Farkas.

Who? Farkas was the head of a relatively small mortgage company called Taylor Bean & Whitaker. In 2002 he started down the primrose path by selling eight fraudulent mortgages to Fannie Mae, all of which defaulted before a single payment was made. In all eight cases, the borrower was Farkas himself! As he admitted at his April 2011 trial (notice the date—*nine years* after the crime), "It was an idea I had that probably wasn't a great idea." No, not that great.

Fannie Mae took umbrage at this practice. But Freddie Mac and Ginnie Mae (the Government National Mortgage Association, a branch of HUD) were still around to be defrauded—and Farkas did so, with gusto. By the time it was all over, *le affaire Farkas* had ballooned into a $2.9 billion web of frauds and conspiracies, for which he was convicted and sent to jail, along with several others from his firm. He is still there.

What is interesting about this case is not the colorful details (example: Farkas once boasted that he "could rob a bank with a pencil"), but the fact that Lee Farkas is apparently the highest-ranking financial official to be convicted and jailed for offenses relating to one of the largest financial crises America has ever seen. There must have been thousands of frauds leading up to the crisis. Some of them must have involved huge companies. And the head of Taylor Bean & Whitaker is the biggest fish to be fried? Can it really be true that the U.S. Department of Justice could find no bigger cases to prosecute? Where was *The Mikado* when we needed him? Only in his January 2012 State of the Union Address did President Obama finally promise to establish a special financial crimes unit in the Justice Department to investigate these cases. Yes, that was *2012!*

The Hated Bank Bailout

The politics of the bank bailout were going to be unpalatable no matter what the Bush or Obama administrations did. Saving the economy necessitated saving the banks, which was going to be politically toxic. But the way our leaders went about saving the banks left much to be desired—both in terms of what was *done* and in terms of what was *said* to explain and justify it. As I have emphasized, Secretary of the Treasury Paulson, presumably with at least the acquiescence if not the support of Bernanke and Geithner at the Fed, let the banks off the hook far too lightly in 2008. Essentially no public-purpose strings were attached to the government's capital injections. It was, *Here, please take public money on highly favorable terms.*

Could the bailout have been done differently? Yes. Minimal lending requirements could have been attached to the public assistance. Dividends could have been banned until the government was paid back. Restrictions on executive compensation could have been tougher. (As secretary of the Treasury, Geithner did toughen them in 2009.) Taxpayers could have been given more of the upside if things turned out well. Instead, many banks were hugely profitable in 2010 while ordinary Americans suffered. (Taxpayers did profit in the end, just not enough.) To add to the public distress, next to nothing was done at first to mitigate foreclosures. And the thirteenth-hour conversion of TARP from buying troubled assets to infusing capital into banks looked like a case of bait and switch.

Perhaps most unforgivably, efforts to *explain* the bank bailout to the public were both *minimal* (give them a D for effort) and highly *ineffective* (give them an F for results). To cite just one example, we have seen that few Americans know that taxpayers came out ahead on what amounted to medium-term loans to banks and Wall Street firms. Nothing would have made the bank bailout popular. But a politically astute government would have made it clear, over and over again, that it viewed aid to the banks as a necessary evil—like collateral damage in wartime. Sadly, neither the Bush nor the Obama government made this case to the public.

Explanations Were Scant

The failure to frame the bank bailout story effectively was symptomatic of a much larger failure to communicate. Amazingly, no one in authority ever really explained to the people what was going on and, more important, *why*. This abject failure to explain the extraordinary policies to ordinary people is a major reason why "we kind of lost the public."

When you are promulgating policies that both feel wrong and are unfair by any objective standard, the communication burden is heavy and doing it well is critical. Explanations by the people in power should have been offered dozens, if not hundreds, of times. Instead, the job was shirked. Can you remember even one speech by President Bush explaining the financial crisis and why his administration took the actions it did? Actually, there was one. It came on September 24, 2008, but it was neither memorable nor repeated. But what about President Obama, who we thought was such a great communicator? He certainly made some speeches on the economic plan. But there was no Clintonian focusing like a laser beam on the economy. There were no Rooseveltian fireside chats. There was no sense that saving the economy was the defining issue of the Obama presidency.

What about the two secretaries of the Treasury? Sadly, neither Hank Paulson in 2008 nor Tim Geithner in 2009 had much to say to the public. Neither man was a talented orator. If there was any doubt about that in Geithner's case, he laid it to rest with his disastrous speech of February 10, 2009. After that he mostly clammed up publicly. Once burned, twice shy.

Journalists, economists, and pundits of all stripes, of course, had lots to say about the crisis and the policy responses thereto. They still do. But they are not the country's leaders, and they were in no way responsible for the policies. In many cases, especially the economists, they had pitifully small audiences.

The dearth of effective communications, unsurprisingly, led to a dearth of understanding—and to widespread confusion, some of which we have encountered already: Like the false notion that the government *gave away* money to the banks. (It actually made loans and equity investments.) Like wrongly identifying the $787 billion stimulus with the $700 billion TARP. (They were two completely different programs.) Like the false notion that the net cost of the financial rescue to taxpayers was enormous. (In fact, it netted a profit.) Like the utter fabrication that Geithner came from Goldman Sachs. (No, that was Paulson.) If you believe that the Obama administration installed a Goldman Sachs fox to guard the public chicken coop, who then proceeded to give away zillions of dollars to undeserving bankers with no benefit to the economy, then you certainly should be hopping mad. Fortunately, none of those awful things were true. Unfortunately, many if not all of them are widely believed.

It is a measure of the Obama administration's ineptitude in communication that the public came to see Geithner, Summers, & Co. as tools of Wall Street while *at the same time* the bankers who were saved from oblivion came to hate the administration for vilifying and scapegoating them. Acquiring one of those two images was excusable, maybe even unavoidable. Acquiring *both* at the same time amounted to gross political negligence.

Did the Fed Overstep Its Authority?

Never mind the Fed's more hysterical critics. More thoughtful observers wondered, sometimes out loud, whether the central bank had overstepped its authority and started acting like a fourth branch of government. Legally, the answer was no. However, the real question is not whether the Fed acted *legally*, but whether it acted *properly*. It loaned massive amounts of money to banks on quite favorable terms—a normal activity for a central bank, but on a huge scale. It also lent impressive sums to *nonbanks*, which is quite unusual, even virtually nationalizing AIG. The Fed purchased for its own portfolio not just ultrasafe Treasury securities, but also a large volume of mortgage-related assets for which there were few other buyers. As the various bailouts were either done or refused, the central bank and the Treasury decided which financial institutions would live on with public support and which would die.

At what point, critics asked, do these extraordinary activities cross the line into tacit appropriations of public funds—a power the Constitution reserves for Congress? At what point do they thrust the technocratic Fed into the political arena? Other critics voiced a different concern: that the Fed was flirting with inflation by blowing up its balance sheet massively. If this were true, the Fed would not be *overstepping* its authority, but *abusing* it.

The Worrisome National Debt

One unhappy side effect of the financial bailouts, and especially of the recession, was the huge increase in the national debt, as shown in figure 13.3. At the end of 2007, the U.S. federal government debt held outside the government itself—that is, not by Social Security and other trust funds, nor

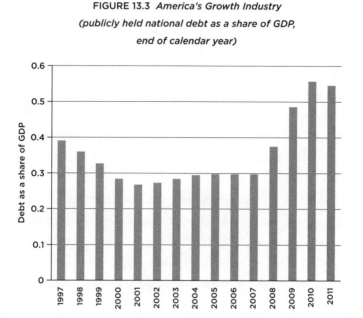

FIGURE 13.3 *America's Growth Industry*
(publicly held national debt as a share of GDP,
end of calendar year)

by the Federal Reserve—was just 30 percent of GDP, right about where it had been since 2004. But by the end of 2011, the debt-to-GDP ratio was over 55 percent—a stunning increase in just four years.

This fiscal development alarmed many observers and gave political salience to the deep-seated American aversion to budget deficits. In fact, however, a Congress riven by partisanship did next to nothing to repair the long-run budget situation in 2010, 2011, or 2012. The December 2010 report of the National Commission on Fiscal Responsibility and Reform, headed by Alan Simpson (a former Republican senator) and Erskine Bowles (a former Democratic White House chief of staff) was widely praised by editorialists and good-government types everywhere. It was almost completely ignored by politicians.

There *was* a rare bipartisan agreement during the lame-duck congressional session that same month, but it *increased* the deficit rather than decreasing it. Democrats wanted to extend President Obama's 2009 payroll tax cuts for American workers but to end President Bush's 2001 and 2003 tax cuts for upper-income groups, while Republicans wanted to do exactly the reverse. So they joined hands to reach a politically courageous "compromise": They would extend *both* tax cuts, without paying for either! The payroll tax cuts were extended for one year, and the Bush tax cuts for two—another case in which Obama seemed to be outbargained. A year later, after several more rounds of brinksmanship, a deal was made in December 2011 to give the payroll tax cut two more months of life. That deal provoked a mixture of chuckling and dismay, plus a near-universal feeling that the other ten months would follow, as, indeed, they did—after more political rancor—in February 2012. Together the December 2011 and February 2012 agreements set up what came to be called the "fiscal cliff" for January 2013.

However, fulmination against budget deficits and the burgeoning national debt did have one notable effect: It more or less ruled out any explicit fiscal stimulus in 2011 or 2012. While the payroll and Bush tax cuts were, in fact, stimulus of sorts, the "S word" was all but banned from political discourse. If anything else was going to be done to speed the nation's sluggish recovery, it would have to come from the Federal Reserve. The only operational question for fiscal policy was how it would *reduce* the deficit— that is, how *contractionary* it would be.

Did President Obama Overextend Himself—and Us?

This is a judgment call, but my answer is an emphatic *yes*. The new president and his team set out to cauterize the bleeding financial system, to stimulate aggregate demand, to reform financial regulation, to transform health care delivery while extending coverage, to devise a new climate/ energy policy built around cap-and-trade, to reform America's K-12 educational system, and much else. When would they come up for air? And that imposing agenda is limited to domestic issues. They also had to deal with the wars in Iraq and Afghanistan, Guantánamo, Pentagon spending, threats from Iran, al Qaeda, North Korea, Pakistan . . . you name it.

It was quite a list and, in truth, the Obama administration turned in a creditable performance in most (though not all) of these policy domains. But the lack of focus took a toll on his political standing—and on the electorate's attitudes. The public could not discern any forest, only lots of trees. What did the new president *really* stand for? Was there a strategy? Americans didn't know.

This is another reason "we kind of lost the public." The final *New York Times*/CBS News poll of the Bush administration, taken in December 2008, found Americans who thought "things [in this country] have pretty seriously gotten off on the wrong track" outnumbering Americans who thought "things are generally going in the right direction" by a whopping 83 percent to 12 percent margin. That lopsided negative attitude improved dramatically during the early months of the Obama presidency. By May 2009, opinion was almost evenly split between the wrong trackers (48 percent) and the right trackers (45 percent). But it was mostly downhill from there. By November 2011, the same CBS poll was showing a 76 percent to 15 percent margin in favor of "on the wrong track," almost as bad as it had been at the end of the Bush presidency. By almost any objective standard,

America was far better off in November 2011 than in May 2009, but the polling results did not reflect that fact. That was not good news for President Obama as he campaigned in 2012.

POPULISM FROM THE RIGHT
AND FROM THE LEFT

Neither was the emergence of the Tea Party. The Tea Party movement began as a (presumptively) grass-roots protest against, first, the bank bailouts (a Bush policy) and, then, the February 2009 fiscal stimulus program (an Obama policy), which protestors derided as larded with pork. A conservative, and even libertarian, movement, the Tea Party received lots of support and attention from Glenn Beck, Rush Limbaugh, Fox News, and Charles and David Koch, to name just a few.

The movement was clearly antitax (remember the *Boston* Tea Party), antispending, antideficit, and, more broadly, antigovernment. It caught fire during the long, hot summer of 2009, when President Obama's health reform proposals were being debated in town hall meetings across the nation.

Though decidedly populist in its attitudes, the Tea Party was almost immediately political and partisan, which meant Republican. It was also successful. Among other races, it helped Senator Scott Brown (R-MA) achieve his upset victory; Senator Mike Lee (R-UT) unseat longtime incumbent Bob Bennett in the Republican primary; and get Senator Rand Paul (R-KY), the libertarian son of libertarian Ron Paul, elected in Kentucky. Other Tea Partiers seemed to do the Republican Party more harm than good, however. For example, Christine ("I am not a witch!") O'Donnell knocked out Congressman Mike Castle (R-DE), a political moderate who would surely have won the general election, in the Republican senatorial primary. Overall, if the criteria are (a) being heard, (b) getting elected, and (c) shifting the national political agenda, the Tea Party must be considered a resounding success. And opposition to everything Obama is one of its bedrock principles. There is no doubt that the Tea Party played a major role in the political backlash.

This thunder from the Right was followed by mere rumblings from the Left, in the form of the Occupy Wall Street movement, which later spawned Occupy Boston, Occupy San Diego, Occupy Denver, Occupy Oakland, and many others. Like the Tea Party, Occupy is a highly populist movement that, for example, hates the Wall Street bailouts. It is more antioligarchy than antigovernment, however, arguing that Wall Street's reckless behavior hurt working-class Americans badly (which is true) and yet has gone unpunished (which is also largely true). But the Occupy movement did not engage much in electoral politics. No Occupy candidates entered any Democratic primaries or ran under a third-party banner for election in November 2012. So while it certainly counts as part of the backlash against the Obama administration, it is by no means clear that Occupy Wall Street is part of the backlash against government activism in general. Maybe it's government passivity they don't like.

A HIGH POLITICAL PRICE

Whatever the cause, and whether the protests came from the Right or from the Left, Americans entered both the 2010 and 2012 political seasons in foul frames of mind. They were in no mood to be told that things would have been even worse, *much worse*, were it not for all the policy interventions by the Bush and Obama administrations and the Fed. Like Howard Beale in the movie *Network*, they were as mad as hell and not going to take this anymore.

Maybe all this anger would have been present even without the mistakes recounted in this chapter. After all, academic studies of voting behavior consistently show that poor economic performance hurts incumbents, and the 2007–2009 recession was a whopper. Since the Democrats held the White House, the Senate, and the House on Election Day 2010, they were squarely in line for a shellacking.

Still, I wonder. Yes, electoral losses were all but inevitable for the Democrats under the circumstances. But would they have been as large if the Obama administration had done the bank bailout differently, had helped more distressed homeowners, had prosecuted more white-collar criminals, had focused more on the economy, and had explained better what it was doing and why? We'll never know. Historians will ponder this question—and the paradox of backlash against government *success*—forever.

Sometime before that, however, when some other music stops playing, we'll learn whether the backlash has damaged the American government's ability to respond to economic crises.

But enough looking backward. The financial crisis, the Great Recession, and the policy responses to both have left a large agenda for the future—a legacy of things that need to be either normalized or fixed. One of them is the Fed's unusual monetary policy.

PART V

LOOKING AHEAD

14

|ıııııııııııııııııııııı|

NO EXIT? GETTING THE FED BACK TO NORMAL

So let it out and let it in, hey Jude, begin . . .

—THE BEATLES

What goes up into the stratosphere, such as bank reserves, must presumably come back down to earth at some point. What drops to rock bottom, such as short-term interest rates, must presumably pop back up eventually. When a central bank opens up all the stops to stimulate its economy, as the Federal Reserve did after September 2008, it must at some point throttle back and return to normalcy.

But when and how? Questions like that constitute what has come to be called the Fed's "exit strategy." Executing the exit strategy well is important to us all. If the Federal Reserve rushes for the door too soon or too abruptly, we could fall back into recession. If it exits too late or too slowly, we could have an inflation problem on our hands.

EXIT FROM WHAT?

Can't the Fed just retrace its steps, like a hiker who cuts bark off trees to mark her path and then follows it back to the trailhead? In large measure, the answer is yes. But the pace and order in which the Fed should "let it in" when the time for exit arrives might not match the pace and order in which the Fed "let it out" after September 2008. And there is much from which to exit, such as:

Extraordinary Lending Programs

As we have seen, the Fed cooked up a thick alphabet soup of lending facilities to cope with the ever-changing financial crisis. Remember TAF, TALF, AMLF, CPFF, PDCF, TSLF, and the others? (Maybe you don't, which is just as well.) Each of these unusual lending programs was designed to meet a particular pressing need for funding or credit. And most of them naturally dwindled away as the need disappeared.

Figure 14.1 is a nice graphical depiction, provided by the Fed, of how the central bank "let it out and let it in" with those extraordinary lending facilities. The ups and downs are impressive. In total, Federal Reserve lending ballooned from roughly zero at the end of 2007 to a peak of about $1.5 *trillion* at the end of 2008 and then fell back to barely above zero by the end of 2010. It was quite a roller coaster! This part of the Fed's exit has already been accomplished. As we will see shortly, it's the only part that has been.

Supersized Balance Sheet

Every loan that underlies figure 14.1 was, of course, an asset on the Federal Reserve's balance sheet. But as the Fed's loan volume plummeted after the frightening winter of 2008–2009, the central bank's total assets did not shrink much. How is that possible, when loans dropped from $1.5 trillion to barely above zero? Figure 14.2 on page 370 shows the answer: The dwindling volume of loans (the dashed line) was replaced by an even larger volume of securities, mainly Treasuries and debt instruments of Fannie Mae and Freddie Mac that the Fed acquired in the two big asset-purchase programs nicknamed QE1 and QE2 (the dotted line). The Fed's total asset holdings (the solid line) fluttered for about a year or so in the neighborhood of $2.25 trillion, and then soared again.

FIGURE 14.1 *The Rise and Fall of Federal Reserve Lending*

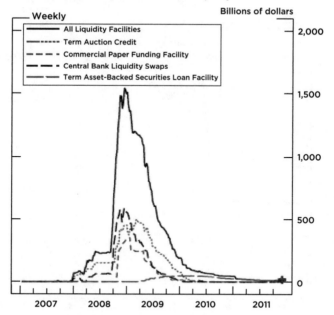

Credit Extended Through Federal Reserve Liquidity Facilities

Figure 14.2 shows the basic story: loans went down, but securities went up. It also shows that the Fed has not even *begun* to exit from this aspect of its unconventional monetary policy: the huge balance sheet. On the contrary, yet another program of quantitative easing (QE3) was announced in September 2012. So the Fed is still entering rather than exiting.

Mountain of Excess Reserves

Balance sheets must balance. As the Fed's total *assets* soared toward the sky, so did its total *liabilities*. Figure 14.3 shows that almost all the growth of the Federal Reserve's liabilities during and after the crisis came from "Deposits of Depository Institutions" (the dotted line)—in plainer language, from *bank reserves*.

FIGURE 14.2 *The Changing Face of Federal Reserve Assets*

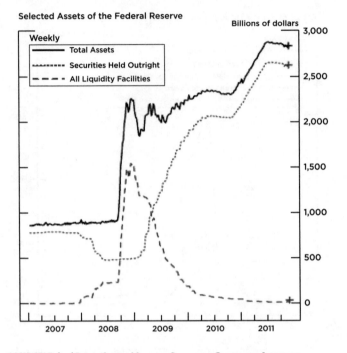

Selected Assets of the Federal Reserve

SOURCE: *Federal Reserve System,* MONTHLY REPORT ON CREDIT AND LIQUIDITY
PROGRAMS AND THE BALANCE SHEET, *December 2011*

The Fed normally pays for any assets it acquires by "printing money"—
that is, by creating new bank reserves, which it deposits into the accounts
of the selling banks. A small portion of these new reserves represents the
minimum reserves *required* by law. These required reserves grow in strict
proportion to banks' transactions deposits—which is to say, modestly.

But as figure 14.4 makes clear, the overwhelming majority of the explosion in bank reserves since September 2008 has been in *excess* (that is,
not required) reserves—deposits that banks hold willingly at the Fed even
though they are just sitting there doing nothing. Excess reserves don't lead
to a bigger money supply or to more bank credit; and they don't earn the
banks much interest. As you can see in the figure, banks' holdings of excess
reserves were essentially zero from January 2000 until Lehman Day, which
is the normal state of affairs. In stark contrast, they topped $1.6 *trillion* in

FIGURE 14.3 *Selected Federal Reserve Liabilities*

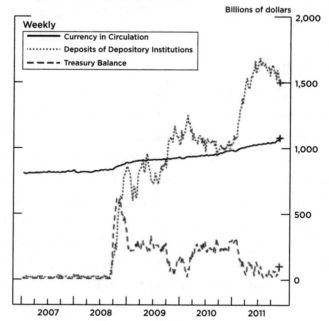

Selected Liabilities of the Federal Reserve

SOURCE: *Federal Reserve System,* Monthly Report on Credit and Liquidity Programs and the Balance Sheet, *December 2011*

FIGURE 14.4 *Total Reserves, Required Reserves, and Excess Reserves (in billions of dollars)*

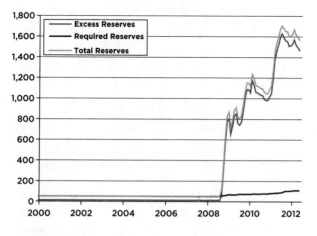

SOURCE: *Federal Reserve Board 2012*

2011. That's not a small discrepancy! An important part of the Fed's eventual exit strategy will be reducing these excess reserves toward zero again.*
It looks like a big job, which they've yet to begin.

Interest Rates Near Zero

Have you checked the interest rates on your bank accounts lately? They are stunningly low. That's because the Federal Reserve's extraordinary monetary policies have been holding the federal funds rate down to a range between zero and 25 basis points since December 2008. To call such a low interest rate abnormal is an understatement. Figure 14.5 displays the history of the federal funds rate from 1990 to 2012. The post-Lehman experience stands out. Except for the period 2002–2004, the funds rate has always been at least 3 percent, and generally higher. Normalizing interest rates is probably the most obvious piece of the Fed's exit strategy; it will certainly be the most obvious to the general public. It needs to be done deftly.

FIGURE 14.5 *The Federal Funds Rate Since 1990*

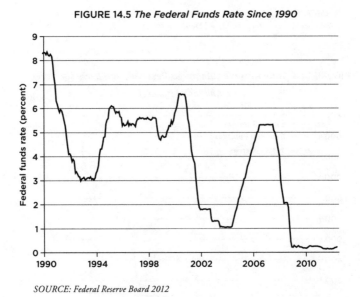

SOURCE: *Federal Reserve Board 2012*

---

*Maybe not quite to zero. By paying a higher interest rate on reserves, the Fed may be able to induce banks to hold more of them. More on this later.

Forward-Looking Prose

The final unconventional monetary policy from which the Fed will eventually exit is its *open-mouth policy*—in particular, how it communicates to the market its intention to maintain the superlow federal funds rate for some time to come. As just noted, the funds rate hit virtually zero in December 2008, from where it can fall no further. But how long will fed funds remain in that rock-bottom 0-to-25-basis-points range?

From March 2009 until August 2011, the FOMC told us that the funds rate would remain that low "for an extended period." These words became almost holy writ in the financial world, even though no one knew exactly what they meant. Market participants were left guessing. Then, at its August 2011 meeting, the FOMC changed the "extended period" wording to "at least through mid-2013." Now the markets had a date—and a pretty distant date at that. By this change in prose, the Fed was still *entering* not *exiting*. It clearly viewed its new wording as an ersatz easing of monetary policy: *It will be longer than you thought, folks.*

The phrase "at least through mid-2013" was heavily criticized, both outside and inside the FOMC, as misleading and even potentially counterproductive by attaching a *date* to the Fed's eventual tightening when exit was actually a function of *economic conditions.* As Charles Plosser, president of the Federal Reserve Bank of Philadelphia, told the *Wall Street Journal,* "Policy needs to be contingent on the economy, not the calendar." He was right. For example, what if the Fed expected to hold the funds rate near zero well into 2014 or beyond? Then might not saying "at least through mid-2013" tacitly make monetary policy a bit tighter than the Fed intended? The Fed's answer came soon: Yes, it might.

At its January 2012 meeting, the FOMC overhauled the nature of its communications in several ways, yet stuck surprisingly close to the "through mid-2013" concept rather than making the commitment "contingent on the economy, not the calendar." Their statement observed that "economic conditions . . . are likely to warrant exceptionally low levels for the federal funds rate [*read: zero to 25 basis points*] at least through late 2014." The eighteen-month extension was a tacit easing of monetary policy, and long-

term interest rates promptly dropped. Here, again, the Fed was still entering, not exiting.

At that meeting, the Fed also began publishing different FOMC members' forecasts of how the federal funds rate should or would evolve over the
coming three years, just as they forecast future GDP, unemployment, and
inflation rates. The views on where the federal funds rate should be at the
end of 2014 varied enormously—from the 0-to-25-basis-points range that
had prevailed since December 2008 (six of the seventeen members) to 2.5
percent or higher (four members). Two members even said that the near-
zero interest-rate policy should continue into 2016. They looked like a
rather fractious bunch, which they were.

Timing Is Everything

That covers the *what* of the Fed's exit. How about the *when*? If the Fed
keeps monetary policy too loose for too long, it will overstimulate the
economy, leading to higher inflation. Given where we've been, a booming
economy doesn't sound so bad. Nonetheless, the fear of accidentally higher
inflation has had the FOMC's hawks clamoring for a faster exit ever since
2009.

The fretting generally starts with the veritable mountain of excess reserves shown in figure 14.4. As conditions normalize, the hawks reason,
banks will not want to hold on to so many excess reserves. Remember, the
historical norm is about *zero*. If the Fed leaves too many reserves hanging
around for too long, banks will lend those funds out rather than hoard
them, leading to large increases in the money supply and bank credit. And
that, economists have taught us since time immemorial, would lead to inflation. In a commonly used metaphor, hawks see the huge accumulation
of reserves as dangerous tinder that may one day catch fire. They'd like to
clean up the tinder before someone drops a match in it.

But there is also an opposite danger. What if the Fed tightens up too
soon, before the economy is strong enough to take it? That potential error
worries the doves. A premature tightening of monetary policy could kick

our still-weak economy down the stairs again, leading to rising unemployment—and, by the way, to *falling* inflation. It seems that the Fed's exit strategy has to be not too fast and not too slow, but *just right*. The Fed is human; it won't get the timing exactly right. Rather, it will err in one direction or the other. But magnitudes matter. And unless FOMC members are derelict in their duties, their error should be modest. Why? Because they should be able to see problems coming and make midcourse corrections.

If the Fed starts to exit too late, as the hawks fear, and the economy begins to heat up, the Fed can *and will* accelerate the exit process. Maybe not quickly enough, so we could wind up with, say, 3 percent or even 4 percent inflation instead of 2 percent—which is the Fed's announced goal. But inflation much higher than that would be gross incompetence. On the other hand, if the Fed exits prematurely and the economy starts slipping again, which is the danger the doves want to avoid, the Fed can *and will* slow down its exit. In that case, we might wind up with 1 percent inflation or maybe even zero, rather than 2 percent. But serious *de*flation seems quite unlikely unless the Fed succumbs to a hawkish feeding frenzy. In short, the risk of exiting either too late or too early is limited by the well-documented *inertia* that characterizes inflation in America. Unlike, say, stock market prices, *core* inflation rarely either leaps upward or drops like a stone.* Rather, it rises or falls gradually, thereby giving policy makers plenty of time to react.

Okay. But which of the two bad outcomes worries the financial markets more? *Neither.* By comparing the *nominal* interest rate on regular 10-year Treasury notes with the *real* interest rate on 10-year TIPS (Treasury Inflation-Protected Securities), one can extract a market-based estimate of expected inflation over a ten-year horizon, as explained in the accompanying box.

Look first at figure 14.6, which shows both the nominal interest rate (upper line) and the real interest rate (lower line) on 10-year U.S. government bonds for the years 2007–2011. The vertical distance between the two

---

*Headline inflation occasionally does, but that's almost always because of either rapidly rising or falling oil prices.

NOMINAL RATES, REAL RATES, AND EXPECTED INFLATION

The interest rates quoted by banks, in the press, and so on are all *nominal* interest rates—the rates at which you can convert *dollars* today into *dollars* at some future date. For example, if the nominal rate on a 2-year bond is 2 percent per annum, and you invest $1,000 today, at the end of two years you will have $(1.02)^2 \times \$1,000$, or $1,040.40, which is roughly 4 percent more *dollars*.

But what about the *purchasing power* of those dollars? That's the question the *real* interest rate is designed to answer. If, for example, the inflation rate is also 2 percent per annum, your gain in purchasing power will be exactly zero. You will have about 4 percent more dollars, but the things you buy will cost about 4 percent more. We say, then, that the *real* interest rate is zero.

This simple notion generalizes. The real interest rate over any holding period is the nominal interest rate *minus* the inflation rate expected over that holding period:

Real interest rate = Nominal interest rate − Expected inflation rate

Now do some lower math. Take the expected inflation rate over to the left and the real interest rate over to the right to get:

Expected inflation rate = Nominal interest rate − Real interest rate

Here is a simple way to observe expected inflation. If you can find both nominal bonds and real (indexed) bonds of exactly the same risk and maturity in the market, you can simply subtract their two interest rates to see what the market expects inflation rate to be over that period. Since the U.S. Treasury borrows routinely in both these forms, market participants perform this calculation every minute of every market day.

is a market measure of the expected inflation rate over the decade to come. To improve your vision, figure 14.7 *subtracts* the real rate from the nominal rate, thereby showing explicitly the vertical distance between the two lines in figure 14.6—that is, the inflation rate that the market expected to prevail.

There is only one really notable movement in figure 14.7, and it happened during the worst months of the financial crisis: the sharp drop in

FIGURE 14.6 *Nominal and Real Interest Rate, 2007–2011*

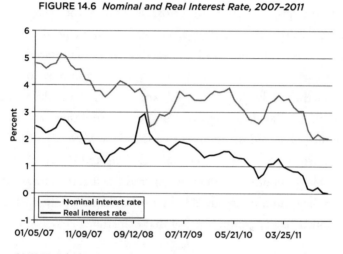

SOURCE: *Federal Reserve Board*

FIGURE 14.7 *A Market-Based Measure of Expected Inflation, 2007–2011*

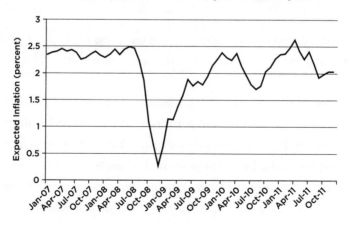

inflationary expectations in late 2008 and its quick rebound in early 2009. Other than that, expected inflation just bounced around in the 1.5 percent to 2.5 percent range. Clearly, the market expects inflation to remain within shouting distance of the Fed's 2 percent target.

WHERE'S THE DOOR?

Some of the more hawkish FOMC members were looking for the exit door already by the spring of 2009. In retrospect, and maybe even in prospect, that was astonishingly premature. The worst of the financial crisis was just receding, the economy was still contracting, and quantitative easing—a central part of the Fed's *entrance* strategy—had begun only in November 2008. Nonetheless, by July 2009, Chairman Ben Bernanke was already sketching the Fed's exit strategy to Congress, stating that "it is important to assure the public and the markets that the extraordinary policy measures we have taken in response to the financial crisis and the recession can be withdrawn in a smooth and timely manner as needed, thereby avoiding the risk that policy stimulus could lead to a future rise in inflation." He explicitly mentioned, as key components of that exit strategy:

- the automatic unwinding of the Fed's extraordinary lending facilities
- extinguishing bank reserves by selling securities out of its portfolio
- raising the interest rate the Fed pays on excess reserves, which he highlighted as "perhaps the most important such tool."

The first of these three was mentioned already. It would happen automatically, and it has. The second constitutes the sort of thing the Fed has been doing on a discretionary basis for generations. The third was novel.

During the crisis, Congress gave the Fed authority to pay interest on bank reserves—and to set the rate thereon. Bernanke argued that once the exit started, the Fed could induce banks to shed their idle reserves more slowly by offering them a higher interest rate, thereby wrapping a kind of fire-resistant blanket around some of the inflationary tinder. Elaborating a few months later, Bernanke observed that while the Fed has "two broad means of tightening monetary policy at the appropriate time—paying interest on reserve balances and taking various actions that reduce the stock of reserves," it would "likely would use both in combination."

The Fed chairman did not, of course, indicate anything about exit *dates*, nor even about what facts on the ground might trigger exit. But he certainly suggested that he had a plan in mind and was waiting for the right moment to put it into effect. An interesting historical question, which Bernanke may never answer, is whether he actually felt the need to have an exit plan ready as early as mid-2009 or was just going through the motions to placate the Fed's hawks—who were itching to exit.

Exit Becomes Reentry

Both Bernanke and the hawks are still waiting. Most of the Fed's attention since July 2009 has been focused instead on whether and how to "let it out" further. Why? Because the aftershocks weren't over, and the Fed worried about a renewed earthquake. The first temblor came from Greece—or did it?

The U.S. economy was beginning to show clear signs of new life by late 2009 and early 2010. Real GDP grew at a 4 percent annual rate in the final quarter of 2009. Payroll employment gains rose sharply to an average of 315,000 per month over the March–May 2010 period, even reaching an eye-popping 516,000 in May. Although those numbers were bloated by the government's hiring of over 500,000 temporary workers to conduct the 2010 Census (which peaked in May), the economy appeared to be reaching "escape velocity."

But then GDP growth dropped off to a modest 2.4 percent average pace in the four quarters of 2010, and to virtually zero in the first quarter of 2011. Following suit, job *losses* reemerged over the four months after May 2010's Census-induced hiring surge. Something went wrong badly

FIGURE 14.8 *The Bottom Drops Out—Again*

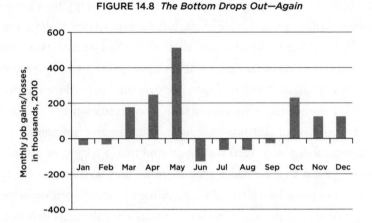

that spring, and as figure 14.8 shows, the change was startlingly abrupt. What happened? The timing certainly points toward Greece. But was it just a coincidence?

That Greece had a serious deficit and debt problem was certainly no secret in 2009 and into 2010. Yet markets seemed not to be terribly concerned until late March 2010. Then, as is so often the case, they became obsessed by it, reacting violently, as if someone had shouted "fire" in a crowded theater. A series of promises of fiscal austerity by the Greek government (quickly broken) and of international assistance from the EU and the IMF followed. But the panic was on. The yield on 10-year Greek government bonds skyrocketed from barely over 6 percent in late March to over 12 percent by early May—doubling in about six weeks. It's hard to hold back a tidal wave.

Twelve percent interest rates when inflation is running about 2 percent are crippling, and so raised serious questions about Greece's financial viability. Could an advanced European country, the cradle of Western civilization no less, actually default on its debt? Unthinkable. Or was it? And since Greece shared the euro with sixteen other countries, markets soon cast a jaundiced eye on other heavily indebted eurozone nations, principally Portugal and Ireland.*

---

*Spain and Italy would get in the crosshairs later. More on the European sovereign debt crisis in chapter 16.

That said, it is hard to understand how the *Greek* sovereign debt crisis could have brought hiring *in the United States* to the screeching halt depicted in figure 14.8. After all, fears of recession in Greece, with a GDP roughly the size of Minnesota's, certainly could not precipitate a U.S. recession. While the U.S. government had a huge fiscal deficit, similar to Greece's, the financial ructions emanating from Athens sent nervous money flocking *to* the United States, not *away*. Interest rates on U.S. Treasury securities therefore dropped, and the dollar rose. Had worldwide investors worried that Greece's debt problems foreshadowed our own, U.S. Treasury rates would have risen instead, and the dollar would have fallen. While financial contagion clearly afflicted Portugal and Ireland, it did not hop the Atlantic. Instead, the U.S. emerged as a major safe haven for frightened capital.

Still, the coincidence in time is striking. Our economy slipped a gear *almost immediately* after the financial panic hit Greece. Of course, other things were happening at the same time. The Fed's QE1 asset-buying program was drawing to a close, and the Obama administration's health care reform bill became law on March 30. The baseball season also started. But it is hard to blame any of these events, or a variety of others, for the abrupt slowdown in the U.S. economy. Perhaps the ructions in Greece (and Portugal and Ireland) just awakened latent fears that we were all headed back into the soup, spooking potential hirers. In any case, what happened happened. And as one corollary, the Federal Reserve stopped talking about exit. Instead, the main question at FOMC meetings became, What else can we do to spur growth?

Well, not quite. That was certainly the view of Chairman Bernanke and the FOMC majority. But the committee's hawks, as always, were unconvinced. The one big hawk who had a vote in 2010 was Thomas Hoenig, then the president of the Federal Reserve Bank of Kansas City (and now an FDIC director). He dissented at every single meeting in 2010—thereby establishing a new FOMC record—fretting out loud about both inflationary tinder and the wisdom of the Fed's commitment to keep rates near zero for "an extended period." More or less the same hawk-dove debate was proceeding outside the Fed, too, with hawkish critics of the Fed arguing for exit and dovish critics goading the Fed to further expansionary action. But as the economy slowed after Greece, the FOMC hawks gradually lost the internal debate to Bernanke and the doves. By the time of its November 2010 meeting, the FOMC was announcing what came to be called QE2—a program of large-scale purchases of longer-dated Treasury securities, designed to push down long-term interest rates.

QE2 kicked off a firestorm of protest, most of it from the political Right. (Ironic reminder: Ben Bernanke is a Republican who described his own political views as libertarian!) But some came from within the FOMC itself. Perhaps the most stunning criticism was that of Fed governor Kevin Warsh, the young Bush appointee who had been one of Bernanke's trusted confidants in the dark days of 2008. On November 3, Warsh voted in favor of QE2 at the FOMC meeting. Five days later, he was on the op-ed page of the *Wall Street Journal* objecting to it. My eyes popped when I opened my *Wall Street Journal* that morning. I guess a lot had changed in five days! Warsh warned that the "Fed's increased presence in the market for long-term Treasury securities poses nontrivial risks that bear watching. . . . Responsible monetary policy . . . requires attention not only to near-term macroeconomic conditions, but also to corollary risks with long-term effects." Bernanke must have had an *Et tu, Brute* moment.

But despite incessant clamoring for its early termination, QE2 ran through its scheduled completion in June 2011, during which time the Fed acquired an additional $600 billion in Treasury securities, mostly with 3- to 10-year terms. Its balance sheet was getting bigger, not smaller. QE2 appears to have achieved its aims, with modest downward effects on medium- to long-term interest rates, though smaller than those from QE1. The Fed was getting down to the light artillery. Was there anything left in its arsenal? Check that: Was there anything left *that the fractious FOMC could agree on?* There certainly were other options. For example, I was urging the Fed to cut the interest rate it paid on excess reserves and to conduct QE in non-Treasury securities.

THE FRACTIOUS FED

Then Greece struck again in the April–July 2011 period. Under pressure from more bad budget news (Greece would fail to meet its deficit-reduction targets) and a sagging Greek economy (which made budget targets much harder to meet), interest rates on Greek sovereign debt spiked anew—from about 12.7 percent on 10-year bonds at the beginning of April to about 17.8 percent by the middle of June. By mid-August Greek rates were higher yet.

As if in step, the U.S. economy foundered again. GDP grew by a paltry 1.3 percent annual rate over the first three quarters of 2011. The economy was no longer earning gentlemen's Cs; it was getting Fs again. These adverse developments strengthened the hands of the FOMC doves—led by Vice Chair Janet Yellen, the New York Fed's Bill Dudley, Boston's Eric Rosengren, and Chicago's Charles Evans. You might have thought such a weak economy would silence the hawks, too. But it didn't.

Instead, a trio of Reserve Bank presidents—Richard Fisher of Dallas, Narayana Kocherlakota of Minneapolis, and Charles Plosser of Philadelphia—dissented loudly in August when the FOMC decided to replace its "extended period" language by the aforementioned pledge to hold the federal funds rate unchanged "at least through mid-2013." Their dissents raised eyebrows because three no votes at a single meeting is virtually unheard of on the consensus-bound FOMC. The dissenters had a point: Economic conditions should trump the calendar. But casting a dissenting vote against *wording*—as opposed to against a policy *action*—is quite unusual.

The FOMC's reentry was not over. With the economy sputtering, the doves ascendant, and the hawkish trio still dissenting, the Fed announced in September 2011 that it would embark on what the media termed "Operation Twist." The objective of Twist was the same as that of QE2: to reduce long-term interest rates, this time by *buying* longer-dated bonds (as QE2 did) while *selling* shorter-dated bonds (which QE2 did not).

Operation Twist could be seen as a kind of compromise. On the one hand, unlike QE1 and QE2, it did not expand the Fed's balance sheet— which was the main bugaboo of inflation hawks both inside and outside the Fed. Largely for this reason, Twist was a weaker stimulus than QE2. On the other hand, it presumably constituted stronger medicine than doing nothing. If Operation Twist succeeded in nudging down longer-term Treasury rates, it would probably nudge down longer-term private borrowing rates as well. The Fed hawks, however, were in no mood to compromise. Messrs. Fisher, Kocherlakota, and Plosser dissented against starting Operation Twist in September. The normally collegial FOMC was getting testy.

Things got worse at the next meeting. Oddly enough, the FOMC's three voting hawks did not repeat their dissents against Operation Twist in November. To further cloud the picture, the Chicago Fed's Evans, who had been arguing for stronger expansionary medicine for months, dissented on the dovish side instead. Chairman Bernanke now faced an almost unprecedented spectacle: He was getting dissents from both sides.

While the Federal Reserve's equivalent of a civil war was going on, what was happening to expected inflation—the presumed fear of the hawks? Figure 14.7 told the tale earlier in this chapter. As measured by the difference between the nominal and real interest rates on 10-year Treasuries, the expected inflation rate was 2.3 percent at the close of 2010, rose to as high as 2.6 percent, and then fell to as low as 1.8 percent during 2011, and closed the year at 2 percent. The hawks may have been harboring inflation fears, but the financial markets weren't.

Is Unconventional Monetary Policy the New Normal?

The Fed ran out of *conventional* monetary policy ammunition on December 16, 2008, the day it reduced the federal funds rate to approximately zero. From that point on, it had two basic choices. It could fold its tent, leaving the economic recovery to the fiscal authorities and the economy's natural recuperative powers. But Bernanke was not about to let that happen. Years earlier he had promised that Federal Reserve passivity would never again cause a depression. Alternatively, the FOMC could resort to a variety of second- and third-best *unconventional* monetary policies, such as quantitative easing and verbal commitments. Which, of course, is exactly what they did—and are still doing. Exit is nowhere in sight.

The likely outlook for the next year or two is for unemployment well above the Fed's target of around 5.6 percent, inflation at or below the Fed's 2 percent target, and extremely low nominal interest rates. If that scenario comes true, the Fed will have to stick with unconventional monetary policies (UMPs) for several more years. Even when things return to normal, we are likely to be living in a world of 1 percent to 2 percent inflation, not 4 percent to 5 percent inflation. In that sort of environment, random events are far more likely to push the federal funds rate down to near zero in the future than in the past—calling again for UMPs. Let's recall briefly what some of those are:

Two classes of UMPs have been discussed extensively in this chapter because the Federal Reserve has deployed them time and again. One is making verbal commitments to keep the fed funds rate low for "an extended period," or "at least through late 2014," or until certain interim targets for inflation and unemployment are achieved. The other is conducting large-scale purchases of assets, as in QE1, QE2, and Operation Twist. We may see more of both of these UMPs from the Fed in the coming years, as we did in September 2012.

But there are other options, and if the economy falters, we may see those, too. As a rule, central bankers disdain these other options because they are so out of the ordinary. In fact, they don't much like even making long-run verbal commitments or conducting large-scale asset purchases— the two UMPs the Fed has already employed. But given the way the U.S., European, and Japanese economies look right now, things may remain unconventional for a while longer yet. As discussed earlier, the Fed can:

- *Peg one or more bond prices:* Instead of purchasing a stated dollar volume of bonds, as in a typical QE program, the Fed can pledge to buy as many bonds as necessary to drive the corresponding

interest rates down to prescribed target levels. *Example:* The Fed
could purchase as many 10-year Treasuries as it takes to drive
their yield down to 1.5 percent.

- *Reduce the interest rate it pays on excess reserves:* Instead of inducing banks to hang on to idle reserves by paying them to do so,
the Fed could pay banks nothing, or even charge them a modest
fee, to encourage bankers to do something more useful with
their money. *Example:* The Fed could *charge* banks 25 basis
points instead of *paying* banks 25 basis points.

ARE WE WAITING FOR GODOT?

Godot took his time. Similarly, the Fed may have to wait a long time for its
opportunity to exit.

In 2012 the U.S. economy just plodded along. The Fed started a
new round of experiments with a different sort of verbal commitment—
publishing forecasts of its own behavior—in January. Those forecasts included widely disperse predictions from FOMC members about when the
exit from near-zero interest rates would start. Then, in September, it extended its super-low interest rate pledge to "at least through mid-2015" and
surprised markets by making QE3 an open-ended commitment to buy
mortgage-backed securities at a rate of $40 billion per month.

As this book went to press, there was not yet much sign that exit is in
sight. Indeed, few people even clamor for it any longer. The time for Federal Reserve exit will come one day. But it's not here yet.

15

|ımı111111111111111111111111|

THE SEARCH FOR
A FISCAL EXIT

The more things change, the more they stay the same.

—English translation of an old French proverb

We Americans take on debt with alacrity, but we hate to see our government do so. At least that's what we tell the pollsters. One of the most prominent, but least beloved, legacies of the Great Recession was the spectacular increase in the federal budget deficit depicted in figure 15.1. The deficit soared from a comparatively benign $161 billion in fiscal year 2007 to a huge $459 billion in fiscal year 2008, which was then the largest deficit ever recorded, and finally to a mind-boggling $1,413 billion in fiscal 2009. At 10 percent of America's gigantic GDP, the fiscal 2009 budget deficit actually exceeded the GDPs of all but eight other countries. And the chart shows that it didn't recede much in the years 2010–2012. In those four fiscal years alone, the cumulative deficit topped $5 trillion. For comparison, the total public debt held *outside* the government itself was only $5.3 trillion at the end of fiscal 2008.

These are eye-popping numbers, far larger than virtually anyone had dreamed possible. To say that they grabbed people's attention would be a gross understatement. Deficit hawks were already railing against the deficit

FIGURE 15.1 *The Exploding Federal Deficit*

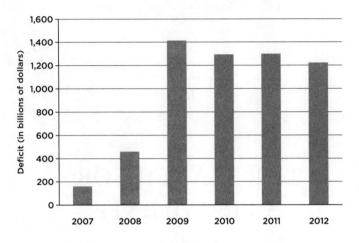

in the dark days of 2009, when the economy was struggling to avoid Great Depression 2.0 and fiscal *stimulus* was desperately needed. As the economy started climbing slowly and haltingly uphill, the deficit became almost a national obsession.

First, an apology: Budgets are about numbers. It is virtually impossible to explain budget developments without trotting out a lot of them. But numbers are boring. To minimize the pain, I will hold the number of numbers in this chapter to a minimum, relying instead on a series of charts. Each picture will, I hope, be worth a thousand numbers.

How Did We Get into This Mess? Part I

The answer is surprisingly simple. As Bill Clinton was turning over the White House keys to George W. Bush, the federal government was staring at budget *surpluses* "as far as the eye can see," as it was put at the time. Those were the days. There was even talk—including loud worries from no less an authority than Federal Reserve Chairman Alan Greenspan—that the government might pay off the entire national debt, after which continuing surpluses would force it to start buying private assets. Greenspan considered that prospect politically unwise, if not dangerous. He strongly urged Congress to prevent it from happening, presumably by passing the 2001 tax cuts. His tacit endorsement of President Bush's controversial policy infuriated many Democrats, who saw it as disingenuous—as a way for Greenspan to ingratiate himself to the new president.

Was Greenspan's worry legitimate? Figure 15.2, which comes from an October 2000 CBO report on the budget outlook, shows the kinds of superoptimistic projections that some people were taking seriously at the time. Three different long-term projections are shown in the graph, but the differences needn't concern us here. Focus instead on the similarities. All three show a remarkable near-term dip in the national debt, actually turning negative in two cases—which was Greenspan's fear. *But then they show a stunningly sharp upturn.* Looking at the far right-hand side of the figure, you see three roughly parallel lines, each heading straight for the wild blue yonder. The only difference is when the upward spiral begins. Thus all three debt paths portrayed a future that could not possibly happen. Something had to give. And that was in 2000!

These projections warned us that the prevailing euphoria over *near-*

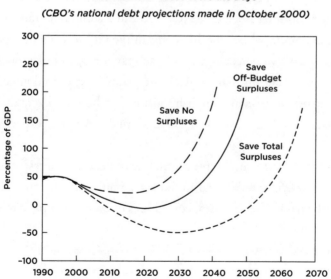

FIGURE 15.2 *Those Were the Days*
(CBO's national debt projections made in October 2000)

term budget prospects was myopic in the extreme. The *long-run* fiscal position of the United States was untenable even then. And the reason was as straightforward then as it is now: rapidly escalating health care costs, mainly for Medicare and Medicaid. America was aging then and is aging now, which raises the bills for Social Security and Medicare. In addition, health care gets more and more expensive each year. We knew even before 2000 that America's public finances were on an unsustainable path. Keep that in mind. It's important.

The unsustainability of the debt-to-GDP paths depicted in figure 15.2 rested on three unforgiving pieces of arithmetic. The first is that when you add 65 to 1945, you get 2010. The significance of this prosaic piece of addition is that cohorts born in 1945 and after started becoming eligible for Medicare in 2010. We knew that 1945 + 65 = 2010 back in 2000, or in 1980 for that matter. So, many years before it actually happened, it was *entirely predictable* that the government's bills for Medicare and Social Security would escalate sharply after 2010—and continue to soar for decades. A smart government would have started squirreling away chestnuts well before 2010. But our government wasn't as smart as your average squirrel.

The second piece of arithmetic is analogous to compound interest. Over the thirty-year period from 1970 to 2000, medical care costs as measured in the Consumer Price Index (CPI) rose at a compound rate of about 7 percent per annum while all other items in the CPI rose about 5 percent per annum. That two percentage point gap may not sound like much, but over thirty years it meant that medical care prices more than doubled relative to other prices. In plain English, health care became *vastly* more expensive relative to almost everything else. Virtually everyone expected this inflation gap to continue, as it has.*

Finally, there is the inexorable arithmetic of deficits, interest, and debt accumulation. *Deficits* today lead to more accumulated *debt*, on which interest must be paid. That, in turn, contributes to even larger *deficits* tomor-

---

*From 2000 to 2011, the two inflation rates were 4 percent and 2.4 percent, respectively.

row. If the government doesn't limit its budget deficit, the national debt can spiral out of control. Figure 15.2 shows that the U.S. national debt was already on such an explosive path by the year 2000. The nation was therefore in no position to afford large *long-term* tax cuts, despite the short-term surpluses. But President Bush recommended them anyway, and Congress passed them in 2001. Two years later, we gorged on a second round of tax cuts. Total federal revenue as a share of GDP quickly declined to its lowest level since 1951.

But that wasn't all. In November 2001, the United States invaded Afghanistan in search of Osama bin Laden and with the expressed intent of deposing the Taliban. The latter mission was accomplished with dispatch, but the war in Afghanistan dragged on. In March 2003, the United States invaded Iraq, starting a war of choice in which American soldiers remained engaged through December 2011. The two wars shared an unusual budget characteristic: Instead of raising taxes to pay for the higher military expenditures, as had been done throughout recorded history, President Bush put them on the national credit card. And when Medicare Part D (the drug benefit) passed Congress in 2003, no funding source was provided for that, either. Just like the tax cuts and the two wars, the bill for the prescription drug benefit was added to the deficit.

All in all, it was an impressive binge of spending and tax cutting—none of which was paid for. The federal budget *surplus* of $128 billion in fiscal year 2001 turned into a $413 billion *deficit* by fiscal 2004. In December 2003, less than two years into the Bush administration, the CBO was already publishing long-run debt-to-GDP projections such as, figure 15.3 on the next page. Forget the details and ignore Scenarios 3, 5, and 6. No one on the planet believed those; the CBO was just being polite. The debate then was over whether we were on a path like Scenarios 2 and 4, which are basically the same, or an even-worse path like Scenario 1, which is literally "off the charts" before 2040. America's long-run budget prospects had gone from horrible to unspeakable.

Keep that image of an exploding national debt in your head. We will return to it later.

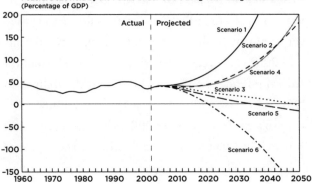

FIGURE 15.3 *Bad to Worse*

(CBO's national debt projections made in December 2003)

How Did We Get into This Mess? Part II

Notice that all this happened *before* the financial crisis and the Great Recession. The federal budget deficit, of course, exploded further in the wake of those unhappy events. As the economy sank, tax revenues declined and expenditures on unemployment insurance, food stamps, and the like all rose. The government also enacted several fiscal stimulus packages, including both tax cuts and higher spending. The biggest of these was the Recovery Act (February 2009), which CBO now scores at $831 billion.

The raw numbers are stunning. Figure 15.1 showed that the federal budget deficit almost tripled from fiscal year 2007 (which ended just after Paribas Day) to fiscal year 2008 (which ended two weeks after Lehman Day). Then it almost tripled again from fiscal 2008 to fiscal 2009, which ended shortly after the recession hit bottom. Most of this astounding increase in the deficit came directly from either the recession or the government's efforts to fight it.

The largest deficit came in fiscal 2009, which began on October 1, 2008 (just before TARP passed), and ran through September 30, 2009. CBO publishes updated budget projections two or three times a year, so we

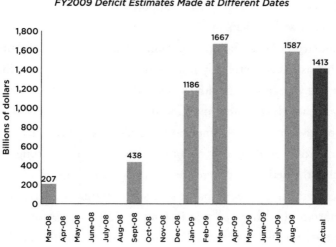

FIGURE 15.4 *How Big a Deficit?*
FY2009 Deficit Estimates Made at Different Dates

can look back and watch how their estimates of the FY2009 budget deficit grew over time. Figure 15.4 displays five different estimates of the FY2009 budget deficit, made between March 2008 and August 2009. In March 2008, before the economy started to deteriorate badly, the CBO was projecting a deficit of just $207 billion. By August 2009, less than two months before the fiscal year ended, it was projecting a staggering $1,587 billion instead. (The actual deficit turned out to be $1,413 billion.) Thus the *estimated* deficit for that fateful year rose by a colossal $1,380 billion in just seventeen months. What happened? The short answer is, Everything.

Public Enemy Number What?

These titanic budget deficits registered with the public—maybe even scared them. The federal government borrowing more than a trillion dollars a year? That's a stupefying number. It sounds not just profligate but dangerous, especially if your views on the deficit are based on false analogies to a family's finances. Partly because the size of the deficit was so shocking, partly because Republicans effectively portrayed the stimulus as a reckless profusion of public spending, but perhaps mostly because Americans have always thought deficits evil, public support for fiscal stimulus sank and public concern with deficits rose.

By January 2011, a Gallup poll found that 84 percent of Americans thought it was either "extremely important" or "very important" that "the president and Congress deal with the federal budget deficit" in the coming year—even though the latest announced unemployment rate was 9.4 percent. Another 12 percent of Americans considered deficit reduction "moderately important. A 96 percent majority looks like a pretty strong mandate for reducing the deficit, but there are two important "buts":

First, those same three response categories (extremely, very, or moderately important) polled 95 percent in January 2007, well before any of the recent budget problems. In fact, they polled 93 percent in January 2002, while George W. Bush was busy cutting taxes and doing virtually everything else he could think of to *increase* the deficit. Such attitudes go back much further. A comparable Gallup poll question in December 1984 found 83 percent of Americans calling the deficit either a "very serious" or "fairly serious problem for the country." A 1939 *Fortune* magazine poll asked, "If you were a member of Congress would you vote for a bill to cut government spending enough to balance the budget immediately?" Remember, doing so would have meant a huge cut in spending while the Depression was still going on. Yet the response was 61 percent in favor, 17 percent opposed. The basic fact is that Americans have always abhorred deficits—in the abstract.

Second, however, Americans in January 2011 were less than enamored of the specific policy changes it would take to make a noticeable dent in the deficit. For example, here is Gallup's favor-oppose polling on cutting specific spending programs:

Foreign aid: 59–37
Aid to farmers: 44–53
National defense: 42–57
Antipoverty programs: 39–55
Medicare: 38–61
Social Security: 32–67

If you are a politician, try doing serious budget cuts with that little public support.

These polling results, too, are typical. You can find similar numbers going back twenty, thirty years and more. For example, a 1981 Harris Survey found Americans overwhelmingly favoring a balanced budget—as always. But Harris could not find majority support for reducing spending on *any* domestic program. In case you're wondering, the desire to cut spending in the abstract but not in the concrete is bipartisan. A YouGov survey in March 2012 showed that cutting foreign aid was the only item that commanded strong majority support among Republican primary voters—the most conservative part of the more conservative party. Less spending on the environment, housing, and unemployment benefits won bare majorities among these small-government stalwarts.

This is not the place for a learned disquisition on the economic costs of large fiscal deficits. Let me mention just two. One stems from the deficit-debt arithmetic alluded to above. If the deficit gets too large, the national debt will grow faster than the economy. Not even the most extreme deficit dove thinks it's fine for the debt-to-GDP ratio to rise without limit. Why not? That brings me to the second point: High levels of public debt tend to push up interest rates—not just for the government but for everyone. That spells less business investment, less homebuilding, fewer automobile sales, and so on. Dick Cheney may have declared that deficits don't matter, but excessively large budget deficits, maintained for a long time, are harmful. But what is "excessive" and what constitutes "a long time"?

The answers depend, among other things, on the willingness of borrowers to extend the government credit. In worst cases, a nation can find itself in the position of Greece, with markets willing to lend only on usurious terms—if at all. Fortunately, the United States is nowhere near that point. In fact, our government is still among the best credits in the world. How do we know that? Just watch the bidding at any auction of Treasury debt, as investors from all over the world eagerly snap up Treasury securities at paltry interest rates. When global financial markets get nervous, U.S. Treasuries remain the ultimate safe haven.

Now look at figure 15.5, which shows the recent behavior of two

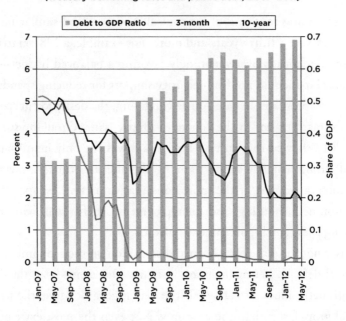

FIGURE 15.5 *The Long and Short of It*
(Treasury borrowing rates and public debt, 2007–2011)

benchmark Treasury borrowing rates: one on 3-month Treasury bills (the lower line), the other on 10-year Treasury bonds (the upper line). The graph also traces the behavior of the federal government debt held by the public, as a ratio to GDP (the vertical bars). You see that 3-month bill rates fell to around zero and remained there, while 10-year bond rates tracked down from around 5 percent to around 2 percent, *even as the national debt mounted* relative to GDP. If anyone was worrying about the U.S. government's creditworthiness, it certainly wasn't bond traders.

SURPLUS OF LIP SERVICE, DEFICIT OF ACTION

In 2009 interest rates were ultralow, and we urgently needed to stimulate our economy out of its worst slump since the 1930s. Nonetheless, reducing the budget deficit became a top political priority—at least at the level of lip service.

In December 2009, Senators Kent Conrad (D-ND) and Judd Gregg (R-NH), two notable deficit hawks, introduced legislation to create a bipartisan fiscal commission to seek politically viable ways to reduce spending and raise revenue. When the commission reported, Congress would have been *compelled* to vote on their recommendations, without filibusters or amendments. That unyielding requirement for an up-or-down vote gave the Conrad-Gregg proposal real teeth. Teeth? Who wanted teeth? The next month, Conrad and Gregg lost on a 53–46 Senate vote. Six Republican cosponsors of their bill turned around and voted against it!

In February 2010, President Obama resurrected a weaker version of their idea by establishing a bipartisan fiscal commission through executive order. The eighteen-member National Commission on Fiscal Responsibility and Reform, cochaired by Alan Simpson and Erskine Bowles, included both politicians and nonpoliticians. But the most important difference between the ill-fated Conrad-Gregg proposal and the Simpson-Bowles commission was that the president lacked the constitutional authority to *compel* a congressional vote. When the Simpson-Bowles recommendations were delivered in December 2010, they were praised lavishly by editorialists and completely ignored by Congress. They were even ignored by the president himself! Here, for once, we had bipartisan agreement: Neither side liked Simpson-Bowles.

As 2010 drew to a close, with Congress and the president at loggerheads, the two parties showed us what bipartisanship really meant when they reached an eleventh-hour agreement to extend the Bush income tax cuts, the Obama payroll tax cut, *and* the unemployment benefits. *All of them*. Did anybody really care about the deficit?

The 112th Congress convened in January 2011 with Republicans running the House and newly elected Tea Party members—feeling their oats and in no mood to compromise—trying to run the Republican Party. The political battle morphed into a two-front war: Democrats against Republicans, and establishment Republicans against Tea Party insurgents. In that complex political environment, it was by no means clear that the new Speaker of the House, John Boehner (R-OH), could cut *any* budget deal. In fact, the U.S government almost shut down in April 2011 over its inability to pass anything that remotely resembled a budget. Congress looked clownish. Its approval ratings—another oxymoron?—fell into the basement.

With partisanship running sky high, Congressman Paul Ryan (R-WI), the youthful new chairman of the House Budget Committee and later the Republican nominee for vice president, threw his own radical budget plan into the hopper. It was not exactly a compromise. The Ryan plan eschewed *any* new tax revenue at all; in fact, it proposed *even more tax cuts* for the most prosperous Americans. Ryan's numbers did produce a balanced budget on paper but not until about 2040. It accomplished that through Draconian spending cuts, especially by gradually replacing Medicare with vouchers to buy private insurance, vouchers whose values were destined to fall ever-further behind the rising cost of health insurance.

The "magic" behind Ryan's budgetary arithmetic was clear to anyone who understood the logic behind the long-run budget mess: If you could—by some wondrous device—take most health care expenditures *off* the federal budget, balancing the rest of the budget would be a piece of cake. Under the Ryan plan, federal health care spending was reduced by *more than two thirds* by 2050. The rest was shunted off to private individuals and state governments to worry about.*

But privatizing Medicare was a political nonstarter, guaranteed to make Democrats see red—or maybe electoral blue. The Republican-dominated House proudly passed Ryan's plan, but the Democratic-led Senate equally proudly rejected it. In fact, Democrats rubbed their hands with glee at the prospect of running against Ryan's Medicare proposal in the 2012 election. But that was a long way off. In the meantime, the U.S. government needed a budget.

After rounds of tortuous negotiations, President Obama and Speaker Boehner came close to agreeing on what came to be called a "grand bargain" in July 2011. It would have reduced the ten-year budget deficit by about $4 trillion, with perhaps 20 percent to 30 percent of that coming from higher taxes. The president might have had trouble selling this deal to congressional Democrats, since some of the cuts came out of Medicare—

---

*When Ryan redid his budget a year later, the cuts of two thirds were reduced to about one half.

which Dems wanted to use as their premier campaign issue. Boehner complained that the president's shifting positions were "like dealing with a bowl of Jell-O." But it never looked likely that the speaker could sell it to his own caucus. One White House aide quipped that Boehner "probably could not deliver a pizza."

Whether Jell-O or pizza, the sticking point was revenue, particularly the difference between 20 percent of the package and 30 percent, where House Republicans wouldn't budge. The grand bargain died in acrimony before it was born. As if to foreclose any possibility of reaching a bipartisan agreement on the budget, Mitt Romney and the other seven Republican presidential candidates at the time declared in an August 2011 debate that they would all reject a budget deal that included even $1 in tax increases for each $10 in spending cuts. When ten-for-one isn't good enough, there isn't much room for compromise.

Meanwhile, congressional hijinks were reaching new heights, and public respect for Congress was plumbing new lows. Throughout June, July, and early August of 2011, the nation witnessed a starkly partisan debate over whether—get ready for this—the U.S. government should *deliberately* default on its debt, even though it could easily pay all its bills! The issue at hand was whether or not to raise the national debt ceiling, a routine action that Congress always takes when necessary—though not without some political posturing.*

Each year's deficit adds to the national debt. Thus voting for a budget with *any* deficit at all, no matter how small, implies, *as a piece of arithmetic*, that the national debt must rise. If the projected increase would push the accumulated debt over the legal limit, the debt limit must be raised. If not, the nation would have two conflicting laws on its books: the budget and the national debt ceiling. A no-brainer, right? Actually, that's an apt cliché, because no-brainers are exactly what many members of Congress looked like.

Finally, on August 2, 2011, with the Treasury on the verge of running

---

*For example, Senator Barack Obama had voted against President Bush's request to raise the national debt ceiling in 2006. But that was a "free vote" because everyone knew the request would pass.

out of cash to pay its daily bills, President Obama and the Republicans made a deal that averted catastrophe. As part of the deal, the two sides agreed on about $900 billion worth of spending cuts—and no tax increases at all—over the next ten years. They also agreed to establish the Joint Select Committee on Deficit Reduction, which was immediately dubbed the "supercommittee." Six senators and six representatives were supposed to come up with another $1.5 trillion in spending cuts and revenue increases. (If you read the fine print, it was actually $1.2 trillion.) If they failed, $1.2 trillion in spending cuts, aimed disproportionately at the defense budget, would trigger in automatically, starting in January 2013. That is, *if* Congress didn't stay the execution—which it started trying to do in May 2012. Note that judgment day was January *2013,* not January *2012.* The can was thus kicked safely past the next election.

Everyone exhaled and went home. The national debt ceiling was raised. The U.S. government did not default on its debt. The supercommittee went to work. But not everyone lived happily ever after.

Standard & Poor's reacted to the spectacle by lowering the U.S. government's credit rating from AAA (the highest possible) to AA+, which made headlines but had no effect whatsoever on U.S. bond rates. Moody's and Fitch did not follow suit. Much more important, after months of partisan wrangling, the supercommittee announced in November 2011 that it was deadlocked, unable to agree on anything, and was giving up. A glance at the calendar revealed that all hope of compromise was now lost: The 2012 election was less than a year away.

PATHS FORWARD

Where do we go from here? The only honest answer is, Nobody knows. Forging a budget agreement is more a matter of politics than of economics. During the 2012 presidential campaign, President Obama sought what he called a "balanced" approach to deficit reduction, which meant including upper-bracket tax increases. But challenger Mitt Romney rejected that idea, and House Speaker John Boehner even threatened to precipitate another crisis over the national debt ceiling. The election outcome could be read as a mandate for Obama's position—but it was a weak one.

Unlike the politics, the budgetary economics are actually not that difficult over the next decade or so. Then they become impossible. The logical solution comes in three parts, one for right now, one for the next decade, and the last for the very long run.

Right Now

With the economy still so weak, the case for near-term fiscal contraction is weak as well. We shouldn't kick away the fiscal crutch until the patient is ready to walk. If I am allowed to indulge in wishful thinking, a two-pronged policy that combines modest fiscal stimulus up front with serious deficit reduction thereafter would be even better.

The Next Decade

Strange as it may seem with trillion-dollar-plus deficits for four years running, the U.S. government still has no *short-run* borrowing problem. On the contrary, investors all over the world are still clambering to lend us money at *negative* real interest rates. In purchasing power terms, they are willing—nay, eager—to pay our government to borrow from them!

Furthermore, the next decade—which is the focus of Simpson-Bowles, the ill-fated "grand bargain," the failed supercommittee, and every other high-profile deficit-reduction plan of recent years—is not really that difficult in budget terms. According to the CBO's January 2012 projections, the federal deficit as a share of GDP will shrink from 9 percent of GDP in fiscal 2011 to roughly 5 percent of GDP in fiscal years 2015–2018, *without any further policy actions*. To be sure, 5 percent of GDP is still too high. But coming from the stunning 10 percent of GDP in 2009, it's a long way down. Besides, how hard can it be to go from 5 percent of GDP deficit down to 3 percent of GDP, a number that is easily manageable?

A reasonable target for deficit *reduction* over the next decade might be 2 to 3 percent of GDP, starting perhaps in fiscal 2014. For the sake of concreteness, let's use 2.5 percent: that translates to about $5 trillion of deficit reduction over the ten-year budget window—close to where the grand bargain, Simpson-Bowles, and all the rest were.

Achieving such an ambitious target will require some compromises. Republicans will have to concede that while it is *arithmetically* possible to do the entire job on the spending side, it is *politically* impossible. Democrats will have to concede that the *majority* of deficit reduction must come on the spending side, including entitlements like Medicare. Accomplishing that will require some painful (to Democrats) choices. Of course, the word "majority" begs the question of whether spending cuts should make up 51 percent or 90 percent of the deficit-reduction package. That issue remains politically contentious. The point is that neither type of political concession looks imminent. Washington looks gridlocked.

The Very Long Run

The truly horrendous budget problems come in the 2020s, 2030s, and beyond. The latest CBO long-term projections show the deficit rising to an alarming 13.1 percent of GDP by 2030, to an unthinkable 18.9 percent of GDP by 2040, and continuing to soar into the stratosphere. That simply cannot happen.

But while the long-run budget problem is vastly larger, it is also far simpler, for two reasons. The first is that the projected deficits are so huge that filling most of the hole with higher revenue is simply out of the question. Spending cuts must bear most of the burden. The second is that there is only one overwhelmingly important factor pushing federal spending up and up and up: rising health care costs. Over the long-term, controlling spending means controlling *health care* spending. It's that simple—and that complex.

Figure 15.6 is designed to illustrate the first of these two points. It shows CBO's latest ultralong budget projection (made in June 2012), which runs out to 2087. Yes, I know, no one should believe any forecast that extends out to the year 2087—or even to the year 2017, for that matter. Don't. It's not even a *forecast;* everyone knows it *cannot* happen. It's just a

FIGURE 15.6 *Our Bleak Budgetary Future*

(CBO's long-term budget projections made in June 2012)

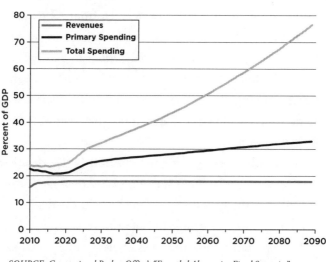

SOURCE: *Congressional Budget Office's "Extended Alternative Fiscal Scenario,"*
extrapolated by Committee for a Responsible Federal Budget

mechanical *extrapolation* of current trends that demonstrates how unsustainable they are. A federal budget deficit topping 25 percent of GDP by 2050, and going much higher after that, is ridiculous. The message in figure 15.6 is that we must get off the unsustainable path sooner or later. Sooner would be better.

The bottom line in the chart, which rises to 18.5 percent of GDP and then stays there, depicts federal revenue. You might call it the Republican dream scenario (no new taxes), though many Republicans prefer revenues even lower than the recent historic norm of 18.5 percent of GDP. The middle line shows total *primary* spending—that is, spending on everything other than interest payments. The top line adds back interest payments to get *total* spending. The vertical gap between total spending (the top line) and total revenue (the bottom line) is, of course, the annual budget deficit. It is clearly exploding over time.

There are four takeaways from figure 15.6. One: The interest bill—which is the vertical gap between primary spending and total spending—eventually comes to dominate the budget. Two: Historically normal levels of taxation (the bottom line) do not come close to covering even primary spending (the middle line), not to mention interest payments. Three: Primary spending as a share of GDP rises steadily, from 22 percent of GDP now to over 32 percent by the 2080s. Four: The government can cover no more than a small fraction of the projected deficits by raising taxes. Sorry, Democrats, but the Republicans are right on this one. Americans are used to federal taxes running about 18.5 percent of GDP; they will not allow them to rise to 32 percent of GDP. Never mind that a number of European countries do so; we won't.

Now on to health care costs. Figure 15.7 adds a fourth line to figure 15.6. It shows *primary* government spending *other than for health care* as a percent of GDP. It is the lowest of the four lines in the diagram, tracking *down* from around 16 percent of GDP now to only about 11 percent of GDP by 2087. In plain English, the costs of everything on which the federal government spends money *except health care and interest*—and that includes Social Security, defense, you name it—are projected to fall over time as a share of GDP. The message is clear: America doesn't have a gen-

FIGURE 15.7 *The Dominant Role of Health Care Spending*
(CBO's long-term budget projection)

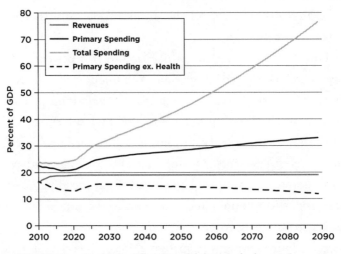

SOURCE: *Congressional Budget Office's "Extended alternative fiscal scenario," extrapolated by Committee for a Responsible Federal Budget*

eralized spending problem that requires severe cuts across the board. We have, instead, a massive problem of exploding health care costs.

The implication for budgeteers is clear: If we can somehow solve the health care cost problem, we will also solve the long-run deficit problem. But if we can't control health care costs, the long-run deficit problem is insoluble. Simple, right? Impossible? We'd better hope not.

SIMPSON-BOWLES REDUX

Eventually, I believe, the nation will return to something like the rejected Simpson-Bowles plan of 2010, though perhaps with some important modifications. Simpson-Bowles was advertised as reducing the cumulative deficit by roughly $4 trillion over the nine fiscal years spanning 2012–2020. But their year-by-year deficit reductions start out small and rise sharply over time. If you stretch the period to ten years and roll it forward to, say, 2014–2023, they would translate to at least $6 trillion in deficit reduction, probably more. My guess is that if and when a multiyear budget agreement is reached, it will be less ambitious than that. The short-run medicine is, in fact, less unpalatable than Simpson-Bowles.

As to composition, the plan contains a bit of everything. And that will be necessary to forge a compromise. A few specifics:

Revenue

The plan derives new tax revenue mainly from tax reform. Simpson and Bowles would raise the federal tax share from its historic average of 18.4 percent of GDP up to 21 percent and then hold it there. An additional 2.6 percent of GDP in tax revenue is a reasonable target that balances Americans' aversion to taxes with the need for revenue implied by the aging of our population. My guess, however, is that it will be quite some time before the Republican Party is willing to go there. Remember, like all the Republican presidential candidates in the 2011–2012 primary season, Mitt

Romney said he would reject even a 10-for-1 offer. Simpson-Bowles can be thought of as 2-for-1.

It is also unrealistic to believe that Congress can squeeze much net revenue out of tax *reform*, rather than by raising tax *rates*, the Romney-Ryan promises notwithstanding. The essence of any good tax reform is to broaden the tax base while lowering tax rates. Economists applaud that. But doing so inevitably creates long lists of winners and losers, making it an uphill fight in our political system, where the status quo has a huge incumbency advantage. If a tax reform proposal is revenue neutral, the winners roughly balance the losers in the lobbying wars. So at least you have a fighting chance. But if tax reform is burdened by the need to raise substantial net revenue, the losers will far outnumber the winners, creating a political hurdle that may be impossible to jump.

Health

Simpson-Bowles takes a small nick out of health care expenditures. As I have emphasized, any serious long-run deficit-reduction plan must *concentrate* on health care cost containment. Simpson and Bowles knew this, of course. But they didn't know how to "bend the cost curve" sufficiently. Neither does anyone else. So they just recommended a target—holding the growth rate of health care spending to GDP growth plus 1 percent—and "requiring action by the President and Congress if growth exceeds the targets." What sort of action? They go on: "If health care costs continue to grow as fast as CBO and the Medicare actuaries project . . . this process will require Congress and the President to consider further actions that make more substantial structural reforms." Got that? In short, Simpson and Bowles, brave as they were, punted on the most critical issue.

I don't blame them. Some people believe that President Obama's health reform, the Affordable Care Act of 2010, contains seeds that will eventually blossom into major cost controls. Others are deeply skeptical. The truth is that, right now, nobody knows how to slow the seemingly inexorable growth of health care costs—short of outright rationing, which no one wants.

Social Security

The Simpson-Bowles plan takes an even smaller nick out of Social Security, though here it's mainly a matter of timing. It is poor public policy—not to mention unfair—to cut the benefits of people nearing retirement, who have little time to adjust. The essence of any sensible Social Security reform is to enact changes *now* that do not take effect for many years. Which is exactly what Simpson and Bowles proposed, with gradual phase-ins of several important "nips and tucks" that will trim benefits and bring in more revenue. If followed, their recommendations would eliminate the entire actuarial deficit in Social Security.

The Rest

The biggest chunk of budget savings actually comes from the "other spending" category—that is, other than on health, Social Security, and interest. Their recommended cuts run the gamut from defense spending to farm subsidies to pensions for civil servants, and much else. The cuts are sizable, but hardly Draconian, amounting to 10 percent of the "other spending" pot.

LAST WORD

Oh, and did I mention that the Simpson-Bowles plan *failed* when it was put to a vote in the commission? Alan Simpson and Erskine Bowles, by then brothers in arms, supported it. But they were joined by only nine of the other sixteen commissioners, leading to a less-than-resounding 11–7 vote, well short of the required supermajority of fourteen. Tellingly, the 11–7 vote broke down as follows:

Republican members of Congress: 3–3
Democratic members of Congress: 3–3
Nonpoliticians: 5–1

Yes, it was a nonpartisan vote! Whereas the nonpoliticians favored Simpson-Bowles overwhelmingly, the politicians were evenly divided. Democrats rebelled against some of the spending cuts, particularly those for Medicare and Social Security. Republicans hated the tax increases.

The vote on Simpson-Bowles should serve as a metaphor. It will be easier to get the citizenry to rally around a comprehensive deficit-reduction plan than it will be to corral the politicians. On the other hand, the 6–6 vote among the politicians can be read as a glass half full. After all, it could have been 0–12. The split vote at least allows for a glimmer of hope. A cool-eyed assessment of the politics does not support much optimism, however. Both Republicans and Democrats look dug in, and our constitutional system makes gridlock easy to sustain. The search for a politically viable fiscal exit strategy continues.

|ııııııııııııııııııııı|

THE BIG AFTERSHOCK:
THE EUROPEAN DEBT CRISIS

Beware of Greeks bearing gifts.

—VIRGIL (*The Aeneid*)

W as it the gift that keeps on taking? What we now know as the European sovereign debt crisis first exploded in Greece in April 2010. It was quite a "gift." This book concentrates on the United States, but Europe's debt crisis is arguably the biggest aftershock from the 2007–2009 financial earthquake. Because the economies and markets of Europe and the United States are linked in so many ways, the crisis in the eurozone also appears to be the biggest threat to continued economic recovery here. The story won't be complete until the "exit" from the European sovereign debt crisis comes. And that may be a long way off.

A serious explanation of the European debt crisis, with all its twists and turns, would require a book in itself, maybe two. And the saga continues. This chapter just scratches the surface, focusing especially on European events that are linked to or parallel to events in the United States.

CRISES HERE AND THERE: SIMILARITIES

The financial crisis in Europe was partly homegrown and partly shipped across the Atlantic from us to them. So it is hardly surprising to find striking similarities.

For openers, both financial crises had their roots in speculative bubbles, most obviously in houses but also in bonds. The real estate craze was particularly pronounced in Ireland, Spain, and the United Kingdom, but it was also visible elsewhere. The financial zaniness we documented in the United States reached tragicomic proportions in Ireland and Iceland, but the UK had a large share, too. Elsewhere in Europe, naïve investors ranging from Belgian widows to German *landesbanken* (state savings banks), deluded by those tempting AAA ratings, scooped up American mortgage-backed securities with glee, thinking they had struck gold: higher returns without greater risk. In fact, they had struck fools' gold. All this sounds eerily like America in the bubble years.

The mortgage mess commanded so much attention that hardly anyone seemed to notice the fact that spreads between, say, Greek government bonds and German government bonds—which, remember, are supposed to represent the differential probabilities of default by the two governments—almost disappeared. Could it really be that profligate Greece was no more likely to default than stolid Germany? The proposition was ludicrous, yet market prices came close to saying so. Vanishing risk spreads, as we know, are a hallmark of a bond bubble—whether in the United States or in Europe.

When the housing and bond bubbles burst, recession quickly descended upon Europe, just as it had here. And if homegrown real estate and bond bubbles weren't enough, virulent infection from the United States after Lehman Day sealed the deal. Virtually every nation in Europe experienced a slump; some were devastatingly long and deep. Greece, Ireland, and Iceland spring to mind as particular horror stories, with the UK and Spain also hit hard. (Spanish unemployment is still over 25 percent.) Even mighty Germany, a stable and conservative country that had no real estate bubble, saw its GDP contract by 6.8 percent between 2008:1 and 2009:1. That's substantially larger than the 4.7 percent contraction in the United States—and we're the ones who started the mess.

Recessions blow holes in government budgets, as Americans learned painfully in 2009 and thereafter. Tax collections in European nations dropped sharply as their economies contracted. Similarly, the already-sizable costs of Europe's social safety net—spending on unemployment benefits, health insurance, public pensions, and the like—rose. Most European governments, turning Keynesian in an emergency, also decided to fight the recession with fiscal stimulus packages of various shapes and sizes. These, of course, also added to their government budget deficits.

And then there were the extraordinary costs of the bank bailouts. In the United States, we created the TARP, which was authorized at about 4.7 percent of GDP but never lent out as much as 3 percent of GDP—and we got it all back with interest. European parliaments enacted myriad mostly ad hoc bailouts on a country-by-country basis, some of them much larger relative to GDP than ours, to prevent their banks from collapsing. And the money didn't always come back. European attitudes toward bank failures differ sharply from our own. Remember the European central banker who declared after Lehman Day that "we don't even let dry cleaners fail."

Finally, in some countries, the government assumed massive amounts of *private* (mostly bank) debt. These decisions, too, had parallels in the United States, where the federal government guaranteed, assumed, or purchased the debts of companies as diverse as Goldman Sachs, Bear Stearns, AIG, General Motors, General Electric, and so on. But here's the difference: The *net* costs in the United States—after interest and repayments—were small, and in most cases *negative*. In some European countries, they were large.

The poster child is Ireland. By guaranteeing essentially all bank liabilities in September 2008, and subsequently assuming those debts as its own, the Irish government added about 40 points to its debt-to-GDP ratio. In theory, the Irish government was a highly creditworthy borrower that could obtain credit on favorable terms and shoulder the debt burden while

Irish banks recovered. In practice, Ireland's rash actions turned a banking crisis into a sovereign debt crisis. Ireland's annual government budget *deficit* in 2010 was a shocking 32 percent of GDP, likely setting a modern-day world record.

Crises Here and There: Differences

So much for similarities. There are also numerous differences, most of them stemming from the fact that the seventeen countries of the eurozone share a common currency and a common central bank—but not a common government.

During and after the crisis, the European Central Bank was not nearly as aggressive a recession fighter as the Federal Reserve. The simplest way to see the difference is to glance at figure 16.1, which displays the main policy interest rates of the two central banks: the federal funds rate for the Fed and the ECB's main refinancing rate. It is evident that the Fed reacted to the burgeoning crisis faster and much more strongly than did the ECB.

FIGURE 16.1 *A Tale of Two Central Banks*
(policy interest rates of the Fed and the ECB)

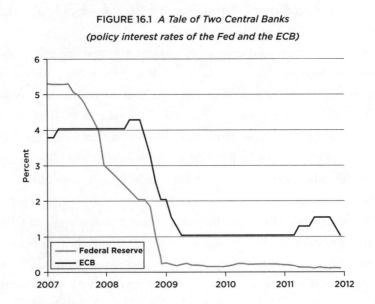

For example, by December 2008, the Fed's rate was already down to virtually zero, while the ECB's was still at 2.5 percent. The ECB even *raised* rates twice in 2011 (what were they thinking?), while the Fed was looking for new ways to give the U.S. economy a boost. One reason for the difference is that the Fed's legal mandate instructs it to pursue *both* low inflation *and* low unemployment, while the ECB's legal mandate is *only* for low inflation.

While the eurozone countries share both a common currency and a common monetary policy, just like the American states, the seventeen countries are far less integrated than the fifty states. It was soon clear that Greece, Portugal, and Ireland were suffering much deeper slumps than, say, Germany, France, and the Netherlands. *In principle*, the weaker countries needed a looser monetary policy than the stronger ones. *In practice*, the ECB cannot run separate monetary policies for individual countries; it's one monetary policy for all.

And also one exchange rate. Because all seventeen countries use the euro, the traditional escape route for a nation mired in a deep slump—a currency depreciation that spurs exports—was ruled out. Which was truly a Greek tragedy. If Greece had its own currency in the summer of 2010, the drachma would have plunged in value, making that sunny Mediterranean land an irresistible destination for vacationers from all over the world. Greece probably would soon have experienced an export boom, led by tourism, and the Greek recession might have ended right there. Instead, the euro kept Greece expensive, and antiausterity riots scared tourists away.

The third critical difference between the United States and Europe is perhaps too obvious to state: They had to deal with Greece; we didn't. The Greek situation is, if you'll pardon the Latin, sui generis. Greece has a dismal fiscal history. Economists Carmen Reinhart and Kenneth Rogoff found that Greece has been in default on its public debt roughly 50 percent of the time since gaining independence in the 1830s! More recently, Greece's budget deficits were large before the crisis and huge thereafter. The Greeks also turn out to be pretty poor tax collectors—some would say they hardly try. And while the government doesn't collect taxes very well, it does keep lots of workers on its payroll—people who expect to be paid and to retire young. All part of Athenian democracy, I suppose.

On top of all this, the worldwide recession hit Greece particularly hard. The reasons are not hard to fathom. The Greek economy relies heavily on two export industries: shipping and tourism. In late 2008 and into 2009, world trade suffered a stunning collapse, comparable to that of the Great Depression. There went shipping. And for millions of people all over the world, the recession meant that vacations in Greece were luxuries they could no longer afford. There went tourism.

Between the third quarter of 2008 (the Lehman quarter) and the end of 2010, real GDP in Greece contracted by 10 percent. And it continued to fall. By the end of 2011, Greek GDP was about 16 percent below its 2008:3 peak—and still falling. By comparison, we considered a 4.7 percent decline in GDP devastating. Here's a scarier comparison: Between 1929 and 1933, real GDP in the United States fell almost 27 percent. We call that the Great Depression. By the end of 2012, Greece was on its way.

And then there was the little matter of lying about its budget deficits and national debt. Greece was admitted to the eurozone in 2001 with a wink and a nod, some fudged numbers, and a public debt well in excess of the Maastricht Treaty's limit of 60 percent of GDP. But hey, who was counting? In November 2009, just a month after his election, Prime Minister George Papandreou revealed that the previous government had run larger deficits than it had admitted. In an ironic link to America's financial mischief, it turns out that some financial engineering by Goldman Sachs had helped the Greek government conceal its mounting debt. The news did not amuse Greece's creditors. The Greek debt-to-GDP ratio, by the way, was already over 120 percent by then—a difficult burden to bear even at modest interest rates. Greek interest rates would soon be immodest.

The United States certainly has badly behaved state and local governments whose fiscal (and other) behavior is roguish or worse. But it is inconceivable that a budgetary disaster in, say, Minnesota—which, proportionately, is to U.S. GDP as Greece is to eurozone GDP—would pull down the entire country. Minnesota would simply, or maybe not so simply, go into default. But starting late in 2009, Greece's fiscal problems shook faith in many eurozone countries, and even in the euro itself. One for all and all for one, right?

BE WARY OF GREECE

The simplest way to assess a European government's perceived creditworthiness is to compare its bond rate to that of Germany, then and now Europe's gold standard. Figure 16.2 displays the spread between the interest rates on Greek and German 10-year government bonds. A few points are evident.

First, the spread was under 1 percent as late as October 2008. In fact, if you look back further, you'll find even smaller spreads in the years 2001–2007—sometimes under 20 basis points. Prior to the crisis, the Greek government apparently was perceived as being almost as good a credit as the German government. Did someone say "bond-market bubble"?

Second, the spread on Greek debt widened to nearly 3 percentage points during the height of the worldwide financial crisis in early 2009, as investors shunned risk in every way they could. But it fell back down

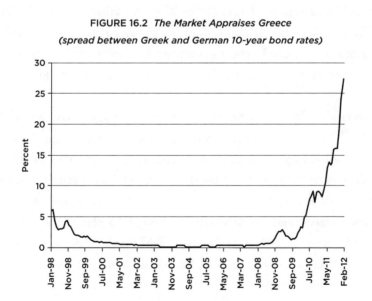

FIGURE 16.2 *The Market Appraises Greece*
(spread between Greek and German 10-year bond rates)

again—though not quite *all the way* down—when global financial conditions improved later that year. If you were a Greek, you could easily convince yourself that the ups and downs of your government's bond rate had more to do with worldwide financial developments than with anything happening in Greece.

Then things began to change. Starting late in 2009, Greek interest rates began to move up as investor fears escalated. The Papandreou government reacted by proposing a succession of fiscal austerity programs that were often announced with fanfare, blessed by the European authorities, and then unraveled. It was a portent of things to come. Some of the programs precipitated protests and even riots on the streets of Athens. Greece's bond rate rose as its credibility sank. Do the math. If your national debt is 150 percent of GDP, and your interest rate is 6 percent, your government must collect 9 percent of GDP just to pay interest. That was about 30 percent of all Greek government revenue. Trouble.

As figure 16.2 shows, things started coming apart around April 2010. Events unfolded quickly: more promises of fiscal austerity; more protests and political turmoil; more downgrades from the rating agencies; more discussions of aid packages from other eurozone countries, and even from the International Monetary Fund (IMF). At one point, Greece's 10-year bond rate breached 12 percent. The cradle of Western civilization was starting to look like a basket case. At the beginning of May 2010, the first "historic" bailout deal was reached, relieving pressure for a while. But as figure 16.2 shows, the relief was short lived. Try doing the math with a bond rate of 12 percent.

Greece's difficulties went beyond mere arithmetic, however. Unlike Ireland, which took the painful medicine willingly, Greece was a poor patient with unmanageable politics. A succession of Greek governments had made deals with its citizens that the state could no longer afford. Suddenly, Greeks were asked to pay higher taxes, do without some public services, earn lower wages, and live less well. And why? To placate foreign bondholders? It's no wonder Greeks protested vehemently and the government failed to deliver on its promises time and time again.

As Greece's slump deepened, its budget targets grew ever harder to meet. After yet another failed European "summit," Papandreou resigned in November 2011. His government was replaced by a coalition led by technocrat Lucas Papademos, a well-respected economist who had previously served as governor of the Bank of Greece and as vice president of the ECB. The Papademos government lasted until May 2012, but it then took two elections to install a viable coalition government. Greece has been teetering on the brink ever since.

The political difficulties over the Greek debt situation were by no means confined to Athens. Across the eurozone bargaining table sat not one country but sixteen, and sometimes other EU countries as well, and sometimes the IMF, too. Henry Kissinger once famously asked, "When I need to call Europe, whom do I call?"* When it came to negotiating a Greek bailout, the inability to answer Kissinger's question posed a serious problem. Who could deliver Europe? Remember, the European Union is a loose confederation of sovereign states, with a minimal central government—more like our Articles of Confederation than the unified nation created by the U.S. Constitution. Remember also that the Articles of Confederation failed. Ironically, one of the major reasons was its inability to deal with government debt.

While lines of authority in Europe are unclear de jure, the Germans and the French normally take the lead de facto. Domestic politics in Germany are particularly intriguing. As Europe's largest economy, Germany is destined to bear the largest share of any bailout. Yet tax-paying, orderly Germans want to know why they should pay for the failings of undisciplined Greeks who—they believe—work shorter hours, retire earlier, and don't pay their taxes. It's a fair question. I often ask Americans to imagine the political reaction here if we were asked to bail out Canada, our friendly neighbor to the north, whose people *do* work hard, *do* pay high taxes, and *do* play by the rules. Yet how many votes in Congress would a Canadian bailout muster? Now change *Canada* to *Mexico* and think again—or re-

---

*This famous quote seems to come in an almost infinite number of variants. Kissinger is not even sure he said it!

member the political donnybrook when our NAFTA partner to the south got in trouble in 1994.

Europe dragged its collective feet, each time kicking the can just far enough down the road to get to the next summit meeting. As they did so, more and more countries were drawn into the muck. Portugal, with its yawning budget deficits and uncompetitive economy, looked too much like Greece for comfort. Ireland, which had experienced a monumental real estate boom and bust, allowed its banks to engage in a surreal array of financial shenanigans, and then bailed them out at colossal public cost, was soon in the crosshairs. Spain, with its whopping real estate bubble and shaky banks, and Italy, with its gigantic public debt and undisciplined government, were next in line. Market participants developed an unflattering name for this list of troubled eurozone countries: the PIIGS (Portugal, Ireland, Italy, Greece, and Spain).

The chances of nipping the crisis in the bud faded away as the list of troubled countries grew. Greece alone was manageable, *if* it could be quarantined and rescued. After all, while Greek public debt was huge relative to its small economy, it amounted to less than 4 percent of eurozone GDP. Could, say, halving a number like that really pose an insurmountable task for Europe? Not arithmetically. But as Portugal and Ireland joined Greece on the bailout list, the problem grew. And Spain, despite its more reasonable public finances, was bigger than Greece, Portugal, and Ireland combined. Then there was Italy, with the third-largest national debt in the world—trailing only the United States and Japan. Italy turned the old cliché on its head: The country was *too big to save*.

THE EURO GIVETH, AND THE EURO TAKETH AWAY

The countries in Europe's so-called periphery benefited enormously from innocence-by-association during the boom years, mainly in the form of lower borrowing rates than they could have achieved on their own. As mentioned, Greek interest rates floated barely above Germany's.

But once the crisis hit, the euro became a straitjacket. With monetary policy for all seventeen countries made in Frankfurt, the PIIGS could not escape from their slumps with easier money. Nor could they escape with currency depreciation, as there was no longer an escudo, a punt, a lira, a drachma, or a peseta—only the euro. That left only one traditional escape route: spending their way out of the slump with fiscal policy. But as government debt mounted in the periphery, these countries' ability to borrow started to disappear. For Greece, the door slammed shut. Eurozone membership became a one-way ticket to a deep, long-lasting recession.

It is notable that the UK, which experienced a huge financial meltdown, a sharp recession, and a government budget deficit almost as large, relative to GDP, as Greece's, fared much better. While it experienced a double-dip recession, there was no British sovereign debt crisis; indeed, British government bond rates are still low. Many economists insist that the main reason is that the UK has its own currency and makes its own monetary policy.

There was also guilt-by-association within the eurozone. As Greece, Ireland, and Portugal crumbled, each requiring a bailout, markets cast a jaundiced eye on Spain and Italy—and interest rates in those countries soared. Even France and Austria lost their cherished AAA credit ratings. Germany, the strongest credit in the eurozone, never worried about rising interest rates—it was the safe haven. But it did worry about a potential breakup of the euro, which would presumably send a new deutsche mark soaring through the roof, thereby killing German exports.

It began to look like the famous old cliché applied to the euro: You can't live with it, and you can't live without it.

DON'T BANK ON IT

So far, I have followed common usage by referring to the mess in Europe as the *sovereign debt crisis*. Investors are worried about the ability of several European governments to pay their bills. But it is also a European *banking crisis*: Investors are worried about the solvency of many of Europe's largest

banks. Indeed, the two crises are inextricably linked. Part of the governments' debt problems derive from the expense of bailing out their banks.
Europe's major banks also own a great deal of government debt, on which
they can ill afford to take losses. Furthermore, the line between banks and
governments is blurrier in Europe than it is here. Don't forget those too big
to fail dry cleaners.

The tight links between European banks and their governments open
up new lines of contagion. I have already mentioned that nervous contagion jumped from Greece to Portugal to Ireland to Spain, and so on. That
was government-to-government contagion. But another line of contagion
also arose in 2010: from Greek *government* debt to Greek *banks* (which own
a lot of Greek government bonds) and then to banks in other European
countries (which have important counterparty relations with Greek banks)
and from there to the whole world financial system. The contagion goes
the other way, too. In 2012 a European bailout of Spanish *banks* cast
further doubt on Spanish sovereign debt because it initially took the form
of new loans to the Spanish *government*.

When the United States designed and conducted its highly successful
bank stress tests in 2009, no one worried that American banks might suffer
losses on their holdings of U.S. Treasury securities. But when Europe conducted similar stress tests on its major banks later that same year, the markets were not reassured. One reason was that European banks held lots of
European government debt, not all of which looked "good as gold." But the
designers of the European stress tests refused to contemplate the possibility
of losses on sovereign debt. Doing so may have been nearly impossible,
politically. Which countries would you name? Nonetheless, assuming away
sovereign risk looked somewhat surreal in the European context.

Nor was Europe as aggressive as the United States in shoring up the
capital positions of its banks. So while market confidence in American
banks came back quickly, doubts remained about European banks. These
doubts were serious and persistent enough that Christine Lagarde, in her
first major speech on becoming head of the IMF, in August 2011, stated
bluntly that Europe's banks "need urgent recapitalization." She went on:
"This is key to cutting the chains of contagion" and should include "using

public funds if necessary." Her stern warning seemed particularly pointed at France, which was remarkable because she had just been France's finance minister. Furthermore, she was seated right next to her countryman, Jean-Claude Trichet, then the president of the ECB, who had been saying reassuring things about Europe's banks. Trichet looked less than delighted as Lagarde spoke.

The Reluctant Rescuer

Which brings us to the ECB.

As Europe's crisis lengthened and deepened, many economists and financial experts concluded that the most plausible way out of the mess was for the ECB to buy massive amounts of government bonds of endangered eurozone countries. Many still feel that way. Why? Because the required amount of money was titanic, and only Europe's central bank can create euros in unlimited amounts—money that, not incidentally, need not be appropriated by European parliaments. The Federal Reserve, the argument went on, had pointed the way with Bear Stearns, AIG, QE1, QE2, and more. These huge asset purchases, financed by creating as much central bank money as necessary, had saved the U.S. financial system. Surely the ECB—and *only* the ECB—could do the same thing for Europe.

But the ECB was reluctant to jump into the sovereign debt fray for several reasons. One was the Maastricht Treaty, which had created the ECB in the first place. The Treaty contains the famous "no bailout" clause:

> The [European] Union shall not be liable for or assume the commitments of central governments, regional, local or other public authorities, other bodies governed by public law, or public undertakings of any Member State. . . .

Sounds definitive, right? And both the ECB and many European governments have appealed to it repeatedly. Wouldn't buying up periphery country debt constitute "bailing out" these nations? Perhaps. But what is often forgotten is that the Maastricht Treaty also contains what might be (but is not) called the "bailout clause":

> Where a Member State is in difficulties . . . caused by natural disas-
> ters or exceptional occurrences beyond its control, the Council, act-
> ing on a proposal from the Commission, may grant . . . Union
> financial assistance to the Member State concerned.

Do self-inflicted wounds qualify as "exceptional occurrences" beyond a nation's control? Well, that depends on how creative your lawyers are. Greece,
Portugal, Ireland, Spain, and Cyprus all received assistance.

The ECB's reluctance to intervene was not, however, based exclusively
on the no-bailout clause. It has long been considered bad central banking
practice to purchase newly issued debt *directly* from the government. Such
monetary financing of government budget deficits is often characterized as
"inflationary finance" for a reason. It was, for example, the main route to
hyperinflation in places as diverse as Weimar Germany, Latin America in
the 1980s, and Zimbabwe recently.

The ECB was consciously built in the image of the Bundesbank and
was well aware of this history. It was also acutely aware that the hallmark
of a truly independent central bank is its ability to resist government pressures to monetize deficits. With this in mind, the Maastricht Treaty clearly
states that:

> Overdraft facilities or any other type of credit facility with the Euro-
> pean Central Bank or with the central banks of the Member
> States . . . in favour of Union institutions . . . or public undertakings
> of Member States shall be prohibited, as shall the purchase directly
> from them by the European Central Bank or national central banks
> of debt instruments.

Prohibited. That seems to be a pretty clear ban on central bank financing
of budget deficits. And the Germans, for one, took the admonition seri-

ously. But the key word here is *directly*. After all, every central bank buys and sells government debt in the secondary market as part of its normal business.

The term "inflationary finance" suggests yet another objection to bond purchases, one that both American hawks and Germans remembering Weimar keep reminding us of: Printing money can be inflationary. In the United States, the Fed appealed to its dual mandate to pursue *both* low inflation *and* high employment. Bond purchases could be instrumental to the latter. But the ECB was created with only one statutory goal: low inflation. Printing money to purchase government debt is traditionally viewed as an *inflationary* policy. It would take a pretty slick lawyer to rebrand it as *anti-inflationary*.

Indeed, as long as Trichet led the ECB, the bank argued that it could never sacrifice its anti-inflation goal to any other cause—not even saving the euro. Quietly, it looked disapprovingly at the Fed's ever-lengthening list of unconventional monetary policies. Wouldn't they ultimately prove inflationary? Indeed, it was fear of inflation that presumably motivated the ECB to *raise* interest rates slightly in 2011, even though Europe was struggling with its debt crisis and weak economic growth.

There was yet another, overtly political reason for the ECB to hold back. Several ECB leaders were quite frank in saying that their reluctance to purchase government bonds stemmed in part from concerns that letting national governments off the hook so easily would ease pressures to get their fiscal houses in order. It was a moral hazard argument, plain and simple: If the ECB started buying Greek, Irish, Portuguese, Spanish, and Italian bonds, that would weaken the incentives of the governments of those countries to solve their budget problems.

In the event, the ECB's attitude probably helped precipitate changes of government in Greece, Spain, and Italy in 2011. In two of those three cases, technocrats temporarily took the helm of what were supposed to be national unity governments.

Super Mario Brothers

One of those technocrats was Mario Monti, an economist by training and sometimes known as "Il Professore," who was installed as prime minister of Italy on November 16, 2011. By coincidence, that was just fifteen days after another highly regarded Italian economist, Mario Draghi, took over as president of the ECB. Though not related, the pair was quickly dubbed the "Super Mario Brothers." And they were super. Monti set about trying to reform Italy—not just its budget but even its restrictive labor laws, licensing provisions, and other ingrained anticompetitive practices. Draghi changed the ECB's course virtually overnight.

It started with interest rates. As mentioned earlier, in an amazing display of obtuseness, the ECB had *raised* its policy rate from 1 to 1.5 percent in two steps in April and July 2011. With mostly the same members still sitting on its governing council but now under Draghi's leadership, the ECB reversed those two increases in November and December 2011. Mistake corrected. But that was just the beginning.

Under President Trichet, the ECB had swallowed its objections and began purchasing modest amounts of Greek, Irish, Spanish, Portuguese, and Italian bonds in May 2010. By October 2011, it had accumulated about €170 billion of such bonds, which sounds like a lot but was a pittance compared with what the Fed had done. Critics said bond purchases needed to be expanded greatly. But the ECB countered with the three objections raised earlier: It was not supposed to finance budget deficits; doing so would let profligate governments off the hook; and the inflation-fighting ECB had to conduct offsetting monetary operations to prevent its balance sheet from exploding like the Fed's. Enter Mario Draghi.

Under President Draghi, the ECB creatively expanded its preexisting Longer-Term Refinancing Operations (LTRO) in entirely new dimensions—both in *size* and in *maturity*. Under the new LTRO strategy, which began in December 2011, banks are not only *allowed* but actually *encouraged* to borrow large amounts of money from the ECB for terms as long as three years—which is a long way from the typical overnight central bank loan. The three-year maturities, by the way, are far longer than any credit the Fed ever extended. When a bank borrows for three years, it is doing much more than tiding itself over a temporary liquidity problem. Three-year money is a stone's throw from capital.

At a stroke, the ECB's new strategy made the European banking crisis far less acute. Banks now had some breathing space. European banks borrowed about €1 trillion from the new LTRO facility in December 2011 and February 2012. That's real money. And cheap money, too: The banks paid the ECB just 1 percent interest. Thus the ECB was now standing squarely behind its banks, much as the Fed and the Treasury had done with the TARP and the stress tests in 2009.

Think about what the new LTRO meant for Europe's sovereign debt crisis. The ECB would not buy more sovereign debt for its own portfolio, as its critics had urged. Draghi continued to talk the talk about how bad that would be, and the old bond-buying program receded into the background. But by granting massive amounts of cheap three-year loans to European banks, the ECB was helping private banks do so. And who doubted that European governments would lean on their banks to buy their bonds? (They did—especially in Spain.) While the ECB was not buying bonds directly, it was enabling others to do so on attractive terms. For example, Spanish banks could now borrow from the ECB at 1 percent and turn around and purchase Spanish government bonds paying 5 percent. A pretty good deal.

The new LTRO looked like a game changer. But it did not solve the sovereign debt crisis. The central bank can't do that, of course, any more than the Fed can solve the U.S. government's mounting debt problem. Only governments can—by cutting spending and raising more revenue. The ECB's actions did buy time. But not as much as was hoped. By June 2012, Spanish banks were getting an explicit bailout and pressure was growing for more LTRO.

A month later, the markets were getting jittery again and the euro was sagging. Talk of a euro-area breakup was in the air. Draghi reacted again, this time with words, telling a conference in London that the ECB would "do whatever it takes to preserve the euro," and "believe me, it will be enough." It was tough talk, and markets immediately began to speculate that the ECB would soon restart, and probably enhance, its suspended program of buying sovereign debt.

They were right. In early September, Draghi announced a new bond-buying program, called "Outright Monetary Transactions" (OMT), that went well beyond the ECB's previous efforts. While restricted to bonds with maturities of three years or less, the *volume* of sovereign debt purchases under OMT is in principle *unlimited*. So the ECB's wallet is wide open. To qualify for the program, however, each debtor nation must agree to conditions (e.g., on its budget) set forth by Europe's bailout fund, the European Stability Mechanism. The ECB will be the financier, but not the judge and jury. Markets cheered the OMT. But at this writing, it is too early to know how it will work in practice. Keep your fingers crossed.

Trojan Horses

Then there is Greece, where it all began. Greece differs from the other PIIGs because its fiscal situation looks hopeless—in at least two respects.

First, Greece seems unable to live up to any of its commitments. It pledges budget cuts; it promises to raise tax collections; it commits itself to economic reforms; but it fails to deliver. Part of that failure is a lack of will. The Greeks simply have not been the dutiful patients that, say, the Irish have been. As any doctor will tell you, the cure won't work unless the patient takes the medicine. And Greek politics are, well . . . Byzantine.

But another reason for failure is beyond Greece's control. Its paymasters in Europe and at the IMF demand ever more fiscal austerity—higher taxes and less government spending—to shrink the budget deficit. Yes, the deficit must shrink. But such profoundly anti-Keynesian policies have exacerbated Greece's depression—and it is a *depression*, not just a *recession*. That, in turn, makes any budget goal harder to achieve.* Slow-moving Greece is chasing a moving target. In the €130 billion bailout agreed on in

---

*Much the same is true of Spain.

February 2012, Greece even had to pledge to reduce its minimum wage by 22 percent. With elections scheduled for May 2012, did anyone really think that would happen? It didn't. And several fringe parties ran successfully against the €130 billion bailout in the May election, creating the need for a second election in June before Greece got a new government. By August, that government was asking its creditors for yet more delays.

Second, even if Greece somehow manages to achieve the promised deficit reductions, all that effort would not be enough. The interim debt-to-GDP target set for Greece is 120 percent by 2020, and virtually no one believes they will achieve it. But suspend disbelief for a moment and imagine they do. If the average interest rate on Greek government debt then drops back to, say, 5 percent—another barely believable assumption—Greece will still have to raise 6 percent of GDP just to meet its interest payments. That's a heavy burden. To achieve budgetary stability, Greece must get its debt-to-GDP ratio well below 120 percent. Is that even possible?

On top of all this, Greece has already defaulted on some of its debt. In a lengthy series of negotiations that began in the summer of 2011 and culminated in March 2012, European governments extracted large *voluntary* concessions from Greece's private creditors, mainly the banks. Did I say voluntary? Yes, about as voluntary as a deal with Tony Soprano. The final deal imposed more than a 75 percent loss on private bondholders, mainly banks, while sparing official bondholders like the IMF and the ECB. A few bondholders are now suing Greece. And the decision to impose losses on the private sector, but *not* on the official sector, made some prospective lenders wary of other governments' bonds—until the ECB promised not to do that in its new bond-buying program.

WHAT'S NEXT?

As this book goes to press, Greece teeters on the brink, struggling—both economically and politically—to live up to its promises. But it has been on the brink for more than two years already. The Greeks apparently know how to teeter. Many economists, including me, wonder why Greece wants to remain in the eurozone in the first place. The price of membership seems excruciatingly high and getting higher. That said, Greek polling continues to show strong support for keeping the euro. Go figure.

By both its words and its deeds, Ireland seems prepared to pay any price—except its status as a corporate tax haven—to remain in the eurozone. Portugal falls somewhere in between, with budget problems like, though not as bad as, Greece's and a will to stay in the euro that is like, but perhaps not as strong as, Ireland's. Spain is less secure, though more for its shaky-looking banks than for its public finances, and rather large for a bailout program. As noted, its banks are a heavy weight on the government. And Italy—we hope!—has started down the road to salvation under the leadership of Super Mario Monti. Meanwhile, Europe's new chief central banker, Super Mario Draghi, seems to be channeling his inner Bernanke.

The Europeans surely live in interesting times. And because of global linkages, so do we. In 2008 a financial panic in the United States quickly infected Europe and the rest of the world. A similar financial panic in Europe in 2013 would quickly infect us, imperiling our still-nascent recovery. That's the so-called Lehman II scenario. No one wants to go there.

17

||||||||||||||||||||||||||||

NEVER AGAIN:
LEGACIES OF THE CRISIS

History doesn't repeat itself, but it does rhyme.

—ATTRIBUTED TO MARK TWAIN

merica has been through a lot since 2007, enough to keep heads spinning, to keep scowls on people's faces, and to fill sixteen chapters of this book. But it isn't over yet. This chapter marks the end of the *book*, not the end of the *story*. Our economy is still limping along, and Washington is still gridlocked, with a new Congress recently installed. Most of the long-awaited "exit" decisions remain in front of us. They will affect our future profoundly.

THE POLICY AGENDA

It's the Economy, Stupid

A logical place to start is with the state of the national economy, which may be the worst legacy of the crisis. More than four years after Lehman

Brothers went under, policy makers are still nursing a frail economy back to health. Having the national unemployment rate near 8 percent is a lot better than having it near 10 percent. But it is far from good. An unemployment rate more like 5 percent to 5.5 percent should be our goal; anything higher is unwarranted defeatism. The Federal Reserve seems to agree, having posted an official target range of 5.2 percent to 6 percent unemployment. But we are not getting there quickly.

The epic hawk-dove battle within the Federal Open Market Committee still rages. The Fed's hawks seem more worried about the inflation *we might get* than about the high unemployment *we still have*. I'm rooting for the doves. Chairman Bernanke's ammunition depot is no longer well stocked, but it is not quite empty, and he seems prepared to fire off more. That's the good news.

Fiscal Policy and the Budget

The bad news is that fiscal policy looks paralyzed, both by the specter of trillion-dollar-plus budget deficits—themselves largely a legacy of the crisis—and by the partisan dysfunction in Congress. The 2012 election left essentially the same partisan split in Congress and did not, by itself, reduce the deficit by a single penny. We'll see. But hope is not a policy— you must enact laws. America's budget mess is starting to look Kafkaesque because the outline of a solution is so clear: We need modest fiscal stimulus today coupled with massive deficit reduction for the future. Some of that will take the form of higher taxes—sorry, Republicans. Most of it will be lower spending—sorry, Democrats.

If you view the world through sufficiently rose-colored glasses, you can perhaps see the two parties inching in that direction. But "inching" isn't good enough. There is plenty of room for partisan bickering over the details, but we need to adopt the Nike solution—*Just do it!*—as soon as possible. The Simpson-Bowles plan points the way, and I imagine that some distant cousin of Simpson-Bowles will be adopted someday. Someday. But not today.

The Fed's Bloated Balance Sheet

Meanwhile, the Federal Reserve is sitting with nearly $3 trillion worth of assets on its books, an uncomfortable legacy of its prodigious efforts to fight the financial crisis and shorten the Great Recession. Before the crisis, it had about $900 billion. The Fed wants to shrink its bloated balance sheet *eventually*. It also wants to normalize interest rates. Chairman Bernanke has sketched the central bank's exit strategy, more or less telling us that the Fed will start raising interest rates well before its balance sheet has been whittled down to size. But they are watching and waiting for either a buoyant economy or signs of inflation before they head for the exits. Neither seems imminent.

The Ghost of Moral Hazard Past

One of the least desirable legacies of the emergency measures of 2008 and 2009 is the creation of moral hazard everywhere. Bailouts, rescues, guarantees, and the like succeeded in saving many investors, companies, and even some executives and traders from oblivion. The moral hazard ayatollahs notwithstanding, doing so was *not* a mistake. Had we stood firmly on the anti-moral–hazard high ground, our principles would have emerged unscathed but our economy would not have. Necessity mothered pragmatism.

But moral hazard is now an undesirable feature of the financial landscape. One important aspect of *Never Again* is convincing financial markets that the government will *not* rescue them from future mistakes. The game of "heads you win, tails the taxpayer loses" is not one we want to keep playing. But innocence has been lost—if, indeed, we ever had it. Investors have seen what the U.S. government did in a dire emergency. Should similar circumstances arise in the future, they'll expect similar treatment.

In that respect, the moral hazard ayatollahs are right. We must convince markets that emergencies are one thing, normal times quite another. Dodd-Frank tries to do that, partly by insisting that dying financial institutions be laid to rest peacefully, not resuscitated at public expense.

Remember the law's key phrase: "Taxpayers shall bear no losses." We'll see how that works out in practice.

Festering Foreclosures

Perhaps the saddest legacy of the financial crisis is the tsunami of fore-closures that continues to wash over us. Many aspects of the crisis caught policy makers by surprise. This one did not. Waves of foreclosures were foreseen well in advance, but we didn't stop them. One foreclosure-mitigation program after another failed, largely because we pinched pennies and made things far too complicated. In February 2012, the U.S. govern-ment and state attorneys general reached yet another "historic" settlement with the nation's largest banks. This one was over the disgraceful number of legal and procedural irregularities in handling foreclosures. To get off the hook, the banks kicked in $26 billion to help underwater homeowners, which is a drop in the proverbial bucket. Even so, news reports in May 2012 revealed that many state governments were intercepting the money before it reached homeowners. Ironically, the biggest near-term effect of the settlement was to allow many foreclosures, previously bottled up by legal wrangling, to proceed. The overhang of foreclosures continues to weigh on our economy.

Is There a Mortgage in Your Future?

As journalist David Frum aptly put it, "The shapers of the American mort-gage system hoped to achieve the security of government ownership, the integrity of local banking and the ingenuity of Wall Street. Instead they got the ingenuity of government, the security of local banking and the in-tegrity of Wall Street." Now that system is gone, swept away by the crisis. Fannie Mae and Freddie Mac limp on as what amount to branches of the U.S. Treasury. No one wants to maintain that arrangement indefinitely. Re-creating a viable system of mortgage finance, one that is safer than the one we had, ranks high on the national agenda. After all, Americans still want to buy houses—and presumably not for cash. The housing market, which was moribund for years, finally seems to be showing some signs of life. Maybe this is a good time to turn some serious attention to reestablishing a mortgage system we can live with.

A New Rule Book for Finance

One final legacy of the financial catastrophe is the 2,319-page Dodd-Frank Act, which rewrote the financial regulatory rulebook. Implementing Dodd-Frank is a huge task that has barely begun. It needs to happen. As I have emphasized, first you write the laws, then you write detailed rules and regulations, then you watch what happens in practice—and make adjustments. The lawmaking phase ended in July 2010, although some Republicans still want to dismantle Dodd-Frank. The rulemaking phase is in progress, and it resembles trench warfare—with neither Dodd nor Frank around to defend it. The practical application phase is in its early stages. More than just the regulatory framework needs to change in the wake of the crisis, so does the way banks and other financial institutions do business. Let's not forget that it was shameful business practices, coupled with regulatory neglect, that got us into this mess.

THE TEN FINANCIAL COMMANDMENTS

So, what are some of the key principles for finance going forward? According to an old joke, there are three secrets to designing a safe and sound financial system—the problem is that nobody knows what they are. Let me instead try to encapsulate the major financial lessons from the crisis into ten commandments for the future of finance.

1. Thou Shalt Remember That People Forget

Looking back, Tim Geithner attributed the crisis, in part, to collective amnesia: "There was no memory of extreme crisis, no memory of what can happen when a nation allows huge amounts of risk to build up." Evidence of forgetting is all around us: in markets, in Congress, and in our nation's vaunted financial institutions. Hyman Minsky, the renegade economist who argued against market efficiency, taught us, or rather *should have* taught us, that it is normal for speculative markets to go to extremes. That's what they do. One key reason, according to Minsky, is that, unlike elephants, people *forget*. When the good times roll, investors expect them to roll indefinitely. But they don't. And when bubbles burst, investors are always surprised. We should remember our Minsky: Markets and people forget.

2. Thou Shalt Not Rely on Self-Regulation

Self-regulation in financial markets is an oxymoron, maybe even a cruel deception. We need *real* regulation, zookeepers watching over the animals. Governments cannot and should not outsource this function to *market discipline* (another oxymoron) or to rating agencies, which are in business to make a profit. It's the government's job, and it needs to be done better. And while, yes, there is a danger of *over*-regulation, I'm not too worried about that now, given where we've just been. Generally speaking, Dodd-Frank reflects these attitudes pretty well, though we will surely discover flaws as time goes by.

3. Thou Shalt Honor Thy Shareholders

If you are a director of a public corporation, you should remember that corporate boards are supposed to understand and monitor the behavior of top executives—who are, in turn, *employees* of the company, not kings and queens—and to protect the interests of shareholders. Too often, directors were asleep at the wheel and did neither. Both their companies and the broader public suffered from the malign neglect. Board members need to pay more attention. We've tried to make them do so before—for example, with the Sarbanes-Oxley Act of 2002—but with only modest success. We need to keep trying.

4. Thou Shalt Elevate the Importance of Risk Management

It turns out that what you don't know *can* hurt you. When heads of business lines are allowed to ride roughshod over risk managers, which is the traditional norm, companies wind up driven too much by greed and not enough by fear. Top executives, boards of directors, and—thanks to Dodd-Frank—regulators all share responsibility for ensuring that financial companies' risk-management systems are up to snuff. Don't trust, verify. Even JP Morgan Chase, long praised for its fine risk management, was caught off guard by London trading losses in 2012. Everyone has to do better.

5. Thou Shalt Use Less Leverage

Thomas Edison, who should know, said, "Genius is one percent inspiration, ninety-nine percent perspiration." There is a lot less genius—and a lot more salesmanship—in the investment world than our overpaid Masters of the Universe would like you to believe. High returns are often illusory, the product of applying high leverage to ordinary investments. (Houses are a good example.) We learn in financial kindergarten that systematically higher returns come only from taking more risk. It's a shame that so many people forget that lesson by the time they reach financial graduate school. Bingeing on leverage is a lot like bingeing on alcohol. Many new postcrisis regulations, not to mention the near-death experiences of many of our leading financial institutions, are now pushing us in the direction of lower leverage. We'll see what happens as people forget.

6. Thou Shalt Keep It Simple, Stupid

Modern finance thrives on complexity; indeed, you might say that the central idea of financial engineering *is* complexity. But ask yourself whether all those fancy financial instruments actually do the economy any good. Or are they perhaps designed to enrich their designers? Economists are accustomed to thinking of innovation as unambiguously good; it raises standards of living. But is that always true in finance? Is it even *usually* true? I do not mean to imply that *all* financial innovations are harmful; as Paul Volcker pointed out, the ATM did a lot of good. So, most likely, did mutual funds, money market funds, and plain-vanilla mortgage pools. But who needed CDO-squared? What did those monstrosities contribute to the betterment of mankind? Of course, simplicity and complexity are in the eye of the beholder. They can't be legislated, probably not even regulated. So we may have to rely on good judgment, transparency, and—here comes that phrase again—*market discipline.* If there is any.

7. Thou Shalt Standardize Derivatives and Trade Them on Organized Exchanges

Derivatives acquired a bad name in the crisis. Did I say *acquired*? Actually, they had a bad name long before. But not all derivatives are financial WMD. When derivatives are straightforward, transparent, well collateralized, traded in reasonably liquid markets by well-capitalized counterparties, *and properly regulated,* they can both hedge risks and reallocate remaining risks to those most willing to bear them—just as their proponents claim. But watch out for customized, opaque, over-the-counter (OTC) derivatives. Those are the dangerous ones, more likely to serve the interests of broker-dealers than those of customers. Dodd-Frank goes some way toward pushing derivatives into greater standardization and more exchange trading, but not nearly far enough. Industry pushback is fierce. They covet the highly profitable, customized, OTC stuff.

8. Thou Shalt Keep Things on the Balance Sheet

Some important financial activities, and even entire financial entities, were taken off banks' balance sheets in order to avoid regulatory capital charges— that is, to boost leverage, contrary to the Fifth Financial Commandment. Sometimes there were other reasons, too. But, to paraphrase the old tune, when you fool the people you seek, you may fool yourself as well. The financial crisis exposed an embarrassing fact: Many CEOs were only dimly aware of all the SIVs, conduits, and other off-balance-sheet entities their companies had. Masters of the Universe? They weren't even masters of their own companies. Dodd-Frank Section 165 specifies that "the computation of capital for purposes of meeting capital requirements shall take into account any off-balance-sheet activities of the company." Good. It's a step toward making off-balance-sheet entities safe, legal, and rare. Now let's make it work.

9. Thou Shalt Fix Perverse Compensation Systems

Dysfunctional compensation systems create incentives for dysfunction. In particular, offering traders monumental rewards for investment success, but mere slaps on the wrist for failure, and offering mortgage brokers commissions based on volume, not on loan performance, invite them to take excessive risks. By which I mean more risk than *shareholders*—or, if the government stands behind the firm, *taxpayers*—want them to take. This commandment ought to be enforced by CEOs and corporate boards; but if they won't do the job, we may need the heavy hand of government.

10. Thou Shalt Watch Out for Ordinary Consumer-Citizens

This last Financial Commandment comes pretty close to the eighth of the real Ten Commandments: *Thou shalt not steal.* We have long known that the meek won't inherit their fair share of the earth if they are constantly being fleeced. We have also long known that morality needs enforcement. What we learned in the crisis is that failure to protect unsophisticated consumers from predatory financial practices can actually undermine the entire economy. That surprising lesson is one we shouldn't forget. The new Consumer Financial Protection Bureau should help.

A Seven-Step Rehab Program for Policy Makers

Perhaps the supreme irony of the entire sorry episode is this: Free and innovative financial markets, inadequately regulated, almost sent us reeling into Great Depression 2.0. The federal government then swooped in to stop the bleeding and clean up the mess. Though far from flawless, its efforts succeeded amazingly well; the worst did not happen. Yet the body politic wound up mad as hell at the government. No one rushed to pin medals on the chests of Ben Bernanke, Hank Paulson, and Tim Geithner—and certainly not on Barack Obama, who has been branded both a socialist for intervening too much and a failure for doing too little. He prevailed in the November 2012 election, but his edge in the popular vote was hardly a vote of confidence.

The stunning combination of *policy success* and *political failure* may be the strangest legacy of the financial crisis, and it carries important lessons for the future. What should policy makers do differently the next time the music stops, even if the particular tune is quite different from what we had in 2007 and 2008? Here's my Seven-Step Rehab Program for wayward (or exhausted) policy makers. They should take the prescribed course of treatment *posthaste*, before the nation has to do something big again.

Step 1: Don't Try to Do Too Many Things at Once

America has a constitutional problem, a partisanship problem, and a bandwidth problem—all of which call for shorter, more focused policy agendas than the one President Obama pursued. The constitutional and bandwidth problems are incurable. The partisanship problem may be curable, but not anytime soon.

The Constitutional Problem

James Madison and his friends deliberately designed a small-government form of government. With all those checks and balances, it is hard for the federal government to get anything done. If you then augment Madison's original design with rabid partisanship (which he knew about), the sixty-vote rule in the Senate (which is *not* in the Constitution), and other obstructionist tactics (mostly in the Senate), you have a generic recipe for extreme logjam. Logjams can be burst by applying enough political force. But it's not easy. And it's especially hard if you're trying to burst through in multiple locations at once. That's why I argued that President Obama should have "focused like a laser beam on the economy."

The Partisanship Problem

The era of good feeling ended long ago. At least since Newt Gingrich's days in the House of Representatives, if not before, American politics has become a blood sport. You don't just oppose the other party's policies, you try to "take out" their leaders—as Gingrich did to the Democratic Speaker of the House in 1989, and tried to do to Bill Clinton in 1998. When Gingrich was asked why House Republicans were trying to impeach Clinton over a sex scandal, his answer was remarkable: "Because we can." That's quite a reason. Similar thinking, I suppose, led Senate Minority Leader Mitch McConnell (R-KY) to declare in October 2010 that "the single most important thing we want to achieve is for President Obama to be a one-term president." How about digging the U.S. economy out of the ditch? Or ending the war in Afghanistan? When partisanship runs that high, you're lucky to accomplish one important thing, never mind twenty-five.

The Bandwidth Problem

Citizens are bombarded by information. Lost in information overload, they are highly vulnerable to deliberate distortions, even to outright lies. And with so many messages to absorb, or to filter out, we the people have limited capacity for deep dives into complicated public policy issues. This behavior is not irrational. After all, who believes that his vote, e-mail, or letter will change national policy? Judging by sound bites is much easier than keeping abreast of complicated issues. Sober policy messages have a hard time penetrating the din.

Step 2: Explain Yourself to the People

Getting anything done in American democracy is devilishly difficult unless the people are behind you. In *parliamentary* systems, the prime minister often can push anything he wants through the legislature. Britain, for example, is sometimes called a dictatorship interrupted by occasional elections. In our *congressional* system, by contrast, the president proposes and Congress *disposes*—often literally. But Congress follows the polling results. So if, in Geithner's phrase, you lose the public, you may lose everything—including your policy initiatives and the next election.

The Obama administration should have trumpeted a consistent four-part message from the get-go:

1. Here is how we got into this mess.
2. This is what we propose to do to fix the problems.
3. We have a coherent plan, and here is why it makes sense.
4. This is going to take time, so please bear with us.

I will never understand why President Obama, who we thought was such a great communicator in 2008, failed to convey this message to the electorate time and time again. But his communication problem went well beyond economic policy. A frustrated *New York Times* columnist, Thomas Friedman, put it this way in 2012: "Barack Obama is a great orator, but he is the worst president I have ever seen when it comes to explaining his achievements, putting them in context, connecting with people on a gut level through repetition and thereby defining how the public views an issue."

Step 3: Say It in Language That Ordinary People Can Understand

Very few people are policy wonks. If you speak wonk-talk, you will probably annoy more people than you enlighten. But Americans have horse sense. If you have a good case, and you make it clearly and concisely, you have a fighting chance of winning in the court of public opinion. Doing so may require the use of clever analogies, slogans, or gimmicks. It will almost certainly require metaphors, for people relate better to stories than to syllogisms. If you want to know what I mean, listen to any explanation by Bill Clinton. He's the master.

Step 4: Repeat Steps 2 and 3

Do it over and over again. Especially when a message is complicated, you can never say it too many times. So repeat, repeat, repeat. President Obama, sadly, didn't.

Step 5: Set Expectations Low

Easy problems are, well, easy to solve. It's the hard ones that matter. Often the government can do little more than practice damage control. For example, once Lehman fell, there was nothing either the Bush or Obama administration could do to prevent a serious recession. Especially when your ability to control events is limited, you don't want to overpromise. When in doubt, *under*promise, for at least two reasons:

One is that progress will probably come slowly. Economic problems rarely disappear overnight. They dissipate slowly, like a dense fog. For a long while, the people will see little or no progress. The public needs to be conditioned to expect that, and not to look for quick fixes. Otherwise, their naturally short attention spans will dominate public discourse.

The other is that there is no political punishment for doing *better* than you indicated, but lots for doing *worse*, as Team Obama learned the hard way. Republicans latched on to the forecasting error made in late 2008 and used it to club the Democrats, even offering it as "proof" that fiscal stimulus failed, despite the fact that unemployment was over 8 percent *even before the 2009 stimulus bill passed*! Amazingly, that same overoptimistic forecast was still used against President Obama and his policies four years later during the 2012 election. Unemployment did go above 8 percent, didn't it?

Step 6: Pay Close Attention to People's Attitudes, Prejudices, and Misconceptions

In politics, as in retailing, the customer is always right. They aren't, really, but a wise retailer treats them that way. So should a wise politician. This is one reason careful explanations are so critical. (See Step 2.) People's basic attitudes are hard to change. Try, for example, to convince a true conservative that redistribution of income from rich to poor is good for society. (I have; it doesn't work.) But misconceptions can sometimes be overcome by facts—provided the facts are simple, credible, and believed. It's not easy, but it's possible—at least for some of the people some of the time. And did I mention Step 4? Say it over and over again.

Step 7: Pay Rapt Attention to Fairness

There is a difference between *close* attention and *rapt* attention. People's sense of fairness demands and deserves the higher-order, drop-everything kind. Because fairness normally matters more than anything else, it should be an obsession with policy makers. If people feel they are being treated fairly, they may go the extra mile with you. Or at least support you in spirit. But if they feel they are being screwed—as they certainly did during the financial crisis, and with good reason—you'll almost certainly lose them, even if you follow Steps 1 through 6 assiduously.

Citizens who feel alienated or mistreated may adopt a "plague on all your houses" attitude, venting their anger indiscriminately at the president, Congress, Democrats, Republicans, the lot—and throw in the Federal Reserve for good measure. *Just say no* may become their answer to everything. Which is not good for policy debates, for policy outcomes, or for our nation's politics. But it seems to encapsulate what happened after the crisis.

RAHM EMANUEL'S QUESTION

I close more or less where I began, with a question derived from the Emanuel Principle: Did we waste the financial crisis or use it well? Nations, like people, learn from their experiences. Or do they? Hegel famously wrote, "What experience and history teaches us is that people and governments have never learned anything from history." But I think they do learn. It's just that they forget, often quickly. (Remember the First Financial Commandment.)

The experience in the United States in the years since the bubbles burst has been tremendously costly; the heavy price we paid was certainly too high for whatever we learned. But we did learn *something*. And we need to remember those lessons the next time big financial ructions strike. Sadly, the forgetting has already begun. Unrepentant financiers, eager to return to the status quo ante, are whining about excessive regulation. Recalcitrant politicians are bemoaning big government and itching to return to laissez-faire. The public has turned its attention elsewhere.

But there's still work ahead. Bubbles will be back. So will high leverage, sloppy risk management, shady business practices, and lax regulation. We need to put in place durable institutional changes that will at least make financial disruptions less damaging the next time the music stops. History really does rhyme. We need to pick up the meter.

Notes

Preface

xv **"We're still dancing"**: Nakamoto and Wighton, "Citigroup chief stays bullish on buy-outs," *Financial Times.*

Chapter 1: What's a Nice Economy Like You Doing in a Place Like This?

12 **for at least a decade or two**: See, for example, Kahn, "The Long-Term Labor Market Consequences of Graduating from College in a Bad Economy," *Labour Economics;* Jacobson, LaLonde, and Sullivan, "Earnings Losses of Displaced Workers," *American Economic Review.*

14 **worst performance since the 1930s**: The 1937–1938 recession was apparently much worse, though there are no official quarterly data for that period. Gordon and Krenn estimate that real GDP declined by 7% over the four quarters spanning 1937:1 to 1938:1. Gordon and Krenn, "The End of the Great Depression," NBER Working Paper.

Chapter 2: In the Beginning . . .

31 **chronicler of the housing bubble**: Figure 2.1 is an adaptation of figure 2.1 in Shiller, *The Subprime Solution*, 33. I have updated his graph with quarterly data available on his public Web site: www.econ.yale.edu/~shiller/data.htm.

33 **"existence of a housing bubble"**: Baker, "The Run-up in Home Prices," CEPR Briefing Paper.

33 **convinced at the time**: Case and Shiller, "Is There a Bubble in the Housing Market?," *Brookings Papers on Economic Activity.*

35 **"strong economic fundamentals"**: Bernanke, "The Economic Outlook," testimony before the Joint Economic Committee, October 20, 2005.

35 **not alone in this judgment**: Lindblad, Boudway, and Winter, "How's Geithner's Home Holding Up?," *Bloomberg Businessweek.*

35 ***Wall Street Journal* article**: Barsky, "What Housing Bubble?," *Wall Street Journal*, A10.

35 **no entry for "bubble"**: Smith and Smith, *Houseonomics.*

37 **substantially more than that**: Shiller, *The Subprime Solution*, 45.

37 **over that same time span**: "Will the walls come falling down?," *Economist.*

38 **central bank's doorstep**: See, for example, Taylor, *Getting Off Track.*

Chapter 3: The House of Cards

58 **already drawing attention**: A March 2002 HUD report called attention to "questionable marketing techniques and borderline or outright fraudulent business practices." U.S. Department of Housing and Urban Development, *Subprime Markets, the Role of the GSEs, and Risk-Based Pricing*, 26.

58 **as early as 2004**: See Andrews, "The Ever More Graspable, and Risky, American Dream," *New York Times.* Ironically, Andrews himself was subsequently caught in a mortgage problem.

58 **sounding alarms there**: Andrews, "Fed Shrugged as Subprime Crisis Spread," *New York Times.* On the Gramlich-Greenspan episode, see also Ip, "Did Greenspan Add to Subprime Woes?," *Wall Street Journal.*

58 **it was too late:** Andrews, "Fed Shrugged as Subprime Crisis Spread," *New York Times.*

59 **commercial bank (Wells Fargo):** Two of the others were Lehman Brothers and Bear Stearns. The data come from a February 2007 Deutsche Bank report to clients, *Shorting Home Equity Mezzanine Tranches.* (It was good advice!)

59 **brokers rather than by banks:** Paulson, *On the Brink,* 69.

59 **supervised banks and thrifts:** Gramlich, *Subprime Mortgages,* 20–21.

60 **conventional banking system:** The size of the shadow banking system depends on what you count. Pozsar, Adrian, Ashcraft, and Boesky, "Shadow Banking," Federal Reserve Bank of New York Staff Report, estimate that the shadow banking system was almost twice as large as the conventional banking system on the eve of the crisis.

60 **history is instructive:** See Tett, *Fool's Gold;* Lewis, *The Big Short;* and others.

63 **bailout by Wall Street firms:** The story is beautifully told by Lowenstein, *When Genius Failed.*

63 **tongue-lashing from Summers:** Schmitt, "Prophet and Loss," *Stanford Magazine.*

63 **more wary about derivatives than Summers:** Rubin and Weisberg, *In an Uncertain World,* 197–98, 287–88.

65 **JP Morgan in the 1990s:** Their story is arrestingly told by Tett, *Fool's Gold.*

67 **financial bets rather than hedges:** "Following the A.I.G. Money," *New York Times,* attributed the 80 percent estimate to Eric Dinallo, then the insurance superintendent for New York State.

69 **marginal at best:** This story has been told in a number of places. See, for example, Wagner, "Unreal Estate," *Metro* (San Jose, Calif.).

69 **FICO scores are below 620:** It is not only the FICO score (for Fair Isaac Company, the inventor) that matters, but it is important. A potential borrower's FICO score is the banker's standard quantitative measurement of creditworthiness. It ranges between 300 and 850, with an average around 725. A score of 620 is pretty low, though not extreme. According to a company news release, roughly 30 percent of FICO scores are below 630.

69 **people become homeowners:** Gramlich, *Subprime Mortgages.*

70 **eighteen-fold increase in just eleven years:** Gramlich, *Subprime Mortgages,* 6.

70 **no-doc variety:** See Barth, *The Rise and Fall of the U.S. Mortgage and Credit Markets,* 93.

71 **failed almost as often:** Foote, Gerardi, and Willen,"Why Did So Many People Make So Many *Ex Post* Bad Decisions?," in *Rethinking the Financial Crisis.*

72 **began to erode:** Acharya, Richardson, Van Nieuwerburgh, and White, *Guaranteed to Fail,* especially chapter 3.

72 **mortgage business fell dramatically:** See Acharya, Richardson, Van Nieuwerburgh, and White, *Guaranteed to Fail,* 51 (table 3.2) and 42 (figure 3.1). Some of this was undoubtedly due to constraints on their growth imposed in reaction to accounting scandals at Fannie and Freddie.

72 **concentrated in the safest tranches:** Financial Crisis Inquiry Commission, *The Financial Crisis Inquiry Report,* 123–24. Henceforth, this document will be referred to as "FCIC Report."

72 **non-GSE mortgages:** Fannie and Freddie held 56 percent of all first mortgages but only 28 percent of seriously delinquent first mortgages, as of September 30, 2011. See Chang and Golding, "Measuring the Effect of Foreclosure Prevention on House Prices and the Spillover Benefit of Reduce[d] Defaults."

72 **Others do not, however:** See, for example, Peter Wallison's dissenting opinion in FCIC Report; Morgenson and Rosner, *Reckless Endangerment.*

78 **"implications of those monstrosities" and "not feeling too guilty about this":** See Tourre, e-mail to Marine Serres. The quotes come from a trove of e-mails that Goldman Sachs made public.

79 **consumers shun all beef:** Paulson, *On the Brink,* 72.

81 **Villain 7:** This section is based on Blinder, "Crazy Compensation and the Crisis," *New York Times.*

82 **flip the big coins, too:** Murphy, "Pay, Politics, and the Financial Crisis," in *Rethinking the Financial Crisis.*

85 **smaller once the bubble burst:** Ellul and Yerramilli, "Stronger Risk Controls, Lower Risk," NBER Working Paper.

86 **"how little our big men know":** Rogers, *Sanity Is Where You Find It,* 120.

Chapter 4: When the Music Stopped

88 **Case-Shiller ten-city composite index:** Christie, "Home futures," CNN *Money.*

88 **"largely contained":** Paulson, *On the Brink,* 66.

88 **"or to the financial system":** Bernanke, "The Subprime Mortgage Market," speech at the Federal Reserve Bank of Chicago's 43rd Annual Conference on Bank Structure and Competition.

89 **("toxic waste") tranches themselves:** Haubrich and Lucas, "Who Holds the Toxic Waste?," Federal Reserve Bank of Cleveland, Policy Discussion Paper.

90 "certain assets fairly": FCIC Report, 250–51.
92 "[in the subprime lending market] was carnage": Gramlich, "Booms and Busts: The Case of Subprime Mortgages," in *Housing, Housing Finance, and Monetary Policy*, 259.
93 "suffer a very serious downturn": Feldstein, "Concluding Remarks," in *Housing, Housing Finance, and Monetary Policy*, 499.
93 initial efforts were clearly inadequate: Wessel, *In Fed We Trust*, 123.

Chapter 5: From Bear to Lehman: Inconsistency Was the Hobgoblin
101 sales over the years 2000–2008: FCIC Report, 285.
101 securities from 2000 to 2007: FCIC Report, 280.
102 world-class bridge game than to his company: Kelly, "Bear CEO's Handling of Crisis Raises Issues, *Wall Street Journal*, A1. See also Wessel, *In Fed We Trust*, 251.
102 "was like Bonds 101": See Cohan, *House of Cards*, 421.
102 most of it overnight: FCIC Report, 281 and 283.
103 "confidence goes, it goes": Quoted in Wessel, *In Fed We Trust*, 151.
103 declining a routine trade: FCIC Report, 287–88.
105 "very hard to say at the time": Wessel, *In Fed We Trust*, 159.
105 "briefed them Friday morning": Wessel, *In Fed We Trust*, 163.
106 "little negotiating leverage": Paulson, *On the Brink*, 121.
107 pony up the cash: Wessel, *In Fed We Trust*, 169.
108 "investment bank's shareholders": Quoted in FCIC Report, 290.
110 "rogue operation": Wessel, *In Fed We Trust*, 174.
110 "what I was taught": Sorkin, *Too Big to Fail*, 78.
110 "someone like that is next?": Sorkin, *Too Big to Fail*, 78.
110 "banking principles and practices": Volcker, speech at the Economic Club of New York.
110 "worst policy mistake in a generation": Quoted in Wessel, *In Fed We Trust*, 174.
111 moral hazard grounds: Wessel, *In Fed We Trust*, 174.
112 "create[d] even bigger losses": FCIC Report, 291.
112 "implications for other firms": FCIC Report, 291.
113 "whole system would be at serious risk": Paulson, *On the Brink*, 102.
114 "just about 45 minutes": FCIC Report, 294.
116 leveraged about 75 to 1: FCIC Report, 65.
116 16 percent in 2001 to 33 percent by 2004: Greenspan, "The Crisis," *Brookings Papers on Economic Activity*, 207 (table 1).
117 "underwriting standards of Fannie Mae and Freddie Mac": Gramlich, *Subprime Mortgages*, 22.
117 "U.S. government housing policy": FCIC Report, 444.
117 "relaxing loan underwriting standards": Morgenson and Rosner, *Reckless Endangerment*, 5.
117 "[as] fundamentally flawed": FCIC Report, 323.
117 "central to the financial crisis": FCIC Report, 323.
118 "'save their ass'": Paulson, *On the Brink*, 144.
118 "you may not have to take it out": Paulson, *On the Brink*, 151.
119 "hardest thing I had ever done": Paulson, *On the Brink*, 170.
120 $200 billion worth of repos outstanding: FCIC Report, 326.
120 "what we learned scared us": Paulson, *On the Brink*, 121.
120 "naked short-selling came after us": FCIC Report, 326–27.
121 better than they actually were: See Latman, "New York Accuses Ernst & Young of Fraud in Lehman Collapse," *New York Times*.
121 longer-term debt by June: FCIC Report, 326.
122 rejected the idea as "gimmicky": FCIC Report, 328.
122 $55 billion loan from the Fed: FCIC Report, 328.
122 Fannie and Freddie were taken over: Sorkin, *Too Big to Fail*, chapter 11.
122 Paulson refused: Paulson, *On the Brink*, 190.
122 "what would you need from us?": Sorkin, *Too Big to Fail*, 94.
123 "'I can't do it again'": Wessel, *In Fed We Trust*, 14.
123 "financial crisis was lunacy" and "statement is way out of line!": Wessel, *In Fed We Trust*, 15–16.
124 "import our cancer": Sorkin, *Too Big to Fail*, 350.
125 "take precautionary measures": Bernanke, "The Economic Outlook," testimony before the Joint Economic Committee, September 24, 2008.

126 **voiced the same opinion:** Sorkin, *Too Big to Fail*, 343.
127 **"secure a Federal Reserve loan":** Bernanke, "Federal Reserve Policies in the Financial Crisis," speech at the Greater Austin Chamber of Commerce.

Chapter 6: The Panic of 2008

129 **"most unbelievable week in America ever":** Quoted in Sorkin, *Too Big to Fail*, 2.
131 **116,000 employees in 130 countries:** FCIC Report, 139.
132 **"irresponsible bets" and "can't think of one, than AIG":** Bernanke at a March 3, 2009, hearing of the Senate Budget Committee, as quoted by Wessel, *In Fed We Trust*, 194.
133 **virtually none of it was hedged:** FCIC Report, 50.
133 **"losing $1 in any of those transactions" and "sleeping a bit easier at night":** Sorkin, *Too Big to Fail*, 160.
134 **Scary stuff:** Sorkin, *Too Big to Fail*, 239.
134 **"imminent danger" and "Fed should bail it out":** Wessel, *In Fed We Trust*, 189–90.
135 **"dealer has exposure to them":** Quoted in FCIC Report, 347.
137 **staggering sum:** Sjostrom, "The AIG Bailout," *Washington & Lee Law Review*, 975. But AIG never actually drew more than $126 billion of its $182 billion line of credit.
137 **"rescuing a failing company":** FCIC Report, 350. This criticism came from a June 2010 report of the Congressional Oversight Panel that was set up to monitor the TARP.
138 **"AIG is the most outrageous":** On ABC's *This Week*, as quoted by Suskind, *Confidence Men*, 216.
138 **"abrogated willy-nilly":** On CBS's *Face the Nation*, transcribed by the author. "Summers: AIG Bonuses Are 'Outrageous'," CBS News, *Face the Nation*.
138 **"rescind the AIG bonuses":** Suskind, *Confidence Men*, 233.
138 **"affronted disbelief":** Scheiber, *The Escape Artists*, 114–15.
138 **25 percent of the money:** See Morgan, "Pay Czar Says AIG Bonus Flap to End in March." Reuters.
139 **"10 percent haircut":** Quoted in Nocera, "Sheila Bair's Bank Shot," *New York Times Magazine*, 29.
140 **"cost for American taxpayers":** Geithner, "The Federal Bailout of AIG," testimony before the Committee on Oversight and Government Reform.
140 **"It was Monday":** This quote appears in many places. See, for example, Paletta, "Barney Frank Celebrates Free Market Day," *Wall Street Journal*.
143 **(leaving all the creditors whole):** See the fund's portfolio manager, Michael Luciano's, testimony. FCIC Report, 356.
144 **"Wednesday and Thursday":** Fed staff economist Patrick McCabe, quoted in FCIC Report, 357.
145 **"commercial paper markets":** FCIC Report, 358.
145 **unable to meet payroll:** Sorkin reports a conversation with GE's CEO, Jeffrey Immelt, to that effect. Sorkin, *Too Big to Fail*, 420.
145 **"run on the dollar":** Paulson, *On the Brink*, 253.
147 **had the same thought:** See Paulson, *On the Brink*, 262.
147 **deposited after that date:** According to Paulson, *On the Brink*, 262, this was Bair's suggestion.
148 **"U.S. issuers of commercial paper":** "Federal Reserve and Other Central Banks Announce Schedules for Term and Forward Auctions of U.S. Dollar Liquidity for Fourth Quarter," Federal Reserve System Monetary Policy Release. Note that this public announcement came a full week after the Board's vote.
151 **"#1 global underwriter of CDOs":** Quoted from Merrill Lynch advertisement, *Derivatives Week*.
151 **"dicing them to CDOs":** Sorkin, *Too Big to Fail*, 144.
151–52 **"super-senior was super safe":** Dow Kim, quoted in FCIC Report, 258. Most of the information in this paragraph comes from the FCIC Report.
152 **"Worst American CEOs of All Time":** Porfolio.com, "Portfolio's Worst American CEOs of All Time," CNBC.
153 **"Now we're next in line":** FCIC Report, 360.
153 **$35 billion on Friday:** FCIC Report, 361.
154 **$55 billion in a single week:** FCIC Report, 362.
154 **"manager should want to have":** FCIC Report, 362.
154 **"real chance they would go under":** FCIC Report, 362.
156 **"same thing for bondholders":** Nocera, "Sheila Bair's Bank Shot," *New York Times Magazine*, 29.
156 **"with serious consequences":** FCIC Report, 366.
156 **"Great Depression":** FCIC Report, 366.
157 **"imprudent and dangerous":** Wessel, *In Fed We Trust*, 220.
157 **"protected, and which are not?":** Wessel, *In Fed We Trust*, 221.
157 **best-run bank in America:** See, for example, "Fed Look at Wachovia in Drug Money Probe," CNN *Money*.

157 **73 cents on the dollar to 29 cents**: FCIC Report, 367.

158 **Let the play begin**: The narrative and events below are based on information in Wessel, *In Fed We Trust*, 221–26, and FCIC Report, 366–71.

158 **"bailed out again"**: FCIC Report, 370.

160 **reflected new due diligence**: FCIC Report, 370.

160 **"conference call with Citi officials"**: Solomon, "Bair's Legacy: An FDIC with Teeth," *Wall Street Journal*. Citi representatives denied this.

161 **Second, throughout its seventy-five-year history**: The FDIC's October 14th press release announced a *temporary* program to insure balances in non-interest bearing transactions accounts (basically, business checking accounts) in *unlimited* amounts. That program wound up being extended twice. "FDIC Announces Plan to Free up Bank Liquidity," FDIC Press Release.

162 **"necessary to avoid or mitigate"**: Quoted from Section 13(c)(4)(G) of the Federal Deposit Insurance Act.

163 **any other financial organization**: For a partial accounting, see Keoun, "Citigroup's 1.1 Trillion of Mysterious Assets Shadows Earnings," *Bloomberg Businessweek*.

163 **"associated hedges"**: The quotation is from the accompanying term sheet in Board of Governors of the Federal Reserve System, Federal Deposit Insurance Corporation, and U.S. Department of the Treasury, "Joint Statement by Treasury, Federal Reserve, and the FDIC on Citigroup," FRB Press Release.

164 **"colossal lack of judgment"**: Paulson, *On the Brink*, 430.

164 **more "candy"?**: Wessel, *In Fed We Trust*, 259.

165 **"firm believer in free markets"**: Paulson, *On the Brink*, 3.

169 **"don't even let dry cleaners fail"**: Wessel, *In Fed We Trust*, 22.

170 **untenable fiscal position**: The story is told, with both pathos and humor by Lewis, *Boomerang*.

170 **What a mess**: Aspects of the mess are recounted by Lewis, *Boomerang*.

171 **"This time, we did not cause it"**: Norris, "Quotes of the Day at Davos," Economix, *New York Times*.

Chapter 7: Stretching Out the TARP

178 **"making it up as we went along"**: Paulson, *On the Brink*, 254.

178 **"only some of it" or "none of it"**: Pew Research Center, Auto Bailout Now Backed, Stimulus Divisive.

178 **"in case things got worse"**: Swagel, "The Financial Crisis: An Inside View," *Brookings Papers on Economic Activity*, 32.

179 **four basic options**: Swagel, "The Financial Crisis: An Inside View," *Brookings Papers on Economic Activity*, 33.

179 **"hold the system together"**: Paulson, *On the Brink*, 254.

179 **"We can't keep doing this"**: Sorkin, *Too Big to Fail*, 431.

180 **"inadequate capital rather than insufficient liquidity"**: Swagel, "The Financial Crisis: An Inside View," *Brookings Papers on Economic Activity*, 33. Remember that Bagehot had counseled central bankers to lend only in order to relieve illiquidity, not insolvency.

180 **"reasons of democratic legitimacy"**: Sorkin, *Too Big to Fail*, 431.

180 **"an economic 9/11"**: Sorkin, *Too Big to Fail*, 417.

181 **Stiglitz also urged that alternative**: Krugman, "Cash for Trash," *New York Times*; Soros, "Paulson Cannot Be Allowed a Blank Cheque," *Financial Times*; Stiglitz, "A Better Bailout," *Nation*.

182 **"I'll be hung out to dry"**: Wessel, *In Fed We Trust*, 203.

182 **"scare the shit out of them"**: Sorkin, *Too Big to Fail*, 445.

183 **"heaven help us all"**: Sorkin, *Too Big to Fail*, 446.

183 **"members of Congress ashen-faced"**: Paulson, *On the Brink*, 259.

183 **"I kind of scared myself"**: Wessel, *In Fed We Trust*, 204.

183 **"selling it to the American people"**: Wessel, *In Fed We Trust*, 205.

183 **"flush the toilets around here" and "we need to do this"**: Wessel, *In Fed We Trust*, 447.

184 **"important to our economy" and "far less than the alternative"**: "Statement by Secretary Henry M. Paulson, Jr. on Comprehensive Approach to Market Developments," U.S. Department of the Treasury Press Release.

184 **account of how their conversation went**: Sorkin, *Too Big to Fail*, 450.

186 **impeached just for proposing it**: Blinder, "Financial Rescue Plan," NPR, *Diane Rehm Show*.

186 **"members would add provisions"**: Paulson, *On the Brink*, 266.

186 **"came across as overreaching"**: Paulson, *On the Brink*, 267.

186 **not worked on the bill**: Sorkin, *Too Big to Fail*, 469.

187 **"wouldn't they?"**: Sorkin, *Too Big to Fail*, 474.

187 **"but our Constitution as well"**: Paulson, *On the Brink*, 283.

187 **"Total Abdication of Responsibility to the Public":** Sorkin, "A Bailout Above the Law," *New York Times.* Rosner later coauthored a muckraking book with the *Times'* Gretchen Morgenson. Morgenson and Rosner, *Reckless Endangerment.*

187 **"communications mistake":** Swagel, "The Financial Crisis: An Inside View," *Brookings Papers on Economic Activity*, 45.

188 **"Fed stands down":** Wessel, *In Fed We Trust*, 205.

189 **"exactly what I didn't want to do":** Paulson, *On the Brink*, 260.

191 **"about as welcome as malaria"** and **"got them into trouble":** Wessel, *In Fed We Trust*, 214. The congressman was Walter Jones.

191 **"sensitive to the public outrage":** Paulson, *On the Brink*, 261.

193 **"We can't say that *now*":** Wessel, *In Fed We Trust*, 227.

194 **was no easy task:** Though the technical problems required thought, they were not insoluble. Swagel reports that "we had reverse auctions to buy MBSs essentially ready to go by late October 2008—including a pricing mechanism." Swagel, "The Financial Crisis: An Inside View," *Brookings Papers on Economic Activity*, 55.

197 **drew huzzahs from many experts:** One example: Krugman, "Gordon Does Good," *New York Times.*

197 **I was one of four people on earth:** Little did I know that Warren Buffett, the Sage of Omaha, was another. Sorkin, *Too Big to Fail*, 510–12.

197 **"we went that route":** Irwin and Cho, "Paulson's Change in Rescue Tactics," *Washington Post*, D1.

197 **"banking system provided greater leverage":** Swagel, "The Financial Crisis: An Inside View," *Brookings Papers on Economic Activity*, 50.

200 **weighed heavily on the officials' minds:** Wessel, *In Fed We Trust*, 238.

200 **"you're not going to like the terms":** Sorkin, *Too Big to Fail*, 527.

201 **"cheap capital":** Wessel, *In Fed We Trust*, 240.

201 **"bailing you out"** and **"you're undercapitalized":** Sorkin, *Too Big to Fail*, 528.

202 **"banks would be unwise to refuse it":** Swagel, "The Financial Crisis: An Inside View," *Brookings Papers on Economic Activity*, 52.

202 **"good, bad, or indifferent":** Sorkin, *Too Big to Fail*, 517–18.

204 **"feet on the ground, and the other guy was not":** Scheiber, *The Escape Artists*, 15.

205 **"new Secretary of the Treasury in about two months":** Blinder, "Whatever Happened to the *Troubled Assets* Relief Program?," testimony before the Committee on Financial Services.

205 **buying troubled assets:** See, for example, Barr, "Banks Want the Old Bailout Back," CNN *Money.*

206 **profit of about $25 billion:** See Congressional Budget Office, *Report on the Troubled Asset Relief Program—March 2012.*

209 **grab bag of financial-market policies:** Almost all of the academic studies focus on the Fed's large-scale asset purchases. See, for example: Gagnon, Raskin, Remache, and Sack, "The Financial Market Effects of the Federal Reserve's Large-Scale Asset Purchases," *International Journal of Central Banking*; Krishnamurthy and Vissing-Jorgensen, "The Effects of Quantitative Easing on Interest Rates," *Brookings Papers on Economic Activity.*

209 **July 2010 by Mark Zandi and me:** Blinder and Zandi, "How the Great Recession Was Brought to an End," *Moody's Analytics.*

Chapter 8: Stimulus, Stimulus, Wherefore Art Thou, Stimulus?

214 **times were demonstrably horrible:** CBS News, "CBS Poll: Americans Optimistic About Obama," CBS News *Opinion.*

214 **"needed feedback and critiques":** Scheiber, *The Escape Artists*, 84.

215 **"bordered on bipartisan bliss":** Connolly, "Obama Chooses Peter Orszag as Chief of Office of Management and Budget," *Washington Post.*

215 **practically at war:** Suskind, *Confidence Men*, 297ff; Scheiber, *The Escape Artists*, 155ff.

215 **"broader discussion by Summers":** Suskind, *Confidence Men*, 151; Scheiber, *The Escape Artists.*

216 **"They weren't":** Suskind, *Confidence Men*, 262.

216 **bit too pro–Wall Street for the times:** Scheiber, *The Escape Artists*, 12.

216 **"health care team?":** Suskind, *Confidence Men*, 277.

218 **Iraq war, polled just 13 percent:** Jones, "Domestic Priorities Top Americans' To-Do List for Obama," Gallup.

219 **"That's not enough for me":** Scheiber, *The Escape Artists*, 15–16.

220 **"ended up having to do":** Scheiber, *The Escape Artists*, 147.

220 **"too serious for this kind of politics":** Obama, Town Hall speech, Raleigh, N.C.

220 **"Republicans would have to be bipartisan":** Scheiber, *The Escape Artists*, 96.

220 **"Obama to be a one-term president"**: Garrett, "Top GOP Priority: Make Obama a One-Term President," *National Journal.*

223 **kicking and screaming (internally)**: Wessel reports that Richard Fisher, president of the Federal Reserve Bank of Dallas, initially lodged a dissent but then withdrew it. So the reported vote was unanimous. Wessel, *In Fed We Trust*, 257–58.

225 **modest shot in the arm**: Parker, Souleles, Johnson, and McClelland, "Consumer Spending and the Economic Stimulus Payments of 2008," NBER Working Paper; Sahm, Shapiro, and Slemrod, "Check in the Mail or More in the Paycheck?," *American Economic Journal.*

225 **"we're in with a bang"**: Goolsbee, "Looking for Lasting Solutions," CBS News, *Face the Nation.*

225 **about in the right place**: Scheiber, *The Escape Artists,* discusses this debate at length.

226 **"shovel-ready as we expected:"**: See his remarks at the Council on Jobs and Competitiveness.

228 **bankers and investors rather than the middle class**: CNN/Opinion Research, "Polls: Stimulus Unpopular, but Its Uses Have Broad Support," CNN *Politics.*

228 **Only 34 percent thought it was President Bush**: Pew Research Center, Political Knowledge Update.

231 **a year and a half later was 1.7 percentage points**: Blinder and Zandi, "How the Great Recession Was Brought to an End," *Moody's Analytics.*

233 **highly publicized study**: Blinder and Zandi, "How the Great Recession Was Brought to an End," *Moody's Analytics.*

233 **several economists of the Right**: See, for example, Cogan, Taylor and Wieland, "The Stimulus Didn't Work," *Wall Street Journal*; Cogan, Cwik, Taylor, and Wieland, "New Keynesian Versus Old Keynesian Government Spending Multipliers," *Journal of Economic Dynamics and Control,* 281–95.

233 **addressed these criticisms**: Feyrer and Sacerdote, "Did the Stimulus Stimulate?," NBER Working Paper.

234 **how does that *destroy* jobs?**: Blinder, "The GOP Myth of 'Job-Killing' Spending," *Wall Street Journal.*

234 **$49 billion dribbling out over fiscal years 2013–2019**: Congressional Budget Office, *The Budget and Economic Outlook: Fiscal Years 2012 to 2022.*

Chapter 9: The Attack on the Spreads

245 **Rogoff (and Krugman again) for the United States**: Krugman, "It's Baaack: Japan's Slump and the Return of the Liquidity Trap," *Brookings Papers on Economic Activity;* Rogoff, "The Bullets Yet to Be Fired to Stop the Crisis," *Financial Times.*

252 **"almost treasonous"**: Daly, "Rick Perry Jabs Bernanke, Says 'Printing More Money . . . Is Almost Treasonous,'" *CBS News Political Hotsheet.*

252 **"magically fix economic problems"**: Palin's letter to the editor appeared on November 18. Blinder, "In Defense of Ben Bernanke," *Wall Street Journal;* Palin, Letter to the Editor, *Wall Street Journal.*

256 **A few have actually done so**: The list includes Chile, Hungary, and Thailand. See, for example, Dalton and Dziobek, "Central Bank Losses and Experiences in Selected Countries," IMF Working Paper. The Banco Central de Chile has operated effectively with negative net worth for years.

257 **"long-term perspective"**: "Remarks by President Obama and British Prime Minister Gordon Brown after Meeting," White House Press Release.

258 **"for those institutions which need it"**: "Secretary Geithner Introduces Financial Stability Plan," U.S. Department of the Treasury Press Release.

259 **Lee Sachs pushing to go ahead**: Scheiber, *The Escape Artists,* 124–29.

Chapter 10: It's Broke, Let's Fix It: The Need for Financial Reform

266 **banking disaster of the last several decades**: Appelbaum, "Citi's Long History of Overreach, Then Rescue," *Washington Post.*

268 **"they are too big"**: King, speech at Lord Mayor's Banquet for Bankers and Merchants. The "distinguished American economist" was Allan Meltzer.

268 **"multi-function, international (financial) firms"**: Quoted in Wessel, "Bernanke: Smaller Banks Not Necessarily the Answer for 'Too Big to Fail' Dilemma," *Wall Street Journal.*

270 **had one existed in 2005**: The next paragraph is based on Blinder, "It's Broke, Let's Fix It: Rethinking Financial Regulation," *International Journal of Central Banking,* 286–87.

276 **Homeland Security, the CIA, and even the IRS!**: Saad, "CDC Tops Agency Ratings; Federal Reserve Board Lowest NASA Ratings Remain High, While Federal Reserve Has Lost Ground," Gallup.

278 **"child's car seat sold on the American market"**: Warren, "Unsafe at Any Rate," *Democracy: A Journal of Ideas.* See also Bar-Gill and Warren, "Making Credit Safer," *University of Pennsylvania Law Review.*

279 **worst decisions he had ever made**: See Hirsh, "The Re-education of Larry Summers," *Newsweek.*

279 **"regulate financial derivatives"**: Clinton, *Back to Work,* 41.

279 **"financial weapons of mass destruction"**: I believe this oft-quoted phrase first appeared in Berkshire Hathaway, *2002 Annual Report*, 15.

279 **"automatic teller machine"**: Volcker, speech at the *Wall Street Journal*'s 2nd Future of Finance Initiative.

282 **"more money than God"**: Mallaby, *More Money Than God*.

289 **policy debate into high gear**: U.S. Department of the Treasury, *Financial Regulatory Reform*.

Chapter 11: Watching a Sausage Being Made

293 **bankruptcy procedures worked well!**: Wallison,"The Argument Against a Government Resolution Authority," Pew Financial Reform Project Briefing Paper; Wallison and Skeel, "The Dodd Bill: Bailouts Forever," *Wall Street Journal*.

305 **"towards subsidized housing"**: Frank at a September 25, 2003, hearing of the Committee on Financial Services, as quoted in "What They Said About Fan and Fred," Opinion, *Wall Street Journal*.

317 **by more than 3 to 1**: Lake Research Partners, "Wall Street Reform: One Year Anniversary."

318 **conservatives rather than to liberals**: Center for Responsive Politics, *Open Secrets*.

Chapter 12: The Great Foreclosure Train Wreck

321 **problem festers to this day**: Cordell, Dynan, Lehnert, Liang, and Mauskopf, "Designing Loan Modifications to Address the Mortgage Crisis and the Making Home Affordable Program," Finance and Economics Discussion Series, table 1. Data come from the Mortgage Bankers Association.

324 **Home Owners' Loan Corporation**: The next several paragraphs draw heavily on Blinder, "From the New Deal, a Way Out of a Mess," *New York Times*, which in turn owes a great deal to Harriss, *History and Policies of the Home Owners' Loan Corporation*.

325 **mortgagees knew their banks**: Actually, Foote, Gerardi, and Willen argue that the apparent novelty of mortgage finance in the 2000s is exaggerated. Foote, Gerardi, and Willen, "Why Did So Many People Make So Many *Ex Post* Bad Decisions?," in *Rethinking the Financial Crisis*.

325 **refinance between 1 million and 2 million homes**: Blinder, "From the New Deal, a Way out of a Mess," *New York Times*. Note the early date of this op-ed, even before Bear Stearns. In August 2012, Senator Jeff Merkley (D-OR) introduced a proposal that was very similar to the HOLC.

326 **other assets of any defaulting borrower**: Feldstein, "How to Stop the Mortgage Crisis," *Wall Street Journal*.

326 **30-year fixed-rate mortgages at 5.25 percent**: Hubbard and Mayer, "First, Let's Stabilize Home Prices," *Wall Street Journal*.

328 **"write a check"**: Swagel, "The Financial Crisis: An Inside View," *Brookings Papers on Economic Activity*, 22.

329 **authority to modify mortgages**: Geanokoplos and Koniak, "Mortgage Justice Is Blind," *New York Times*.

330 **insured only 762 houses**: U.S. Department of Housing and Urban Development, *FHA Annual Management Report, FY 2011*, 16.

330 **"bankers and investors compared to foreclosure"**: "FDIC Implements Loan Modification Program for Distressed IndyMac Mortgage Loans," FDIC Press Release.

331 **$11,000 per loan**: Luhby, "FDIC's Bair Pushes Aggressive Mortgage Plan," CNN *Money*.

333 **$50 billion from TARP would ever be utilized**: Congressional Budget Office, *Report on the Troubled Asset Relief Program—March 2012*.

334–35 **60,000 mortgages had been refinanced**: Timiraos, "Confusion Roils HARP Program for Refinancing," *Wall Street Journal*.

335 **short of the administration's goal**: Gopal, "Banks Block Obama's Mortgage Stimulus Plan," *Bloomberg Businessweek*.

336 **57,000 short sales had been arranged**: U.S. Department of the Treasury, *Making Home Affordable Program Performance Report through June 2012*, 5.

339 **In his words**: Oddly, CNBC has no transcript of the rant, even though it may be the most famous words ever uttered on that network. An Internet search surfaces numerous alleged "transcripts," but they are inaccurate. I compiled this one directly from the video clip. Santelli, "Rick Santelli and the 'Rant of the Year,'" YouTube.

339 **origin of the Tea Party**: See, for example, Zernike, "'Boiling Mad': A Tea Party Origin Story," NPR, *All Things Considered*.

340 **whopping 64 percent to 33 percent margin**: Newport, "Views on Government Aid Depend on the Program," Gallup.

Chapter 13: The Backlash

345 **"inject the government into the private sector"**: Paulson, *On the Brink*, 3.

345 **catastrophe into something that was merely awful**: Blinder and Zandi, "How the Great Recession Was Brought to an End," *Moody's Analytics*. Remember, some economists dispute our methodology.

345 **ideologically conservative:** This is a very old idea in American political science. See, for example, Free and Cantril, *The Political Beliefs of Americans.* For more recent evidence, see Fiorina and Abrams, *Disconnect: The Breakdown of Representation in American Politics.*

346 **"government hands off my Medicare":** This quote was reported in many places. One example is Cesca, "Keep Your Goddamn Government Hands off My Medicare!," *Huffington Post.*

348 **"join in the government-bashing":** Clinton, *Back to Work,* 7.

349 **Cochrane excoriated the bailouts:** Cochrane, "Lessons from the Financial Crisis," *Regulation.*

349 **Meltzer accused Bernanke:** Meltzer wrote that "Chairman Ben Bernanke seemed willing to sacrifice much of the independence that Paul Volcker restored in the 1980s. He worked closely with the Treasury and yielded to pressures from the chairs of the House and Senate Banking Committees and others in Congress." Meltzer, "Policy Principles: Lessons from the Fed's Past," in *The Road Ahead for the Fed,* 13.

349 **Taylor argued that the Fed's:** In Taylor's words: "In my view, the financial crisis was caused, prolonged, and worsened by the Fed's departure from traditional monetary policy." Taylor, "The Need for a Clear and Credible Exit Strategy," in *The Road Ahead for the Fed,* 85.

351 **"Reagan proved that deficits don't matter":** See Suskind, *The Price of Loyalty,* 291.

351 **"determined to stamp out":** "The Rise of the Anti-Keynesians: Paul Ryan's Intellectual Hinterland," *Economist.*

351 **reduce federal spending, not to increase it:** Hirsh, "The Party of Goldwater?," *Newsweek.*

351 **despite costing over $800 billion:** This work is summarized in Taylor, "An Empirical Analysis of the Revival of Fiscal Activism in the 2000s," *Journal of Economic Literature.*

351–52 **"stimulating the economy" and "finding should come as a surprise":** Taylor, "The 2009 Stimulus Package: Two Years Later," testimony before the Committee on Oversight and Government Reform, Subcommittee on Regulatory Affairs.

352 **"unprecedented policy regime" and "return to traditional monetary policy":** Taylor, "The Need for a Clear and Credible Exit Strategy," in *The Road Ahead for the Fed,* 85.

352 **formulaic rule for interest-rate setting:** Taylor, "Discretion Versus Policy Rules in Practice," *Carnegie-Rochester Series on Public Policy.*

352 **"Fed's departure from traditional monetary policy":** Taylor, "The Need for a Clear and Credible Exit Strategy," in *The Road Ahead for the Fed,* 85–100.

353 **"broad-based robust economic recovery":** Greenspan, "Activism," *International Finance,* 1 and 7.

353 **"Liquidate labor" and "pick up the pieces from less competent people":** Hoover, *The Memoirs of Herbert Hoover,* 30.

355 **Taylor Bean & Whitaker:** The details of the story come from Norris, "After Years of Red Flags, a Conviction," *New York Times.*

355 **largest financial crises America has ever seen:** Protess, "Mortgage Executive Receives 30-Year Sentence," *New York Times.*

Chapter 14: No Exit? Getting the Fed Back to Normal

373 **"the economy, not the calendar":** Di Leo and Hilsenrath, "Fed Could Keep Short-Term Interest Rates Near Zero Well Beyond Mid-2013," *Wall Street Journal.* Plosser dissented against the language change in August 2011.

378 **"future rise in inflation":** Bernanke, "Semiannual Monetary Policy Report to the Congress," testimony before the Committee on Financial Services. This quotation and others in the next paragraph come from this testimony.

379 **"reduce the stock of reserves" and "both in combination":** Bernanke, "The Federal Reserve's Balance Sheet: An Update," speech at the Federal Reserve Board Conference on Key Developments in Monetary Economics.

382 **"corollary risks with long-term effects":** Warsh, "The New Malaise and How to End It," *Wall Street Journal.*

382 **smaller than those from QE1:** Krishnamurthy and Vissing-Jorgensen, "The Effects of Quantitative Easing on Interest Rates," *Brookings Papers on Economic Activity.*

382 **in non-Treasury securities:** Blinder, "The Fed Is Running Low on Ammo," *Wall Street Journal.*

385 **never again cause a depression:** Bernanke, "On Milton Friedman's Ninetieth Birthday," remarks at Conference to Honor Milton Friedman.

Chapter 15: The Search for a Fiscal Exit

389 **CBO report on the budget outlook:** Congressional Budget Office, *The Long-Term Budget Outlook,* October 1, 2000.

391 **long-run debt-to-GDP projections:** Congressional Budget Office, *The Long-Term Budget Outlook*, December 1, 2003, 12.

392 **CBO now scores at $831 billion:** Congressional Budget Office, *The Budget and Economic Outlook: Fiscal Years 2012 to 2022*.

394 **"moderately important":** Jones, "Americans Want Congress, Obama to Tackle Economic Issues," *Gallup Politics*.

394 **61 percent in favor, 17 percent opposed:** Stein, *The Fiscal Revolution in America*, 117–18. Stein noted, "Public opinion seems to have been in 1939 what it had always been."

395 **reducing spending on *any* domestic program:** Blinder and Holtz-Eakin, "Public Opinion and the Balanced Budget," *American Economic Review*, 145.

395 **small-government stalwarts:** Sides, "Republican Primary Voters Embrace Government," *Model Politics*, YouGov.

399 **"bowl of Jell-O" and "could not deliver a pizza":** Wallsten, Montgomery, and Wilson, "Obama's Evolution: Behind the Failed 'Grand Bargain' on the Debt," *Washington Post*.

401 **"*without any further policy actions*":** Congressional Budget Office, *The Budget and Economic Outlook: Fiscal Years 2012 to 2022*, table 1-7. I use here numbers from the CBO's "Alternative Fiscal Scenario."

405 **some important modifications:** The commission's recommendations are in *Moment of Truth: Report of the National Commission on Fiscal Responsibility and Reform*.

406 **"if growth exceeds the targets" and "substantial structural reforms":** *Moment of Truth: Report of the National Commission on Fiscal Responsibility and Reform*, 41–42.

Chapter 16: The Big Aftershock: The European Debt Crisis

410 **UK had a large share, too:** For an entertaining account of the craziness in Iceland and Ireland, and the aftermath in both countries, see Lewis, *Boomerang*.

412 **modern-day world record:** Whelan, "Ireland's Sovereign Debt Crisis," Centre for Economic Research Working Paper, University College Dublin.

413 **gaining independence in the 1830s!:** Reinhart and Rogoff, *This Time Is Different*, 98.

414 **conceal its mounting debt:** Story, Thomas, and Schwartz, "Wall St. Helped to Mask Debt Fueling Europe's Crisis," *New York Times*.

414 **go into default:** California, a much larger state, resorted to issuing scrip in 2009. But that strange event didn't shake the national financial markets. The last state to default on its debt was Arkansas in 1933. See Davey, "The State That Went Bust," *New York Times*.

417 **deal with government debt:** Sargent, "United States Then, Europe Now," Nobel Prize in Economic Sciences Lecture.

420–21 **"urgent recapitalization," "chains of contagion," and "using public funds if necessary":** Lagarde, "Global Risks Are Rising, but There Is a Path to Recovery," in *Achieving Maximum Long-Run Growth: A Symposium Sponsored by the Federal Reserve Bank of Kansas City*.

421 **"public undertakings of any Member State":** Article 125 of the version of the treaty posted on the ECB's Web site. European Central Bank, "Consolidated versions of the Treaty on European Union and the Treaty on the Functioning of the European Union," *Official Journal of the European Union*. It was formerly Article 103.

422 **"assistance to the Member State concerned":** European Central Bank, "Consolidated Versions of the Treaty on European Union and the Treaty on the Functioning of the European Union," *Official Journal of the European Union*, Article 122 (formerly 100).

422 **"central banks of debt instruments":** European Central Bank, "Consolidated Versions of the Treaty on European Union and the Treaty on the Functioning of the European Union," *Official Journal of the European Union*, Article 130 (formerly 108).

425–26 **"it will be enough":** McHugh, "Draghi: ECB to Do 'Whatever It Takes' to Save Euro," Associated Press.

Chapter 17: Never Again: Legacies of the Crisis

432 **"integrity of Wall Street":** Frum, "Full Comment," *National Post*.

433 **"amounts of risk to build up":** Geithner, "Financial Crisis Amnesia," *Wall Street Journal*.

439 **"Because we can":** From a November 1998 conversation with then White House chief of staff Erskine Bowles, related in Clinton, *My Life*, 824.

440 **"public views an issue":** Friedman, "Obama Should Seize the High Ground," *New York Times*.

443 **"learned anything from history":** Hegel, *Introduction to the Philosophy of History*.

Sources

|ıııııııııııııııııııııı|

Acharya, Viral V., Matthew Richardson, Stijn Van Nieuwerburgh, and Lawrence J. White. *Guaranteed to Fail: Fannie Mae, Freddie Mac, and the Debacle of Mortgage Finance.* Princeton, N.J.: Princeton University Press, 2011.

Andrews, Edmund L. "The Ever More Graspable, and Risky, American Dream." *New York Times,* June 24, 2004.

————. "Fed Shrugged as Subprime Crisis Spread." *New York Times,* December 18, 2007.

Appelbaum, Binyamin. "Citi's Long History of Overreach, Then Rescue." *Washington Post*, March 11, 2009.

Baker, Dean. "The Run-up in Home Prices: Is It Real or Is It Another Bubble?" CEPR Briefing Paper, Center for Economic and Policy Research, Washington, D.C., August 2002.

Bar-Gill, Oren, and Elizabeth Warren. "Making Credit Safer." *University of Pennsylvania Law Review* 157 (2008): 1–101.

Barr, Colin. "Banks Want the Old Bailout Back." CNN *Money,* January 9, 2009. http://money.cnn .com/2009/01/09/news/classic.tarp.fortune/index.htm?postversion=2009010916.

Barsky, Neil. "What Housing Bubble?" *Wall Street Journal,* July 28, 2005.

Barth, James R., *The Rise and Fall of the U.S. Mortgage and Credit Markets.* Hoboken, N.J.: John Wiley & Sons, 2009.

Bebchuk, Lucian A., and Holger Spamann. "Regulating Bankers' Pay." *Georgetown Law Journal* 98/2 (2010): 247–87.

Berkshire Hathaway. *2002 Annual Report.* Omaha, Nebr.: Berkshire Hathaway, 2003. www .berkshirehathaway.com/2002ar/2002ar.pdf.

Bernanke, Ben S. "The Economic Outlook." Testimony before the Joint Economic Committee, U.S. Congress, Washington, D.C., October 20, 2005.

————. "The Economic Outlook." Testimony before the Joint Economic Committee, U.S. Congress, Washington, D.C., September 24, 2008.

————. "Federal Reserve Policies in the Financial Crisis." Speech at the Greater Austin Chamber of Commerce, Austin, Tex., December 1, 2008.

————. "The Federal Reserve's Balance Sheet: An Update." Speech at the Federal Reserve Board Conference on Key Developments in Monetary Economics, Washington, D.C., October 8, 2009.

————. "Nonmonetary Effects of the Financial Crisis in Propagation of the Great Depression." *American Economic Review* 73/3 (June 1983): 257–76.

————. "On Milton Friedman's Ninetieth Birthday." Remarks at Conference to Honor Milton Friedman, University of Chicago, November 8, 2002.

————. "The Recent Financial Turmoil and Its Economic and Policy Consequences." Speech at the Economic Club of New York, New York, October 15, 2007.

————. "Semiannual Monetary Policy Report to the Congress." Testimony before the Committee on Financial Services, U.S. House of Representatives, Washington, D.C., July 21, 2009.

————. "The Subprime Mortgage Market." Speech at the Federal Reserve Bank of Chicago's 43rd Annual Conference on Bank Structure and Competition, *The Mixing of Banking and Commerce*, Chicago, May 17, 2007.

Blinder, Alan S. "Crazy Compensation and the Crisis." *New York Times,* May 28, 2009.

————. "The Fed Is Running Low on Ammo." *Wall Street Journal,* August 26, 2010.

————. "Financial Rescue Plan," interview by Katty Kay. NPR *Diane Rehm Show*, September 22, 2008. http://thedianerehmshow.org/shows/2008-09-22/financial-rescue-plan.

————. "From the New Deal, a Way out of a Mess." *New York Times,* February 24, 2008.

————. "The GOP Myth of 'Job-Killing' Spending." *Wall Street Journal,* June 21, 2011.

————. "In Defense of Ben Bernanke." *Wall Street Journal,* November 15, 2010.

————. "It's Broke, Let's Fix It: Rethinking Financial Regulation." *International Journal of Central Banking* 6/4 (December 2010): 277–330.

————. "Whatever Happened to the *Troubled Assets* Relief Program?" Testimony before the Committee on Financial Services, U.S. House of Representatives, Washington, D.C., November 17, 2008.

Blinder, Alan S., and Douglas Holtz-Eakin. "Public Opinion and the Balanced Budget." *American Economic Review* 74/2 (May 1984): 144–49.

Blinder, Alan S., and R. Glenn Hubbard. "Blanket Deposit Insurance Is a Bad Idea." *Wall Street Journal*, October 15, 2008.

Blinder, Alan S., Andrew Lo, and Robert Solow, eds. *Rethinking the Financial Crisis*. New York: Russell Sage Foundation, 2012.

Blinder, Alan S., and Mark Zandi. "How the Great Recession Was Brought to an End." *Moody's Analytics,* July 27, 2010. www.economy.com/mark-zandi/documents/End-of-Great-Recession.pdf.

Board of Governors of the Federal Reserve System, Federal Deposit Insurance Corporation, and U.S. Department of the Treasury. "Joint Statement by Treasury, Federal Reserve, and the FDIC on Citigroup." FRB Press Release, November 23, 2008. www.federalreserve.gov/newsevents/press/bcreg/bcreg20081123a1.pdf.

Case, Karl E., and Robert J. Shiller. "Is There a Bubble in the Housing Market?" *Brookings Papers on Economic Activity* 34/2 (Fall 2003): 299–362.

Cassidy, John. "No Credit." *New Yorker*, March 15, 2010, 26–30.

CBS News. "CBS Poll: Americans Optimistic About Obama." CBS News *Opinion*, February 11, 2009. www.cbsnews.com/stories/2009/01/17/opinion/polls/main4729887.shtml.

Center for Responsive Politics. *Open Secrets*. www.opensecrets.org/lobby/top.php?showYear=2009&indexType=i.

Cesca, Bob. "Keep Your Goddamn Government Hands off My Medicare!" *Huffington Post*, August 5, 2009. www.huffingtonpost.com/bob-cesca/get-your-goddamn-governme_b_252326.html.

Chang, Yan, and Edward L. Golding, "Measuring the Effect of Foreclosure Prevention on House Prices and the Spillover Benefit of Reduce[d] Defaults." Presentation at the Wharton School, University of Pennsylvania, Philadelphia, Pa., April 27, 2012.

Christie, Les. "Home Futures: Price-drop Seen for 10 Top Markets." CNN *Money*, September 19, 2006. http://money.cnn.com/2006/09/19/real_estate/futures_trading_indicates_housing_drop/index.htm.

Clinton, Bill. *Back to Work*. New York: Alfred A. Knopf, 2011.

————. *My Life*. New York: Alfred A. Knopf, 2004.

CNN *Money*. "Fed Look at Wachovia in Drug Money Probe," CNN *Money*, April 26, 2008. http://money.cnn.com/2008/04/26/news/companies/wachovia_mexico.

CNN/Opinion Research. "Polls: Stimulus Unpopular, but Its Uses Have Broad Support." CNN *Politics*, January 29, 2010. http://articles.cnn.com/2010-01-29/politics/stimulus.poll_1_stimulus-bill-stimulus-plan-cnn-survey?_s=PM:POLITICS.

Cochrane, John H. "Lessons from the Financial Crisis." *Regulation* 32/4 (Winter 2009–2010): 34–37.

Cogan, John F., Tobias Cwik, John B. Taylor, and Volker Wieland. "New Keynesian Versus Old Keynesian Government Spending Multipliers." *Journal of Economic Dynamics and Control* 34/3 (March 2010): 281–95.

Cogan, John F., John B. Taylor, and Volker Wieland. "The Stimulus Didn't Work." *Wall Street Journal,* September 17, 2009.

Cohan, William D. *House of Cards: A Tale of Hubris and Wretched Excess on Wall Street.* New York: Doubleday, 2009.

Congressional Budget Office. *The Budget and Economic Outlook: Fiscal Years 2012 to 2022.* Washington, D.C.: U.S. Government Printing Office, January 31, 2012.

———. *The Long-Term Budget Outlook.* Washington, D.C.: U.S. Government Printing Office, October 1, 2000.

———. *The Long-Term Budget Outlook.* Washington, D.C.: U.S. Government Printing Office, December 1, 2003.

———. *Report on the Troubled Asset Relief Program—March 2012.* Washington, D.C.: U.S. Government Printing Office, March 28, 2012.

Connolly, Ceci. "Obama Chooses Peter Orszag as Chief of Office of Management and Budget." *Washington Post,* November 26, 2008.

Cordell, Larry, Karen Dynan, Andreas Lehnert, Nellie Liang, and Eileen Mauskopf. "Designing Loan Modifications to Address the Mortgage Crisis and the Making Home Affordable Program." Finance and Economics Discussion Series (FEDS), Board of Governors of the Federal Reserve System, Washington, D.C., 2009-43.

Dalton, John, and Claudia Dziobek. "Central Bank Losses and Experiences in Selected Countries." IMF Working Paper 5/72, International Monetary Fund, Washington, D.C., April 2005.

Daly, Corbett B. "Rick Perry Jabs Bernanke, Says 'Printing More Money . . . Is Almost Treasonous.'" CBS News *Political Hotsheet,* August 16, 2011. www.cbsnews.com/8301-503544_162-20092885-503544. html?tag=contentMain;contentBody.

Davey, Monica. "The State That Went Bust." *New York Times,* January 22, 2011.

Deutsche Bank Securities. "Shorting Home Equity Mezzanine Tranches: A Strategy to Cash in on a Slowing Housing Market," February 2007. In *Fact Sheet,* compiled by U.S. Department of the Treasury, Office of the Comptroller of the Currency, formerly Office of Thrift Supervision, September 25, 2008. Accessed at Committee on Homeland Security & Governmental Affairs, U.S. Senate, http://hsgac.senate.gov/public/_files/Financial_Crisis/FN107-1342.pdf.

Di Leo, Luca, and Jon Hilsenrath. "Fed Could Keep Short-Term Interest Rates Near Zero Well Beyond Mid-2013." *Wall Street Journal,* December 22, 2011.

Economist. "The Rise of the Anti-Keynesians: Paul Ryan's Intellectual Hinterland." April 14, 2011. www.economist.com/node/18560739.

———. "Will the Walls Come Falling Down?" April 20, 2005. www.economist.com/node/3886356.

Ellul, Andrew, and Vijay Yerramilli. "Stronger Risk Controls, Lower Risk: Evidence from U.S. Bank Holding Companies." NBER Working Paper 16178, National Bureau of Economic Research, Cambridge, Mass., July 2010.

European Central Bank. "Consolidated Versions of the Treaty on European Union and the Treaty on the Functioning of the European Union." *Official Journal of the European Union,* 2008/C 115/01 (May 9, 2008): 1–200. www.ecb.int/ecb/legal/pdf/fxac08115enc_002.pdf.

Fair Isaac Corp. "FICO Scores Drift Down as Economic Factors Weigh on Consumer Credit Risk." FICO News Release, July 13, 2010. www.fico.com/en/Company/News/Pages/07-13-10.aspx.

Federal Deposit Insurance Corp. "FDIC Announces Plan to Free up Bank Liquidity." FDIC Press Release, October 14, 2008.

———. "FDIC Implements Loan Modification Program for Distressed IndyMac Mortgage Loans." FDIC Press Release, August 20, 2008.

Federal Open Market Committee and the Board of Governors of the Federal Reserve System. "Federal Reserve and Other Central Banks Announce Schedules for Term and Forward Auctions of U.S. Dollar Liquidity for Fourth Quarter." Federal Reserve System Monetary Policy Release, October 7, 2008.

———. Minutes of the Federal Open Market Committee (FOMC), Washington, D.C., 2010 (January 26–27, March 16, April 27–28, August 10, and November 2–3).

Federal Reserve Bank of Kansas City. *Housing, Housing Finance, and Monetary Policy:* A Symposium Sponsored by the Federal Reserve Bank of Kansas City, Jackson Hole, Wyo., August 30–September 1, 2007.

Feldstein, Martin. "Concluding Remarks," in *Housing, Housing Finance, and Monetary Policy:* A Symposium Sponsored by the Federal Reserve Bank of Kansas City, Jackson Hole, Wyo., August 30–September 1, 2007: 489–500.

———. "How to Stop the Mortgage Crisis." *Wall Street Journal,* March 7, 2008.

Feyrer, James, and Bruce Sacerdote. "Did the Stimulus Stimulate? Real Time Estimates of the Effects of the American Recovery and Reinvestment Act." NBER Working Paper 16759, National Bureau of Economic Research, Cambridge, Mass., February 2011.

Financial Crisis Inquiry Commission. *The Financial Crisis Inquiry Report: Final Report to the National Commission on the Causes of the Financial and Economic Crisis in the United States.* Washington, D.C.: U.S. Government Printing Office, January 2011.

Fiorina, Morris P., and Samuel J. Abrams. *Disconnect: The Breakdown of Representation in American Politics,* Julian J. Rothbaum Distinguished Lecture Series, Vol. 11. Norman: University of Oklahoma Press, 2009.

Foote, Christopher L., Kristopher S. Gerardi, and Paul S. Willen. "Why Did So Many People Make So Many *Ex Post* Bad Decisions? The Causes of the Foreclosure Crisis," in *Rethinking the Financial Crisis.* Edited by Alan S. Blinder, Andrew Lo, and Robert Solow. New York: Russell Sage Foundation, 2012.

Free, Lloyd A., and Hadley Cantril. *The Political Beliefs of Americans: A Study of Public Opinion.* New Brunswick, N.J.: Rutgers University Press, 1967.

Friedman, Thomas L. "Obama Should Seize the High Ground." *New York Times,* May 26, 2012.

Frum, David. Full Comment, *National Post,* July 11, 2008. http://fullcomment.nationalpost.com/author/dfrumnp.

Gagnon, Joseph, Matthew Raskin, Julie Remache, and Brian Sack. "The Financial Market Effects of the Federal Reserve's Large-Scale Asset Purchases." *International Journal of Central Banking* 7/1 (March 2011): 3–44.

Garrett, Major. "Top GOP Priority: Make Obama a One-Term President." *National Journal,* October 23, 2010. http://nationaljournal.com/member/magazine/top-gop-priority-make-obama-a-one-term-president-20101023?mrefid=site_search.

Geanakoplos, John D., and Susan P. Koniak. "Mortgage Justice Is Blind." *New York Times,* October 29, 2008.

Geithner, Timothy F. "The Federal Bailout of AIG." Testimony before the Committee on Oversight and Government Reform, U.S. House of Representatives, Washington, D.C., January 27, 2010.

———. "Financial Crisis Amnesia." *Wall Street Journal,* March 1, 2012.

Goolsbee, Austan. "Looking For Lasting Solutions," interview by Bob Schieffer. CBS News, *Face the Nation,* November 23, 2008. www.cbsnews.com/htdocs/pdf/FTN_112308.pdf.

Gopal, Prashant. "Banks Block Obama's Mortgage Stimulus Plan." Bloomberg, August 16, 2011. www.bloomberg.com/news/2011-08-16/banks-block-obama-on-mortgage-stimulus-plan.html.

Gordon, Robert J., and Robert Krenn. "The End of the Great Depression: VAR Insight on the Roles of Monetary and Fiscal Policy." NBER Working Paper 16380, National Bureau of Economic Research, Cambridge, Mass., September 2010.

Gramlich, Edward M. "Booms and Busts: The Case of Subprime Mortgages," in *Housing, Housing Finance, and Monetary Policy:* A Symposium Sponsored by the Federal Reserve Bank of Kansas City, Jackson Hole, Wyo., August 30–September 1, 2007: 257–265.

———. *Subprime Mortgages: America's Latest Boom and Bust.* Washington, D.C.: Urban Institute Press, 2007.

Greenspan, Alan. "Activism." *International Finance* 14/1 (Spring 2011): 165–82.

———. "The Crisis." *Brookings Papers on Economic Activity* 41/1 (Spring 2010): 201–61.

———. "Outlook for the Federal Budget and Implications for Fiscal Policy." Testimony before the Committee on the Budget, U.S. Senate, Washington, D.C., January 25, 2001.

Harriss, C. Lowell. *History and Policies of the Home Owners' Loan Corporation.* New York: National Bureau of Economic Research, 1951.

Haubrich, Joseph G., and Deborah Lucas. "Who Holds the Toxic Waste? An Investigation of CMO Holdings." Federal Reserve Bank of Cleveland Policy Discussion Paper 20 (June 2007).

Hegel, Georg Wilhelm Friedrich, 1770–1831. *Introduction to the Philosophy of History: With Selections from the Philosophy of Right.* Translated, with introduction, by Leo Rauch. Indianapolis, Ind.: Hackett Publishing Co., 1988.

Hirsch, Michael. "The Party of Goldwater?" *Newsweek,* January 28, 2009.

———. "The Re-education of Larry Summers." *Newsweek,* February 20, 2009.

Hoover, Herbert. *The Memoirs of Herbert Hoover,* Vol. 1, *Years of Adventure, 1874–1920.* New York: Macmillan, 1951.

Hubbard, R. Glenn, and Chris Mayer. "First, Let's Stabilize Home Prices." *Wall Street Journal,* October 2, 2008.

Ip, Greg. "Did Greenspan Add to Subprime Woes?" *Wall Street Journal,* June 9, 2007.

Irwin, Neil, and David Cho. "Paulson's Change in Rescue Tactics." *Washington Post,* October 15, 2008.

Jacobson, Louis S., Robert J. LaLonde, and Daniel G. Sullivan. "Earnings Losses of Displaced Workers." *American Economic Review* 83/4 (September 1993): 685–709.

Jones, Jeffrey M. "Americans Want Congress, Obama to Tackle Economic Issues." *Gallup Politics,* January 14, 2011. www.gallup.com/poll/145592/americans-congress-obama-tackle-economic-issues.aspx.

———. "Domestic Priorities Top Americans' To-Do List for Obama." Gallup, January 19, 2009. www .gallup.com/poll/113869/domestic-priorities-top-americans-list-obama.aspx.

Kahn, Lisa B. "The Long-Term Labor Market Consequences of Graduating from College in a Bad Economy." *Labour Economics* 17/2 (April 2010): 303–16.

Kelly, Kate. "Bear CEO's Handling of Crisis Raises Issues." *Wall Street Journal,* November 1, 2007.

Keoun, Bradley. "Citigroup's 1.1 Trillion of Mysterious Assets Shadows Earnings." Bloomberg, July 13, 2008. www.bloomberg.com/apps/news?pid=newsarchive&sid=a1liVM3tG3aI.

King, Mervyn. Speech at Lord Mayor's Banquet for Bankers and Merchants, Mansion House, London. Bank of England, June 17, 2009. www.bankofengland.co.uk/publications/Documents/speeches/2012/speech587.pdf.

Krishnamurthy, Arvind, and Annette Vissing-Jorgensen. "The Effects of Quantitative Easing on Interest Rates: Channels and Implications for Policy." *Brookings Papers on Economic Activity* 42/2 (Fall 2011): 215–87.

Krugman, Paul R. "Cash for Trash." *New York Times,* September 21, 2008.

———. "Gordon Does Good." *New York Times,* October 12, 2008.

———. "It's Baaack: Japan's Slump and the Return of the Liquidity Trap." *Brookings Papers on Economic Activity* 29/2 (Fall 1998): 137–205.

Lagarde, Christine. "Global Risks Are Rising, but There Is a Path to Recovery," in *Achieving Maximum Long-Run Growth:* A Symposium Sponsored by the Federal Reserve Bank of Kansas City, Jackson Hole, Wyo., August 25–27, 2011: 421–26.

Lake Research Partners. "Wall Street Reform: One Year Anniversary." Presentation at Americans for Financial Reform, Washington, D.C., July 18, 2011. www.lakeresearch.com/news/AFR/Presentation .WallStreetReform.f.071811.pdf.

Latman, Peter. "New York Accuses Ernst & Young of Fraud in Lehman Collapse." *New York Times,* December 22, 2010.

Lewis, Michael. *The Big Short: Inside the Doomsday Machine.* New York: W. W. Norton, 2010.

———. *Boomerang.* New York: W. W. Norton, 2011.

Lindblad, Cristina, Ira Boudway, and Caroline Winter. "How's Geithner's Home Holding Up?" *Bloomberg Businessweek,* May 20, 2010.

Lowenstein, Roger. *When Genius Failed: The Rise and Fall of Long-Term Capital Management.* New York: Random House, 2000.

Luhby, Tami. "FDIC's Bair Pushes Aggressive Mortgage Plan." CNN *Money,* November 14, 2008. http:// money.cnn.com/2008/11/14/news/economy/fdic_bair/index.htm.

Mallaby, Sebastian. *More Money Than God.* New York: Penguin Press, 2010.

McHugh, David. "Draghi: ECB to Do 'Whatever It Takes' to Save Euro." Associated Press, July 26, 2012. http://bigstory.ap.org/article/draghi-ecb-do-whatever-it-takes-save-euro.

Meltzer, Allan H. "Policy Principles: Lessons from the Fed's Past," in *The Road Ahead for the Fed.* Edited by John D. Ciorciari and John B. Taylor. Stanford, Calif.: Hoover Institution Press, Stanford University, 2009: 13–32.

Merrill Lynch advertisement. *Derivatives Week*, November 7, 2005.

Morgan, David. "Pay Czar Says AIG Bonus Flap to End in March." Reuters, February 3, 2010. www
.reuters.com/article/2010/02/03/us-aig-feinberg-idUSTRE6122ZH20100203.

Morgenson, Gretchen, and Joshua Rosner. *Reckless Endangerment: How Outsized Ambition, Greed, and Corruption Led to Economic Armageddon.* New York: Henry Holt, 2011.

Murphy, Kevin J. "Pay, Politics, and the Financial Crisis," in *Rethinking the Financial Crisis.* Edited by Alan S. Blinder, Andrew Lo, and Robert Solow. New York: Russell Sage Foundation, 2012.

Nakamoto, Michiyo, and David Wighton. "Citigroup Chief Stays Bullish on Buy-Outs." *Financial Times*, July 9, 2007.

National Commission on Fiscal Responsibility and Reform. *Moment of Truth: Report of the National Commission on Fiscal Responsibility and Reform.* Washington, D.C.: U.S. Government Printing Office, December 1, 2010.

Newport, Frank. "Views on Government Aid Depend on the Program." Gallup, February 24, 2009. www
.gallup.com/poll/116083/views-government-aid-depend-program.aspx.

New York Times. "Following the A.I.G. Money." Opinion, March 15, 2009. www.nytimes.com/2009/03/15/
opinion/15sun1.html.

Nocera, Joe. "Sheila Bair's Bank Shot." *New York Times Magazine,* July 9, 2011.

Norris, Floyd. "After Years of Red Flags, a Conviction." *New York Times*, April 21, 2011.

———. "Quotes of the Day at Davos." Economix, *New York Times*, January 25, 2008. http://economix
.blogs.nytimes.com/2008/01/25/quotes-of-the-day-at-davos.

Obama, Barack. Town Hall speech, Raleigh, N.C., August 19, 2008.

———. Remarks at the Council on Jobs and Competitiveness, Durham, N.C., June 13, 2011.

Palin, Sarah. Letter to the Editor, *Wall Street Journal,* November 18, 2010.

Paletta, Damian. "Barney Frank Celebrates Free Market Day." *Wall Street Journal,* September 17, 2008.
http://blogs.wsj.com/economics/2008/09/17/barney-frank-celebrates-free-market-day.

Parker, Jonathan A., Nicholas S. Souleles, David S. Johnson, and Robert McClelland. "Consumer Spending and the Economic Stimulus Payments of 2008." NBER Working Paper 16684, National Bureau of Economic Research, Cambridge, Mass., January 2011.

Paulson, Henry M., Jr., *On the Brink: Inside the Race to Stop the Collapse of the Global Financial System.* New York: Business Plus, 2010.

Pew Research Center. *Auto Bailout Now Backed, Stimulus Divisive.* Washington, D.C.: Pew Research Center Publications, February 23, 2012. www.people-press.org/2012/02/23/auto-bailout-now-backed-
stimulus-divisive.

———. *Political Knowledge Update.* Washington, D.C.: Pew Research Center Publications, July 15, 2010.
http://pewresearch.org/pubs/1668/political-news-iq-update-7-2010-twitter-tarp-roberts.

Porfolio.com. "Portfolio's Worst American CEOs of All Time." CNBC, April 30, 2009. www.cnbc.com/
id/30502091?slide=1.

Pozsar, Zoltan, Tobias Adrian, Adam Ashcraft, and Hayley Boesky. "Shadow Banking." Federal Reserve Bank of New York Staff Report 458 (July 2010).

Protess, Ben. "Mortgage Executive Receives 30-Year Sentence." *New York Times*, June 30, 2011.

Reinhart, Carmen M., and Kenneth Rogoff. *This Time Is Different: Eight Centuries of Financial Folly.* Princeton, N.J.: Princeton University Press, 2009.

Rogers, Will. *Sanity Is Where You Find It.* Selected and edited by Donald Day. Boston, Mass.: Houghton Mifflin, 1955.

Rogoff, Kenneth. "The Bullets Yet to Be Fired to Stop the Crisis." *Financial Times,* August 8, 2011.

Rubin, Robert E., and Jacob Weisberg. *In an Uncertain World: Tough Choices from Wall Street to Washington.* New York: Random House, 2003.

Saad, Lydia. "CDC Tops Agency Ratings; Federal Reserve Board Lowest NASA Ratings Remain High, While Federal Reserve Has Lost Ground." Gallup, July 27, 2009. www.gallup.com/poll/121886/
cdc-tops-agency-ratings-federal-reserve-board-lowest.aspx.

Sahm, Claudia, Matthew D. Shapiro, and Joel Slemrod. "Check in the Mail or More in the Paycheck: Does the Effectiveness of Fiscal Stimulus Depend on How It Is Delivered?" *American Economic Journal: Economic Policy* 413 (August 2012): 216–50.

Santelli, Rick. "Rick Santelli and the 'Rant of the Year.'" YouTube, February 19, 2009. www.youtube.com/watch?v=bEZB4taSEoA.

Sargent, Thomas J. "United States Then, Europe Now." Nobel Prize in Economic Sciences Lecture, Stockholm University, December 8, 2011.

Scheiber, Noam. *The Escape Artists: How Obama's Team Fumbled the Recovery.* New York: Simon & Schuster, 2011.

Schmitt, Rick. "Prophet and Loss." *Stanford Magazine,* March/April 2009.

Shiller, Robert J. *The Subprime Solution: How Today's Global Financial Crisis Happened, and What to Do about It.* Princeton, N.J.: Princeton University Press, 2008.

Sides, John. "Republican Primary Voters Embrace Government. No, Really." *Model Politics,* YouGov, March 22, 2012. http://today.yougov.com/news/2012/03/22/republican-primary-voters-embrace-government-no-re.

Sjostrom, William K., Jr. "The AIG Bailout." *Washington & Lee Law Review* 66 (2009): 943–91.

Smith, Gary N., and Margaret H. Smith. *Houseonomics: Why Owning a Home Is Still a Great Investment.* Upper Saddle River, N.J.: FT Press, 2008.

Solomon, Deborah. "Bair's Legacy: An FDIC with Teeth." *Wall Street Journal,* July 7, 2011.

Sorkin, Andrew Ross. "A Bailout above the Law." *New York Times,* September 22, 2008.

———. *Too Big to Fail: The Inside Story of How Wall Street and Washington Fought to Save the Financial System—and Themselves.* New York: Viking Penguin, 2010.

Soros, George. "Paulson Cannot Be Allowed a Blank Cheque." *Financial Times,* September 24, 2008.

Stein, Herbert. *The Fiscal Revolution in America.* Chicago: University of Chicago Press, 1969.

Stiglitz, Joseph E. "A Better Bailout." *Nation,* September 26, 2008.

Story, Louise, Landon Thomas Jr., and Nelson D. Schwartz. "Wall St. Helped to Mask Debt Fueling Europe's Crisis." *New York Times,* February 13, 2010.

Summers, Lawrence. "Summers: AIG Bonuses Are 'Outrageous,'" interview by Kevin Hechtkopf. CBS News, *Face the Nation,* March 15, 2009. www.cbsnews.com/8301-503544_162-4866598-503544.html.

Suskind, Ron. *Confidence Men: Wall Street, Washington, and the Education of a President.* New York: HarperCollins, 2011.

———. *The Price of Loyalty: George W. Bush, the White House, and the Education of Paul O'Neill.* New York: Simon & Schuster, 2004.

Swagel, Phillip. "The Financial Crisis: An Inside View." *Brookings Papers on Economic Activity* 40/1 (Spring 2009): 1–78.

Taylor, John B. "Discretion Versus Policy Rules in Practice." *Carnegie-Rochester Series on Public Policy* 39 (1993): 195–214.

———. "An Empirical Analysis of the Revival of Fiscal Activism in the 2000s." *Journal of Economic Literature* 49/3 (September 2011): 686–702.

———. *Getting Off Track: How Government Actions and Interventions Caused, Prolonged, and Worsened the Financial Crisis.* Stanford, Calif.: Hoover Institution Press, Stanford University, 2009.

———. "The Need for a Clear and Credible Exit Strategy," in *The Road Ahead for the Fed.* Edited by John D. Ciorciari and John B. Taylor. Stanford, Calif.: Hoover Institution Press, Stanford University, 2009: 85–100.

———. "The 2009 Stimulus Package: Two Years Later." Testimony before the Committee on Oversight and Government Reform, Subcommittee on Regulatory Affairs, U.S. House of Representatives, Washington, D.C., February 16, 2011.

Tett, Gillian. *Fool's Gold: How Unrestrained Greed Corrupted a Dream, Shattered Global Markets and Unleashed a Catastrophe.* New York: Free Press, 2009.

Timiraos, Nick. "Confusion Roils HARP Program for Refinancing." *Wall Street Journal,* September 2, 2009.

Tourre, Fabrice. E-mail to Marine Serres, January 23, 2007. Accessed at *Telegraph* (London). http://i.telegraph.co.uk/multimedia/archive/01623/Fabrice_Tourre_ema_1623617a.pdf.

U.S. Department of Housing and Urban Development. *Annual Report to Congress: Financial Status of the FHA Mutual Mortgage Insurance Fund (MMI Fund), Fiscal Year 2011*. Washington, D.C.: U.S. Government Printing Office, November 15, 2011.

———. *Subprime Markets, the Role of the GSEs, and Risk-Based Pricing*. Washington, D.C.: U.S. Government Printing Office, March 2002.

U.S. Department of the Treasury. *Financial Regulatory Reform: A New Foundation—Rebuilding Financial Supervision and Regulation*. Washington, D.C.: U.S. Government Printing Office, June 23, 2009.

———. *Making Home Affordable Program Performance Report through March 2012*. Washington, D.C.: U.S. Government Printing Office, May 4, 2012.

———. "Secretary Geithner Introduces Financial Stability Plan." U.S. Department of the Treasury Press Release, February 10, 2009.

———. "Statement by Secretary Henry M. Paulson, Jr. on Comprehensive Approach to Market Developments." U.S. Department of the Treasury Press Release, September 19, 2008.

Volcker, Paul A. Speech at the Economic Club of New York, New York, April 8, 2008. http://online.wsj .com/public/resources/documents/volckerspeech040808.PDF.

———. Speech at the *Wall Street Journal*'s 2nd Future of Finance Initiative, Horsham, West Sussex, UK, December 8, 2009.

Wagner, Paul. "Unreal Estate." Metroactive, *Metro* (San Jose, Calif.), September 10, 2008. www .metroactive.com/metro/09.10.08/news-0837.html.

Wallison, Peter J. "The Argument Against a Government Resolution Authority." Pew Financial Reform Project Briefing Paper 4 (August 18, 2009).

Wallison, Peter J., and David Skeel. "The Dodd Bill: Bailouts Forever." *Wall Street Journal*, April 7, 2010.

Wallsten, Peter, Lori Montgomery, and Scott Wilson. "Obama's Evolution: Behind the Failed 'Grand Bargain' on the Debt." *Washington Post*, March 17, 2012.

Wall Street Journal. "What They Said About Fan and Fred." Opinion, *Wall Street Journal*, October 2, 2008. http://online.wsj.com/article/SB122290574391296381.html.

Warren, Elizabeth. "Unsafe at Any Rate." *Democracy: A Journal of Ideas* 5 (Summer 2007): 8–19.

Warsh, Kevin M. "The New Malaise and How to End It." *Wall Street Journal*, November 8, 2010.

Wessel, David. "Bernanke: Smaller Banks Not Necessarily the Answer for 'Too Big to Fail' Dilemma." *Wall Street Journal*, October 23, 2009.

———. *In Fed We Trust: Ben Bernanke's War on the Great Panic*. New York: Random House, 2009.

Whelan, Karl. "Ireland's Sovereign Debt Crisis." Centre for Economic Research Working Paper 11/09, University College Dublin, May 2011.

The White House, Office of the Press Secretary. "Remarks by President Obama and British Prime Minister Gordon Brown after Meeting." White House Press Release, March 3, 2009.

Zernike, Kate. "'Boiling Mad': A Tea Party Origin Story," interview by David Greene. NPR, *All Things Considered*, September 14, 2010. www.wbur.org/npr/129865403/boiling-mad-a-tea-party-origin-story.

INDEX

|IIIIIIIIIIIIIIIIIIIIIIIIIIII|